Simon and Schuster
New York, London,
Toronto, Sydney,
Tokyo

Glorious Chocolate

*Mary Goodbody
and the Editors of*

Chocolatier

M a g a z i n e

Simon and Schuster
Simon & Schuster Building
Rockefeller Center
1230 Avenue of the Americas
New York, New York 10020

Copyright © 1989 by *Chocolatier* Magazine
Illustrations copyright © 1989 by Glenn Wolff
All rights reserved
including the right of reproduction
in whole or in part in any form.

SIMON AND SCHUSTER and colophon are registered trademarks
of Simon & Schuster Inc.

Designed by Levavi and Levavi/Mary Beth Kilkelly
Manufactured in the United States of America

10 9 8 7 6 5 4 3 2 1

Library of Congress Cataloging in Publication Data

Goodbody, Mary.
  Glorious chocolate / Mary Goodbody and the Editors of *Chocolatier*
Magazine
      p. cm.
    1. Cookery (Chocolate) I. *Chocolatier*. II. Title.
TX767.C5G66   1989   89–34826
641.6′374—dc20   CIP

ISBN 0–671–67289–4

A Note from the Editor-in-Chief of Chocolatier Magazine

All of us at *Chocolatier* are very enthusiastic about *Glorious Chocolate*. This book signifies that the magazine has been around long enough to provide us with a solid group of recipes to make up the definitive work on chocolate, our very favorite flavor.

This book has special meaning to all of us who are or have been connected to *Chocolatier*, the people who I consider the nucleus of our far-reaching "*Chocolatier* family." Not only do we now have an easy-to-carry collection of treasured recipes and photographs, but the book represents our relationships with some outstanding people.

In general, "chocolate people" (for lack of a better way to describe them) are a great bunch of folks—they may be chefs, those who attend chocolate festivals, bakers, cookbook authors, employees of the world's major chocolate companies, or readers of our magazine. Because each recipe we publish is carefully screened, we frequently have a chance to get acquainted with the people connected to it. Happily, we have found that they are nearly always "one of us." I have to think that if you are reading this book, you too, must be part of this big chocolate-loving family. And, honestly, I can't think of a better way for all of us to be connected than by our abiding passion for the wonderful and delicious flavor of chocolate.

Mary Goodbody, the author of *Glorious Chocolate*, has been at *Chocolatier* almost from the beginning. As a seasoned food professional, cookbook author, and former editor-in-chief of *COOK'S* Magazine, she was the perfect person to take charge of the monumental task of organizing the best recipes from *Chocolatier* into a cookbook.

Enjoy the book. I hope you take pleasure reading it as well as learning, cooking, and baking from it. And as you continue to indulge your love of chocolate, please keep sharing your ideas and recipes with us so that we can plan for a second volume in the very near future.

—*Barbara Albright*
April 1989

Acknowledgments

A cookbook containing recipes and information from a magazine owes so much to so many people that it is hard to single out just a few. One person who does stand out, however, is Joan Steuer, the first editor-in-chief of *Chocolatier*. Joan's vision, her exuberant creativity, and her unfailing love for the magazine (not to mention for chocolate) still linger within the offices and on the pages of *Chocolatier*. Surely they are evident in this book, too.

We would also like to thank Janice Wald Henderson for her dedication, loyalty, and great ideas over the years. And without the much appreciated efforts of Rick Rodgers, Debbie Sachs, Susan Spedalle, and Susan Shapiro during their tenure with the magazine, this book would not be nearly as complete as it is.

We offer our heartfelt thanks as well to the following people for their valuable help with the cookbook: Mary Dauman, Melanie Falick, Maurice Goodbody, Kathryn Knapp, Julie Naughton, Harriet Schary, and Lynn Sallaberry. Without the long hours and hard work they contributed to the manuscript at different stages, it would not have been possible.

The Editors of *Chocolatier*
Mary Goodbody—Cookbook Coordinator
Barbara Albright—Editor-in-Chief
Adrienne Welch—Food Editor/Test Kitchen Director
Cathy Garvey—Associate Editor
Teri Griffing—Assistant Editor

Contents

Foreword

New York, October 1985. A taxicab pulls up at the curb. While the driver unloads my two suitcases of baking equipment, I knock on the door. It opens and I enter a photographer's studio to shoot photographs for a *Chocolatier* magazine article.

How excited I was to have this opportunity! Shooting a baking class for an issue of *Chocolatier* touched several of my passions at once: love of baking, teaching, and chocolate.

Ever since the first issue of *Chocolatier* appeared on the newsstands in February 1984, I awaited each magazine with great anticipation. Chocolate, the most popular and talked-about sweet ingredient of the decade, immediately found its showcase in *Chocolatier*. The magazine provided a major link to chocolate's millions of fans. With its enticing color pictures and delicious recipes, every issue celebrated chocolate as never before and soon *Chocolatier* became the chocolate lovers' Pied Piper.

Looking back to the day I walked into the photographer's studio, I was not only becoming a participant in the important work that *Chocolatier* was doing, but I was also entering the warm wonderful world of the *Chocolatier* family. Today I have the same feeling of excitement and pride in writing the Foreword for this book.

For years before *Chocolatier*, I was obsessed with chocolate. I not only loved the taste of chocolate, but I believed that an understanding of chocolate basics gave you the freedom to improvise. I wanted to teach it in simpler terms in order to make it less frustrating and more fun.

I read every book on chocolate I could get my hands on; like a mad scientist, I added chocolate to all sorts of baking recipes—chocolate puff pastry being one of my proudest feats; I talked with every chef about chocolate—once I even called *the* master, Albert Kumin, when he was pastry chef at the White House; I visited Boldemann and World Finest as well as other chocolate manufacturers; I enrolled in several professional confectionery courses such as Ecole LeNôtre in France and Richardson Researches in California; I was chairperson of the International Association of Cooking Professionals' Chocolate Consumer Information committee to help clarify chocolate facts for the food professional.

How is chocolate made? How much cocoa butter is in each brand? Why are the standards for manufacturing it in the United States stricter than in Europe? What is the difference between semisweet and bittersweet? Is one chocolate better than another for making curls, leaves, ruffles, and even truffles? Are chocolates interchangeable in recipes? I was grappling with all these questions.

Finally, here are the answers—all in one book. It's the best of the *Chocolatier* collection, so that forever you can say it with chocolate. Thanks to good old-fashioned teamwork, *Chocolatier* has passed, in a short period of time, from the infancy stage to full-bloom maturity. The proof is in the publishing of *Glorious Chocolate* for all to enjoy. No other book captures chocolate's spirit like this one. *Chocolatier*'s passion will bring the magical world of chocolate right into your kitchen.

From the time I first saw the magazine, I was awed by the talent and imagination of the *Chocolatier* staff. Working with them only increased my awareness of their strengths. Joan Steuer was the creative force behind the magazine, Mary Goodbody was the editorial wizard, Barbara Albright had a crystal-ball intuition of the needs, wants, and expectations of chocolate lovers across the country, and Adrienne Welch was the consummate student of chocolate, scholarly and dedicated, with exceptional knowledge and experience. I will always smile when I think of Rick Rodgers and his energy as he trotted around the country demonstrating *Chocolatier* recipes as their representative. And I was sincerely touched by the professionalism of Dennis Andes, Janice Wald Henderson, Cathy Garvey, Teri Griffing, Debbie Sachs, Melanie Falick, and Susan Spedalle.

Such writers as Richard Sax, Barbara Kafka, Philip Schulz, and the late James Beard and Bert Greene contributed to the wealth of information contained in the magazine. Recipes and decorating ideas by other writers such as Jim Fobel and Rose Levy Beranbaum added dimension to *Chocolatier*'s voice. There was news, upcoming events of interest, kitchen-tested recipes, desserts from professionals, and pages and pages of valuable advice on techniques, ingredients, and equipment.

Thanks to *Chocolatier*, America's view of chocolate has changed forever. There's now a greater-than-ever variety of chocolate available, and white chocolate, partly by virtue of its name, has become enormously popular. We understand more of chocolate's chemistry and so we are suitably reverent when melting it, but we are no longer afraid to temper. We know that it's possible to make exceptional chocolate desserts without a lot of special equipment and training, and with little persuasion we're happy to taste our chocolate to make sure it's just right for the recipe we're preparing.

Chocolatier's *Glorious Chocolate* is what I always wished for. Now the world can be a little sweeter. Chocolate fans have everything they need to make chocolate desserts like the experts. Once you share this book's rich chocolate secrets with family and friends, no other ingredient will ever be able to reign supreme.

—*Flo Braker*

Introduction

et *Chocolatier* join you in the kitchen as you create some of the best chocolate desserts and confections ever printed on the pages of our magazine. We are devoted to chocolate with a passion, a passion you no doubt share. We love to bake and cook with chocolate, to look at it, feel it, smell it, and taste it. During the more than five years that we have been publishing *Chocolatier,* scarcely a day has passed that we have not learned something new and intriguing about this capricious ingredient. With this sense of fantastic discovery, we invite you to open our book and celebrate the joys and wonders of chocolate. As you make these recipes, we hope you, too, will learn about, explore, and enjoy chocolate in all its glory.

Baking and cooking with chocolate is a rewarding challenge and we trust that this collection of recipes will appeal to you, your family, and your friends. We could not have compiled it without the help of the food writers, chefs, recipe developers, and caterers who, over the years, have provided us with mouth-watering, quality recipes and smashing ideas. These men and women are listed at the end of the book. We are truly grateful for their contributions and dedication to the magazine and to this book. And we are also grateful to the photographers who made the food look so beautiful.

Finally, but not of least importance, *Chocolatier* is most fortunate to have Food Editor/Test-Kitchen Director Adrienne Welch on staff. A number of the following recipes are her own exquisite creations, and she painstakingly tested and retested many of the other recipes, making adjustments and suggestions when necessary. Adrienne knows far more about chocolate and chocolate cookery than most people, and we are lucky that she has been able to share her expertise and love of chocolate with us and our readers.

All of us at the magazine hope you will get as much pleasure from this book as we have gotten from putting it together.

1

Michael Weiss

About Chocolate: Ingredients, Equipment, and Techniques

olid chocolate may be unsweetened, bittersweet, semisweet, milk, or white. Because white chocolate contains no chocolate liquor, it is not officially considered chocolate by the U.S. Standard of Identity and is not labeled as such. Chocolate also comes as a powder, called cocoa. All chocolates, even those in the same category, taste different, depending on the quality of the beans and how they are processed.

How Chocolate Is Made

To understand chocolate—and to be able to select the right one for a particular baking or cooking need—it is helpful to understand a little about how it is made. Cocoa beans, which are grown in equatorial areas of Africa, South and Central America, the West Indies, New Guinea, Malaysia, and Samoa, are fermented for up to six days after they are harvested. The fermented beans are then dried, cleaned, blended, and roasted much as coffee beans are. Roasting develops the chocolate flavor and, as the shell cracks with the heat, exposes the nib (meat) of the bean. The heated nib is ground into a thick paste, which is called either cocoa mass or, more commonly, chocolate liquor. Approximately 53 percent of this mass is cocoa butter. The chocolate liquor, after further refining, becomes what we know as unsweetened chocolate. Depending on the amount of sugar added, it becomes sweet, semisweet, or bittersweet chocolate. When milk solids are added, it becomes milk chocolate.

Once the beans have been roasted—and the various ways of roasting affect the final flavor of the chocolate—the chocolate liquor is then rolled between huge rollers to refine it by reducing the particle size of the mass. Even after sugar and other ingredients are added, the chocolate is refined further. Most chocolate is also conched. Tremendous conching machines spin large blades through the heated liquor for 12 to 72 hours to knead it and allow volatile acids and moisture to evaporate. During conching, more cocoa butter and other emulsifiers, such as lecithin, are added, which provide the chocolate with its smooth, rich, unique texture, so indescribably unlike any other.

The Different Kinds of Chocolate

Clearly, all chocolate is different. The type and blend of beans, the roasting, refining, and conching contribute to the final flavor and texture, as does the amount of sugar and milk solids, if any, and any extra cocoa butter, lecithin, and flavorings that are mixed into the liquor. All chocolate, except white chocolate, contains chocolate liquor and additional cocoa butter.

Unsweetened Chocolate: This is chocolate liquor. Sometimes called bitter or plain chocolate, it must, according to the U.S. Standard of Identity, contain a minimum of 50 percent and a maximum of 58 percent cocoa butter. The percentages vary from brand to brand.

Bittersweet and Semisweet Chocolate: These chocolates must contain *at least* 35 percent chocolate liquor. Within this extremely broad guideline, manufacturers produce chocolates that vary greatly, depending on the amounts of sugar, additional cocoa butter, milk solids and lecithin, and flavorings (such as vanillin and vanilla) as well as the overall amount of chocolate liquor. If a recipe that was originally developed with one manufacturer's bittersweet chocolate is made with another brand of bittersweet or semisweet, the results can be subtly or drastically different from the original in both texture and taste. Please refer to the box on page 16 for a listing of the brands of chocolate we use in the recipes. European-style recipes generally call for bittersweet chocolate, while American-style recipes call for semisweet. Likewise, European companies usually refer to their chocolate as bittersweet or dark, while American companies generally label it semisweet.

Sweet Chocolate: This is a blending of chocolate liquor and varying amounts of sugar, cocoa butter, lecithin, and flavorings, but to qualify as sweet chocolate, it must contain at least 15 percent chocolate liquor.

Milk Chocolate: Milk chocolate is America's favorite eating chocolate. To earn the nomenclature, the chocolate must contain no less than 3.66 percent milk fat (butterfat), no less than 12 percent milk solids, and at least 10 percent chocolate liquor. Manufacturers add varying amounts of sugar, cocoa butter, lecithin, and flavorings such as vanilla and vanillin to the chocolate. The milk proteins in milk chocolate make it more sensitive to heat than dark chocolates. Because of the lesser amount of chocolate liquor in milk chocolate, it cannot be substituted for dark chocolate in a recipe calling for sweet dark chocolate.

White Chocolate: Because the U.S. Standard of Identity does not consider this to be chocolate, there are no strict standards for white chocolate in this country. It is a combination of varying amounts of sugar, cocoa butter, butterfat, milk solids, lecithin, and flavorings. When produced in the United States, the confection is labeled a confectionery coating; produced in Europe, it is called white chocolate, although European companies sometimes label their white chocolate for U.S. distribution as confectionery bars. Because products made with vegetable fat rather than cocoa butter are also called confectionery or summer coatings, it is imperative to read the label to be certain the product you are buying contains cocoa butter. If the chocolate is not labeled, its color is a good indication of its identity. White chocolate is ivory colored, while vegetable fat-based summer coatings are bright white. As is true with milk chocolate, white chocolate is more sensitive to heat than dark chocolate. Take care when melting it—keep the water in the double boiler between 110° and 120° F—and be especially careful when melting white chocolate morsels or chips, as they contain the least amount of cocoa butter of any form of white chocolate.

Cocoa Powder: Cocoa powder is made from chocolate liquor that has had nearly all the cocoa butter removed by hydraulic pressure. The pressure forms what is called a press cake, which is then ground into powder. The cocoa powder available to the consumer is known as breakfast cocoa and contains at least 22 percent cocoa butter. Dutch processed cocoa is alkalized cocoa powder, which means that an alkali is added to the chocolate during processing to produce a less harsh tasting, dark cocoa. Nonalkalized cocoa powder, sometimes called natural cocoa powder, is usually lighter in color than alkalized but generally has more chocolate flavor. Nearly every brand of imported cocoa is alkalized. Hershey's and Nestlé make nonalkalized cocoa powders. For many recipes, we prefer the bold chocolate flavor of nonalkalized cocoa powder, although in other recipes we specify alkalized. Cocoa powder is alkalized purely to control flavor and color.

Selecting and Storing Chocolate

Check the recipe before setting out to buy the chocolate for it. Be sure to buy the kind of chocolate called for in the recipe. It's important to familiarize yourself with the nationally available brands of chocolate we use and describe on page 16.

To store the chocolate, wrap it first in foil and then plastic and keep it in a cool, dry place with good air circulation. Ideally, it should be somewhere with a constant temperature of 65°F and a relative humidity of 50 percent. Five degrees higher and 10 percent more humidity are acceptable, although the chocolate will not last quite as long. Perfectly stored unsweetened and dark chocolates will keep for as long as 10 years. Milk chocolate keeps for about a year and white chocolate for 7 or 8 months. We do not recommend storing baking or couverture chocolate in the refrigerator or freezer for any length of time. The humidity may cause sugar bloom and affect the taste and texture of the chocolate. On the other hand, truffles and pralines can be stored in the freezer if well wrapped and kept in an airtight container. Thaw the chocolates, still wrapped, overnight in the refrigerator, and then bring them to room temperature the following day before serving.

Brands of Chocolate

When we tested the recipes in this book we used the nationally available brands of chocolate listed here. Be sure to check the recipe before setting out to buy the chocolate for it—if you use the wrong type of chocolate, all your efforts may be wasted, certainly the results may be different. Within the following categories, you may use the brands we name interchangeably with only subtle differences in taste and/or texture.

Unsweetened chocolate: Baker's or Hershey's

Bittersweet chocolate: Lindt Excellence or Tobler Tradition (bittersweet chocolate often is labled Swiss Dark Chocolate)

Semisweet chocolate Baker's or Hershey's

Semisweet chocolate chips Baker's, Hershey's, or Nestlé

Sweet chocolate: Baker's German Sweet Chocolate

Milk chocolate: Lindt or Tobler (milk chocolate often is referred to as Swiss Milk Chocolate)

Milk chocolate chips: Baker's, Hershey's, or Nestlé

White chocolate: Lindt or Tobler (white chocolate is often labled Swiss Confectionery Chocolate)

Couverture chocolate: For coating, use Cacao Barry couverture, Callebaut couverture, Carma couverture, Guittard couverture, Lindt Excellence couverture, or Nestlé couverture. For fillings, we suggest Lindt Excellence couverture.

Bloom

Chocolate that has not been stored correctly will bloom. There are two kinds of bloom: sugar bloom and fat bloom. Sugar bloom occurs when the chocolate has been stored in damp conditions causing moisture to collect on its surface. As the moisture evaporates, tiny sugar crystals leach out of the chocolate and leave the surface feeling rough. Fat bloom occurs when the chocolate has been allowed to get too warm during storage. Stable cocoa butter crystals melt and re-form as unstable crystals. These transform back into large stable crystals that show up on the surface of the chocolate as gray-white blotches and streaks. For the most part, tempering erases this sort of bloom by melting and re-forming smaller, more stable cocoa butter crystals. Chocolate with sugar bloom is usable for cooking and baking, but not for candy work. In most cases, chocolate with fat bloom can be used for baking and candy work.

Why Temper Chocolate?

Throughout the book you will be instructed to temper chocolate. If you have never tempered before, you may decide to turn the page and try another recipe instead. Please don't. There are good reasons for tempering and it really is not difficult. We explain how to do it beginning on page 22, describing three methods. You will have to decide which one best suits you.

Tempering is the process of heating chocolate to 110° to 120°F. These temperatures are high enough to melt out unstable as well as stable cocoa butter crystals. The chocolate is cooled to a temperature between 82° and 84°F (depending on the kind and brand of chocolate), a temperature at which the stable (beta) crystals are able to re-form but the unstable ones are not. The chocolate is now "seeded" and is heated to a temperature ranging from 84° to 91°F to give it a consistency with a workable viscosity appropriate for the type and brand of chocolate being tempered. This temperature range must be maintained while you are working with the chocolate. These ranges, as well as the melted temperatures, may differ slightly from one brand of chocolate to another. Most bulk couvertures include temperature guidelines, which should be followed.

Dark, sweet chocolate (semisweet and bittersweet)	86° to 91°F
Milk chocolate	84° to 88°F
White chocolate	84° to 86°F

But what is all the fuss? Who cares if the cocoa butter crystals are unstable? As explained, unstable crystals may bloom and will cause the chocolate to be grainy, dull, and splotchy. Properly tempered chocolate looks glossy and velvety and is so finely textured that it breaks with a gentle snap and melts smoothly in your mouth. We feel that if you are going to take the time to make dipped or enrobed chocolates, chocolate ribbons, leaves, or curls, or fashion delicate molded bars, you deserve to end up with beautiful-looking chocolate. And this is why we encourage tempering.

It is helpful to keep in mind that all solid chocolate, whether it is a 10-pound block or a small bar, is tempered before it leaves the factory. Provided it was cooled correctly by the manufacturer and stored properly along the way, the chocolate will be in good temper when you buy it. As soon as you melt it, however, it goes out of temper. Of course it is not necessary to temper melted chocolate that will be incorporated into cake batters, cookie doughs, frostings, mousses, and so on.

About Our Recipes and Ingredients

All the recipes in this book have been kitchen tested and adapted so that you can easily reproduce them in your own kitchen. Every one of them appeared first in *Chocolatier* magazine and while we may have altered the style of particular recipes to make all those in the book consistent, their content has not been changed. We rate each recipe according to its degree of difficulty. One-bar (■) recipes are, we think, foolproof. Two-bar (■■) recipes are fairly simple and should be no problem to anyone who enjoys cooking and baking. Three-bar (■■■) recipes are more challenging and may require advance preparation and a number of steps.

We do our very best to use ingredients found in most supermarkets. When an ingredient is only available from a specialty store or through mail order, we pass this information on to you. At the back of the book you will find a list of mail order sources.

Flour, Eggs, and Sugar: Unless otherwise indicated, we use large grade A eggs and nationally available brands of bleached all-purpose flour. We

are careful to specify when eggs need to be at room temperature. When we do not specify, you may use cold eggs. We also always indicate whether to use granulated, superfine, confectioners', and light or dark brown sugar in each recipe.

All-purpose flour is made from a blending of hard and soft wheats to produce a flour with medium strength and protein content of 10.5 to 13 percent. All-purpose flour is widely marketed by the major food companies and works well for many baking purposes.

Cake flour, on the other hand, has weak gluten-forming capabilities. Milled from soft winter wheat, it is more refined than all-purpose and is low in protein. This flour produces a soft, delicate crumb, which is why it is often specified for cakes—but never for breads. We use cake flour in a number of recipes and recommend that when we specify it, you make an effort to use it rather than substitute all-purpose. But be sure you do not buy *self-rising* cake flour.

Mixes: Throughout the book and particularly in chapter 10, "Chocolate in a Hurry," you will come across recipes that list a mix or two with the ingredients. We purposely developed these recipes because there are so many good mixes in the stores capable of saving time while producing a dessert that is truly special.

Couverture Chocolate: Couverture is the chocolate of choice for most serious chocolate work. It is not a brand or type of chocolate but rather a term used to describe professional-quality coating chocolate with a high percentage of cocoa butter—at least 32 percent and often as high as 39 percent for good-quality couverture. The extra cocoa butter allows the chocolate to form a thinner coating shell than noncouverture chocolate. It also gives the melted chocolate good fluidity and workable viscosity. Couverture used to make something that is to be held at room temperature must be tempered. Otherwise the chocolate will not set properly and its texture will be grainy.

Quality varies from brand to brand, but the best couvertures are almost always European. The best have an exquisitely fine texture and well-balanced flavor and melt to a thick, flawless pool that is ideal for molding, enrobing, and hand dipping. Couverture chocolate may be purchased through a baker's supply house or a specialty mail order supply source. It should be wrapped in foil and then plastic, and stored in a dark, dry, cool place (ideally at 65°F) with good air circulation and a relative humidity of about 50 percent.

Cocoa Butter: A few of our recipes call for additional cocoa butter. As explained earlier, this is the fat present in all chocolate. During processing, it may be removed from the chocolate liquor and added to chocolate in varying amounts, depending on need. Pure cocoa butter, an especially rich emulsifier, is available from some pharmacies, baking supply houses and specialty shops, and through mail order.

Food Colors: The most easily available food colorings are liquid, sold in supermarkets usually in tiny plastic bottles. They generally come in four colors: red, yellow, green, and blue. Cake decorators and candy makers often rely on paste food colors for the rainbow of hues they require. These produce brighter, deeper colors than liquids and mix well to make subtle or exotic shades. Paste colors are sold at specialty shops and bakers' and candy makers' supply houses.

Coffee Powder and Espresso Coffee Powder: Although in some cases they may be used interchangeably, espresso powder is stronger than coffee powder. If a recipe calls for one, try to use what is specified. Powder dissolves more readily than freeze-dried crystals, although if the coffee or espresso powder will be dissolved in very hot or boiling water before being added to the rest of the ingredients, you may use the crystals if they are all you have on hand.

Chocolate Plastic: Chocolate plastic, also known as chocolate leather, is a mixture of chocolate and corn syrup. It is pliable and thus easy to wrap, bend, and otherwise manipulate into shapes. When it is required, we provide a recipe for making it. Essentially, it is made by mixing together room temperature melted chocolate and corn syrup until they make a dull-looking mixture. This is then set aside at room temperature until slightly stiffened. At this point, it can be rolled into sheets or ribbons or formed into flowers such as roses and carnations as well as all different kinds of decorations and wraps for chocolate desserts and confections.

Gianduja: Gianduja (pronounced john-doo-ya) is a combination of chocolate and hazelnuts devised by European chocolatiers as a filling for truffles and pralines (a European term for chocolate candies). It is also used in cakes, frostings, and pastries. The chocolate part of gianduja is generally milk chocolate couverture, although dark chocolate is sometimes used instead. This is melted and mixed with a smooth nut paste known as *duja*, made from confectioners' sugar, roasted hazelnuts, and sometimes almonds. The mixture is further refined so that the particle size of the finished product is extremely fine. Gianduja is then tempered, molded into blocks, and packaged for sale to candy makers and bakers. Large blocks of gianduja are obtainable from mail order sources or professional chocolatiers. Well wrapped and stored in a cool, dry place away from sunlight, it will keep for 6 to 8 months.

Vanilla: Vanilla is an essential ingredient in almost all chocolate dessert recipes because it enhances the flavor of the chocolate. Whether you use vanilla extract or the dried vanilla bean, it will most likely have come from the Bourbon Islands—Madagascar, Réunion, and the Comoros—or from Tahiti. Tahitian vanilla, which is rapidly becoming popular in the United States, has a bolder flavor and larger beans.

Vanilla is generally used in the form of the extract derived from cured, chopped vanilla beans. Alternatively, the whole, cured bean is infused in hot liquid—sugar syrup or milk—to release its flavor. You can't infuse the bean more than once, but you can use the infused bean to make vanilla-flavored sugar. Just rinse and dry the bean and store it in a container of granulated or confectioners' sugar. Within a few days, the sugar will take on the flavor of vanilla.

Nuts: If possible, buy nuts from a health food or specialty store where they are sold loose and in bulk. Shelled or unshelled, these tend to be fresher (and more economical) than those sold prepackaged. Shelled nut meats should be firm but not dry, moist but not soft.

Because of their high oil content, nuts can easily turn rancid and should be used as quickly as possible after buying. At home, store them in a cool, dry, dark place, well protected from heat, light, and moisture. Nuts in their shells keep their freshness better than unshelled, but shelled nuts may be kept in the refrigerator for a month or so in a tightly closed plastic bag in an airtight container. If you do not plan to use the nuts within a month, it is a good idea to freeze them. Place the nut meats in an airtight plastic bag in an airtight container and they will keep for several months.

Coconut: Many of our recipes call for unsweetened coconut flakes. These are available in natural food stores and in most markets that sell ingredients in bulk.

Equipment

Most of the equipment used in these recipes is found in every kitchen. At the beginning of each recipe, we list any special equipment or unusual pan sizes to alert readers to check their inventory. Turn to the mail order sources at the end of the book for hard-to-find equipment.

You will notice right away that we use a hand-held electric mixer most of the time. Surveys we have taken indicate that most households rely on this sort of mixer, and so, with a few duly noted exceptions, we test all our recipes using this convenient, handy appliance. Since a good percentage of our readers undoubtedly also own large standing mixers such as KitchenAids, we urge you to follow our visual descriptions rather than time constraints when using these more powerful machines.

We suggest that our readers be sure their kitchens are stocked with standard-size cake pans (8, 9, or 10 inches by 2 inches deep), jelly-roll pans (10½ inches by 15½ inches and 11½ inches by 17½ inches), muffin tins (6- to 7-tablespoon-size cups), loaf pans, a Bundt pan or other tube pan, and 9-by-3- and 10-by-3-inch springform pans. You will also need 9- or 10-inch glass Pyrex pie plates and an 11-inch tart pan. Also have measuring cups appropriate for dry and liquid measures; cake spatulas, both flat and offset (with a crooked handle); rubber spatulas for scraping bowls; wooden spoons; a long serrated knife; wire racks for cooling; a sifter; fine sieves; a rolling pin; wire whisks; an accurate oven thermometer; a chocolate thermometer; a candy thermometer; assorted pastry brushes; a kitchen scale; and several heavy-duty baking sheets. A pastry bag with assorted tips is necessary if you plan to decorate your desserts, as is parchment paper for making paper cones. Otherwise, keep baking parchment and a good supply of waxed paper, foil, and plastic wrap on hand.

In each recipe we indicate where in the oven the rack(s) should be placed. Most cakes bake best in the middle of the oven, but there are times when we request, for instance, that the rack be placed in the top or bottom third of the oven. For the best results, try to follow these instructions. Also, be sure to use an oven thermometer to ensure that your oven is accurate. If it is not, have the oven calibrated and adjusted.

Buying and Caring for Chocolate Molds

Chocolate molds can be made of plastic or metal. The advantage of using metal is that it cools more rapidly than plastic and so the chocolate sets more quickly. Before buying a metal mold—either new or antique—make sure the molding surface is not scratched and shows no sign of rusting or pitting.

Plastic molds, made from FDA-approved polycarbonate plastic materials, can be flexible and transparent or hard and opaque. Transparent molds make it easier to see when the chocolate is set. Both types are durable—they will not dent when dropped and will not rust (both of which are liabilities with metal molds). The price of plastic molds depends on the quality and may vary greatly. Whether you buy metal or plastic, choose molds with clearly defined patterns so that the molded chocolate will reproduce the design clearly and cleanly.

When you buy a new mold, wash it in warm water with a soft cloth or sponge. Do not use a cleanser and add only a drop or two of mild soap if you feel it is necessary. If you use soap, be sure to rinse the mold thoroughly. Dry it with a soft cloth and if you are not using it right away, store it in a cool, dry place.

Be sure the mold is at room temperature before you use it. Wipe it carefully with a lint-free cloth or a cotton ball. If the mold is clean and dry when you coat it with chocolate (according to recipe instructions) and if the chocolate is properly tempered, you will have no trouble releasing the chocolate from the mold when it is set.

When you have finished using it, wipe any chocolate residue from the mold. Leftover chocolate on the mold can cause your next batch to stick or it may leave marks on a new batch.

To clean the mold, wipe it with a soft cloth or wash it in warm water without using soap. Soap will wash away the transparent film of cocoa butter that seeps from the chocolate onto the mold while the chocolate sets and facilitates future unmoldings. Dry the mold well before storing it.

Techniques

Detailed instructions for preparing each dessert or sweet are included with each recipe. What follows are some techniques that are used so often and in so many recipes that we decided to explain them here and refer you to these pages as you come across the instructions in the individual recipes.

Measuring Dry Ingredients: Keep in mind that we measure flour and all dry ingredients (including cocoa) by spooning them lightly into the appropriate measuring cup and leveling them with the straight edge of a knife or spatula. Tapping the measure will alter the measurement.

Roasting Nuts: This is a simple procedure called for in any number of recipes, well worth the little bit of extra effort required, since the process

releases natural oils and therefore makes the nuts more flavorful.

The nuts we most frequently suggest roasting are whole almonds, either natural or blanched, and sliced or slivered almonds, walnuts, pecans, and hazelnuts. Each nut requires slightly different treatment, although the preliminary steps are the same. The instructions that follow are tailored for 1 to 2 cups of nuts.

Position a rack in the center of the oven and preheat to correct temperature. Spread the nuts in a single layer on a baking sheet in preparation for roasting. The oven temperature and roasting time vary slightly according to the type of nut.

• Whole almonds, natural or blanched: Roast in a 350°F oven for 10 to 15 minutes, shaking the pan two or three times during roasting, or until the nuts are done. Blanched almonds should be golden; natural almonds should be an even light brown all the way through when cut in half. Transfer the nuts to another baking sheet to stop cooking, and cool completely.

• Sliced or slivered almonds: Roast in a 325°F oven for 5 to 10 minutes, shaking the pan two or three times during roasting, or until the nuts are lightly browned. Transfer the nuts to another baking sheet to stop cooking, and cool completely.

• Walnuts and pecans: For lightly roasted nuts, roast in a 350°F oven for 5 to 10 minutes, shaking the pan two or three times during roasting, or until fragrant. Transfer the nuts to another baking sheet to stop cooking, and cool completely.

• Hazelnuts: Roast in a 350°F oven for 10 to 15 minutes, shaking the pan two or three times, or until golden beneath the skins. Wrap the nuts in a clean towel and cool completely. Transfer the cooled hazelnuts to a large sieve and rub them back and forth to remove the loose skins.

Choosing a Candy Thermometer and Checking It for Accuracy: Candy thermometers often are called frying thermometers. Look for one with the mercury bulb and column mounted on a protective metal casing and with a clip for attaching it to the side of the pan. If the thermometer is not set in a metal frame, you must not allow the bulb to touch the bottom of the pan and this can be inconvenient. The thermometer's temperature range should be from 100° to 400°F.

An accurate thermometer is an essential factor in successful candy making. If you're not sure about the accuracy of yours, it's a good idea to test it before you start. Put it in a pot of rapidly boiling water for 1 to 2 minutes. If it registers above or below 212°F—boiling point—adjust the temperatures in the candy recipe accordingly.

Making Chocolate Curls: Chocolate curls add a professional touch to a cake and are easy to make. Warm a 3-ounce bar or 1-ounce square of chocolate by putting it in the microwave oven for 20-second intervals at medium (50 percent) power until it starts to soften. This can take five or six tries, depending on the wattage of the microwave oven, the type of chocolate, and the heat of the kitchen. The chocolate should not begin to melt—just soften. You can also soften the chocolate by putting it about 6 inches from a desk lamp for 5 to 10 minutes, turning it every couple of minutes until it starts to soften.

Line a baking sheet with waxed paper. Grip the bar of chocolate with a paper towel so that your hand does not melt the chocolate. Using a vegetable peeler, scrape one of the edges of the chocolate bar in a downward motion, forming tight curls. Chocolate that is too cool will produce shavings; overly heated chocolate will curl very little. As you form the curls, let them fall onto the waxed paper. Refrigerate the baking sheet until you are ready to use the curls.

Melting Chocolate in the Microwave Oven: Using a microwave oven is the quickest and most efficient way to melt chocolate. Although many manufacturers suggest melting chocolate with the microwave oven at high (100 percent) power, we have found that for even melting and to avoid scorching, it is better to set it at medium (50 percent) power. The amount of time it takes to melt the chocolate depends on the wattage of the microwave oven, the amount of cocoa butter in the chocolate, and the size of the container holding the chocolate. It's more important to watch the

appearance of the chocolate than the clock. It will not become liquid, as it does when melted by traditional methods, but, instead, takes on a shiny appearance. At this point, it is time to take it from the microwave oven and stir for at least 1 minute to complete the melting process and stabilize the temperature.

Softening Ice Cream: If you leave most containers of ice cream in the refrigerator for 30 minutes, the ice cream will soften enough so that it can be spread between brownie and cake layers or in a pie shell. You can also soften it in the microwave oven, a pint at a time, for 20-second intervals at medium (50 percent) power until it reaches the right consistency.

Toasting Coconut: As with nuts, this improves the flavor of the coconut. Preheat the oven to 350°F. Spread about a cup of coconut in an even layer on a baking sheet and bake for 6 to 10 minutes, stirring three or four times, until golden. Transfer the coconut to another baking sheet to stop the cooking process. Cool completely. Coconut may be toasted up to one or two days ahead of time and stored in an airtight container.

Making Dry Bread Crumbs: For a cup of bread crumbs, preheat the oven to 400°F. Trim the crusts from four slices of bread and put the slices on a baking sheet. Bake for 10 to 15 minutes, turning once, until the slices are dry but not browned. Cool completely. Cut the slices into cubes and process in a food processor or blender until finely ground. Pass the crumbs through a sifter. These will keep in a covered, airtight container for several weeks.

Freezing Pie and Tart Shells: Pie and tart shells made from pastry are easy to freeze and good to have on hand when you want to make a pie or tart in a hurry. Press the pastry into the pie plate, trim the sides, and crimp the edges to make it pretty. Wrap the unbaked pie shell first in plastic and then in a double layer of foil. Freeze it for up to a month. When you are ready to bake it, take it from the freezer and unwrap it carefully. By the time you fill the shell, it will be thawed sufficiently so that you need not adjust the baking time, but, nevertheless, judge its doneness more by visual checks than time.

Lining Cake Pans: Lining cake pans with waxed paper or baking parchment prevents a skin of flour from forming on the bottom of the baked cake. To line a pan, first lightly butter the bottom and sides and then cover the bottom of the pan with a piece of waxed paper or baking parchment cut to fit. Dust the sides of the pan—but not the paper-lined bottom—with flour and tap out the excess. When you remove the cake from the oven and invert it on a wire rack to cool, carefully peel off the paper or parchment, but do not discard it: leave the paper loosely set on the cake layer to protect the cake from being cut by the wire cooling racks.

Splitting Cake Layers and Assembling a Cake for Frosting: Many recipes require that you split one or more baked cake layers in half horizontally and then sandwich these layers with filling. Most often this is done with two cake layers to make a four-layer cake. To assure success, follow these simple guidelines.

First, make sure the cake layers are completely cool before attempting to slice them. Otherwise, they will crumble. Set one layer on a cake-decorating stand, a lazy Susan, or a cardboard circle. If necessary, trim the top of the layer so that it is flat and not domed in the center.

Use a serrated knife that is longer than the diameter of the cake. Make a small notch length-wise down the side of the cake layer. Lay one hand lightly on the top of the cake layer and horizontally score the layer by holding the knife at the midpoint of the cake and simultaneously turning the cake with the other hand. Using the scored line as a guide, carefully saw straight through the cake layer. Slice the second cake layer (if applicable) in the same way so that all four layers are of equal thickness.

Assemble the layers with the filling by starting with the original bottom. Spread it evenly with filling and then position the top of the same layer over the filling, lining them up by matching the vertical notch. Spread filling over the second layer and top it with the bottom of the other cake layer. Set the top of this layer on top of the final application of filling and align it by using the notch as a guide. The cake is now ready to frost.

Frosting a Cake: We suggest you start frosting a cake by beginning on the top and ending with the sides. When the frosting is as thick and even as you want it to be, smooth the rim of frosting that may have built up around the top edge of the cake with a cake spatula. Hold the spatula at an angle and spread the frosting in toward the center of the cake.

In some cases, we suggest beginning with a crumb coat. A crumb coat is a thin layer of frosting that has been allowed to set, holding any loose cake crumbs in place while a second layer of frosting is applied. These are most useful with white or light-colored frostings, especially if the cake is very dark, such as a chocolate cake. Novices may want to apply a crumb coat most of the time, since after it has set (usually by sitting in the refrigerator for 15 to 25 minutes), the second layer of frosting glides flawlessly over the cake.

In all cases, take your time when you frost a cake. Work with sure, steady strokes and do not try to cover too much of the cake at one time. It is also a good idea to wipe the knife or spatula clean with a damp cloth every time you lift it from the cake.

Tempering Chocolate

Because so many of our recipes call for tempered chocolate, we decided the procedure warranted its own section. Tempering is a way of controlling the crystalline structure of the cocoa butter in chocolate by a process of heating and cooling. All solid chocolate is tempered before it leaves the factory but loses temper when melted. Therefore, chocolate that will be used for molding, dipping or coating, or formed into curls, leaves, ribbons, and other intricate shapes needs to be re-tempered. If not, the finished product could turn out dull and grainy, instead of glossy and smooth.

First, the chocolate is heated to a high enough

temperature—110° to 120°F—to melt both stable and unstable cocoa butter crystals. The melted chocolate is cooled to 82° to 84°F, the temperature range at which the stable crystals, but not the unstable ones, are able to re-form. The chocolate is then heated again to 84° to 91°F until it reaches the appropriate consistency for its intended use.

Tempering Equipment: You do not need a lot of special equipment for tempering and perhaps the most crucial piece is a good thermometer. Look for one that reads below 80°F and up to 130°F in increments of one or two degrees, such as a lab thermometer or instant-read thermometer. Standard candy or frying thermometers cannot be used for tempering because they generally begin registering temperature at 100°F.

A heating pad of the kind normally used to relieve backaches is useful for holding tempered chocolate at the right temperature while you work.

You will need a large sharp knife for chopping the chocolate and an accurate kitchen scale for weighing it. A marble slab is the ideal surface for working with chocolate, but any smooth work surface will do as long as it is clean and dry.

Checking the Temperature of Tempered Chocolate: It is essential to get an accurate temperature reading when tempering chocolate. Be sure to submerge the thermometer into the melted chocolate to at least 1 inch above the mercury, and do not rest it against the sides or bottom of the pan.

Tempering Methods: There are several methods of tempering chocolate. The instructions that follow are for couverture chocolate (see page 17), which is the best sort of chocolate to use for most confectionery work, but they apply to any chocolate you choose to temper.

MICROWAVE-TABLE METHOD

Using a microwave oven in conjunction with the time-honored method of tempering chocolate on a smooth, hard surface (such as marble or Formica) takes no longer than 15 to 20 minutes. Always stir chocolate thoroughly for at least 1 minute after removing it from the microwave oven before checking the temperature, since the temperature will continue to climb even after it is out of the microwave oven. Bear in mind that both milk and white chocolate need to be removed from the microwave oven and stirred sooner than dark chocolate to ensure that the milk proteins do not overheat and cause graininess.

1¼ pounds dark, milk, or white chocolate couverture, coarsely chopped

1. Put half of the chopped chocolate in a microwave-safe 2-quart glass or ceramic container. (Do not use plastic.) Put the chocolate in the microwave and heat at medium (50 percent) power for 90 seconds to 3 minutes or until shiny. Check after 90 seconds if using milk or white chocolate. Stir the chocolate to make sure it is completely melted and then add the remaining chopped chocolate. Return the chocolate to the microwave oven and heat at medium (50 percent) power for another 90 seconds to 3 minutes. Gently stir the chocolate and when it is completely melted, check the temperature. It should read between 110° and 120°F or the temperature recommended by the couverture manufacturer. If necessary, put the chocolate back in the microwave oven and heat at low (10 percent) power for 5 to 20 seconds, until it reaches the correct temperature. Stir the chocolate for at least 1 minute before checking the temperature.

2. Transfer the melted chocolate to a microwave-safe 1-quart glass or ceramic container, preferably a glass bowl. This will bring the temperature of the chocolate down to 95° to 100°F.

3. Wrap a heating pad in plastic to protect it from chocolate stains. Set the control dial to the lowest setting.

4. Pour one third of the chocolate onto a clean, dry work surface, such as marble or Formica. Keep the remaining chocolate in the bowl on the heating pad.

5. Using an offset metal cake spatula, spread the chocolate evenly across the work surface into a 12-inch rectangle. Using a pastry scraper, bring the chocolate together and as you do so, scrape the excess chocolate from the pastry scraper. Continue this spreading and scraping process until the chocolate cools to 82° to 84°F, loses its shine, and forms a thick paste with a dull matte finish. Work quickly so that the chocolate does not lump. This process can take anywhere from 5 to 10 minutes, depending on the type and brand of chocolate as well as the temperature of the kitchen. The chocolate is now seeded. The professional term for the paste is "mush."

6. Add the mush to the bowl of 95°F chocolate and using a rubber spatula, stir the chocolate gently until smooth. Be careful not to create air bubbles as you stir.

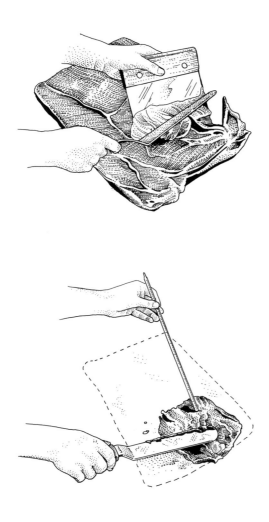

7. Check the temperature of the chocolate. It should register between 84° and 91°F, depending on the type of chocolate being tempered. If necessary, heat the bowl of chocolate in the microwave oven at low (10 percent) power for 5- to 10-second intervals to raise the temperature of the chocolate to the required level. Stir the chocolate for at least 1 minute before checking the temperature again and be very careful not to overheat. The chocolate is now ready to work with. As you work, regularly stir the chocolate and check its temperature. If it begins to lose its fluidity, simply reheat it in the microwave oven at low (10 percent) power for 5 to 10 seconds. Remember to stir the chocolate for at least 1 minute before rechecking the temperature. Never let its temperature exceed 91°F, or the stable cocoa butter crystals will start to melt and the temper will be lost.

POT METHOD

This method takes longer than the microwave-table or direct method, about 30 to 40 minutes, and does not seed the chocolate as efficiently. You will need a ¼-pound chunk of chocolate to seed the melted chocolate. Make sure the chunk of choco-late is in good temper—it should have even color and smooth grain, and show no evidence of streak-ing or blotching. You may use a hot tray or double boiler to melt the chocolate.

1¼ pounds dark, milk, or white chocolate couverture

1. Chop 1 pound of the chocolate into small pieces. Reserve the remaining ¼-pound chunk to use when you cool the chocolate. Put half of the chopped chocolate in the top of a double boiler or a heavy 2-quart saucepan. If using a double boiler, fill the bottom with enough 125°F water to touch the bottom and sides of the top portion without making it float. Maintain this water temperature throughout the melting process. If using a sauce-pan, melt the chocolate by setting the pan on a hot tray adjusted to the medium-low setting.

2. Stir the chocolate and gradually add the re-maining chopped chocolate until all the chocolate is melted. Dark chocolate should be stirred fre-quently; milk chocolate should be stirred almost constantly; white chocolate should be stirred con-tinuously to ensure that the crystals melt com-pletely and evenly.

3. Heat the melted chocolate until it reaches 110° to 120°F or the temperature recommended by the couverture manufacturer.

4. Remove the top part of the double boiler from the bottom, or remove the pan from the hot tray. If using a double boiler, wipe the bottom of the pan dry. Transfer the chocolate to a 1-quart bowl. This will bring the temperature of the chocolate down to 95° to 100°F.

5. Add the ¼-pound chunk of chocolate to the melted chocolate. Lower the temperature of the chocolate by stirring constantly. This room-temperature piece of chocolate will help lower the temperature gradually and evenly. It will also seed the melted chocolate with stable cocoa butter crys-tals, which helps keep it in good temper as it hardens.

6. Check the temperature of the chocolate. It should be between 84° and 91°F, depending on the type of chocolate being tempered and the brand. Remove what is left of the remaining chunk of chocolate and set it aside for use in other baking or candy making. Remember, it must be tempered again.

7. Wrap a heating pad in plastic to protect it from chocolate stains. Set the control dial to the lowest setting.

8. Put the bowl of tempered chocolate on the heating pad. The chocolate is now ready to work with. As you work, regularly stir the chocolate to check the temperature. If the melted chocolate cools too much and loses its fluidity, simply raise the temperature by adjusting the setting on the heating pad. Do not let the temperature exceed 91°F, or the stable cocoa butter crystals will start to melt and the temper will be lost.

DIRECT METHOD

This method breaks the rules of the most traditional methods of tempering in that the cocoa butter crystals are not melted and re-formed. The chocolate is heated very carefully in the microwave oven just until it melts, so that the temperature never exceeds 91°F. It is absolutely essential that the couverture chocolate (see page 17) be in good temper when using this method—it should have even color and smooth grain, and show no evidence of streaking or blotching. This method is very easy and takes about 15 to 20 minutes, but you must watch the temperature of the chocolate very carefully. Always stir the chocolate for at least 1 minute before checking the temperature, since the temperature of the chocolate will continue to climb even after it has been removed from the microwave oven.

1¼ pounds dark, milk, or white chocolate couverture, coarsely chopped

1. Put the chocolate in a microwave-safe 1½-quart glass or ceramic container. (Do not use plastic.) Put the chocolate in the microwave oven and heat at medium (50 percent) power for 90 seconds to 3 minutes or until the chocolate is shiny and half melted. Check milk or white chocolate after 90 seconds. Let the chocolate stand at room temperature, stirring frequently, until the chocolate is almost completely melted.

2. Check the temperature of the chocolate. It should read between 84° and 91°F. If necessary, put the chocolate back in the microwave oven at low (10 percent) power for 5- to 10-second intervals, until it reaches the correct temperature and the chocolate is completely melted. Stir the chocolate for at least 1 minute before checking the temperature.

3. Wrap a heating pad in plastic to protect it from chocolate stains. Set the control dial to the lowest setting. Put the bowl of tempered chocolate on the heating pad. The chocolate is now ready to work with. As you work, regularly stir the chocolate and check its temperature. If it begins to lose its fluidity, simply reheat it in the microwave oven at low (10 percent) power for 5- to 10-second intervals. Never let the temperature of the chocolate exceed 91°F, or the cocoa butter crystals will start to melt and the temper will be lost.

Using Leftover Tempered Chocolate

Leftover tempered chocolate may be reused for baking or candy making so long as it is correctly handled. To keep the chocolate until you want to use it again, line a baking sheet with foil and pour the melted chocolate onto it. Spread it evenly with a metal cake spatula and refrigerate it for 8 to 10 minutes, until set. Let the chocolate sit at room temperature for 30 minutes and then break it into pieces for easy storage. If you plan to use it later for any purpose that requires tempered chocolate, you will need to temper it again.

Chocolate Bark: Making chocolate bark is a delicious way to use up leftover tempered chocolate if you have some nuts and dried fruit on hand. Line a baking sheet with aluminum foil. Check the temperature of the tempered chocolate. Stir a handful of mixed nuts and chopped dried fruits into the bowl of tempered chocolate. Spread the mixture onto the prepared baking sheet and refrigerate for 10 minutes or until firm. Let the chocolate bark stand at room temperature for 30 minutes. Break into pieces and store in an airtight container.

Molded Candy Bars: Another good way to use up leftover tempered chocolate is to make chocolate bars or mini-chocolate bars in molds. To do so, stir together a handful of mixed roasted nuts, some crisped rice cereal, and some chopped dried fruit.

Check the temperature of the chocolate and if it has cooled lower than the tempering temperature, reheat it before stirring the nut mixture into the chocolate.

Fill clean, dry chocolate bar molds or rectangular tartlet molds—for mini-chocolate bars—with the chocolate mixture. (See page 19 for information on preparing molds for filling.) Tap the molds several times on a flat surface to release any air bubbles in the chocolate and refrigerate them for 30 to 60 minutes or until the chocolate is firm. In metal molds, the chocolate will contract slightly from the edges of the mold cavities when it is firm. In plastic molds, the surface of the chocolate against the mold will look frosty. Unmold the chocolate bars by inverting the molds and giving them a gentle tap. It is a good idea to unmold the bars over a folded dish towel so that they do not break, as they might on a hard surface. Wrap the bars individually in plastic, and store them at room temperature in airtight containers for up to 2 weeks.

2

John Paul Endress

Not-
Just-for-Kids
(Everyday Chocolate)

Fudgy Food-Processor Brownies
Chocolate Linzer Bars
Peanut Butter Chocolate Chip Bars
Chilled Peanut Butter Brownies
Cashew-Praline Blondies
Hollywood Hills
The Most Chocolate Chip Cookies
Buffalo Chip Cookies
Walnut Brownies
Chocolate-Dipped Peanut Brittle Fingers
The World's Best Rugelach
Chunky Chocolate Coconut Bars
Reverse Chocolate Hazelnut Cookies
White Chocolate Cocomacs
San Francisco Fudge Foggies®
Brownies in the Round
Trump's Mini-Cupcakes
Chunky Peanut Butter Chocolate
Chunk Cookies
Mocha Macadamia Nut Chocolate
Chunk Cookies
Oatmeal Bittersweet Chocolate Chunk
Cookies
Chocolate-Dipped Chocolate Chunk
Cookies
Crème de Menthe Brownies
Peanut Butter Cupcakes
Ever-So-Delicious Brownies
Chocolate Chubbies

We can hardly imagine a day without chocolate, which is why we grouped some of our favorite recipes in this chapter. These are easy recipes for the brownies, cookies, and bars everyone likes to grab "on the run," munch on after lunch, or eat with a late-afternoon glass of ice-cold milk or cup of hot tea. As good as they are as snacks, most do very well as dessert, too. Put a plate of brownies and a bowl of fresh fruit on the table after dinner and no one will be disappointed. These recipes also "travel" well, which means they are ideal for taking along as a hostess gift or to a sick friend, or for toting on board plane or train for respite during a long journey.

Kids adore these recipes, and as adults we might find ourselves baking a batch of chocolate chip cookies or fudgy brownies for the children in our lives, knowing all the while that the kids are simply providing an excuse. We will, naturally, *share* the cookies with our children and we might even tuck a few in their lunch boxes, but these goodies are most definitely "not just for kids." They are for everyone who likes quick, simple, unadorned chocolate treats. And who doesn't?

～ *Fudgy Food-Processor Brownies* ～

You won't find any brownies quicker to make. We devised this recipe specifically for the food processor and were excited by the fudgy, moist result. As fast as they are to mix up in the processor, don't forget that they really should cool for a couple of hours to allow time for their good chocolaty flavor to develop.

YIELD: 8 to 16 servings

DIFFICULTY: ◼

PREPARATION TIME: 15 minutes plus baking and cooling times

---

8 tablespoons (1 stick) unsalted butter
½ cup packed light brown sugar
¼ cup granulated sugar
9 ounces bittersweet chocolate, broken into pieces
1 ounce unsweetened chocolate
2 large eggs
1½ teaspoons vanilla extract
½ cup all-purpose flour
⅛ teaspoon salt
1 cup walnuts

1. Position a rack in the center of the oven and preheat to 350°F. Line an 8-inch square baking pan with aluminum foil so that the foil extends 2 inches beyond two opposite sides of the pan. Lightly butter the bottom and sides of the foil-lined pan.

2. In a medium saucepan, combine the butter and sugars. Over medium heat, stir them with a wooden spoon for 4 to 6 minutes or until the butter is melted.

3. Put the chocolates in a food processor fitted with the metal chopping blade and process for 15 to 20 seconds or until finely chopped. Add the hot

butter-sugar mixture and process for 15 to 20 seconds or until smooth, scraping down the sides of the work bowl as necessary. Add the eggs and vanilla and process for 10 to 15 seconds or until combined. Add the flour and salt and process for 5 to 7 seconds, until just combined, scraping down the work bowl if needed. Add the walnuts and pulse 10 times to incorporate them into the mixture and to chop them slightly.

4. Scrape the batter into the prepared pan and smooth the top with a rubber spatula. Bake the brownies for 25 to 30 minutes or until a cake tester or toothpick inserted 2 inches away from the center comes out slightly moist. Do not overbake.

5. Cool the brownies in the pan on a wire rack for 30 minutes. Using the two ends of the foil as handles, lift the brownies out of the pan. Leaving the brownies on the foil, cool on a wire rack for at least 2 hours.

6. Invert the brownies onto a large plate and gently peel off the foil. Invert again onto a smooth surface and cut into bars. Store in an airtight container.

NOTE: These brownies can be baked in an 8-inch round pan and cut into wedges. The baking time is the same whether the pan is square or round.

～ *Chocolate Linzer Bars* ～

There's nothing tricky about these bars, but the addition of chocolate to the traditionally raspberry-flavored sweets gives them a new twist we're sure you'll appreciate.

YIELD: Approximately 36 bars plus trimmings

DIFFICULTY: ▰

PREPARATION TIME: 25 minutes plus baking and cooling times

¾ *cup blanched whole almonds*
¾ *cup granulated sugar, divided*
1¼ *cups all-purpose flour*
¼ *cup unsweetened alkalized cocoa powder*
½ *teaspoon ground cinnamon*
¼ *teaspoon salt*
⅛ *teaspoon ground cloves*
8 *tablespoons (1 stick) unsalted butter, chilled and cut into 12 pieces*
1 *large egg, at room temperature*
1 *teaspoon grated lemon zest*
1 *teaspoon vanilla extract*
3 *ounces unsweetened chocolate, coarsely chopped*
⅔ *cup strained raspberry preserves*
½ *cup sliced almonds*

1. Position a rack in the center of the oven and preheat to 325°F. Generously butter a 10-by-15-by-1-inch jelly-roll pan.

2. In a food processor fitted with the metal chopping blade, combine the whole blanched almonds with ¼ cup of the sugar. Pulse 15 to 20 times or until the almonds are coarsely ground. Transfer the ground-almond mixture to a small bowl. Do not wash the work bowl.

3. Put the remaining ½ cup sugar, the flour, cocoa, cinnamon, salt, and cloves in the food processor. Pulse briefly to mix. Distribute the butter evenly over the dry ingredients and pulse 15 to 20 times or until the mixture resembles coarse meal. Add the egg, lemon zest, vanilla, and ground-almond mixture and pulse about 10 times, just until the mixture begins to cling together.

4. Transfer the dough to the prepared pan. Using the heel of your hand, firmly press the dough into an even layer over the bottom of the pan. Bake for 18 to 22 minutes or until firm and just beginning to brown.

5. While the dough is baking, melt the chocolate in the top of a double boiler, over hot, not simmering, water, stirring occasionally until smooth.

6. When the cocoa cookie base is ready, remove the pan from the oven, brush the melted chocolate evenly over the cookie, and cool for 5 minutes. Using a flexible metal spatula, spread the raspberry preserves in a layer over the chocolate. Sprinkle the sliced almonds evenly over the preserves. Return the pan to the oven for 15 to 17 minutes or until the preserves are bubbling and the almonds are light brown. Cool on a wire rack for 10 minutes. With the short end of the pan facing you, use a sharp knife to make diagonal slices, 1½ inches apart, beginning in the lower left corner. Then, starting from the top of the pan, make five vertical cuts, 2 inches apart. Using a metal spatula, remove the diamond-shaped bars and the trimmings from the pan. Store the cooled bars in an airtight container.

Peanut Butter Chocolate Chip 〜 Bars 〜

For a wallop of chocolate and peanut butter—and who doesn't love the combination?—try these simple bars. Your kids will love them—and so will your Saturday night dinner guests.

YIELD: 12 bars

DIFFICULTY: ▰

PREPARATION TIME: 20 minutes plus baking and cooling times

1⅓ cups all-purpose flour

1 teaspoon double-acting baking powder

¼ teaspoon baking soda

¼ teaspoon salt

⅔ cup extra-chunky peanut butter

4 tablespoons (½ stick) unsalted butter, softened

1 cup packed light brown sugar

2 large eggs, at room temperature

1 teaspoon vanilla extract

6 ounces (about 1 cup) semisweet chocolate chips

1. Position a rack in the center of the oven and preheat to 350°F. Line a 9-inch square baking pan with aluminum foil so that the foil extends 2 inches beyond two opposite sides of the pan. Lightly butter the bottom and sides of the foil-lined pan.

2. In a small bowl, stir together the flour, baking powder, baking soda, and salt.

3. In a large bowl, using a hand-held electric mixer set at medium-high speed, beat the peanut butter, butter, and brown sugar for 2 to 3 minutes or until well combined. Beat in the eggs and vanilla. Using a wooden spoon, stir in the flour mixture until just combined. Stir in the chocolate chips. Scrape the batter into the prepared pan and spread evenly.

4. Bake for 25 to 30 minutes or until a cake tester or toothpick inserted into the center of the pan comes out with a few moist crumbs clinging to it. Do not overbake the brownies. Cool in the pan on a wire rack for 30 minutes. Using the two ends of the foil as handles, lift the bars out of the pan. Leaving the bars on the foil, cool on the wire rack for at least 2 hours. Invert the bars onto a plate and carefully peel off the foil. Invert again onto a smooth surface and cut into 12 bars. Store the bars in an airtight container.

∼ *Chilled Peanut Butter Brownies* ∼

These layered brownies illustrate yet another way to combine the good flavors of peanut butter and chocolate . . . we don't think there are *too many* ways.

YIELD: 12 brownies

DIFFICULTY: ■

PREPARATION TIME: 20 minutes plus baking and chilling times

Peanut butter layer:

1 cup smooth peanut butter
⅓ cup granulated sugar
1 large egg, at room temperature

Chocolate layer:

5 tablespoons unsalted butter, softened
¾ cup granulated sugar
2 large eggs, at room temperature
1 teaspoon vanilla extract
¼ cup sifted unsweetened alkalized cocoa powder
½ cup all-purpose flour
5 ounces milk chocolate, cut into ¼-inch pieces

1. Position a rack in the center of the oven and preheat to 350°F. Line an 8-inch square baking pan with aluminum foil so that the foil extends 2 inches beyond two opposite sides of the pan. Lightly butter the top and sides of the foil-lined pan.

Make the peanut butter layer:

2. In a medium bowl, using a hand-held electric mixer set at medium speed, beat the peanut butter, sugar, and egg for 1 minute or until just combined.

(continued)

Scrape the mixture into the prepared pan. Using your fingertips, press the peanut butter layer evenly into the bottom of the pan.

Make the chocolate layer:

3. In a medium bowl, using a hand-held electric mixer set at high speed, beat the butter and sugar for 4 minutes or until light. Add the eggs and vanilla and continue beating for 2 minutes or until creamy and smooth. At low speed, beat in the cocoa and flour until just combined. Stir in the chocolate.

4. Scrape the batter into the baking pan and spread it evenly over the peanut butter layer. Bake the brownies for 30 to 35 minutes or until a cake tester or toothpick inserted 2 inches away from the center comes out clean.

5. Cool the brownies in the pan on a wire rack for at least 1 hour. Cover and refrigerate for at least 2 hours. Using the foil as handles, lift the brownies out of the pan. Invert the brownies onto a large plate and carefully peel off the foil. Invert again onto a smooth surface and cut into 12 brownies.

～ Cashew-Praline Blondies ～

The cashew praline gives these blondies a little crunch and fine flavor; the grated white chocolate makes them pretty as well as tasty.

YIELD: 8 bars

DIFFICULTY: ▰

PREPARATION TIME: 45 minutes plus roasting (the nuts), baking, and cooling times

Cashew praline:

¼ cup granulated sugar
2 tablespoons brandy or rum
¾ cup unsalted roasted cashews (for roasting instructions, see page 20)

Blondies:

3 ounces white chocolate, coarsely chopped
4 tablespoons (½ stick) unsalted butter, softened
½ cup packed light brown sugar
1 large egg, at room temperature
¼ teaspoon salt
1 tablespoon brandy or rum
1 cup all-purpose flour
1½ ounces white chocolate, coarsely grated

Make the cashew praline:

1. Lightly oil a 6-inch square space on a baking sheet. In a small, heavy saucepan, combine the sugar and liquor. Cook over medium heat, stirring constantly, until the sugar dissolves. Increase the heat to high and bring the syrup to a boil. Cook without stirring for 4 minutes or until the syrup

caramelizes. Immediately add the roasted cashews and stir to coat with the syrup. Quickly turn the cashew mixture out onto the oiled baking sheet. Cool for 20 minutes or until hardened. Finely chop the cashew praline with a sharp knife. Set the chopped praline aside.

Make the blondies:

2. Position a rack in the center of the oven and preheat to 350°F. Line an 8-inch square baking pan with aluminum foil so that the foil extends 2 inches beyond the two opposite sides of the pan. Lightly butter the bottom and sides of the foil-lined pan.

3. In the top of a double boiler over hot, not simmering, water, melt the white chocolate, stirring constantly. When smooth, remove the top of the double boiler and cool the chocolate for 5 to 10 minutes or until tepid. Whisk in the butter 1 tablespoon at a time and blend after each addition until smooth.

4. In a large bowl, using a hand-held electric mixer, combine the brown sugar, egg, and salt. Beat at high speed for 2 to 3 minutes or until it forms a thick ribbon when the beaters are lifted. At low speed, beat in the liquor. With a rubber spatula, fold in the white chocolate mixture. Stir in the flour and ⅓ cup of the chopped cashew praline. Transfer the batter to the prepared pan and spread evenly.

5. Bake for 18 minutes. Sprinkle the blondies with the remaining praline and bake 6 to 8 minutes more or until a cake tester or toothpick inserted in the middle comes out clean. Sprinkle the hot blondies with the grated white chocolate. Cool the blondies in the pan on a wire rack for at least 1 hour. Using the foil as handles, lift the blondies from the pan. With a sharp knife, cut them in half. Cut each half into 4 bars and carefully lift them off the foil. Store the completely cooled bars in an airtight container.

⌒ *Hollywood Hills* ⌒

The dough for these simple little chocolate cookies can be made as much as a month before baking. Roll it into a log and freeze it until you decide it's time to slice and bake the cookies.

YIELD: Approximately 2 dozen cookies
DIFFICULTY: ◼
PREPARATION TIME: 25 minutes plus shaping, freezing, baking, and cooling times

1½ cups all-purpose flour

¼ cup whole wheat flour

¾ teaspoon baking soda

Pinch of salt

12 tablespoons (1½ sticks) unsalted butter, softened

½ cup granulated sugar

½ cup packed light brown sugar

1 large egg plus 1 large egg yolk, at room temperature

1 teaspoon vanilla extract

8 ounces German sweet chocolate, coarsely chopped

2 cups coarsely chopped walnuts

1. In a medium bowl, stir together the flours, baking soda, and salt.

2. In another medium bowl, using a hand-held electric mixer set at low speed, beat the butter for

1 to 2 minutes or until creamy. Increase the speed to medium and beat in the sugars until combined. Add the egg, egg yolk, and vanilla, and continue beating for 1 to 2 minutes or until light. Decrease the mixer speed to low and slowly beat in the flour mixture. Stir in the chocolate and nuts.

3. Scrape the mixture onto a sheet of waxed paper or plastic wrap. Using the paper, shape the dough into a 10-by-2½-inch cylinder. Wrap well and freeze the dough for at least 1 hour or refrigerate for at least 2 hours until firm.

4. Position a rack in the center of the oven and preheat to 350°F. Remove the cookie dough from the freezer and thaw 5 to 10 minutes or until it is just soft enough to be sliced with a thin, sharp knife. Cut the dough into ½-inch thick slices. Put the cookies on a baking sheet, leaving 3 inches between cookies.

5. Bake the cookies for 8 to 10 minutes or until lightly puffed, brown edged, and dry on top. Cool the cookies on the baking sheet for 2 to 3 minutes, just until firm enough to lift with a spatula. Transfer the cookies to wire racks and cool completely. Store at room temperature in an airtight container.

The Most Chocolate Chip ∽ Cookies ∾

Chunks, chips, and mini-chips combine to give these cookies their name. The recipe comes from one of our best resources: a reader.

YIELD: Approximately 4 dozen cookies

DIFFICULTY: ■

PREPARATION TIME: 30 minutes plus chilling, baking, and cooling times

2¾ cups all-purpose flour

1 teaspoon baking soda

1 teaspoon salt

¾ cup granulated sugar

¾ cup packed light brown sugar

1½ cups (3 sticks) unsalted butter, melted and cooled slightly

2 large eggs, at room temperature

1 teaspoon vanilla extract

24 ounces (about 4 cups) semisweet chocolate chips

8 ounces (about 1 cup) miniature semisweet chocolate chips

6 ounces semisweet chocolate, cut into ¼-inch chunks

¾ cup walnuts, coarsely chopped

1. In a medium bowl, stir together the flour, baking soda, and salt.

2. In a large bowl, using a hand-held electric mixer set at low speed, gradually beat the sugars

into the melted butter for 1 to 2 minutes or until completely emulsified and creamy. Beat in the eggs and vanilla. Using a wooden spoon, stir in the flour mixture. Add both kinds of chocolate chips, the chocolate chunks, and the walnuts, and stir until well combined. Cover the bowl with plastic wrap and refrigerate for at least 1 hour or overnight.

3. Position a rack in the center of the oven and preheat to 350°F. Line two baking sheets with baking parchment paper or aluminum foil.

4. Using about 2 tablespoons of dough for each cookie, drop the dough onto the baking sheets, leaving about 2 inches between each cookie. Bake for 12 to 14 minutes or until lightly browned around the edges. Cool the cookies on the pans for 3 to 5 minutes. Transfer to wire racks and cool completely. Store the cookies in an airtight container at room temperature.

⌒ *Buffalo Chip Cookies* ⌒

Generous and domed, these cookies combine the crunchy flavors of corn flakes, coconut, and rolled oats with (what else?) chocolate. Baking takes a little while, since only three fit on a cookie sheet at one time, which is why we suggest using two levels in the oven.

YIELD: About 27 cookies
DIFFICULTY: ▰
PREPARATION TIME: 30 minutes plus baking and cooling times
SPECIAL EQUIPMENT: ⅓-cup measuring cup or ice cream scoop with ⅓-cup capacity

4 cups all-purpose flour

2 teaspoons double-acting baking powder

2 teaspoons baking soda

1 teaspoon salt

2 cups granulated sugar

2 cups packed light brown sugar

2 cups (4 sticks) unsalted butter, melted

4 large eggs, at room temperature

2 teaspoons vanilla extract

2 cups uncooked old-fashioned rolled oats

2 cups corn flakes

12 ounces (about 2 cups) semisweet chocolate chips

1 cup pecans, coarsely chopped

1 cup sweetened flaked coconut

1. Position one rack in the top third and another rack in the bottom third of the oven and preheat to 350°F. Lightly butter two baking sheets.

2. In a medium bowl, stir together the flour, baking powder, baking soda, and salt.

3. In a large bowl, using a hand-held electric mixer set at low speed, gradually beat the sugars into the melted butter for 2 to 3 minutes or until

creamy and completely combined. Beat in the eggs and vanilla. Using a wooden spoon, stir in the flour mixture. Add the rolled oats, corn flakes, chocolate chips, pecans, and coconut, and stir until well combined.

4. Using a ⅓-cup measuring cup or an ice cream scoop with a ⅓-cup capacity, measure the dough and drop three scoops onto each of the prepared baking sheets, leaving about 3 inches between each cookie. Bake for 20 to 25 minutes or until lightly browned around the edges but still slightly soft in the center. Cool the cookies for 3 to 5 minutes on their pans before transferring to wire racks to finish cooling. Repeat with the remaining dough. Store the cooled cookies in an airtight container at room temperature.

⌣ *Walnut Brownies* ⌣

Here is the classic brownie, well studded with walnuts.

YIELD: 16 brownies
DIFFICULTY: ◼
PREPARATION TIME: 30 minutes plus baking and cooling times

¾ cup granulated sugar
½ cup packed light brown sugar
8 tablespoons (1 stick) unsalted butter, cut into tablespoons
2 ounces unsweetened chocolate, coarsely chopped
1 tablespoon light corn syrup
½ cup all-purpose flour
½ teaspoon double-acting baking powder
2 large eggs, at room temperature
1 teaspoon vanilla extract
2 cups walnuts, coarsely chopped

1. Position a rack in the center of the oven and preheat to 350°F. Line an 8-inch square baking pan with aluminum foil so that the foil extends 2 inches beyond two opposite sides of the pan. Lightly butter the bottom and sides of the foil-lined pan.

2. Combine the sugars, butter, chocolate, and corn syrup in a medium saucepan. Over medium-low heat, stir the mixture with a wooden spoon for 4 to 6 minutes or until it is melted and smooth. Remove the pan from the heat and let it cool for 15 to 20 minutes or until tepid.

3. In a small bowl, stir together the flour and baking powder.

4. Whisk the eggs and vanilla into the cooled chocolate mixture, blending until smooth. Using a wooden spoon, stir in the flour mixture and walnuts.

5. Scrape the batter into the prepared pan and smooth the top with a rubber spatula. Bake the brownies for 30 to 40 minutes or until a cake tester or toothpick inserted into the center comes out

with a few moist crumbs clinging to it. Do not overbake the brownies.

6. Cool the brownies in the pan on a wire rack for at least 30 minutes. Using the two ends of the foil as handles, lift the brownies out of the pan and cool on the foil for at least 2 hours. Invert the brownies onto a large plate and carefully peel off the foil. Invert again onto a smooth surface and cut into 16 squares.

Chocolate-Dipped Peanut Brittle
∾ Fingers ∾

A triple taste treat: a buttery cookie topped with peanut brittle and then dipped in a semisweet chocolate glaze.

YIELD: Approximately 6 dozen cookies

DIFFICULTY: ◼◼

PREPARATION TIME: 45 minutes plus baking and cooling times

Butter pastry:

9 tablespoons (1 stick plus 1 tablespoon) unsalted butter, softened
½ cup plus 1 tablespoon granulated sugar
1 large egg plus 1 large egg yolk, at room temperature
1 teaspoon vanilla extract
2¼ cups all-purpose flour

Peanut brittle topping:

¼ cup plus 2 tablespoons light corn syrup
½ cup packed light brown sugar
4 tablespoons (½ stick) unsalted butter
¼ cup heavy (whipping) cream
2 cups coarsely chopped, salted dry-roasted peanuts
1 teaspoon vanilla extract
A few drops of lemon juice

Chocolate glaze:

6 ounces semisweet chocolate, coarsely chopped, or 6 ounces (about 1 cup) semisweet or milk chocolate chips
2 tablespoons solid vegetable shortening

Make the butter pastry:

1. In a medium bowl, using a hand-held electric mixer set at medium-high speed, cream the butter with the sugar for 2 to 3 minutes or until light. Stir in the egg, egg yolk, and vanilla. Stir in the flour just until combined.

2. Position a rack in the center of the oven and preheat to 350°F. Press the mixture into an un-

greased 10½-by-15-by-2-inch jelly-roll pan (do not use a nonstick pan), pressing it up the sides slightly. Chill the dough for 15 minutes.

3. Prick the surface of the dough with a fork. Bake for 18 to 20 minutes or until the pastry is light brown. Remove the pastry from the oven and let it cool while you make the peanut brittle topping.

Make the peanut brittle topping:

4. In a heavy, medium-sized saucepan set over low heat, combine the corn syrup and brown sugar and stir to dissolve. Add the butter and cream, raise the heat to medium high, and bring to a rolling boil. Remove the pan from the heat and stir in the peanuts, vanilla, and lemon juice. Pour the mixture over the crust and gently spread it evenly over the surface with a spatula. Bake for 15 to 20 minutes or until bubbly and light brown.

5. Remove the pan from the oven to a wire rack and cool completely. Use a sharp knife to trim the edges of the pastry and cut into 1-by-2-inch bars.

Make the chocolate glaze:

6. When the bars are cool and ready to be dipped, melt the chocolate and vegetable shortening in the top of a double boiler over hot, not simmering, water, stirring occasionally until smooth. Scrape the mixture into a shallow bowl and dip each peanut brittle bar into the warm chocolate, coating it halfway. Cool the bars on a wire rack until set. Store in an airtight container at room temperature.

⌁ The World's Best Rugelach ⌁

These pretty cookies take a little time to assemble, and the dough needs to be chilled for a couple of hours before you can begin to roll and bake the rugelach, but the combination of the sour cream pastry and the chocolate-walnut filling is hard to beat.

> YIELD: 48 cookies
>
> DIFFICULTY: ◣◣
>
> PREPARATION TIME: 1 hour plus 2 hours for chilling the dough before baking

Sour cream pastry:

2 cups all-purpose flour
¼ teaspoon salt
1 cup (2 sticks) chilled unsalted butter, cut into tablespoons
¾ cup sour cream, chilled
1 large egg yolk, at room temperature

Chocolate walnut filling:

2 ounces semisweet chocolate, coarsely chopped, or 2 ounces (about ⅓ cup) semisweet chocolate chips
½ ounce unsweetened chocolate, coarsely chopped
⅓ cup walnuts
3 tablespoons granulated sugar
½ teaspoon ground cinnamon

Topping:

2 tablespoons unsalted butter, melted
3 tablespoons granulated sugar
½ teaspoon ground cinnamon

Make the sour cream pastry:

1. In a food processor fitted with the metal chopping blade, combine the flour and salt. Process for 5 seconds or until blended. Evenly distribute the butter cubes and sour cream over the flour mixture. Add the egg yolk and process for 10 to 20 seconds or just until the dough starts to hold together and comes away from the sides of the work bowl. Wrap the dough in plastic and refrigerate for at least 2 hours or overnight or until firm.

Make the filling:

2. In a food processor fitted with the metal chopping blade, combine the chocolates, walnuts, sugar, and cinnamon, and process until finely chopped. Transfer to a small bowl.

Assemble the cookies:

3. Position one rack in the top third and another rack in the bottom third of the oven and preheat to 350°F.

4. Divide the dough into quarters. Keeping three quarters of the dough in the refrigerator, put the fourth on a lightly floured work surface and roll it into a 9-inch circle. Sprinkle 3 tablespoons of the filling evenly over the dough and press it down gently with your fingers.

5. Use a sharp knife to cut the circle into 12 wedges. Beginning with the widest edge, roll each wedge tightly. Put the rugelach, point side down, on an ungreased baking sheet, leaving ½ inch between each cookie. Prepare the remaining quarters of dough in the same fashion, keeping the remaining dough and the assembled rugelach in the refrigerator while you work.

Make the topping:

6. Brush the rugelach with the melted butter. Stir the sugar and cinnamon together and sprinkle over the cookies. Bake the rugelach for 25 to 30 minutes or until golden brown. With a spatula, transfer them to a wire rack to cool completely. Store the cookies in an airtight container for up to 1 week.

∾ *Chunky Chocolate Coconut Bars* ∾

The name says it all. Chunky, chocolate, and darkly delicious.

YIELD: 24 bars

DIFFICULTY: ◼

PREPARATION TIME: 20 minutes plus baking and cooling times

1 cup plus 2 tablespoons all-purpose flour
½ teaspoon baking soda
¼ teaspoon salt
8 tablespoons (1 stick) unsalted butter, softened
⅓ cup granulated sugar
⅓ cup packed light brown sugar
1 large egg, at room temperature
1 teaspoon vanilla extract
1¼ cups sweetened flaked coconut
6 ounces (about 1 cup) semisweet chocolate chips
½ cup pecans, coarsely chopped

1. Position a rack in the center of the oven and preheat to 350°F. Line a 9-inch square baking pan with aluminum foil so that the foil extends 2 inches beyond the two opposite sides of the pan. Lightly butter the bottom and sides of the foil-lined pan.

2. Stir together and then sift the flour, baking soda, and salt. In a large bowl, using a hand-held electric mixer set at medium speed, cream the butter with the sugars for 2 to 3 minutes or until light and fluffy. Beat in the egg and vanilla. Reduce the speed to low and add the flour mixture, beating just until combined. Stir in the coconut, chocolate chips, and pecans. Scrape the batter into the prepared pan and spread evenly.

3. Bake for 20 to 25 minutes or until the surface is dry and golden and a cake tester or toothpick inserted in the center comes out slightly moist. Remove the pan from the oven to a wire rack and cool completely. Using the two ends of the foil as handles, lift the bars from the pan and invert them on a plate. Carefully peel off the foil. Invert again onto a flat surface and cut into 24 bars. Store the completely cooled bars in an airtight container.

Reverse Chocolate Hazelnut ～ *Cookies* ～

We think you'll agree that these chocolate cookies with white chocolate chips are a heavenly change from the usual.

YIELD: Approximately 24 cookies
DIFFICULTY: ▰
PREPARATION TIME: 15 minutes plus chilling and baking

1 cup all-purpose flour
⅓ cup unsweetened nonalkalized cocoa powder
½ teaspoon double-acting baking powder
¼ teaspoon salt
½ cup (1 stick) unsalted butter, softened
½ cup packed dark brown sugar
½ cup granulated sugar
1 teaspoon vanilla extract
1 large egg, at room temperature
8 ounces white chocolate, coarsely chopped
¾ cup roasted hazelnuts, coarsely chopped (for roasting instructions, see page 20)

1. Stir together the flour, cocoa, baking powder, and salt in a medium bowl.

2. In another medium bowl, cream the butter with the sugars and vanilla for 1 minute or until light and fluffy, using a hand-held electric mixer set at medium-high speed. Beat in the egg. With a wooden spoon, stir in the flour mixture. Add the white chocolate and hazelnuts and stir until well combined. Cover the bowl with plastic wrap and refrigerate for at least 6 hours or overnight.

3. Lightly butter two large baking sheets. Position one rack in the top third and another rack in the bottom third of the oven and preheat to 325°F.

4. Using 2 tablespoons of dough for each cookie, roll the dough into 1½-inch balls between the palms of your hands. Put the balls on the baking sheets, leaving 2½ inches between each cookie. Bake for 12 to 14 minutes or until no impression is left when a cookie is lightly touched with a fingertip. Do not overbake. Cool the cookies on the baking sheet on a wire rack for 1 minute and then, with a metal spatula, transfer them to a wire rack. Cool completely and store in an airtight container.

⌒ *White Chocolate Cocomacs* ⌒

Macadamia nuts and white chocolate are one of our favorite flavor combinations, and these jumbo cookies with crispy edges have the added benefit of coconut.

> **YIELD:** Approximately 24 4-inch cookies
>
> **DIFFICULTY:** ▰
>
> **PREPARATION TIME:** 15 minutes plus at least 2 hours for chilling the dough before baking
>
> **SPECIAL EQUIPMENT:** 2⅜-inch diameter ice cream scoop

¾ *cup macadamia nuts*
2 *cups all-purpose flour*
1 *teaspoon baking soda*
1 *teaspoon salt*
1 *cup (2 sticks) unsalted butter, softened*
1 *cup packed dark brown sugar*
¼ *cup packed light brown sugar*
¼ *cup granulated sugar*
2 *large eggs, at room temperature*
2½ *teaspoons vanilla extract*
12 *ounces white chocolate, coarsely chopped*
1⅓ *cups sweetened flaked coconut*

1. Rub the macadamia nuts between two paper towels to remove as much salt as possible. Chop the nuts coarsely.

2. In a medium bowl, stir together the flour, baking soda, and salt. In a large bowl, using a hand-held electric mixer on medium-high, beat the butter, brown sugars, and sugar until well mixed. Beat in the eggs and vanilla until the mixture is light and fluffy. Beat in the flour mixture only until no white streaks remain. Stir in the white chocolate chunks, coconut, and macadamia nuts until combined. Cover the dough with plastic wrap and refrigerate for at least 2 hours. It will keep this way for 2 days.

3. Position a rack in the center of the oven and preheat to 350°F. Line a baking sheet with baking parchment or aluminum. Use a 2⅜-inch diameter ice cream scoop to form the cookies. Pack the dough into the scoop so it is even with the edge and then release it onto the baking sheet. Put five scoops on the sheet. Bake for 18 to 20 minutes or until the cookies are golden around the edges. Cool the cookies on the baking sheet until they are just warm. The cookies will become slightly crisp around the edges as they cool. Remove the cookies to a wire rack to cool completely. Repeat with the remaining dough. Store completely cool cookies in an airtight container at room temperature.

∽ *San Francisco Fudge Foggies*® ∾

We think these foggies break new ground—not really a brownie (they're just *too* fudgy), they are more like "baked" fudge. Easy to mix up, they're so moist after baking that you have to let them chill thoroughly for at least 6 hours before cutting, so be sure to give yourself enough time.

YIELD: 16 foggies
DIFFICULTY: ◣
PREPARATION TIME: 25 minutes plus baking and chilling times

1 pound bittersweet chocolate, coarsely chopped
1 cup (2 sticks) unsalted butter, cut into tablespoons
⅓ cup strong brewed coffee
4 large eggs, at room temperature
1½ cups granulated sugar
½ cup all-purpose flour
2 cups walnuts, coarsely chopped

1. Position a rack in the center of the oven and preheat to 375°F. Line a 9-by-13-inch baking pan with aluminum foil so that the foil extends 2 inches beyond the two long sides of the pan. Butter the bottom and sides of the foil-lined pan.

2. In the top of a double boiler over hot, not simmering, water, melt the chocolate and butter with the coffee, stirring frequently, until smooth. Remove the top part of the double boiler from the bottom and cool the mixture, stirring it occasionally, for 10 minutes or until tepid.

3. In a large bowl, using a hand-held electric mixer set at high speed, beat the eggs for 30 seconds or until foamy. Gradually add the sugar, and continue to beat for 2 minutes or until the mixture is very light. Reduce the mixer speed to low and gradually beat in the chocolate mixture until just blended. Stir in the flour with a wooden spoon and then use the same spoon to stir in the walnuts. Do not over beat.

4. Scrape the batter into the prepared pan and spread evenly. Bake for 28 to 30 minutes or until the foggies are just set around the edges. They will be moist in the center.

5. Cool the foggies in the pan on a wire rack for 30 minutes. Cover the pan tightly with aluminum foil and refrigerate overnight or for at least 6 hours. Remove the top foil and run a sharp knife around the edge of the foggies. Using the two ends of the foil as handles, lift the foggies out of the pan and invert them onto a large plate. Carefully peel off the foil and then invert them again onto a smooth surface and cut into 16 rectangles.

~ *Brownies in the Round* ~

You could also call this a chocolate pizza. The white chocolate garnishing the top looks a little like melted cheese! If you're in a hurry or do not have white chocolate on hand, make this chocolate pie anyhow, leaving off the decorative drizzles of white chocolate.

> YIELD: 16 wedges
>
> DIFFICULTY: ▬
>
> PREPARATION TIME: 30 minutes plus baking and cooling times
>
> SPECIAL EQUIPMENT: 12-inch diameter pizza pan

2 ounces unsweetened chocolate, coarsely chopped
6 ounces bittersweet chocolate
3 ounces milk chocolate
1 cup small pecan halves
¾ cup all-purpose flour
⅛ teaspoon salt
8 tablespoons (1 stick) unsalted butter, softened
1 cup packed dark brown sugar
2 large eggs, at room temperature
1½ teaspoons vanilla extract
3 ounces white chocolate, coarsely chopped

1. Position a rack in the center of the oven and preheat to 325°F. Lightly butter the bottom and sides of the pizza pan.

2. In the top of a double boiler over hot, not simmering, water, melt the unsweetened chocolate. Remove the top part of the double boiler from the bottom and cool for 5 to 10 minutes or until the chocolate is tepid.

3. Chop the bittersweet and milk chocolates into ½-inch squares. Set aside half of the bittersweet chocolate squares, half of the milk chocolate squares, and half of the pecan halves; these will be sprinkled over the batter just before baking.

4. In a small bowl, stir together the flour and salt. In a large bowl, using a hand-held electric mixer set at medium speed, beat the butter and brown sugar until light. Beat in the eggs one at a time, mixing well after each addition. Beat in the melted unsweetened chocolate and the vanilla until blended. Beat in the flour mixture until just com-

bined. Fold in half of the chopped bittersweet and milk chocolate squares and half of the pecans. Scrape the batter into the prepared pan and smooth the surface with a spatula. Sprinkle with the reserved chopped chocolate pieces and pecans.

5. Bake for 25 to 30 minutes or until a cake tester or toothpick inserted 2 inches away from the center comes out clean. Remove the pan to a wire rack to cool.

6. In the top of a double boiler over hot, not simmering, water, melt the white chocolate, stirring constantly, until smooth. Fill a small paper cone with the melted white chocolate and cut a ⅛-inch opening at the tip (for instructions on making a paper cone, see page 187). Drizzle the white chocolate over the surface of the brownies. Cut into wedges to serve.

NOTE: To make a diamond pattern with the white chocolate, first drizzle white chocolate in diagonal stripes about 1 inch apart. Cross these with horizontal stripes that are also about 1 inch apart.

Trump's Mini-Cupcakes

Ever wonder how they get the creamy filling inside cupcakes? Try this recipe and find out. It's easy. The bite-sized cupcakes may look familiar to devotees of cream-filled chocolate cupcakes, but we think they are much better than any you can buy. And they're such fun!

> YIELD: 24 miniature cupcakes
>
> DIFFICULTY: ■■
>
> PREPARATION TIME: 1 hour plus baking, cooling, and chilling times
>
> SPECIAL EQUIPMENT: 24 1¾-by-¾-inch (1 ounce) muffin or biscuit cups; pastry bag fitted with a plain tip (such as Ateco #1)

Cupcakes:

½ cup plus 2 tablespoons all-purpose flour
2½ tablespoons unsweetened nonalkalized cocoa powder
¾ teaspoon baking soda
¼ teaspoon salt
½ cup granulated sugar
½ cup water
3 tablespoons vegetable oil
1½ teaspoons distilled white vinegar
1 teaspoon vanilla extract

Filling:

⅓ cup heavy (whipping) cream
2 teaspoons granulated sugar
¼ teaspoon vanilla extract

Chocolate glaze:

3 ounces bittersweet chocolate, finely chopped
3 tablespoons boiling water

White icing:

1 tablespoon egg white, at room temperature
Pinch of cream of tartar
½ cup plus 2 to 3 tablespoons sifted confectioners' sugar

Make the cupcakes:

1. Position a rack in the center of the oven and preheat to 325°F. Lightly butter muffin or biscuit cups.

2. In a medium bowl, stir and then sift together the flour, cocoa, baking soda, and salt. Add the sugar until combined. Make a well in the center of the dry ingredients. Pour the water, oil, vinegar, and vanilla into the well and whisk until smooth. The batter will be thin.

3. Spoon the batter into the prepared cups. Bake for 12 to 14 minutes or until a cake tester or toothpick inserted into the center of one of the cupcakes comes out clean. Cool the cupcakes in

the pan(s) for 5 minutes on a wire rack. Remove the cupcakes from the pan(s) and finish cooling on the rack.

Make the filling:

4. In a chilled bowl, whip the cream with the sugar and vanilla until stiff peaks start to form. Transfer the whipped cream to a pastry bag fitted with a ⅜-inch plain tip (such as Ateco #1). Insert the pastry tip ¼ inch into the bottom of each cooled cupcake and squeeze a little filling into each one.

Make the chocolate glaze:

5. Put the chocolate into a small bowl. Whisk in the boiling water and blend until smooth. Dip the top of each cupcake into the warm glaze, turn it right side up, and set it on a wire rack that is set over a baking sheet. Refrigerate the cupcakes for 5 minutes to set the glaze.

Make the white icing:

6. In a medium bowl, whisk the egg white until frothy. Stir in the cream of tartar. Gradually mix in enough of the confectioners' sugar to make a fairly stiff and smooth icing. Fill a small paper cone with the icing and cut a 1/16-inch opening at the tip (for instructions on making a paper cone, see page 187). Remove the cupcakes from the refrigerator. Pipe a crisscross design on top of each cupcake. Store in a single layer in an airtight container until ready to serve.

Chunky Peanut Butter Chocolate Chunk Cookies

Beginning with this recipe and following are four versions of chunk cookies—a variation on traditional chocolate chip cookies that use chopped-up chocolate bars rather than packaged chocolate chips. These chunks are larger than most chips and are meltingly wonderful in the baked cookies. For these recipes you don't even need an electric mixer to make the batter—but you do need to chill it for several hours (or overnight) before baking, which makes them a good choice for plan-ahead occasions.

YIELD: Approximately 25 cookies

DIFFICULTY: ■

PREPARATION TIME: 15 minutes plus chilling and baking times

---

1 cup all-purpose flour
½ teaspoon baking soda
¼ teaspoon salt
8 tablespoons (1 stick) unsalted butter, softened
⅓ cup chunky peanut butter
¾ cup packed dark brown sugar
¼ cup granulated sugar
1 large egg, at room temperature
1 teaspoon vanilla extract
12 ounces bittersweet chocolate, coarsely chopped
¾ cup unsalted roasted peanuts, coarsely chopped
Vegetable shortening, for the baking sheets

1. In a small bowl, stir together the flour, baking soda, and salt. In a large bowl, using a wooden spoon, beat together the butter, peanut butter, brown sugar, and sugar until creamy. Beat in the egg and vanilla. Stir in the flour mixture and then the chocolate and peanuts. Cover the surface of the dough with plastic wrap and refrigerate until firm, about 4 hours or overnight.

2. Position one rack in the top third and another rack in the bottom third of the oven and preheat to 350°F. Lightly coat two baking sheets with vegetable shortening. Using 2 tablespoons of dough for each cookie, shape the dough into balls and put them on the baking sheets, leaving about 1 inch between the cookies. Bake for 10 to 12 minutes or until the cookies spring back when very lightly touched. Do not overbake or the cookies will dry out.

3. Cool the cookies on their baking sheets for 2 minutes. Transfer the cookies to paper towels for 2 minutes and then to wire racks to cool completely. Repeat the baking procedure with the remaining dough, using cool baking sheets and coating them with additional vegetable shortening for each batch. Store the cookies in an airtight container.

Mocha Macadamia Nut
〜 Chocolate Chunk Cookies 〜

YIELD: Approximately 25 cookies	
DIFFICULTY: ◼	
PREPARATION TIME: 15 minutes plus chilling and baking times	

1 cup plus 2 tablespoons all-purpose flour
2 tablespoons unsweetened cocoa powder
½ teaspoon baking soda
¼ teaspoon salt
1½ teaspoons instant espresso coffee powder
1 teaspoon boiling water
8 tablespoons (1 stick) unsalted butter, softened
6 tablespoons packed dark brown sugar
6 tablespoons granulated sugar
1 large egg, at room temperature
1 teaspoon vanilla extract
12 ounces mocha or semisweet chocolate, coarsely chopped
¾ cup macadamia nuts, coarsely chopped and rinsed if salted
   (see Note)
Vegetable shortening, for the baking sheets

1. In a small bowl, stir together the flour, cocoa, baking soda, and salt. In a small cup, stir together the expresso coffee powder and water until dissolved. In a large bowl, using a wooden spoon, beat

together the butter, brown sugar, and sugar until creamy. Beat in the egg, espresso mixture, and vanilla. Stir in the flour mixture and then the chocolate and nuts. Cover the surface of the dough with plastic wrap and refrigerate until firm, about 4 hours or overnight.

2. Position one rack in the top third and another rack in the bottom third of the oven and preheat to 325°F. Lightly coat two baking sheets with vegetable shortening. Using 2 tablespoons of the dough for each cookie, shape the dough into balls and put them on the baking sheets, leaving about 2 inches between the cookies. Bake for 12 to 14 minutes or until the cookies spring back when very lightly touched. Do not overbake or the cookies will dry out.

3. Cool the cookies on their baking sheets for 2 minutes. Transfer the cookies to paper towels for another 2 minutes and then to wire racks to cool completely. Repeat the baking procedure with the remaining dough, using cool baking sheets and coating them with additional vegetable shortening for each batch. Store the cookies in an airtight container.

NOTE: To remove salt from the macadamia nuts, put them in a strainer and rinse under cool running water. Pat the nuts dry with paper towels before chopping.

Oatmeal Bittersweet Chunk ～ Chocolate Cookies ～

YIELD: Approximately 25 cookies

DIFFICULTY: ▬

PREPARATION TIME: 15 minutes plus chilling and baking times

---

1 cup uncooked old-fashioned rolled oats
¾ cup all-purpose flour
½ teaspoon baking soda
½ teaspoon salt
8 tablespoons (1 stick) unsalted butter, softened
½ cup packed dark brown sugar
½ cup granulated sugar
1 large egg, at room temperature
1 teaspoon water
1 teaspoon vanilla extract
12 ounces bittersweet chocolate, coarsely chopped
¾ cup walnuts or pecans, coarsely chopped
Vegetable shortening, for the baking sheets

1. In a small bowl, stir together the oats, flour, baking soda, and salt. In a large bowl, using a wooden spoon, beat together the butter, brown sugar, and sugar until creamy. Beat in the egg,

water, and vanilla. Stir in the oat mixture and then the chocolate and walnuts. Cover the surface of the dough with plastic wrap and refrigerate until firm, about 4 hours or overnight.

2. Position one rack in the top third and another in the bottom third of the oven and preheat to 350°F. Lightly coat two baking sheets with vegetable shortening. Using 2 tablespoons of dough for each cookie, shape the dough into balls and put them on the baking sheets, leaving about 2 inches between the cookies.

Bake for 10 to 12 minutes or until the cookies spring back when very lightly touched. Do not overbake.

3. Cool the cookies on their baking sheets for 2 minutes. Transfer the cookies to paper towels for another 2 minutes and then to wire racks to cool completely. Repeat the baking procedure with the remaining dough, using cool baking sheets and coating them with additional vegetable shortening for each batch. Store the cookies in an airtight container.

Chocolate-Dipped Chocolate ⌒ Chunk Cookies ⌒

If you don't temper the chocolate for dipping the cookies, it will lose its shine and smooth texture. Of course, you may decide that they are just fine without the extra chocolate coating—and they are! But for intense chocolate flavor, try dipping them.

YIELD: Approximately 20 cookies

DIFFICULTY: ◣

PREPARATION TIME: 25 minutes plus chilling and baking times

1 ounce unsweetened chocolate, coarsely chopped
1 cup all-purpose flour
½ teaspoon baking soda
½ teaspoon salt
8 tablespoons (1 stick) unsalted butter, at room temperature
½ cup packed dark brown sugar
⅓ cup granulated sugar
1 large egg, at room temperature
1 teaspoon vanilla extract
12 ounces bittersweet chocolate, coarsely chopped
Vegetable shortening, for the baking sheets
8 ounces tempered couverture chocolate, for dipping (for tempering instructions, see page 22)

1. In the top of a double boiler over hot, not simmering, water, melt the unsweetened chocolate, stirring frequently until smooth. Remove the top part of the double boiler from the bottom and cool for 5 to 10 minutes or until tepid.

2. In a small bowl, stir together the flour, baking soda, and salt. In a large bowl, using a wooden spoon, beat together the butter, brown sugar, and sugar until creamy. Beat in the chocolate, egg, and vanilla. Stir in the flour mixture and then the

bittersweet chocolate. Cover the surface of the dough with plastic wrap and refrigerate until firm, for about 4 hours or overnight.

3.   Position one rack in the top third and another in the bottom third of the oven and preheat to 325°F. Lightly coat two baking sheets with vegetable shortening. Using 2 tablespoons of dough for each cookie, shape the dough into balls and put them on the baking sheets, leaving about 2 inches between the cookies. Bake for 12 to 14 minutes or until the cookies spring back when very lightly touched. Do not overbake.

4.   Cool the cookies on their baking sheets for 2 minutes, transfer them to a paper towel for another 2 minutes, and then transfer them to wire racks to cool completely. Repeat the baking procedure with the remaining dough, using cool baking sheets and coating with additional shortening for each batch.

5.   Put the tempered chocolate in a small bowl and dip a third to a half of each cookie into the chocolate. Coat the top of the cookie first and then the bottom, scraping the bottom of the cookie along the edge of the bowl to remove the excess chocolate. Put the cookies on an aluminum foil-lined baking sheet. Let the cookies set at room temperature for 20 minutes before transferring them to an airtight container.

～ *Crème de Menthe Brownies* ～

These brownies are made in three stages—first, you bake the brownie base; next, you spread the refreshingly minty filling over the brownies; and, finally, after the filling has set in the refrigerator, you top it with a simple chocolate glaze. The result is spectacular, certainly fancy enough to serve with after-dinner coffee at your next party.

YIELD: 24 brownies

DIFFICULTY: ◼

PREPARATION TIME: 1 hour plus baking, cooling, and chilling times

---

Brownies:

1 cup all-purpose flour

½ teaspoon salt

1 cup granulated sugar

8 tablespoons (1 stick) unsalted butter, softened

4 large eggs, at room temperature, lightly beaten

2 cups chocolate syrup

1 teaspoon vanilla extract

½ cup walnuts or pecans, coarsely chopped

Crème de menthe filling:

8 tablespoons (1 stick) unsalted butter, softened

2 cups confectioners' sugar

¼ cup crème de menthe liqueur

Glaze:

¼ cup water

3 tablespoons unsalted butter, cut into tablespoons

6 ounces (about 1 cup) semisweet chocolate chips

Make the brownies:

1. Position a rack in the center of the oven and preheat to 350°F. Line a 9-by-13-inch baking pan with aluminum foil so that it extends 2 inches beyond the two long sides of the pan. Lightly butter the bottom and sides of the foil-lined pan.

2. In a medium bowl, stir together the flour and salt.

3. In a large bowl, using a hand-held electric mixer set at medium speed, cream together the sugar and butter for 2 to 3 minutes, until light. At low speed, slowly beat in the eggs. The mixture may look curdled, but do not worry if it does. Using a wooden spoon, stir in the chocolate syrup and vanilla. Stir in the flour mixture until smooth. Fold in the nuts with a rubber spatula.

4. Scrape the batter into the prepared pan and smooth the top with a rubber spatula. Bake for 30 to 35 minutes or until a toothpick inserted into the center of the brownies comes out with a few moist crumbs clinging to it. Cool completely in the pan on a wire rack for about 1 hour.

Make the crème de menthe filling:

5. In a large bowl, using a hand-held electric mixer set at medium high speed, beat the butter, sugar, and crème de menthe for 2 to 3 minutes, until light. Using a metal cake spatula, spread the crème de menthe filling evenly over the cooled brownies. Refrigerate the brownies for 50 to 60 minutes or until the filling is firm.

Prepare the glaze:

6. In a small saucepan, combine the water and butter. Over medium heat, stirring constantly, bring the water-butter mixture to a boil. Remove the pan from the heat and add the chocolate chips. Let the mixture sit for 1 to 2 minutes to melt the chocolate. Whisk the glaze until smooth, and let cool for 3 to 5 minutes or until tepid.

7. Remove the brownies from the refrigerator. Pour the glaze over the crème de menthe filling. Using an offset metal cake spatula, quickly spread the glaze smoothly over the brownies and refrigerate for 10 minutes to set the glaze.

8. Using the two long ends of the foil as handles, lift the brownies out of the pan. Carefully remove the foil and cut the brownies into 24 squares. Refrigerate the brownies in an airtight container until ready to serve.

～ *Peanut Butter Cupcakes* ～

Peanut butter-flavored cupcakes are sure to be a hit with the kids, as well as with many adults. They're good without the glaze, but we think the chocolate coating makes them extra special. If you're not up to using a pastry bag, simply spread a little glaze over the cupcakes with a table knife.

YIELD: 12 cupcakes

DIFFICULTY: ▬

PREPARATION TIME: 30 minutes plus baking and cooling times

SPECIAL EQUIPMENT: pastry bag fitted with a plain writing tip (such as Ateco #1)

Cupcakes:

1½ cups cake flour (not self-rising)
1 cup granulated sugar
2 teaspoons double-acting baking powder
¼ teaspoon salt
¾ cup milk, at room temperature
⅓ cup vegetable oil
2 large eggs, at room temperature, lightly beaten
1 teaspoon vanilla extract
¾ cup chunky peanut butter, at room temperature

Chocolate glaze (optional):

3 ounces bittersweet chocolate, finely chopped
3 tablespoons heavy (whipping) cream

Make the cupcakes:

1. Position a rack in the center of the oven and preheat to 350°F. Line 12 2⅝-by-1⅛-inch (3-ounce) muffin or cupcake cups with paper liners.

2. In a large bowl, stir and then sift together the flour, sugar, baking powder, and salt. Make a well in the center of the flour mixture.

3. In a medium bowl, stir together the milk, oil, eggs, and vanilla with a wire whisk and pour into the flour well. Whisk the mixture until combined. Stir in the peanut butter.

4. Divide the batter evenly among the prepared cupcake or muffin cups. Bake the cupcakes for 25 to 30 minutes or until a cake tester or toothpick inserted into the center of one of the cupcakes comes out clean. Cool the cupcakes in their pan(s) set on a wire rack for 5 minutes. Transfer the cupcakes from the pan(s) to a wire rack to cool completely.

Make the chocolate glaze:

5. In the top of a double boiler, over hot, not simmering, water, melt the chocolate, stirring occasionally until smooth. Remove the top part of the double boiler from the bottom and cool the chocolate for about 5 minutes or until tepid.

6. In a small pan set over medium heat, heat the cream until bubbles begin to form around the edge of the pan. Remove the pan from the heat and whisk in the cooled chocolate until smooth.

7. Put the cupcakes on a wire rack set over a baking sheet. Fill a paper cone or a pastry bag fitted

with a plain writing tip (such as Ateco #1) with the glaze. Using quick back-and-forth strokes, pipe a crisscross pattern over the cupcakes. Refrigerate the cupcakes for 5 minutes to set the glaze. Store the cupcakes in an airtight container at room temperature.

⌒ *Ever-So-Delicious Brownies* ⌒

One of our readers submitted this recipe. With its coconut-chocolate chip topping—melted to a soft yet crunchy turn under the broiler—we found it a winner and ever so deserving of its name.

YIELD: 16 brownies
DIFFICULTY: ◾
PREPARATION TIME: 45 minutes plus baking and cooling times

Brownies:

½ cup all-purpose flour

3 tablespoons unsweetened nonalkalized cocoa powder

¼ teaspoon salt

8 tablespoons (1 stick) unsalted butter, softened

1 cup granulated sugar

2 large eggs, at room temperature

1 teaspoon vanilla extract

3 ounces (about ½ cup) semisweet chocolate chips

½ cup walnuts, coarsely chopped

½ cup sweetened flaked coconut

Topping:

8 tablespoons (1 stick) unsalted butter, softened

½ cup packed light brown sugar

¼ cup heavy (whipping) cream

1 cup sweetened flaked coconut

3 ounces (about ½ cup) semisweet chocolate chips

Make the brownies:

1. Position a rack in the center of the oven and preheat to 350°F. Line an 8-inch square baking pan with aluminum foil so that the foil extends 2 inches beyond two opposite sides of the pan. Lightly butter the bottom of the foil-lined pan.

2. In a medium bowl, stir together the flour, cocoa, and salt.

3. In a large bowl, using a hand-held electric mixer set at medium-high speed, beat the butter for 30 seconds until creamy. Gradually beat in the sugar. Beat in the eggs one at a time and continue beating for 2 to 3 minutes until light. Beat in the vanilla. Reduce the speed to low and add the flour mixture, mixing until smooth. Using a wooden spoon, stir in the chocolate chips, walnuts, and coconut.

(continued)

4. Scrape the batter into the prepared pan and smooth the top with a rubber spatula. Bake for 25 to 30 minutes or until a cake tester or toothpick inserted into the center of the brownies comes out with a few moist crumbs clinging to it. Cool the brownies in the pan on a wire rack for 10 minutes.

Make the topping:

5. Preheat the broiler. In a medium bowl, mix together the butter and brown sugar with a wooden spoon until creamy. Stir in the cream and coconut.

Using a metal cake spatula, spread the topping over the warm brownies.

6. Put the brownies under the broiler for 1 to 2 minutes or until the topping begins to bubble and turns golden brown. Remove the pan from the broiler and sprinkle the chocolate chips over the hot brownies.

7. Cool the brownies in the pan on a wire rack for 30 minutes. Using the two ends of the foil as handles, lift the brownies out of the pan. Cool the brownies on the foil on a wire rack for at least 2 hours. Cut into 16 squares. Store in an airtight container.

∿ Chocolate Chubbies ∿

Three kinds of chocolate and two kinds of nuts make these brownies, well, "chubby" with rich flavor.

YIELD: 24 brownies

DIFFICULTY: ◼

PREPARATION TIME: 30 minutes plus baking and cooling times

6 ounces (about 1 cup) semisweet chocolate chips
4 ounces unsweetened chocolate, coarsely chopped
10 tablespoons (1 stick plus 2 tablespoons) unsalted butter, cut into tablespoons
½ cup all-purpose flour
1 teaspoon double-acting baking powder
6 medium eggs, at room temperature
2 cups granulated sugar
1 pound white chocolate, cut into ¼-inch chunks
3 cups pecans, coarsely chopped
3 cups walnuts, coarsely chopped

1. Position a rack in the center of the oven and preheat to 325°F. Line a 12-by-18-inch rectangular roasting pan with a double thickness of aluminum foil so that the foil extends 2 inches beyond the short sides of the pan. Lightly butter the bottom of the foil-lined pan.

2. In the top of a double boiler over hot, not simmering, water, melt the chocolate chips, unsweetened chocolate, and butter, stirring frequently until smooth. Remove the top part of the double boiler from the bottom and cool the mixture for 10 to 15 minutes or until tepid.

3. In a small bowl, first stir then sift together the flour and baking powder.

4. In a large bowl, beat the eggs with a wire whisk until foamy. Add the sugar and beat until blended. Add the cooled chocolate mixture and mix until smooth. Stir in the flour mixture until well combined. Using a rubber spatula, fold in the white chocolate chunks and nuts.

5. Scrape the batter into the prepared pan and smooth the top with a rubber spatula. Bake the brownies for 20 to 25 minutes or until a toothpick inserted in the middle comes out with a few moist crumbs clinging to it.

6. Cool the brownies in the pan on a wire rack for 30 minutes. Using the two ends of the foil as handles, lift the brownies from the pan and cool on the foil for at least 2 hours.

7. Invert the brownies onto a large cutting board and gently peel off the foil. Invert again onto a smooth surface and cut into 24 brownies. Store the brownies in an airtight container.

3

Michael Weiss

Cakes Take It

All-American Dixie Devil's Food Cake
Boston Cream Pie
Microwave Walnut Brownie Cake
Microwave Walnut Brownie Cake à la Mode
Microwave Walnut Brownie Cake with Whipped-Cream Frosting
Triple Chocolate Sour Cream Cake
Chocolate Cheesecake Triangles
Chocolate Marble Cheesecake
White Chocolate Sour Cream Cheesecake
Andrea's Fudge Cake
Cocoa Blackout Cake
Chocolate Raspberry-Ganache Cake
White Chocolate Pound Cake
Betsy's Best Wishes Cake
Chocolate Walnut Torte
White Chocolate Strawberry Obsttorte
Florentine Chocolate Cake
White Chocolate Lemon Cheesecake
Oregon Hazelnut Pavé
Chocolate Indulgence
Triple Chocolate Espresso Cake
Chocolate Walnut-Praline Cake
Chocolate Orange Truffle Cake
Crème Fraîche
Adrienne Welch's Rigo Jancsi
Chocolate Fig Cake with Gianduja Glaze
Incredible Chocolate Cake
Kathy Fleegler's Chocolate Strawberry Patch
Chocolate Orange Marble Cake

There is good reason why cakes spring to the minds of so many of us when we think about baking and entertaining. They are delicious, versatile, and beautiful. A birthday wouldn't be complete without a cake ablaze with candles, for example, and many of us could not imagine planning a large party without baking a cake or two. Here we have collected some of our very favorite cake recipes. These are not the elaborate creations you will find in chapter 6 but the simpler, more approachable cakes you might make for a Saturday night dinner party, a small family gathering, a club meeting, or a friend's birthday.

We believe that cakes are meant to taste as good as they look, and we have taken great care to garnish and decorate our cakes with fillings, frostings, and flourishes that enhance the flavors in the cake itself. Our cakes are complete creations, in which, we think, all flavors and textures complement each other in perfect balance. This does not mean that your own preferences cannot guide you—if you prefer a buttercream where we have specified a ganache, please follow your instincts. If you are in a bit of a hurry and do not have time to do more than dust the cake with confectioners' sugar, go right ahead. Most of all, cakes are meant to be enjoyed for their beauty and flavor, and we think the tortes, cheesecakes, pound cakes, and other kinds of cakes easily meet these criteria. We hope you will agree.

All-American Dixie Devil's Food Cake

It's not unusual to find cocoa rather than melted chocolate in recipes for devil's food cake, sweet milk instead of buttermilk, or brown sugar instead of granulated. What *is* unusual, however, is for a devil's food cake to lack a slightly reddish hue, provided by the reaction of the acidic ingredients (vinegar, brown sugar, buttermilk, etc.) with alkaline ones. Some folks even add red food coloring to heighten the cake's color—we rely on more conventional methods. Color aside, the flavor is always pleasantly mild and the texture light, which make it the perfect cake to serve with a snowy white whipped-cream frosting.

YIELD: 8 to 12 servings

DIFFICULTY: ◼

PREPARATION TIME: 1½ hours plus baking and cooling times

Cake:

2 ounces unsweetened chocolate, coarsely chopped
2 cups sifted cake flour (not self-rising)
1 teaspoon baking soda
½ teaspoon salt
8 tablespoons (1 stick) unsalted butter, softened
1½ cups granulated sugar
2 large eggs, at room temperature
1 cup buttermilk, at room temperature
1 tablespoon distilled white or apple cider vinegar
1 teaspoon vanilla extract

Whipped-cream frosting:

2¼ cups heavy (whipping) cream
4½ tablespoons granulated sugar
1 teaspoon vanilla extract

Make the cake:

1. Position a rack in the center of the oven and preheat to 350°F. Lightly butter the bottoms and sides of two 8-by-2-inch round cake pans. Line the bottom of each pan with a circle of baking parchment or waxed paper. Dust the sides with flour and tap out the excess.

2. In the top of a double boiler over hot, not simmering, water, melt the chocolate, stirring often, until smooth. Remove the top part of the double boiler from the bottom and cool the chocolate for 5 to 10 minutes or until tepid.

3. In a medium bowl, stir together and then sift the flour, baking soda, and salt.

4. In a large bowl, using a hand-held electric mixer set at medium speed, beat the butter while gradually adding the sugar for 2 to 3 minutes or until well combined. Beat in the eggs one at a time. On low speed, alternately beat in the flour mixture and the buttermilk in two additions each. Beat in the cooled chocolate, vinegar, and vanilla. Scrape the batter into the prepared pans and bake for 25 to 30 minutes or until a cake tester or toothpick inserted into the center of each cake layer comes out clean. Cool the layers in their pans set on wire

racks for 10 minutes. Run the tip of a sharp knife around the top edges of the layers to loosen them from the pans. Invert the layers onto other wire racks and carefully peel off the papers, leaving them loosely attached to the bottoms of the layers. Holding the papers in place, invert the layers onto other racks so they are right side up. Cool the layers completely.

Make the whipped-cream frosting:

5. In a large bowl, using a hand-held electric mixer set at medium speed, beat the cream and sugar until soft peaks start to form. Add the vanilla and beat until stiff peaks form.

6. Using a long, serrated knife, trim the top of each cooled cake layer if it is not already level. Horizontally slice each layer in half to make four equal layers. Place a 10-inch round cake platter on a revolving cake-decorating stand or an inverted cake pan and set the bottom cake layer on it. Using a metal cake spatula, spread the top of the cake layer evenly with ¾ cup of the whipped-cream frosting. Repeat the filling procedure again with the second and third layers, being careful to spread the frosting evenly, so that the cake will be level. Place the fourth layer on top and cover the entire cake with the remaining frosting.

∽ *Boston Cream Pie* ∾

Boston Cream Pie is not a pie at all; it's a sponge cake layered with pastry cream and then topped with a chocolate glaze. Why it is called a pie rather than a cake remains a matter of good-natured debate, but considering that the name has been used to describe this particular confection since the 1800s (and perhaps earlier), it would, most likely, be futile to change the name to Boston Cream Cake—albeit more accurate.

YIELD: 8 servings
DIFFICULTY: ▰▰
PREPARATION TIME: 1 hour plus chilling, baking, and cooling times

Pastry cream:

¼ cup plus 2 tablespoons granulated sugar
¼ cup cornstarch
1 large egg, at room temperature, lightly beaten
1½ cups milk
3 strips fresh lemon zest (each about ¾ inch by 2 inches)

Sponge cake:

1 cup sifted cake flour (not self-rising)
¼ teaspoon salt
6 large eggs, at room temperature
¾ cup granulated sugar
¾ teaspoon freshly grated lemon zest
1 teaspoon vanilla extract
6 tablespoons unsalted butter, melted and cooled until tepid

To assemble:

½ teaspoon vanilla extract
½ cup heavy (whipping) cream
1 teaspoon granulated sugar

Chocolate glaze:

½ cup heavy (whipping) cream
4 ounces bittersweet chocolate, finely chopped
½ teaspoon vanilla extract

Make the pastry cream:

1. In a large, heavy saucepan, stir together the sugar and cornstarch. Slowly whisk in the beaten egg to make a smooth paste. Gradually stir in the milk. Add the lemon zest.

2. Cook the mixture over medium-low heat, stirring constantly with a whisk, for 4 to 6 minutes or until thick and boiling. Remove the pan from the

heat and discard the strips of lemon zest. Immediately strain the pastry cream through a fine sieve into a medium bowl. Put plastic wrap directly on the surface of the pastry cream to prevent a skin from forming and cool to room temperature. Refrigerate for 1 to 2 hours or until well chilled.

Make the sponge cake:

3. Position a rack in the center of the oven and preheat to 350°F. Lightly butter the bottoms and sides of two 9-by-2-inch round cake pans. Line the bottom of each pan with a circle of baking parchment or waxed paper.

4. In a small bowl, stir together the flour and salt and then sift onto a piece of waxed paper. In a large, heatproof mixing bowl, whisk the eggs until the whites and yolks are blended. While continuing to whisk, add the sugar in a steady stream. Set the bowl over a pot of hot, not simmering, water. (The bottom of the bowl must touch the water.) Continue whisking the egg mixture constantly for 3 to 4 minutes, until the sugar crystals dissolve and the mixture is hot to the touch (110° to 120°F). Remove the bowl from the water.

5. Using a hand-held electric mixer set at medium-high speed, beat the egg mixture for 8 to 10 minutes or until it has tripled in volume and the batter is pale yellow and forms a thick yellow ribbon when the beaters are lifted. The batter should hold a crease after your finger has been drawn 1½ inches across the top. Beat in the lemon zest and vanilla.

6. Resift a quarter of the flour mixture over the batter. Using a large whisk or a rubber spatula, fold the flour into the batter, making sure to draw the whisk or spatula along the bottom and up the sides of the bowl to free any clinging flour. Resift the remaining flour mixture over the batter a quarter at a time, and fold it in.

7. Skim off and discard as much as possible of the white solids that have floated to the surface of the melted butter. Gently fold the skimmed butter into the batter, being careful not to deflate it. Scrape the batter into the prepared pans and smooth with a spatula.

8. Bake the sponge cake layers for 28 to 32 minutes or until the edges pull away from the sides of the pans and the center of each cake layer springs back when gently pressed. Cool the cake layers in their pans on wire racks for 10 minutes. Run the tip of a sharp knife around the edges of the cake layers to loosen them from the pans. Invert the sponge cake layers onto other wire racks and carefully separate the papers from the layers, leaving them loosely attached. Holding the papers in place, invert the layers onto other wire racks, so that they are right side up. Cool the cake layers completely.

Assemble the cake:

9. Remove the pastry cream from the refrigerator and whisk in the vanilla.

10. In a chilled bowl, beat the cream and sugar until soft peaks start to form. Fold one third of the whipped cream into the pastry cream to lighten it and then fold in the rest of it.

11. Place one layer of sponge cake on a serving plate. Using a metal cake spatula, spread the pastry cream evenly over the layer. Place the second cake layer on top of the pastry cream. Refrigerate the cake while making the chocolate glaze.

Make the chocolate glaze:

12. In a small, heavy saucepan set over medium heat, bring the cream to a gentle boil. Remove the pan from the heat and stir in the chocolate. Let the mixture stand for 1 to 2 minutes to melt the chocolate. Whisk until smooth and stir in the vanilla.

13. Remove the cake from the refrigerator. Pour the warm glaze over the top of the cake, allowing some of it to dribble down the sides. Refrigerate until almost ready to serve and then let the cake sit at room temperature for 20 minutes before serving.

NOTE: If desired, the cooled sponge cake layers may be wrapped in plastic and then in aluminum foil and frozen for up to 1 month before completing the cake.

Microwave Walnut Brownie
〜 Cake 〜

Food Editor and Test Kitchen Director Adrienne Welch developed this wonderful chocolate cake expressly for the microwave oven. The instructions look long, we know, but since baking in the microwave is new to so many people, we feel our explicit directions are necessary for your success. We developed this cake using a food processor with a large work bowl that measured 7 inches across the inside and 4⅞ inches high on the inside of the bowl. A much smaller bowl cannot hold all the batter.

What is so fantastic about this cake (aside from its good taste) is that it really can be made in less than 1 hour—baking time included. And it is just as delicious served with no more embellishment than a spoonful of ice cream and a little chocolate sauce as when it is "dressed up" with frosting and chocolate curls. The cake can be frozen for as long as a month and then defrosted in a microwave set on low (20 percent) power for 3 to 4 minutes. We suggest you carefully read through the recipe and the baking notes before beginning.

YIELD: 6 servings

DIFFICULTY: ▬

PREPARATION TIME: 25 minutes plus baking, setting, and cooling times

SPECIAL EQUIPMENT: microwave-safe 8-inch round glass cake dish (such as Pyrex)

---

3 chocolate cookie wafers (see Ingredient Note)
½ cup plus 2 tablespoons sifted cake flour (not self-rising)
½ cup plus 2 tablespoons granulated sugar, divided
½ teaspoon baking soda
¼ teaspoon double-acting baking powder
⅛ teaspoon salt
⅓ cup walnuts
3 ounces unsweetened chocolate, coarsely chopped
⅓ cup packed dark brown sugar
¾ teaspoon instant espresso coffee powder
¼ cup water
4 tablespoons (½ stick) unsalted butter, chilled and cut into
    ½-inch cubes
1 tablespoon dark rum
⅓ cup sour cream, chilled
1 large egg, chilled
2 teaspoons vanilla extract

INGREDIENT NOTE: If you cannot find chocolate cookie wafers, process 3 vanilla wafers with ¾ teaspoon unsweetened alkalized cocoa powder (see step 2).

1. Lay two 9-inch long sheets of baking parchment or waxed paper on top of each other on a work surface. Put the glass cake dish on top of the paper. With the tip of a small, sharp knife, trace the outline of the bottom of the dish onto the paper, then cut out the paper circles. Lightly grease the bottom of the cake dish with vegetable shortening and then line the bottom of the dish with both paper circles, one on top of the other. (The bottom circle will absorb excess moisture from the cake batter and the top circle will enable you to easily lift the cake out of the dish.)

2. Put the chocolate wafers in a food processor fitted with the metal chopping blade. Process for 20 to 30 seconds, until finely ground. Transfer the cookie crumbs to a small bowl and reserve to sprinkle over the baked cake.

3. Without washing the food processor, combine the flour, 2 tablespoons of the granulated sugar, the baking soda, baking powder, and salt. Process for 4 seconds and add the walnuts. Pulse 8 to 10 times or until the walnuts are finely chopped. Transfer to a small bowl.

4. Again without washing the food processor, combine the chocolate, the remaining ½ cup of the granulated sugar, the brown sugar, and espresso powder. Process for 30 to 40 seconds, until the mixture is finely ground. Leave in the processor.

5. In a microwave-safe 2-cup glass measuring cup, combine the water, butter, and rum. Tightly cover the top of the measuring cup with a piece of microwave-safe plastic wrap and fold back one corner so that the pouring spout is uncovered. Heat in the microwave on high (100 percent) power for 1½ to 2 minutes or until the mixture comes to a boil. Remove from the microwave, and with the food processor running, pour the hot butter mixture through the feed tube. Process for 15 to 20 seconds, until the chocolate mixture is smooth.

6. Add the sour cream, egg, and vanilla. Process for no longer than 5 seconds or just until the mixture is creamy. Using a spatula, scrape down the sides of the bowl. Add half of the flour mixture and pulse 4 to 6 times, until there is barely a trace of the flour left. Add the remaining flour mixture and pulse 4 to 6 times until there is barely a trace

of flour in the batter. Scrape down the sides of the bowl again. Do not over process.

7. Pour the batter into the prepared pan and smooth the top with a spatula. To ensure even baking, put an inverted microwave-safe saucer or bowl on the microwave floor or turntable and put the cake dish on top of the bowl or saucer. If you do not have a turntable, rotate the cake dish a quarter turn every 3 minutes. Microwave on medium (50 percent) power for 9 to 11 minutes or until the cake starts to pull away from the side of the dish and there are no large wet patches on the surface of the cake. A cake tester or toothpick inserted into the center of the cake will come out with a few moist crumbs clinging to it. Check the cake after 9 minutes and if necessary microwave for 30-second intervals at medium (50 percent) power until the cake is done. Place the cake dish on a heatproof work surface for 10 minutes.

8. Sprinkle the cookie-crumb mixture evenly over the top of the warm cake. (This will prevent the cake from sticking to the plate or cardboard when you invert it.) Run the tip of a sharp knife around the edge of the cake to loosen it from the pan. With a gentle tap, invert the cake onto a 9-inch plate or foil-covered cardboard circle. If the cake does not unmold easily, let it sit 5 more minutes. Carefully peel off the paper and leave it loosely set on the bottom of the layer. Holding the paper in place, reinvert the layer onto a second plate or cardboard cake circle so that it is crumb side up. Wrap the sides of the cake with a large piece of plastic wrap that has been folded into a long strip. Put the cake on its plate or cardboard circle onto a wire rack to cool completely. Invert the cake onto a serving plate, crumb side down, and remove the paper. Serve the cake warm or at room temperature with a dollop of whipped cream or a dusting of confectioners' sugar along with some fresh berries. Or try one of the following variations (see pages 66 to 68) for finishing the cake.

BAKING NOTES:

• We tested the recipe in microwaves with 650 and 700 watts. If your microwave has a different wattage, adjust the baking times accordingly.

• Be sure the waxed paper circles completely cover the bottom of the pan, or the cake may stick when it is time to unmold it.

• During baking, don't worry about opening the microwave—the cake won't fall and it is perfectly safe.

• When checking for doneness, don't mind any small wet patches on the surface of the cake—these will quickly disappear as the cake cools.

Microwave Walnut Brownie Cake à la Mode

If you would prefer to leave out the liquor in the chocolate sauce, simply increase the amount of heavy cream by 1 tablespoon. And if the ice cream is too hard to scoop when it comes time to serve it, soften it in the microwave for 15 to 20 seconds on medium (50 percent) power. This is an easy and wonderful way to serve the cake.

YIELD: 6 servings
DIFFICULTY: ◼
PREPARATION TIME: 25 minutes plus baking, setting, and cooling times

1 recipe Microwave Walnut Brownie Cake (see page 64)

Chocolate sauce:

8 ounces bittersweet chocolate, broken into 1-inch pieces
⅔ cup heavy (whipping) cream
⅓ cup light corn syrup
A few grains of salt
1 tablespoon dark rum, coffee liqueur, or cognac
1 teaspoon vanilla extract
1½ pints vanilla or coffee ice cream

1. Prepare the Microwave Walnut Brownie Cake.

Make the chocolate sauce:

2. Put the chocolate in a food processor fitted with the metal chopping blade. Pulse the chocolate 5 to 6 times or until coarsely chopped. Process for 25 to 35 seconds or until finely chopped.

3. In a microwave-safe 1-quart glass measuring cup, combine the cream, corn syrup, and salt. Tightly cover the top of the container with a piece of microwave-safe plastic wrap and fold back the corner over the pouring spout. Heat in the microwave on high (100 percent) power for 1 minute. Remove the container from the microwave and turn back the plastic wrap so that you can stir the cream

mixture with a wooden spoon. Replace the plastic wrap so that only the corner over the pouring spout is left open, and microwave for 1 to 1½ minutes on high power or until the cream mixture comes to a boil. Remove the container from the microwave and carefully remove the plastic wrap with the open spout facing away from you (the hot steam will vent through the spout). Add the chocolate and let the mixture sit for 1 to 2 minutes to melt the chocolate. Whisk until smooth. Stir in the liquor or liqueur, and vanilla.

4. Serve the Microwave Walnut Brownie Cake warm or at room temperature, cut into wedges, with a scoop of ice cream and a ladleful of warm chocolate sauce.

Microwave Walnut Brownie Cake with Whipped-Cream ⌒ *Frosting* ⌒

The trick here is making the chocolate curls. The secret is to make sure the chocolate is the right temperature: if it is too cold, it will yield only shavings; if it is too warm, the chocolate will hardly curl. This is where the microwave comes in handy: with it, it's pretty easy to achieve just the right temperature for the chocolate. Decorating the cake like this is a fast way to turn a quick dessert into an elegant one.

YIELD: 6 servings
DIFFICULTY: ◼
PREPARATION TIME: 25 minutes plus baking, setting, and cooling times
SPECIAL EQUIPMENT: pastry bag fitted with a star tip (such as Ateco #2)

1 recipe Microwave Walnut Brownie Cake (see page 64)

Chocolate curls:

3 ounces semisweet chocolate

Whipped-cream frosting:

1¼ cups heavy (whipping) cream
1 tablespoon plus 1 teaspoon granulated sugar
1 tablespoon dark rum
¾ teaspoon vanilla extract

1. Prepare the Microwave Walnut Brownie Cake.

Make the chocolate curls:

2. Warm a 1-ounce square of semisweet chocolate by putting it in the microwave for 20-second intervals at low (20 percent) power until it starts to soften but not melt.

3. Put a sheet of waxed paper on a work surface. Grip the square of chocolate with a paper towel, so that your hand does not melt the chocolate. Using a vegetable peeler, scrape one of the edges of the chocolate square in a downward motion, forming small, tight curls. As you form the curls, let them fall onto the waxed paper. Continue making curls in the same manner with the two remaining squares of chocolate.

Make the whipped-cream frosting:

4. In a chilled large bowl, using a hand-held electric mixer set at medium speed, beat the cream and sugar until soft peaks start to form. Add the rum and vanilla and continue beating until stiff peaks start to form.

5. If desired, surround the base of the cake with strips of waxed paper to prevent the serving plate from getting messy. Reserve ¾ cup of the whipped cream for piping rosettes. Using an offset metal cake spatula, frost the top and sides of the cake with the remaining whipped cream.

6. Using a baker's scraper or metal spatula, scoop up some of the chocolate curls and gently press them against the sides of the frosted cake.

7. Fill a pastry bag fitted with a star tip (such as

Ateco #2) with the ¾ cup of reserved whipped cream. Pipe a shell border around the top edge of the cake. Pipe one large rosette in the center of the cake. Store the cake in the refrigerator. Let the cake sit at room temperature for 30 minutes before serving.

Food Processor Shortcuts

As well as simplifying numerous basic cooking techniques, the food processor can help out with baking in several ways.

• If you forget to soften butter in advance for baking, cut it into 1-inch pieces, drop it in the work bowl, and process with the metal blade for about 20 seconds.

• Instead of sifting flour and other dry ingredients to aerate them, process them with the metal blade for 15 to 30 seconds.

• Eggs may be added directly to the other ingredients in the work bowl. They do not need to be beaten first.

• Nuts, dried fruits, or cranberries may be added to batter in the work bowl without chopping them in advance. Just pulse several times after adding.

• To melt chocolate when it is to be used in a food processor recipe together with butter or a liquid ingredient, first chop it finely using the metal blade. Heat the butter or liquid ingredient and pour it through the feed tube with the machine running. Process for 20 to 30 seconds or until the chocolate is melted. This saves using another utensil and also eliminates the risk of burning the chocolate.

Triple Chocolate Sour Cream
⌒ Cake ⌒

Bittersweet and unsweetened chocolate are combined in the batter for this cake to produce deep chocolate flavor, which is nicely balanced by the additions of sour cream and brown sugar. The mocha glaze provides sweet contrast to the chocolate. Decorate the cake with swirls of melted white chocolate for a formal occasion, or if you just can't wait, serve it with unglazed spoonfuls of whipped cream and juicy strawberries soon after it's taken from the oven. Whatever suits your fancy, the cake is easy to mix up since it's done completely in the food processor.

YIELD: 12 servings

DIFFICULTY: ◼◼

PREPARATION TIME: 50 minutes plus baking, cooling, and chilling times

SPECIAL EQUIPMENT: 12-cup fluted tube pan; pastry bag fitted with a small writing tip (such as Ateco #1)

Cake:

2 cups plus 1 tablespoon sifted cake flour (not self-rising), divided

1½ cups granulated sugar, divided

1½ teaspoons baking soda

¾ teaspoon double-acting baking powder

¼ teaspoon salt

5 ounces bittersweet chocolate, coarsely chopped

1 cup walnuts, coarsely chopped

⅓ cup packed dark brown sugar

6 ounces unsweetened chocolate, coarsely chopped

1½ teaspoons instant espresso coffee powder

¾ cup water

12 tablespoons (1½ sticks) unsalted butter, cut into tablespoons

⅔ cup coffee liqueur, divided

½ cup sour cream

2 large eggs plus 1 large egg yolk

2 teaspoons vanilla extract

Mocha glaze:

9 ounces bittersweet chocolate, coarsely chopped

¾ teaspoon instant espresso coffee powder

¾ cup heavy (whipping) cream

3 tablespoons light corn syrup

3 tablespoons coffee liqueur

¾ teaspoon vanilla extract

Decoration:

1 ounce white chocolate, coarsely chopped

Whipped cream, for garnish (if you are serving the cake warm from the oven)

Strawberries, for garnish (optional)

Make the cake:

1. Position a rack in the center of the oven and preheat to 350°F. Generously butter the fluted tube pan. Dust with flour and tap out the excess.

2. In a food processor fitted with the metal chopping blade, combine 2 cups of the flour, ¼ cup of the granulated sugar, the baking soda, baking powder, and salt. Pulse 3 to 4 times and transfer the mixture to a medium bowl. In another medium bowl, toss the bittersweet chocolate and the walnuts with the remaining tablespoon of flour.

3. Without washing the food processor, combine the remaining granulated sugar, the brown sugar, unsweetened chocolate, and espresso powder. Process for 20 to 25 seconds or until the mixture is finely ground.

4. In a small saucepan, combine the water and butter. Cook over medium heat, stirring frequently, until the mixture comes to a boil and the

butter melts. Remove the pan from the heat. With the motor running, pour the hot butter mixture through the feed tube of the food processor. Process for 15 to 20 seconds or until the mixture is smooth. Pour ⅓ cup of coffee liqueur through the feed tube and process 5 seconds. Add the sour cream, eggs, egg yolk, and vanilla. Process for 15 to 20 seconds or until the mixture is smooth. Add half the flour mixture and pulse 4 to 5 times or until there is barely a trace of flour left. Add the remaining flour mixture and pulse 4 to 5 times, again until there is barely a trace of flour left in the batter. Add the chocolate-walnut mixture and pulse 2 to 3 times or until just mixed.

5. Scrape the batter into the prepared pan and smooth the top with a spatula. Bake for 55 to 60 minutes or until a cake tester or toothpick inserted into the center of the cake comes out with a few moist crumbs clinging to it. Let the cake cool in the pan on a wire rack for 20 minutes. Run the tip of a sharp knife around the top edge of the cake to loosen it from the pan. Invert the cake onto the wire rack and brush with the remaining ⅓ cup of coffee liqueur. Cool completely.

Make the mocha glaze:

6. Put the chocolate and espresso powder into a food processor fitted with the metal chopping blade. Process for 15 to 20 seconds or until finely ground.

7. In a small saucepan, combine the heavy cream and corn syrup. Bring the mixture to a gentle boil and remove from the heat. With the motor of the food processor running, pour the hot cream mixture through the feed tube. Process for 15 to 20 seconds or until smooth. Add the coffee liqueur and vanilla and process for 3 to 5 seconds, until blended. Strain the glaze through a fine sieve into a measuring cup to remove any air bubbles.

8. Set the cake on its wire rack over a baking sheet. Pour the warm glaze over the cake, covering it completely. Chill the cake for 5 minutes to set the glaze.

Decorate the cake:

9. In the top of a double boiler over hot, not simmering, water, melt the white chocolate, stirring constantly, until smooth. Remove the top part of the double boiler from the bottom.

10. Fill a paper cone or a pastry bag fitted with a small writing tip (such as Ateco #1) with the white chocolate (for instructions on making a paper cone, see page 187). Pipe delicate, slightly curved lines of white chocolate over the glazed cake, following the fluted design created by the tube pan. Refrigerate the cake 5 minutes to set the white chocolate. Cover the cake and store at room temperature. Garnish with whipped cream and strawberries before serving, if desired.

NOTE: After the cake has cooled completely, it can be wrapped in aluminum foil and left to sit overnight or frozen for up to a month before glazing.

∽ *Chocolate Cheesecake Triangles* ∽

Do you have a bag of chocolate chips and some cream cheese handy? Then you can make these charming little cheesecake triangles with very little effort. The gingersnap crust adds an irresistible "zing," and when garnished with rosettes of whipped cream and strips of orange zest, the triangles make a special dessert. Of course, if you prefer, you can cut them into more traditional rectangles or squares and serve them to your eager family without fuss. Packed in an insulated container, these make good lunch box fare.

YIELD: 18 servings
DIFFICULTY: ■
PREPARATION TIME: 45 minutes plus baking and cooling times
SPECIAL EQUIPMENT: pastry bag fitted with a star tip (such as Ateco #4 or #5)

Crust:

4 tablespoons (½ stick) unsalted butter, cut into tablespoons
2 cups gingersnap cookie crumbs

Cheesecake:

8 ounces (about 1⅓ cups) semisweet chocolate chips
1½ pounds cream cheese, softened
1 14-ounce can sweetened condensed milk
2 large eggs, at room temperature
1 cup sour cream, at room temperature
2 tablespoons brandy
½ teaspoon ground cinnamon
½ teaspoon almond extract

Garnish (optional):

¾ cup heavy (whipping) cream
2 tablespoons granulated sugar
Ground cinnamon
Strips of orange zest
Fresh mint leaves

Make the crust:

1. Position a rack in the center of the oven and preheat to 325°F. Line a 9-by-13-inch baking pan with two layers of aluminum foil so that the foil extends 2 inches beyond the short ends of the pan.

2. In a medium saucepan, melt the butter over low heat. Remove the saucepan from the heat and stir in the gingersnap crumbs. Evenly press the mixture onto the bottom of the foil-lined pan.

Refrigerate the crust until ready to fill.

Make the cheesecake:

3. In the top of a double boiler over hot, not simmering, water, melt the chocolate, stirring occasionally until smooth. Remove the top part of the double boiler from the bottom and cool the chocolate for 5 to 10 minutes or until tepid.

4. In a large bowl, using a hand-held electric

mixer set at medium-high speed, beat the cream cheese for 2 to 3 minutes or until light and smooth. With the mixer at low speed, gradually beat in the milk. Scrape down the sides of the bowl frequently. Beat in the eggs one at a time, beating well after each addition. Gradually beat in the melted chocolate and sour cream. Stir in the brandy, cinnamon, and almond extract.

5. Scrape the batter into the prepared pan. Bake the cheesecake for 55 to 65 minutes or until set and puffed and a cake tester or toothpick inserted into the center comes out with moist crumbs. Cool the cheesecake in the pan on a wire rack for 1 to 2 hours or until it reaches room temperature. Cover the cheesecake with plastic wrap and refrigerate for 8 hours or overnight, until thoroughly chilled.

Decorate the cheesecake:

6. Using the ends of the aluminum foil as handles, gently lift the cheesecake out of its pan. Put it on a board and, using a sharp knife, cut it into 18 triangles. Put the triangles on individual serving plates.

7. In a chilled large bowl, beat the heavy cream and sugar with a hand-held electric mixer set at medium speed until stiff peaks start to form. Put the whipped cream into a pastry bag fitted with a star tip (such as Ateco #4 or #5) and pipe rosettes of whipped cream onto each plate next to the cheesecake triangles. Sprinkle the rosettes with ground cinnamon and garnish each triangle with strips of orange zest and mint leaves.

◠ *Chocolate Marble Cheesecake* ◠

As with all cheesecakes, cooling is important. This one requires at least 4 hours, so be sure to allow for the time. What makes the cake especially pretty, we think, is the delicate way the chocolate is marbled with the rest of the creamy filling. Although we usually suggest using a hand-held electric mixer in our recipes, for this one we recommend a stand-up one, since the batter is a little heavy for hand-held models.

YIELD: 12 servings

DIFFICULTY: ▰▰

PREPARATION TIME: 45 minutes plus baking and cooling times

SPECIAL EQUIPMENT: stand-up electric mixer; 9-by-3-inch round springform pan

---

Crumb crust:

1½ cups crushed graham crackers
3 tablespoons unsalted butter, melted

Cheesecake:

2 pounds cream cheese, softened
1½ cups granulated sugar
⅓ cup all-purpose flour
1 teaspoon grated orange zest
1¾ cups sour cream, at room temperature
4 large eggs, at room temperature
1 teaspoon vanilla extract
4 ounces semisweet chocolate, finely chopped
2 teaspoons solid vegetable shortening

Make the crumb crust:

1. Position a rack in the center of the oven and preheat to 300°F. Lightly butter the bottom and sides of the springform pan. Using two 12-by-15-inch pieces of heavy-duty aluminum foil, tightly wrap the outside of the pan.

2. In a medium bowl, stir together the cracker crumbs and the melted butter until well combined. Put the mixture into the springform pan and using your fingers, press it firmly and evenly over the bottom of the pan. Refrigerate the crust in the pan.

Make the cheesecake filling:

3. In the large bowl of a stand-up electric mixer set at medium-high speed, beat the cream cheese for 5 minutes or until smooth. With the beater running, add the sugar, flour, and orange zest. Continue to beat for 3 minutes or until light, scraping down the sides of the bowl with a rubber spatula as needed. Beat in the sour cream, eggs, and vanilla, and continue beating for 2 minutes or until the filling is very smooth. Pour the batter into the prepared crust.

4. In the top of a double boiler over hot, not simmering, water, melt the chocolate with the shortening, stirring occasionally, until smooth. Pour the chocolate mixture in ¼-inch wide parallel lines, about 1 inch apart, on top of the filling. Insert the tip of a small knife about ¼ inch deep into the filling. Working perpendicular to the chocolate stripes, draw the knife back and forth in lines to create a feathery marbled effect.

5. Put the springform pan in a larger roasting pan. Put the roasting pan in the oven and add enough very hot water to come two-thirds up the side of the springform pan. Bake for 1 hour and 30 to 40 minutes or until the center of the cheesecake is set and the top is beginning to brown lightly. Remove the springform pan from the water bath and remove the aluminum foil wrapping. Run a thin knife around the edge of the pan to release the cheesecake. (This step will reduce the chances of the cheesecake cracking as it cools.) Cool the cake completely on a wire rack.

6. Cover the top of the springform pan tightly with plastic wrap and refrigerate overnight or for at least 4 hours, until well chilled. Take the cheesecake from the refrigerator 30 minutes before serving and remove the sides of the springform pan. Cut the cheesecake with a sharp, thin knife, dipping the blade into hot water between each slice to ensure clean, even slices.

White Chocolate Sour Cream
∼⟩ Cheesecake ⟨∼

White on white, this seductively sweet cheesecake, generously flavored with white chocolate, requires at least 6 hours to chill. Rather than a conventional water bath, the cake is baked with a pan of hot water positioned on a lower oven rack to produce a steamy environment.

YIELD: 12 servings
DIFFICULTY: ▃▃
PREPARATION TIME: 45 minutes plus baking, cooling, and chilling times
SPECIAL EQUIPMENT: 9-by-3-inch round springform pan

Cheesecake:

12 ounces white chocolate, coarsely chopped
1½ pounds cream cheese, softened
½ cup granulated sugar
1 teaspoon fresh lemon juice
Pinch of salt
1½ cups sour cream, at room temperature
4 large eggs, at room temperature
2½ teaspoons vanilla extract

Sour cream topping:

1¾ cups sour cream, at room temperature
2 tablespoons granulated sugar
¼ teaspoon vanilla extract

Strawberry sauce (see Note):

6 cups fresh hulled strawberries, divided
½ cup water
½ cup plus 2 tablespoons granulated sugar
4 teaspoons cornstarch
2 tablespoons orange liqueur, such as Grand Marnier

Garnish (optional):

Fresh mint leaves
Fresh strawberries, cut into fan shapes

Make the cheesecake:

1. Position one rack in the middle and another rack in the bottom third of the oven and preheat to 400°F. Remove the sides from the springform pan. Trim a 9-inch round cardboard cake circle so that it fits snugly within the curved lip of the bottom of the springform pan. Cover the top of the cardboard-lined springform bottom with aluminum foil so that there is a 2-inch overhang all around the edge. Attach the sides of the springform pan, being careful not to tear the aluminum foil. Fit the aluminum foil halfway up the sides and lightly butter the foil-covered bottom and inside of the

pan. (Lining the bottom of the pan this way gives the cheesecake an even, flat base, which makes it easier to remove from the pan.)

2. In the top of a double boiler over hot, not simmering, water, melt the white chocolate, stirring constantly, until smooth. Remove the top part of the double boiler from the bottom and cool the chocolate for 5 to 10 minutes or until tepid.

3. In a food processor fitted with a metal chopping blade, combine the cream cheese, sugar, lemon juice, and salt. Process the mixture for 30 seconds and scrape down the sides of the container with a rubber spatula. Process for 1 minute or until creamy. Add the melted chocolate, sour cream, eggs, and vanilla. Process the mixture for 30 seconds and scrape clean the sides of the work bowl. Process for 1 minute more or until smooth.

4. Pour the cheesecake batter into the prepared springform pan. Tap the pan several times on a work surface to deflate any large air bubbles. Place the cheesecake on the middle rack of the oven. Place a roasting pan on the bottom rack. Pour 4 to 6 cups of boiling water into the roasting pan so that it reaches a depth of 2 inches. Bake the cheesecake for 10 minutes. Lower the oven temperature to 300°F. Continue baking the cheesecake 45 to 55 minutes or until the cheesecake is firm to the touch. Do not open the oven door for the first 45 minutes of baking. Remove the cheesecake from the oven and set it on a wire rack to cool for 10 to 15 minutes. Raise the oven temperature to 350°F.

Make the sour cream topping:

5. In a medium bowl, whisk together the sour cream, sugar, and vanilla until smooth. Pour the sour cream mixture over the baked cheesecake and spread it evenly with a spatula. Return the cheesecake to the oven and bake for 3 to 5 minutes or until the sour cream topping is set. Run a thin-bladed knife around the inside of the pan to release the

cheesecake. (This will help prevent the cheesecake from cracking as it cools.) Put the cheesecake in its pan on a wire rack to cool for 1 hour. Refrigerate the cheesecake in its pan overnight or for at least 6 hours, until firm.

Make the strawberry sauce:

6. In a medium saucepan, combine 4 cups of the strawberries, the water, and sugar. Cook over medium heat, stirring constantly, until the sugar dissolves and the strawberries start to soften. Raise the heat to medium high and bring the mixture to a boil. Boil for 3 to 5 minutes or until the strawberries turn into a puree. Strain the hot strawberry mixture through a sieve into a bowl.

7. In a medium saucepan, make a paste by stirring together a small amount of the strained strawberry liquid with the cornstarch. Stir in the remaining strawberry liquid. Cook the mixture over medium heat, stirring constantly, until the mixture comes to a boil. Boil for 1 minute. Remove the pan from the heat and strain the sauce through a sieve into a bowl. Cool to room temperature.

8. Slice the remaining 2 cups of strawberries. Stir the orange liqueur into the sauce and gently fold in the sliced strawberries. Cover and refrigerate. Allow the sauce to sit at room temperature for 30 minutes before serving.

9. Remove the sides of the springform pan. Slide two metal cake spatulas underneath the cheesecake and transfer it to a serving platter.

10. Cut the cheesecake with a sharp, thin knife, dipping the blade into hot water between each slice. Serve each slice with a large spoonful of the sauce, and garnish with fresh mint and a strawberry fan, if desired.

NOTE: The strawberry sauce can be made up to 2 days ahead and refrigerated. Try it over ice cream, too.

Cooling Cheesecakes

Home cooks commonly battle cracked cheesecakes. While the cakes crack most often during cooling, they sometimes split during baking, which is why they are baked at moderate temperatures. If you are topping a cheesecake, cracking is not really a problem, since the flaw will be well hidden.

Traditionally, cheesecakes are cooled gradually in a switched-off oven with the door propped slightly open. (If your oven won't stay open on its own, prop it with the handle of a wooden spoon.) This gives the filling time to settle slowly with little opportunity for splitting. It is also helpful to first run a knife around the just-baked cake to loosen it from the sides of the pan.

Cheesecakes should always be cooled to room temperature before they are refrigerated. They should not be refrigerated until they are cool. Most cheesecakes are served thoroughly chilled.

∽ Andrea's Fudge Cake ∾

This is one of our most popular cakes—one for which we constantly get requests for copies of the recipe.

YIELD: 8 to 10 servings

DIFFICULTY: ▬

PREPARATION TIME: 10 minutes plus baking and cooling times

SPECIAL EQUIPMENT: 9-by-3-inch round springform pan

---

12 ounces semisweet chocolate, coarsely chopped
5 tablespoons espresso or strong coffee
2 cups granulated sugar
1 cup (2 sticks) unsalted butter
6 large eggs, at room temperature, separated
1 cup all-purpose flour
Confectioners' sugar, for garnish (optional)

1. Position a rack in the center of the oven and preheat to 350°F. Lightly butter the springform pan. Dust the pan with flour and tap out the excess.

2. In the top of a double boiler over hot, not simmering, water, melt together the chocolate and espresso, stirring occasionally until smooth. Scrape the chocolate into a large bowl and cool for 10 to 15

minutes or until tepid.

3. In a large bowl, using a hand-held electric mixer set at medium-high speed, cream the sugar and butter together until light and fluffy. One at a time, add the egg yolks to the mixture, beating well after each addition. Beat in the flour.

4. In a large, grease-free bowl, using a hand-held electric mixer set at medium-high speed, beat the egg whites until they form stiff, shiny peaks. Fold one-fourth of the egg whites into the chocolate mixture to lighten. Then fold in the remaining egg whites. Fold in the creamed sugar mixture.

5. Scrape the batter into the prepared pan and bake for 60 to 70 minutes or until the top is crusty and cracked and the middle is still slightly moist. Remove the cake to a wire rack to cool completely. Remove the sides of the springform pan and transfer the cake to a serving plate. If desired, place a doily on top of the cake and sprinkle with confectioners' sugar to form a pattern. Remove the doily carefully.

⌒ *Cocoa Blackout Cake* ⌒

Here's a simple way to make a deep, dark chocolate cake look particularly intriguing: baked along with the two cake layers that compose the traditional layer cake is a third layer. This "extra" layer is cut into cubes and attached to the frosted cake. The assembled cake is next dusted with confectioners' sugar for a richly textured and appealing final effect. Lots of chocolate flavor, too.

YIELD: 12 servings

DIFFICULTY: ▰▰

PREPARATION TIME: 1½ hours plus baking, cooling, and chilling times

Cocoa cake:

2 cups granulated sugar

1¾ cups all-purpose flour

1 cup unsweetened nonalkalized cocoa powder

2 teaspoons baking soda

1 teaspoon double-acting baking powder

¼ teaspoon salt

1 cup freshly brewed strong coffee or 2 teaspoons instant espresso coffee powder dissolved in 1 cup boiling water, cooled to room temperature

1 cup buttermilk, at room temperature

8 tablespoons (1 stick) unsalted butter, melted and cooled to room temperature

3 large eggs, at room temperature

2 teaspoons vanilla extract

2 teaspoons orange zest

(ingredients continued)

Whipped-cocoa frosting:

1 cup granulated sugar
1 cup unsweetened nonalkalized cocoa powder
1 cup heavy (whipping) cream
1 teaspoon honey or light corn syrup
2 tablespoons unsalted butter
4 teaspoons vanilla extract

Confectioners' sugar, to dust over cake
Orange slices, for garnish (optional)

Make the cake layers:

1. Position a rack in the center of the oven and preheat to 350°F. If the oven rack will not hold three pans across, set one rack in the upper third and one rack in the lower third of the oven, so that you can bake all three layers of the cake at once. Lightly butter the bottoms and sides of three 8-by-2-inch round cake pans. Line the bottom of each pan with a circle of baking parchment or waxed paper. Dust the sides of the pan with cocoa powder and tap out the excess.

2. In a large bowl, first stir together the sugar, flour, cocoa, baking soda, baking powder, and salt, and then sift the mixture. Using a hand-held electric mixer set at low speed, add the coffee, buttermilk, butter, eggs, vanilla, and orange zest. Beat for 1 to 2 minutes or until the batter is smooth.

3. Scrape the batter into the prepared pans. Bake for 25 to 30 minutes or until a cake tester or toothpick inserted into each layer comes out clean.

4. Cool the layers in their pans on wire racks for 10 minutes. Gently run the tip of a sharp knife around the edges of the layers to loosen, and invert them onto wire racks. Carefully peel off the papers and leave them loosely set on the bottom of the layers. Holding the papers in place, invert the layers onto other racks and cool completely. Wrap the cake layers in plastic and refrigerate overnight.

Make the whipped-cocoa frosting:

5. The same day or an hour or so before you plan to serve the cake, stir together the sugar and cocoa in a small bowl and then sift the mixture. In a heavy, medium saucepan, over low heat, combine the cream and honey. Add the sugar-cocoa mixture and butter. Using a wooden spoon, stir occasionally for 8 to 10 minutes, until the mixture is completely smooth. Do not let it boil. Remove the pan from the heat and stir in the vanilla.

6. Strain through a fine sieve into a medium bowl to remove any unincorporated bits. Cover the surface of the frosting directly with plastic wrap and refrigerate for 45 to 60 minutes or until slightly firm. Using a hand-held electric mixer set at low speed, beat the mixture for 1 to 2 minutes or until light and fluffy. Refrigerate until ready to use.

Assemble the cake:

7. Remove the baking parchment from the cake layers. Put one layer on a serving plate. Using a metal cake spatula, spread one third of the frosting on top of it. Put the second layer on top, and cover the top and sides with the remaining frosting.

8. Using a long, serrated knife, horizontally slice the third layer into two even layers. Keeping the two layers together, cut the cake into strips about ½ to ¾ inch wide. Turn the cake 90° and make cuts perpendicular to the first cuts to make cubes out of the cake.

9. Gently press the cake cubes one at a time all over the frosted cake until the entire surface is covered. Cover the cake loosely with plastic wrap until 20 minutes before serving time. Just before serving, dust the cake lightly with confectioners' sugar. Garnish with orange slices, if desired.

Chocolate Raspberry-Ganache 〜 *Cake* 〜

We have long thought the combination of raspberry and chocolate is close to unbeatable—and one bite of this cake should explain why. The next bite will taste even more of raspberry, and so on and on until you have finished your (first) slice! What is more, the cake is easy to make, since it is made in the food processor. When you make the ganache frosting, try to leave enough time so that it can sit at room temperature for 7 or 8 hours or overnight. Otherwise, it may not have the correct consistency for spreading. Refrigerating it for 90 minutes instead also works fine.

YIELD: 16 servings

DIFFICULTY: ▬▬ ▬

PREPARATION TIME: 1 hour plus baking, cooling, and setting times

SPECIAL EQUIPMENT: pastry bag fitted with a star tip (such as Ateco #2)

Raspberry ganache:

18 ounces bittersweet chocolate, coarsely chopped
1⅓ cups heavy (whipping) cream
A few grains of salt
2 tablespoons unsalted butter, cut into 4 pieces
⅔ cup seedless raspberry preserves
¼ cup black raspberry liqueur, such as Chambord
1 teaspoon vanilla extract

Chocolate cake:

1¾ cups all-purpose flour
2 cups granulated sugar, divided
1½ teaspoons baking soda
¼ teaspoon double-acting baking powder
¼ teaspoon salt
5 ounces unsweetened chocolate, coarsely chopped
¾ cup water
12 tablespoons (1½ sticks) unsalted butter, cut into 12 pieces
¼ cup black raspberry liqueur, such as Chambord
½ cup sour cream
2 extra-large eggs
2 teaspoons vanilla extract
¼ cup seedless raspberry preserves

Raspberry cream:

1 cup heavy (whipping) cream
¼ cup seedless raspberry preserves
1½ teaspoons black raspberry liqueur, such as Chambord

½ pint fresh raspberries, for garnish

(continued)

Make the raspberry ganache:

1. Put the chocolate in a food processor fitted with the metal chopping blade and process for 25 to 30 seconds or until finely chopped.

2. In a small saucepan, bring the heavy cream and salt to a boil. Remove the pan from the heat. With the motor of the food processor running, pour the hot cream through the feed tube. Process for 15 to 20 seconds or until the mixture has liquefied. Scrape down the sides of the work bowl and add the butter. Process for 10 to 15 seconds more or until smooth. Add the preserves, raspberry liqueur, and vanilla, and process for 10 to 15 seconds or until creamy. Transfer the ganache to a medium metal bowl and cover tightly with plastic wrap. Let the ganache thicken at room temperature for 7 or 8 hours or overnight. If you would rather make the ganache the day you plan to frost the cake layers, refrigerate it for no longer than 1½ hours or until the consistency is thick enough to frost the cake.

Make the cake:

3. Position one rack in the top third and another in the bottom third of the oven and preheat to 350°F. Lightly butter the bottoms of two 10-by-2-inch round cake pans. Line the bottom of each pan with a circle of baking parchment or waxed paper.

4. In a food processor fitted with the metal chopping blade, combine the flour, ¼ cup of the sugar, the baking soda, baking powder, and salt. Pulse 3 to 4 times and transfer the flour mixture to a medium bowl.

5. Without washing the container of the food processor, combine the remaining sugar and chocolate. Process for 20 to 25 seconds or until the mixture is finely ground.

6. In a small saucepan, combine the water and butter. Cook over medium heat, stirring frequently, until the mixture comes to a boil and the butter melts. Remove the pan from the heat. With the motor of the food processor running, pour the hot butter mixture through the feed tube. Process

for 15 to 20 seconds or until the mixture is smooth. Pour the liqueur through the feed tube and process for 5 seconds or until smooth.

7. Scrape down the sides of the bowl and then add the sour cream, eggs, and vanilla to the butter mixture. Process for 15 to 20 seconds or until the mixture is smooth. Add half of the flour mixture and pulse 4 to 6 times or until there is barely a trace of flour left. Add the remaining flour mixture and pulse 4 to 6 more times or until there is barely a trace of flour left in the batter.

8. Scrape the batter into the prepared pans and bake for 25 to 30 minutes or until a cake tester or toothpick inserted into the center of each cake layer comes out clean. Cool the cake layers in the pans set on wire racks for 10 minutes. Run the tip of a sharp knife around the edges of the cake layers to loosen them from the pans. Invert the cake layers onto wire racks. Carefully peel off the paper circles and leave them loosely placed on the bottoms of the layers. Invert the layers onto other racks, so that they are right side up. Cool the layers completely.

Assemble the cake:

9. Remove the papers from the cake layers. Place one cake layer on a serving plate. Surround the cake layer with strips of waxed paper to keep the border of the plate clean. Using a metal cake spatula, spread the raspberry preserves over the top of the cake layer. Spread 1 cup of the prepared raspberry ganache over the preserves. Place the second cake layer on top of the ganache. Using a metal cake spatula, frost the top and sides of the cake with a smooth, even coating of the ganache. If desired, use the spatula to create a decorative swirling pattern on top of the frosted cake. Discard the strips of waxed paper. Keep the cake refrigerated until 45 minutes before serving.

Make the raspberry cream:

10. In a large bowl, using a hand-held electric mixer set at medium-high speed, beat the cream until soft peaks start to form. Add the raspberry

preserves and the black raspberry liqueur. Continue beating the cream mixture until stiff peaks start to form.

11. Fill a pastry bag fitted with a star tip (such as Ateco #2) with the raspberry cream. Pipe stars around the top edge of the cake. Pipe a scroll border around the bottom edge of the cake. Top alternating stars with the fresh raspberries to finish the decoration.

～ White Chocolate Pound Cake ～

Do you love plain pound cake but sometimes wish for one with a little more glamour? If so, this version may be just the cake. The white chocolate adds subtle chocolate flavor as well as just the right amount of sweetness. We don't think it's too sweet but suggest that you adjust the amount of sugar to suit your own taste.

> YIELD: 10 to 12 servings
>
> DIFFICULTY: ▬▬
>
> PREPARATION TIME: 1 hour plus baking and cooling times
>
> SPECIAL EQUIPMENT: 10-inch Bundt or tube cake pan; stand-up electric mixer

1 tablespoon pecans, finely chopped
4 ounces white chocolate, coarsely chopped
3 cups all-purpose flour
½ teaspoon salt
¼ teaspoon baking soda
1 cup (2 sticks) unsalted butter, softened
2 to 3 cups granulated sugar
1 cup heavy (whipping) cream
2 teaspoons vanilla extract
6 large eggs, at room temperature
Confectioners' sugar, for dusting
Whipped cream and berries or White Chocolate Almond Ice
*   Cream (see page 255), as an accompaniment (optional)*

1. Position a rack in the center of the oven and preheat to 300°F. Lightly butter the Bundt cake pan. Dust the pan with flour and tap out the excess. Sprinkle the pecans evenly over the bottom.

2. In the top of a double boiler over hot, not simmering, water, melt the white chocolate, stirring constantly until smooth. Remove the top part of the double boiler from the bottom and cool the chocolate for 5 to 10 minutes or until tepid.

3. In a large bowl, stir together the flour, salt, and baking soda, and then sift the mixture.

4. In the large bowl of a stand-up electric mixer, beat the butter at medium speed for 1½ to 2 minutes or until creamy. Add the sugar, 1 cup at a time, beating well after each addition. (After you have added 2 cups, you may want to taste the batter to decide if you want to add the third cup, or a portion of it.) Beat in the cream, the melted white chocolate, and the vanilla. Add the eggs one at a time, beating for 45 to 60 seconds after each addition. Reduce the speed to low. Add the flour mixture 1 cup at a time. Mix 20 to 30 seconds after each addition or until the batter is just blended.

(continued)

5. Scrape the batter into the prepared pan, smoothing it on top. Bake for 1 hour and 15 minutes to 1½ hours or until a cake tester or toothpick inserted in the center of the cake comes out clean. Transfer the cake in the pan to a wire rack and cool for 15 minutes. Using a small spatula, loosen the cake from the sides of the pan and invert it onto a wire rack. Cool completely. Sift confectioners' sugar lightly over the top of the cake. Serve with freshly whipped cream and berries or white chocolate ice cream, if desired.

NOTE: The pound cake can be wrapped in plastic and stored at room temperature for up to 1 week or frozen for up to a month.

⟶ *Betsy's Best Wishes Cake* ⟶

Even without the embellishment, this is a delicious carrot cake. But if you take the extra time to fashion the cake so that it actually looks like a gift-wrapped package, your efforts will be received with exciting enthusiasm. The "tag" is made from white chocolate plastic, a sturdy, edible mixture of chocolate and corn syrup that holds a firm shape when cut. It is an easy matter to pipe letters and flourishes on the tag.

YIELD: 15 to 20 servings

DIFFICULTY: ◼◼◻

PREPARATION TIME: 2½ hours plus baking, cooling, setting, and drying times

SPECIAL EQUIPMENT: paper cone for decorating; 5 yards of ⅜-inch-wide satin ribbon and 2 yards of ⅝-inch-wide satin ribbon, in colors of your choice

Chocolate chip carrot cake:

1¾ cups sifted unbleached all-purpose flour
1 cup whole wheat flour
2 teaspoons double-acting baking powder
2 teaspoons baking soda
2 teaspoons ground cinnamon
1 teaspoon ground nutmeg
¾ teaspoon ground allspice
¼ teaspoon salt
4 large eggs, at room temperature
1 cup packed light brown sugar
1¼ cups vegetable oil
2 cups grated carrots (2 to 3 large whole carrots)
1 cup drained, canned crushed pineapple in juice
6 ounces (about 1 cup) miniature semisweet chocolate chips
⅔ cup raisins

White chocolate plastic:

2½ ounces white chocolate, finely chopped
1½ tablespoons light corn syrup

White chocolate buttercream:

9 ounces white chocolate, finely chopped
¾ cup granulated sugar
3 large egg whites, at room temperature
1½ cups (3 sticks) unsalted butter, softened

Decoration:

3 ounces semisweet chocolate, coarsely chopped
2½ cups shredded sweetened coconut
5 yards ⅜-inch-wide satin ribbon in the color of your choice
2 yards ⅝-inch-wide satin ribbon in another color

Make the cake:

1. Position a rack in the center of the oven and preheat to 325°F. Lightly butter the bottom and sides of a 9-by-13-inch pan. Line the bottom and the long sides of the pan with aluminum foil so that the foil extends beyond the sides by about 2 inches. Lightly butter the foil. Dust the bottom and sides of the pan with flour and tap out the excess.

2. In a medium bowl, stir together the flours, baking powder, baking soda, spices, and salt, and then sift the mixture.

3. In a large bowl, using a hand-held electric mixer, beat the eggs at low speed for 30 to 60 seconds or until foamy. Gradually add the brown sugar and beat for 1 to 2 minutes or until well blended. Pour in the oil in a slow, steady stream and beat for 2 to 3 minutes longer or until well emulsified. Using a wooden spoon, gradually stir in the flour mixture. Fold in the carrots, pineapple, chocolate chips, and raisins. Scrape the batter into the prepared pan. Bake for 40 to 50 minutes or until a cake tester or toothpick inserted in the center of the cake comes out clean.

4. Cool the cake in its pan on a wire rack for 15 minutes. Using the ends of the foil as handles, lift the cake out of the pan and place it on a wire rack to finish cooling. When the cake is cool, invert the cake onto an 8-by-12-inch cardboard rectangle. Carefully peel off the aluminum foil.

Make the white chocolate plastic:

5. In the top of a double boiler over hot, not simmering, water, melt the white chocolate. Stir constantly until smooth and remove from the heat. Transfer the chocolate to a bowl and cool for 10

minutes or until tepid. Stir in the corn syrup and mix for 30 to 60 seconds or until the mixture thickens and starts to lose its shine. Cover with plastic wrap and let it stand at room temperature for at least 1 hour.

Make the white chocolate buttercream:

6. In the top of a double boiler over hot, not simmering, water, melt the white chocolate, stirring constantly until smooth. Remove the top part of the double boiler from the bottom and let the chocolate cool for 10 minutes or until tepid.

7. In a large, grease-free bowl, combine the sugar and egg whites. Set the bowl over a pot of hot, not simmering, water. Whisk the mixture constantly until it is white and creamy and is hot to the touch (about 110°F). Rub a small amount of the mixture between your fingers to make sure the sugar is completely dissolved. Remove the bowl from the pot of water.

8. Beat the egg white mixture with a hand-held electric mixer set at medium speed until foamy. Gradually increase the speed to high and beat 8 to 10 minutes or until the mixture is thick and shiny. Reduce the speed to medium and gradually beat in the softened butter a tablespoon at a time. Stir in the melted chocolate.

Make the gift tag:

9. Dust a work surface very lightly with cornstarch. Roll the white chocolate plastic with a rolling pin into a 6¾-by-5½-inch rectangle, about ³⁄₁₆ inch thick. Dust off any excess cornstarch. Using the pattern provided on page 89, cut out the tag with a small, thin knife and set it aside to dry.

(continued)

10. In the top of a double boiler over hot, not simmering, water, melt the semisweet chocolate, stirring constantly until smooth, and remove the top part of the double boiler from the bottom and cool the chocolate for about 10 minutes or until tepid. Transfer the chocolate to a small paper cone and cut a 1/16-inch opening at the tip (for instructions on making a paper cone, see page 187). Using the pattern as a guide, pipe "Best Wishes" onto the gift tag. Use a paper puncher to make a hole in the end of the tag.

Frost the cake:

11. Using a long, serrated knife, slice the cake horizontally in half to make two layers. Carefully slide the top layer onto a large piece of cardboard. Evenly spread the bottom layer with 1½ cups of the buttercream. Gently slide the top layer back onto the bottom layer. Using a metal cake spatula, frost the top and sides of the cake with the rest of the buttercream. Sprinkle the coconut all over the cake, gently pressing it so that it adheres to the buttercream.

Decorate the cake:

12. Cut one 19-inch and one 15-inch piece of each width of ribbon so that you have four lengths. Put the two corresponding 19-inch pieces together and extend them across the center of the cake. Secure the ribbon by taping the ends to the cardboard. Put the two 15-inch pieces of ribbon together and cross them over the other ribbons to resemble a gift box. Run a small piece of the ⅜-inch wide ribbon through the hole on the gift tag and tie the gift tag to the ribbons at their crossing point. Use the remaining ⅜-inch wide ribbon to tie a bow, and tie the bow to the ribbons at their crossing point.

～ Chocolate Walnut Torte ～

When you're in the mood for a classic European-style cake, try our walnut torte frosted with a rich, dark, buttery ganache. Take care not to overbake and dry out the cake—it should not spring back when lightly pressed, as an American-style layer cake would, but should hold a slight indentation. Both the torte and the frosting fare best held at room temperature for 8 to 10 hours, or overnight, before eating. Refrigerating the torte makes it overly moist and heavy, although you may chill the ganache for an hour and a half before frosting the cake.

YIELD: 12 servings

DIFFICULTY: ▰▰▰

PREPARATION TIME: 1½ hours plus baking, cooling, and setting times

---

Torte:

10 ounces bittersweet chocolate, coarsely chopped
¼ cup dark rum
2 tablespoons water
⅔ cup chopped walnuts
¼ cup confectioners' sugar
1 cup plus 2 tablespoons sifted cake flour (not self-rising)
¼ teaspoon salt
14 tablespoons (1¾ sticks) unsalted butter, softened
¾ cup plus 1 tablespoon granulated sugar, divided
5 large eggs, at room temperature, separated
2 teaspoons vanilla extract

Ganache:

8 ounces bittersweet chocolate, coarsely chopped
1 vanilla bean, split in half lengthwise
1 cup heavy (whipping) cream
5 tablespoons unsalted butter, cut into tablespoons
A few grains of salt

Chocolate glaze:

¾ cup heavy (whipping) cream
3 tablespoons light corn syrup
A few grains of salt
6 ounces bittersweet chocolate, finely chopped
2 teaspoons dark rum
½ cup walnuts, finely chopped

Make the torte:

1. Position a rack in the center of the oven and preheat to 350°F. Lightly butter the bottom and sides of a 10-by-2-inch round cake pan. Line the bottom of the pan with a circle of baking parchment or waxed paper. Dust the sides of the pan with flour and tap out the excess.

2. In the top of a double boiler over hot, not simmering, water, melt the chocolate with the rum and water. Stir frequently until smooth. Remove the top of the double boiler from the bottom and cool the chocolate for 5 to 10 minutes or until tepid.

3. In a food processor fitted with the metal chopping blade, combine the walnuts and confectioners' sugar. Process for 5 to 10 seconds or until the walnuts are coarsely ground. Transfer the nut mixture to a medium bowl and stir in the flour and salt until well combined.

4. In a large bowl, using a hand-held electric mixer set at medium-high speed, beat the butter with ¾ cup of the granulated sugar for 1 to 2 minutes or until creamy. Add the egg yolks and vanilla and continue beating for 30 to 60 seconds or until light. Blend in the melted chocolate.

5. In a large, grease-free bowl, using a hand-held electric mixer set at low speed, beat the egg whites until frothy. Gradually increase the speed to me-

dium high and continue to beat the whites until they start to form soft peaks. Add the remaining 1 tablespoon of granulated sugar and continue to beat the whites until they form stiff, shiny peaks when the beaters are lifted.

6. Fold one third of the egg whites along with one third of the walnut-flour mixture into the chocolate batter. Gently fold in the remaining egg whites and walnut-flour mixture, one third at a time. Scrape the batter into the prepared pan and use a spatula to spread it evenly. Bake for 30 to 32 minutes or until a cake tester or toothpick inserted 3 inches from the side of the pan comes out with a few moist crumbs clinging to it. Cool the torte in the pan set on a wire rack for 20 minutes. Run a knife around the edges of the torte to loosen it from the sides of the pan and invert it onto a wire rack. Leave the paper attached to the bottom and invert it onto another rack so that the torte is right side up. Cool completely. Wrap the torte in plastic and let it set at room temperature overnight.

Make the ganache:

7. Put the chocolate in a food processor fitted with the metal chopping blade. Process the chocolate for 10 to 15 seconds or until finely chopped.

8. Scrape the tiny black seeds from inside the vanilla bean into a heavy, medium saucepan. Add

the scraped vanilla bean pod, cream, butter, and salt. Slowly bring the mixture to a boil over medium-low heat. Take the pan off the heat and remove the scraped vanilla bean pod. Reserve it for making the chocolate glaze. With the motor of the food processor running, pour the hot cream mixture through the feed tube. Process for 15 to 20 seconds or until the mixture is smooth. Transfer the ganache to a small bowl and cover the surface with plastic wrap. Let the ganache thicken at room temperature overnight, or make the ganache the day after you bake the torte and refrigerate it for no longer than 1½ hours or until it is thick enough to frost the torte.

9. Put the torte paper-side up onto a 10-inch cardboard circle and carefully peel off the paper. Transfer the torte to a revolving cake-decorating stand or lazy Susan. Using a metal cake spatula, frost the top and sides of the torte with a smooth, even coating of the ganache. Refrigerate the torte for no more than 15 to 20 minutes or just until the ganache is firm.

Make the chocolate glaze:

10. In a medium saucepan over medium-low heat, slowly bring the cream, corn syrup, salt, and reserved vanilla bean pod to a gentle boil. Take the pan off the heat and remove the vanilla bean. Gently stir in the chocolate until smooth. Blend in the rum and then strain the chocolate glaze into a medium bowl. Let the glaze cool to 84° to 86°F, stirring frequently but gently so that it cools evenly without creating too many air bubbles.

11. Remove the torte from the refrigerator and put it on an inverted 8-inch cake pan set on a baking sheet. Pour the glaze over the top of the torte and spread it evenly over the top and sides with a metal cake spatula. Using the spatula, smooth any drips clinging to the bottom of the torte. Use the tip of the spatula to create a decorative pattern on the top and sides of the torte. Sprinkle the walnuts around the top edge. Refrigerate the torte for no more than 10 minutes or until the glaze has set. Transfer the torte to a serving plate and serve at room temperature.

White Chocolate Strawberry ⁓ Obsttorte ⁓

This simple sponge cake, filled with a cloud of sweetened whipped cream and decorated with overlapping circles of juicy red strawberries, is far easier to make than you might imagine. We recommend using an obsttortenform, which is a round cake pan with a raised center that creates an indentation in the baked sponge, but an everyday cake pan works nearly as well. As the cake cools, it naturally sinks a little in the center, forming a hollow that can be filled. Try this light dessert after a special dinner party, or serve it for an afternoon tea party.

YIELD: 6 to 8 servings

DIFFICULTY: ◼

PREPARATION TIME: 1 hour plus baking, roasting (the nuts), and cooling times

SPECIAL EQUIPMENT: an obsttortenform, available at all Williams-Sonoma stores or through their catalog, (415) 421-7900. If you cannot locate a form, use a 9½-inch or 10½-inch sponge cake shell, sold at most supermarkets.

Sponge cake:

2 large eggs, at room temperature
¼ cup granulated sugar
Pinch of salt
½ teaspoon vanilla extract
3 tablespoons sifted cake flour (not self-rising)

White chocolate filling:

½ cup heavy (whipping) cream
1½ teaspoons orange liqueur, such as Grand Marnier
1½ ounces white chocolate, finely grated

To assemble:

2 pints medium strawberries, hulled and sliced
½ cup red currant jelly
¼ cup roasted sliced almonds (for roasting instructions, see page 20)
White chocolate curls, for garnish (optional)

Make the sponge cake:

1. Position a rack in the center of the oven and preheat to 350° F. Butter a 9½-inch obsttorten-form. Lightly dust with flour; tap out the excess.

2. In a medium heatproof bowl, whisk together the eggs, sugar, and salt. Set the bowl over a pot of hot, not simmering, water (the bottom of the bowl must touch the water). Continue whisking the mixture 1 to 2 minutes or until the sugar crystals have dissolved and the mixture is warm to the touch. Remove the bowl from the hot water.

3. Using a hand-held electric mixer set at medium-high speed, beat the mixture for 3 to 4 minutes or until it has tripled in volume and the batter forms a thick ribbon when the beaters are lifted. Beat in the vanilla.

4. Sift one third of the flour over the batter and fold it in briskly but gently. Fold in the remaining flour a third at a time. Scrape the batter into the prepared pan and spread it evenly. Tap the pan on a work surface to release any large air bubbles. Bake for 10 to 12 minutes or until the center of the cake springs back when lightly touched and the cake has started to pull away from the sides. Cool the cake in the pan on a wire rack for 10 minutes. Using a small knife, loosen the edges of the cake

from the sides of the pan and invert the cake onto a serving plate.

Make the filling:

5. In a chilled, medium bowl, whip the cream with the orange liqueur until soft peaks start to form. Fold in the white chocolate. Spread the filling into the indentation created by the cake mold. At this point, the filled cake can be covered with plastic wrap and refrigerated for up to 2 hours before it is assembled.

Assemble the cake:

6. Starting at the outer edge of the filled sponge cake, arrange the strawberry slices in a circle with points facing out. Continue making circles, slightly overlapping the berries, until the center.

7. Strain the currant jelly through a sieve to liquefy it. Carefully brush the strawberries with the currant jelly. Lightly brush the sides of the sponge cake with the remaining jelly. Crush the almonds slightly with your hand and gently press the almonds against the sides of the cake. If desired, pile white chocolate curls in the center of the glazed strawberries. Serve immediately, or keep the assembled sponge cake refrigerated for no more than an hour before serving.

〜 *Florentine Chocolate Cake* 〜

This cake, filled with a light, frothy low-calorie mousse, is meant to be served chilled, adorned with slices of bright tropical fruits. After it is filled, it is refrigerated for at least 4 hours, held in place in a springform pan that is easily removed just before serving. Such treatment makes the cake an ideal choice for entertaining when you don't want to have to fuss with dessert during the party.

YIELD: 10 servings
DIFFICULTY: ▰▰
PREPARATION TIME: 1 hour plus baking, cooling, and chilling times
SPECIAL EQUIPMENT: 10-by-2-inch round springform pan

Chocolate almond sponge cake:

⅓ cup sliced blanched almonds
½ cup plus 3 tablespoons cake flour, divided (not self-rising)
1½ ounces bittersweet chocolate, very finely chopped
3 large eggs, at room temperature
½ cup granulated sugar
Pinch of salt
1 teaspoon vanilla extract

Chocolate mousse filling:

¼ cup low-fat (2 percent) milk
4 ounces bittersweet chocolate, finely chopped
1 teaspoon vanilla extract
6 large egg whites
⅓ cup granulated sugar
1½ teaspoons unflavored gelatin

To assemble:

1 tablespoon confectioners' sugar
2 kiwifruit, pared and sliced
¼ papaya, peeled, seeded, and sliced

Make the chocolate almond sponge cake:

1. Position a rack in the center of the oven and preheat to 350°F. Lightly butter the bottom and sides of the pan. Line the bottom of the pan with a circle of baking parchment or waxed paper. Dust the sides of the pan with flour and tap out the excess.

2. In a food processor fitted with the metal chopping blade, combine the almonds and 3 tablespoons of the flour. Process for 15 to 25 seconds or until the almonds are finely ground. Transfer the mixture to a medium bowl and stir in the remaining ½ cup of flour and the chocolate until well blended.

3. In a large heatproof bowl, whisk the eggs, sugar, and salt together. Set the bowl over a saucepan of hot, not simmering, water. Continue whisking the mixture for 3 to 5 minutes, until it is warm to the touch and the sugar has dissolved. Remove the bowl from the heat and stir in the vanilla.

4. Using a hand-held electric mixer set at medium-high speed, beat the egg mixture for 4 to 6

minutes, until it has tripled in volume and forms a thick ribbon when the beaters are lifted.

5. Sprinkle the flour mixture, a third at a time, over the batter and fold it in carefully so that the batter does not deflate. Scrape the batter into the prepared pan and spread it evenly. Bake for 20 to 25 minutes or until a cake tester or toothpick inserted into the center of the cake comes out clean. Cool the cake in the pan on a wire rack for 10 minutes. Run a knife around the edge of the cake to loosen, and invert it onto a wire rack. Carefully peel the paper off the bottom of the cake and invert it again so that the cake is right side up. Cool the cake completely.

Make the chocolate mousse filling:

6. In a small saucepan, bring the milk to a gentle boil. Remove the pan from the heat and stir in the chocolate until melted. Stir in the vanilla until smooth. Transfer the chocolate mixture to a large bowl.

7. In a large grease-free, heatproof bowl, whisk the egg whites, sugar, and gelatin together. Set the bowl over a saucepan of hot, not simmering, water. Continue whisking the mixture for 2 to 4 minutes or until the sugar and gelatin have dissolved and the mixture is warm and frothy.

8. Using a hand-held electric mixer set at medium-high speed, beat the egg-white mixture for 2 to 4 minutes or until it is cool and forms a stiff, shiny meringue. Fold one third of the meringue into the chocolate mixture to lighten it. Fold in the remaining meringue.

Assemble the cake:

9. Using a serrated knife, slice the sponge cake in half to make two ½-inch layers. Put the sides of a 10-inch round springform pan on a large serving plate. Set one cake layer inside the springform on the plate. Use a metal spatula to spread the mousse filling evenly over the cake layer. Lay the second layer of cake on top and gently press it so that it is level. Cover the cake with plastic wrap and refrigerate for at least 4 hours or overnight.

10. Use a hot metal spatula that has been warmed in hot water and then dried to cut around the edge of the cake to free it from the springform pan. Remove the sides of the pan. Lightly sprinkle the top of the cake with confectioners' sugar. Arrange slices of kiwifruit and papaya around the top edge of the cake. Serve the cake chilled.

White Chocolate Lemon
∿ Cheesecake ∿

Created by one of our readers, this version of America's favorite dessert combines the sweetness of white chocolate with the tartness of lemon—an unbeatable team. And to top it off, the cake is glazed with dark chocolate. What could be better? The cheesecake bakes for a short time and will look undercooked. Resist the temptation to bake it longer; it firms up very nicely in the refrigerator after it cools—cools *completely,* don't forget—on the kitchen counter.

YIELD: 10 servings

DIFFICULTY: ▬▬

PREPARATION TIME: 45 minutes plus baking and chilling times

SPECIAL EQUIPMENT: 10-by-3-inch round springform pan

Crust:

4½ ounces chocolate wafer cookies, finely crushed (about 1½ cups)

5 tablespoons unsalted butter, melted

Filling:

8 ounces white chocolate, finely chopped
½ cup heavy (whipping) cream
1½ pounds cream cheese, softened
1½ cups granulated sugar
4 large eggs, at room temperature
⅓ cup freshly squeezed lemon juice
1 tablespoon grated lemon zest
1 teaspoon vanilla extract
½ teaspoon lemon extract
¼ cup white rum (optional)

Lemon zest garnish:

3 large lemons
1 cup granulated sugar
½ cup water

Bittersweet chocolate glaze:

6 ounces bittersweet chocolate, finely chopped
1 ounce unsweetened chocolate, finely chopped
2 tablespoons light corn syrup
3 tablespoons unsalted butter, softened

Make the crust:

1. Position a rack in the center of the oven and preheat to 350°F. Lightly butter the bottom and sides of the springform pan.

2. In a medium bowl, combine the cookie crumbs and melted butter. Stir the mixture with a wooden spoon until it is well blended. Transfer the mixture into the springform pan. Using your fingers, firmly press the mixture evenly into the bottom of the pan. Refrigerate the crust while you make the filling.

Make the filling:

3. In the top of a double boiler over hot, not simmering, water, melt the white chocolate with the cream, stirring often, until smooth. Remove the top part of the double boiler from the bottom and allow the mixture to cool for 10 minutes, stirring occasionally.

4. In a large bowl, using a hand-held electric mixer set at high speed, beat the cream cheese with the sugar for about 1 minute or until it is light. Beat in the cooled white chocolate mixture until well combined. One at a time, add the eggs, beating well after each addition. Beat in the lemon juice, lemon zest, vanilla and lemon extracts, and rum, if desired, until well combined. Pour the filling into the chilled crust.

5. Bake for 45 to 50 minutes or until the cake is barely set in the center. Remove the cake from the oven to a wire rack. With a small, sharp knife, cut around the sides to release the cake from the pan. Leave the cake in the pan and cool it completely on a wire rack. Remove the sides of the springform pan and refrigerate the cheesecake for 1 to 2 hours or until firm. Insert a large metal cake spatula between the crust and the bottom of the springform pan to loosen. Using two large metal cake spatulas, lift the cake off the bottom of the springform and place it on a 10-inch cardboard cake circle. Set the cake on its cardboard circle on a wire rack set over a baking sheet.

Make the garnish:

6. Use a vegetable peeler to remove strips of zest from the lemons, avoiding the white pith underneath. With a sharp knife, cut the zest into 2-by-$\frac{1}{16}$-inch pieces. Put the strips in a small saucepan filled with cold water. Bring the water to a boil over medium-high heat. Boil the strips for about 10 minutes or until they are tender. Drain the lemon zest strips, rinse under cold water, and drain again. Dry the strips well on paper towels.

7. In a small saucepan over medium-high heat, combine the sugar and water. Bring the syrup to a boil, stirring with a wooden spoon, until it is clear and the sugar is dissolved. Stop stirring and let it boil until it reaches 230°F on a candy thermometer. Remove the pan from the heat. Stir in the lemon zest. Let the lemon zest soak in the syrup for at least 1 hour.

Make the glaze:

8. In the top of a double boiler over hot, not simmering, water, melt the bittersweet and unsweetened chocolates with the corn syrup, stirring often, until smooth. Remove the pan from the heat and with a wooden spoon, stir in the butter 1 tablespoon at a time, mixing well after each addition.

Assemble the cheesecake:

9. Spoon the warm glaze over the top of the cheesecake. With a large metal cake spatula, spread the glaze over the top of the cake, letting the excess rundown the sides of the cake. Smooth the glaze over the top and sides of the cake. Arrange the lemon zest garnish in a circle around the rim of the cake. Refrigerate the cake for 1 hour or until the glaze is set. Cover the cake and refrigerate if not serving immediately.

∾ *Oregon Hazelnut Pavé* ∾

In French cooking, *pavé* means "brick," yet the homely connotation does little justice to this magnificent creation of hazelnut-flavored chocolate mousse generously layered between chocolate-hazelnut sponge cake, frosted with sweetened whipped cream and garnished with more chopped hazelnuts. Since the cake, the mousse, and the garnish all call for roasted hazelnuts, it's advisable to roast them all at the same time. The pavé chills for 8 hours or so before it is decorated, so be sure to allow plenty of time. You might want to make it the day before your next party—we promise rave reviews.

YIELD: 8 servings

DIFFICULTY: ▰▰▰

PREPARATION TIME: 1½ hours plus roasting (the nuts), baking, cooling, and setting times

SPECIAL EQUIPMENT: 11-by-17½-inch jelly-roll pan; 5¼-by-9¼-by-2½-inch loaf pan; pastry bag fitted with a large star tip (such as Ateco #3)

Hazelnut sponge cake:

¼ cup all-purpose flour
¼ cup unsweetened alkalized cocoa powder
⅛ teaspoon salt
¼ cup roasted hazelnuts, coarsely ground (for roasting instructions, see page 20)
4 large eggs, at room temperature, separated
½ cup granulated sugar, divided
1 teaspoon hazelnut liqueur

Sugar syrup:

¾ cup water
⅓ cup granulated sugar
2 tablespoons hazelnut liqueur

Chocolate hazelnut mousse:

7 ounces bittersweet chocolate, coarsely chopped
1½ tablespoons unsalted butter, softened
2 large eggs, at room temperature, separated
¼ cup hazelnut liqueur
½ teaspoon vanilla extract
½ cup heavy (whipping) cream
¼ cup roasted hazelnuts, finely chopped

Decoration:

1⅓ cups heavy (whipping) cream
⅓ cup sifted confectioners' sugar
8 strawberries or 8 hazelnuts
3 ounces (about ¾ cup) roasted hazelnuts, finely chopped

Make the hazelnut sponge cake:

1. Position a rack in the center of the oven and preheat to 350°F. Lightly butter the jelly-roll pan and line it with baking parchment or waxed paper. Make 1½-inch slits in each corner of the paper. Fold the cut ends over one another to make neat corners. Lightly butter the paper. Dust the pan with flour and tap out the excess.

2. In a medium bowl, stir together the flour, cocoa, and salt. Sift the mixture. Stir in the ground hazelnuts.

3. In a large bowl, using a hand-held electric mixer set at medium-high speed, beat the egg yolks with ¼ cup of the sugar and the hazelnut liqueur for 2 to 3 minutes, until the mixture forms a thick pale-yellow ribbon when the beaters are lifted.

4. In a large, grease-free bowl, beat the egg whites with a hand-held electric mixer set at low speed until frothy. Gradually increase the speed to medium high and continue beating until soft peaks start to form. Add the remaining ¼ cup of sugar 1 tablespoon at a time, and continue beating 1 to 2 minutes or until the whites form stiff, shiny peaks.

5. Fold the beaten egg whites and the flour-nut mixture into the egg yolk mixture. Scrape the batter into the prepared pan and spread it evenly with a spatula. Bake for 10 to 15 minutes or until the top of the sponge cake springs back when gently pressed. Cool the cake in the pan on a wire rack for 15 minutes. Remove the sponge cake from the pan by covering it with a large piece of waxed paper and the back of another baking sheet. Carefully invert the sponge cake onto the waxed paper-covered baking sheet and gently peel off the paper. Cool completely.

Make the sugar syrup:

6. In a small saucepan, combine the water and sugar. Cook over medium heat, stirring with a wooden spoon until the sugar dissolves. Increase the heat to medium high and bring the syrup to a simmer. Remove the pan from the heat and cool the syrup to room temperature. Stir in the hazelnut liqueur.

Make the chocolate hazelnut mousse:

7. In the top of a double boiler over hot, not simmering, water, melt the chocolate. Stir frequently until smooth. Remove the top of the double boiler and cool the chocolate for 5 to 10 minutes or until tepid.

8. In a large bowl, whisk the butter and egg yolks together. Stir in the hazelnut liqueur, vanilla, and ¼ cup of the sugar syrup. Stir in the chocolate until the mixture is smooth.

9. In a medium bowl, using a hand-held electric mixer set at low speed, beat the egg whites until frothy. Gradually increase the speed to medium high and continue beating the whites for 1 to 2 minutes or until they form stiff, shiny peaks. Fold the egg whites into the chocolate mixture.

10. In a chilled medium bowl, whip the cream until stiff peaks start to form. Fold the cream and the chopped hazelnuts into the chocolate-egg white mixture.

Assemble the pavé:

11. Line the loaf pan with a large piece of plastic wrap, leaving a 3-inch overlap on the short ends. Cut the sheet of sponge cake into three 9¼-by-5¼-inch rectangles. Put one of the trimmed sponge cake layers into the bottom of the lined loaf pan. Brush the layer with the sugar syrup until the cake is quite moist. Put half of the chocolate hazelnut mousse over the sponge cake layer, spreading it evenly. Top the mousse with a second layer of sponge cake. Brush this layer with more sugar syrup until it is moist. Spread the remaining mousse over the second sponge cake layer. Top the mousse with the third sponge cake layer and brush it with sugar syrup. Cover the pavé with the overlapping pieces of plastic wrap and refrigerate for 8 hours or overnight, until firm.

Decorate the pavé:

12. Uncover the top of the chilled pavé and turn it out onto a rimless baking sheet. Carefully remove the plastic wrap. In a chilled large bowl, beat the cream and confectioners' sugar with a hand-held

electric mixer set at medium-high speed until stiff peaks start to form.

13. Using a metal cake spatula, frost the top and sides of the pavé with the whipped cream. Put the remaining whipped cream into a pastry bag fitted with a large star tip (such as Ateco #3). Using the edge of the metal cake spatula, lightly score the top of the pavé into eight equal portions. Pipe a rosette in the center of each slice and top each rosette with a strawberry or hazelnut. Cupping manageable amounts of the chopped hazelnuts in your hand, gently press the nuts onto all four sides of the pavé. Using two metal cake spatulas, carefully transfer the decorated pavé to a rectangular serving platter. Keep the pavé refrigerated until serving time.

～ *Chocolate Indulgence* ～

An almost flourless, decadently chocolaty cake (a whole pound of chocolate!), the dessert bakes in 15 minutes and needs no more garnish than a few spoonfuls of whipped cream and a simple sauce made from frozen raspberries. If fresh raspberries are in the markets, they look pretty set on the plate with the cake and the sauce.

YIELD: 8 servings

DIFFICULTY: ■■

PREPARATION TIME: 1 hour plus baking and cooling times

SPECIAL EQUIPMENT: 8-by-3-inch round springform pan

Cake:

1 pound bittersweet chocolate, coarsely chopped
10 tablespoons (1 stick plus 2 tablespoons) unsalted butter, cut into tablespoons
4 large eggs, at room temperature
1 tablespoon granulated sugar
1 tablespoon all-purpose flour

To assemble:

2 10-ounce packages frozen raspberries in light syrup, thawed and drained
1 tablespoon Framboise or Pear William liqueur
1 cup heavy (whipping) cream
½ pint fresh raspberries, for garnish (optional)

Make the cake:

1. Position a rack in the center of the oven and preheat to 400°F. Lightly butter the bottom and sides of the springform pan. Line the bottom of the pan with a circle of baking parchment or waxed paper. Dust the sides of the pan with flour and tap out the excess.

2. In the top of a double boiler over hot, not simmering, water, melt 8 ounces of the chocolate with 5 tablespoons of the butter. As the chocolate and butter melt, gradually stir in the remaining chocolate and butter until the mixture is completely melted and smooth. Remove the top of the double boiler from the bottom and let the chocolate mixture cool for 15 minutes or until tepid.

3. In a large heatproof bowl, stir together the eggs and sugar with a whisk until frothy. Set the bowl over a saucepan of hot, not simmering, water. (The water should touch the bottom of the bowl.) Continue whisking the egg mixture for 2 to 3 minutes or until it is warm to the touch and the sugar crystals have dissolved. Remove the bowl from the heat.

4. Using a hand-held electric mixer set at medium-high speed, beat the egg mixture for 4 to 5 minutes or until it has tripled in volume and forms soft peaks when the beaters are lifted.

5. Sift the flour over the batter and gently fold it in. Fold one fourth of the batter into the chocolate mixture to lighten it. Carefully fold the lightened chocolate mixture into the remaining batter. Scrape the batter into the prepared pan and spread it evenly with a spatula.

6. Bake for 15 minutes or until a cake tester or toothpick inserted into the center of the cake comes out slightly moist. Set the cake in the pan on a wire rack for 45 minutes or until completely cool. Remove the sides of the springform pan and invert the cake onto a plate. Carefully peel off the paper.

Assemble the cake:

7. In a food processor or blender, puree the raspberries until smooth. Strain the puree through a sieve into a bowl. Stir in the liqueur.

8. In a chilled bowl, using a hand-held electric mixer set at medium-high speed, beat the cream for 3 to 5 minutes or until soft peaks begin to form.

9. Cut the cake into slices. Serve each slice with a large dollop of the whipped cream and spoon 2 to 3 tablespoons of the raspberry sauce around the base of each slice. If desired, garnish each serving with fresh raspberries.

⟞ *Triple Chocolate Espresso Cake* ⟝

This simple glazed cake is made even easier because we start with a mix—the sort available in every supermarket. We add instant chocolate pudding, sour cream, chocolate chips, and espresso powder for improved texture and heightened flavor, and bake the cake in a fluted tube pan to make it attractive and easy to glaze.

YIELD: 12 to 16 servings

DIFFICULTY: ◼

PREPARATION TIME: 40 minutes plus baking, cooling, and setting times

SPECIAL EQUIPMENT: stand-up electric mixer; 12-cup fluted tube pan

Cake:

9 ounces (about 1½ cups) semisweet chocolate chips
1 tablespoon all-purpose flour
1 18.25-ounce box chocolate cake mix
1 4-ounce package instant chocolate pudding mix
2 tablespoons instant espresso coffee powder
1 cup sour cream, at room temperature
¾ cup vegetable oil
½ cup water
4 large eggs, at room temperature

(ingredients continued)

Bittersweet chocolate glaze:

12 ounces (about 2 cups) semisweet chocolate chips
½ cup water
1 tablespoon light corn syrup
2 teaspoons instant espresso powder
1 tablespoon sifted confectioners' sugar

Make the cake:

1. Position a rack in the center of the oven and preheat to 350°F. Lightly butter and flour the fluted tube pan and tap out the excess flour.

2. In a medium bowl, toss the chocolate chips with the flour until evenly coated. In the large bowl of a stand-up electric mixer, combine the cake mix, instant pudding mix, espresso powder, sour cream, vegetable oil, water, and eggs. Mix on low speed until moistened. Beat at medium-high speed for 2 minutes or until very thick and well blended. Fold in the floured chocolate chips. Pour the batter into the prepared pan, smoothing the top with a spatula.

3. Bake for 50 to 60 minutes or until a cake tester or toothpick inserted into the center of the cake comes out clean. Cool the cake in the pan on a wire rack for 10 minutes. Invert it onto a rack and cool the cake completely.

Make the bittersweet chocolate glaze:

4. In the top of a double boiler over hot, not simmering, water, melt the chocolate chips. Stir frequently until smooth, then remove the top part of the double boiler from the bottom and cool the chocolate for 5 to 10 minutes or until tepid. In a small saucepan, combine the water, corn syrup, and espresso powder. Bring to a gentle boil over medium-high heat. Remove the pan from the heat and pour the mixture into a medium bowl. Using a whisk, stir in the melted chocolate and mix until smooth.

5. Put the cake, still on the wire rack, onto a jelly-roll pan. Carefully pour the warm glaze over the cake and spread it evenly with a metal cake spatula. Let the glaze set at room temperature for 1 hour. Lightly sift the confectioners' sugar over the cake, and store in an airtight container at room temperature.

～ *Chocolate Walnut-Praline Cake* ～

This stunning dessert took top honors in the cake category of our 1986 recipe contest. It masterfully combines the flavor of walnuts with a subtle touch of chocolate in its moist, tender crumb, which is accented by a white chocolate ganache laced with crushed praline. More praline is gently pressed on the sides of the cake after it is frosted with a silky white chocolate buttercream.

YIELD: 12 servings

DIFFICULTY: ◼︎◼︎◼︎

PREPARATION TIME: 2 hours plus baking, setting, and chilling times

SPECIAL EQUIPMENT: pastry bag fitted with large star tip (such as Ateco #3)

Caramelized walnuts and walnut praline:

¾ cup granulated sugar
⅓ cup water
6 perfect walnut halves
1 cup chopped walnuts

Chocolate diamonds:

2 ounces bittersweet chocolate, coarsely chopped

Walnut cake:

2 cups walnut pieces
1 cup blanched slivered almonds
1 cup granulated sugar, divided
½ cup sifted dry rye bread crumbs
¼ cup unsweetened alkalized cocoa powder
2 ounces bittersweet chocolate, finely chopped
¼ teaspoon ground cinnamon
10 large eggs, at room temperature, separated
3½ teaspoons instant coffee powder
½ cup boiling water
1 teaspoon fresh lemon juice
¼ teaspoon salt

White chocolate ganache with praline:

1 cup heavy (whipping) cream
8 ounces white chocolate, coarsely chopped
4 tablespoons (½ stick) unsalted butter, softened

White chocolate cream cheese buttercream:

15 ounces white chocolate, coarsely chopped
12 ounces cream cheese, softened
1½ cups (3 sticks) unsalted butter, softened
1½ cups sifted confectioners' sugar
1 teaspoon fresh lemon juice

To assemble:

¾ cup apricot preserves

Make the caramelized walnuts and walnut praline:
1. Lightly oil a large baking sheet. In a small saucepan, combine the sugar and water. Stir over medium heat until the sugar dissolves. Increase the heat to medium high and continue to cook without stirring for 4 to 6 minutes or until the syrup caramelizes. Immediately remove the pan from the heat. Add the 6 walnut halves to the caramel and toss to coat. With an oiled fork, remove the halves one at a time, letting the excess caramel drip back into the pan, and place them at one end of the prepared baking sheet. Quickly stir the 1 cup of walnut halves into the remaining hot caramel. Pour the walnut praline onto the other end of the baking

sheet. Cool the praline for 30 minutes or until hard. Reserve the 6 individual caramelized walnut halves for decorating the cake.

2. Coarsely chop the praline on a cutting board using a large knife. In a food processor fitted with the metal chopping blade, process the praline for 35 to 45 seconds or until finely ground, and then transfer to a bowl.

Make the chocolate diamonds:

3. In the top of a double boiler over hot, not simmering, water, melt the bittersweet chocolate. Stir frequently until smooth. Remove the top of the double boiler from the bottom and cool for 5 minutes, stirring occasionally.

4. Cut a 2-inch-long-by-¾-inch wide diamond-shaped pattern out of cardboard. Line a baking sheet with aluminum foil. Using an offset metal cake spatula, spread the melted chocolate evenly over the foil to form a ⅛-inch thick layer. Refrigerate the baking sheet for 5 to 8 minutes or until the chocolate is just set but not hard. Using a small, sharp knife, use the pattern to cut out six diamonds. Return the baking sheet to the refriger-

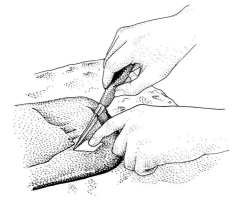

ator for 15 to 20 minutes or until the chocolate is hard. Peel the chocolate from around the diamonds, taking care to handle the diamonds as little as possible. Refrigerate until ready to decorate the cake.

Make the walnut cake layers:

5. Position a rack in the center of the oven and preheat to 350°F. Lightly butter the bottom and sides of two 10-by-2-inch round cake pans. Line the bottom of each pan with a circle of baking parchment. Dust the sides of the pans with flour and tap out the excess.

6. In a food processor fitted with the metal chopping blade, process the walnuts and almonds with ½ cup of the sugar for 10 to 15 seconds or until finely ground. In a medium bowl, stir together the ground-nut mixture, bread crumbs, cocoa, bittersweet chocolate, and cinnamon.

7. In a very large bowl, using a hand-held electric mixer set at medium-high speed, beat the egg yolks with the remaining ½ cup of sugar for 3 to 4 minutes or until the mixture is pale yellow and forms a thick ribbon when the beaters are lifted. Dissolve the coffee powder in the boiling water and slowly beat it into the egg yolk mixture. Add the lemon juice and then fold in the ground-nut mixture.

8. In a large, grease-free bowl, using a hand-held electric mixer set at low speed, beat the egg whites until foamy. Add the salt and gradually increase the speed to medium high. Continue beating the whites until they form stiff, shiny peaks. Carefully fold one third of the whites into the batter to lighten it. Fold in the remaining whites. Scrape the batter into the prepared pans and spread evenly.

9. Bake for 30 minutes or until a cake tester or toothpick inserted into the center of each layer comes out clean. Cool the cake layers in their pans on wire racks for 10 minutes. Run a knife around the edges of the cake layers to loosen them, and invert them onto wire racks. Leave the papers attached to the bottoms of the cake layers and invert them again, so that the tops face up. Cool the layers completely.

Make the ganache:

10. In a small saucepan, bring the heavy cream to a gentle boil over medium heat. In a food processor fitted with the metal chopping blade, process the white chocolate for 15 to 20 seconds or until finely chopped. With the motor running, pour the hot cream through the feed tube. Process 15 to 20 seconds or until the chocolate is melted. Add the butter and process for 5 to 10 seconds or until the ganache is smooth. Scrape the ganache into a medium bowl. Cover the surface of the ganache with plastic wrap and refrigerate for no longer than 1 hour, until thickened. (Do not overchill, or it will be too stiff to beat.)

Make the buttercream:

11. In the top of a double boiler over hot, not simmering, water, melt the white chocolate. Stir constantly until smooth. Remove the top of the double boiler from the bottom and cool for 5 to 10 minutes or until the chocolate is tepid.

12. In a medium bowl, using a hand-held electric mixer set at medium-high speed, beat the cream cheese and butter for 1 minute or until smooth. Stir in the confectioners' sugar and continue beating until smooth. Add the lemon juice and the chocolate, and continue beating 1 minute more or until well combined and fluffy. Hold the buttercream at room temperature.

Assemble the cake:

13. Using a hand-held electric mixer set at medium speed, beat the ganache with ½ cup of the praline powder for 10 to 15 seconds, just until soft peaks start to form. Do not overbeat, or the ganache will separate.

14. Carefully remove the baking parchment from the bottoms of the cake layers. With a serrated knife, trim the tops of the cake layers so that they are level. Spread a large dab of the buttercream in the center of a 9-inch cardboard circle and set the first cake layer on top. Press gently so that the layer adheres to the cardboard. Spread the white chocolate ganache evenly over the top of the cake layer. Place the second layer on top, over the ganache.

Using a pastry brush, brush any loose crumbs from the top and sides of the cake.

15. In a small saucepan over low heat, melt the apricot preserves, stirring constantly until hot. Strain the hot preserves through a sieve into a bowl, pressing the solids with the back of a wooden spoon. Using a pastry brush, coat the top and sides of the cake with a thin layer of the warm apricot glaze. Refrigerate the cake uncovered for 10 minutes or until the glaze is set.

(continued)

16. Put the cake on a revolving cake stand or an inverted 9-inch round cake pan. Set aside 1½ cups of the buttercream to decorate the cake and use the rest to frost it. Using a metal cake spatula, frost the top and sides of the cake with an even layer of buttercream. Smooth the top of the cake by holding the spatula at a slight angle, working from the edge inward.

17. Set the cake on its stand over a large sheet of waxed paper. In small, slightly cupped handfuls, gently press the walnut-praline powder around the sides of the cake, letting the excess fall onto the waxed paper.

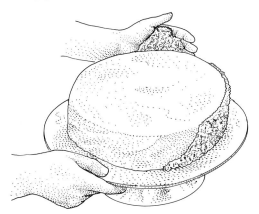

18. Transfer the cake to a serving plate or cake stand. Fill a pastry bag fitted with a large star tip (such as Ateco #3), with the remaining buttercream. Pipe a border of rosettes or scrollwork around the top and bottom edges of the cake. Arrange the chocolate diamonds in a starburst pattern in the center of the cake and set the caramelized walnut halves between the diamonds. Refrigerate the cake until the buttercream is set and then loosely cover with plastic wrap. Remove the plastic wrap and let the cake stand at room temperature for about 15 minutes before serving. Serve the cake at room temperature.

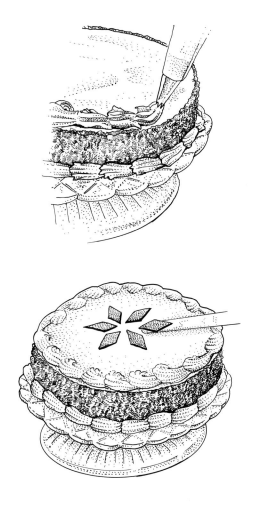

Chocolate Orange
∽ Truffle Cake ∽

Orange and chocolate are a delightful combination and we were thrilled to get a recipe from the world-famous Bel-Air Hotel in California that blended the two so artfully. Of course, with the wonderful oranges grown in California, it comes as no surprise that local chefs would use them whenever possible. The two flavors are bound together with a rich, satisfying filling that uses crème fraîche as its base. You can buy excellent crème fraîche in many specialty stores or you can make your own. If you make your own, be sure to allow enough time for it before starting the cake. The cake itself, baked in springform pans, is layered back into one of the pans after it is baked and filled, and then left overnight to chill.

YIELD: 16 servings

DIFFICULTY: ▬▬▬

PREPARATION TIME: 1½ hours plus baking, cooling, and chilling times

SPECIAL EQUIPMENT: 2 10-by-3-inch round springform pans; stand-up electric mixer

Cake:

14 ounces bittersweet chocolate, coarsely chopped
12 tablespoons (1½ sticks) unsalted butter, cut into ½-inch pieces
8 large eggs, at room temperature, separated
6 tablespoons granulated sugar, divided
Grated zest of 3 medium oranges (about 2 teaspoons)
Pinch of salt
2 tablespoons all-purpose flour

Filling:

12 ounces bittersweet chocolate, coarsely chopped
⅔ cup heavy (whipping) cream
4 tablespoons (½ stick) unsalted butter
1 tablespoon instant espresso coffee powder
1½ teaspoons water
2 cups homemade (for recipe, see page 103) or store-bought crème fraîche

Frosting:

10 ounces bittersweet chocolate, coarsely chopped
½ cup plus 2 tablespoons heavy (whipping) cream
3 tablespoons unsalted butter

Candied orange peel, for garnish (optional)

(continued)

Make the cake:

1. Position a rack in the center of the oven and preheat to 350°F. Lightly butter the bottom and sides of the springform pans. Line the bottom of each pan with a circle of baking parchment or waxed paper. Do not dust with flour.

2. In the top of a double boiler over hot, not simmering, water, melt the chocolate and butter. Stir frequently until smooth. Remove the top of the double boiler from the bottom and cool the chocolate for 10 to 15 minutes or until tepid, stirring occasionally.

3. In the large bowl of a stand-up electric mixer, beat the yolks with 3 tablespoons of the sugar at high speed for 3 minutes or until the mixture forms a thick yellow ribbon when the beaters are lifted. Beat in the orange zest.

4. In a grease-free bowl, beat the egg whites at low speed until they start to foam. Add the salt and gradually increase the speed to medium high. Continue beating until the whites start to form soft peaks. Gradually add the remaining 3 tablespoons of sugar and beat the whites until they form stiff, shiny peaks.

5. Fold the chocolate mixture into the yolk mixture. Fold in one third of the egg white mixture to lighten the batter. Top with the remaining whites. Sift the flour over the whites and fold the batter together until well combined. Divide the mixture between the two prepared pans. Bake for 35 minutes or until a cake tester or toothpick inserted in the middle of each cake layer comes out clean. Cool the layers in their pans set on wire racks for 10 minutes. Remove the sides of the pans and invert the layers onto wire racks. Remove the pan bottoms and carefully peel off the papers. Invert the layers onto other racks and cool them completely.

Make the filling:

6. Using a food processor fitted with the metal chopping blade, process the chocolate for 20 seconds or until it is finely chopped.

7. In a medium saucepan over medium heat, bring the heavy cream and butter to a gentle boil. With the motor of the food processor running, pour the hot cream-butter mixture through the feed tube. Process for 20 seconds or until smooth. Transfer the mixture to a medium bowl and at room temperature cool for 20 minutes.

8. In a small bowl, dissolve the espresso powder in the water. In the bowl of a stand-up electric mixer, whip the crème fraîche for 1 minute at medium-high speed or until it starts to form soft peaks. Beat in the dissolved coffee powder. Fold the crème fraîche into the chocolate mixture.

Assemble the cake:

9. Using a serrated knife, trim the tops of the cake layers to make them flat. Put one layer of cake in a 10-inch round springform pan. Add half of the filling and spread it evenly over the layer and into the surrounding empty space between the edge of the cake layer and the sides of the springform pan. Lay the second layer on top and press gently so that it is level. Top with the rest of the filling and again spread it evenly over the cake as well as into the surrounding empty space. Cover with plastic wrap and refrigerate for about 1½ hours or until the filling is set.

Make the frosting:

10. In a food processor fitted with the metal chopping blade, process the chocolate for 20 seconds or until it is finely chopped. In a medium saucepan over medium heat, bring the heavy cream and butter to a gentle boil. With the motor of the food processor running, pour the hot cream-butter mixture through the feed tube and process for 20 seconds or until smooth. Transfer the mixture to a bowl and allow to cool for 20 minutes or until it is spreading consistency.

Decorate the cake:

11. Using a hot, narrow metal cake spatula, warmed in hot water and then dried, cut around the edge of the cake to free it from the sides of the springform pan, and remove the sides. With two

large cake spatulas, lift the cake off the bottom of the springform pan and put it on a 10-inch cardboard cake circle or large serving plate. Smoothly ice the top and sides of the cake. Decorate with candied orange peel, if desired. Serve at room temperature.

⌒ *Crème Fraîche* ⌒

Serve this with the Chocolate Orange Truffle Cake, but don't stop there. Crème fraîche has so many uses, it is a good idea to keep a recipe for it close at hand. For instance, try it spooned over scones, with quick breads, or as a topping for fresh berries and fruit.

YIELD: 2 cups

DIFFICULTY: ▰

PREPARATION TIME: 10 minutes plus standing time (allow 12 to 24 hours for the crème fraîche to thicken)

2 cups heavy (whipping) cream
2 tablespoons buttermilk

1. In a medium saucepan over low heat, gently heat the heavy cream and the buttermilk to 90°F and immediately pour the mixture into a warm thermos. Cover and let stand in a warm spot for 12 to 24 hours or until the mixture thickens.

2. Transfer to a noncorrosive container, cover tightly, and refrigerate overnight.

~ *Adrienne Welch's Rigo Jancsi* ~

The old Hungarian tale goes that a beautiful princess fell so wildly in love with a handsome gypsy named Rigo Jancsi that she left her wealthy husband, her children, and her home to be with him. Shortly after their wedding night, a sentimental pastry chef created a cake for the lovers meant to be as exotic as their romance. To this day, the sumptuous chocolate cake remains part of the cuisine of Hungary. We have developed our own version, spreading an airy ganache between two bittersweet torte layers and enrobing the cake in an elegantly patterned milk chocolate and dark chocolate glaze.

YIELD: 16 servings

DIFFICULTY: ▬▬▬

PREPARATION TIME: 2 hours plus baking and cooling times, and 4 hours chilling time

SPECIAL EQUIPMENT: 2 9-by-3-inch round springform pans; stand-up electric mixer

Bittersweet ganache:

1½ cups heavy (whipping) cream
12 tablespoons (1½ sticks) unsalted butter, cut into 1-inch pieces
A few grains of salt
2 vanilla beans, split in half lengthwise (see Ingredient Note)
12 ounces bittersweet chocolate, coarsely chopped
2 large egg yolks

Bittersweet chocolate cake:

6 ounces bittersweet chocolate, coarsely chopped
½ ounce unsweetened chocolate
5 tablespoons unsalted butter, cut into 1-inch pieces
4 large eggs, at room temperature, separated
⅓ cup granulated sugar
1 teaspoon vanilla extract
Pinch of salt

Apricot filling:

⅓ cup apricot preserves
2 teaspoons cognac

Milk chocolate glaze:

9 ounces Swiss milk chocolate, coarsely chopped
¼ cup plus 1 tablespoon boiling water

Dark chocolate glaze:

1½ tablespoons water
1½ ounces bittersweet chocolate, finely chopped

INGREDIENT NOTE: You may substitute 1½ teaspoons of vanilla extract for the vanilla beans, although the flavor will not be as full. Stir the vanilla into the ganache after you have blended the chocolate, egg yolks, and hot cream (see step 2).

Make the bittersweet ganache:

1. In a 1-quart saucepan, combine the heavy cream, butter, and salt. Scrape the tiny black seeds from the inside of the vanilla beans into the cream mixture. Add the scraped bean pods and bring the mixture to a gentle boil over medium heat. Remove the pan from the heat and cool for 5 minutes. Remove the vanilla pods.

2. In a food processor fitted with the metal chopping blade, blend the chocolate for 20 seconds or until finely chopped. Add the egg yolks and pulse twice. Pour the hot cream mixture through the feed tube while the machine is running. Blend for 20 seconds or until the mixture is smooth. Pour it into a metal mixing bowl. Cover and refrigerate for no longer than 1½ hours or until the ganache has thickened to the consistency of chocolate pudding. Using a hand-held electric mixer set at medium speed, beat for 20 seconds or until the ganache is lighter in color and forms soft peaks (do not overbeat, or it will become grainy).

Make the cake:

3. Position a rack in the center of the oven and preheat to 350°F. Butter the bottoms and sides of the two springform pans and line each bottom with a circle of baking parchment or waxed paper. Dust the sides of the pans with flour and tap out the excess.

4. In the top of a double boiler over hot, not simmering, water, melt the two chocolates and butter, stirring occasionally until smooth. Remove the top part of the double boiler from the bottom and cool the chocolate for 15 minutes or until tepid.

5. In a large bowl of a stand-up electric mixer, beat the egg yolks with the sugar at medium-high speed for 4 minutes or until they form a thick yellow ribbon when the beaters are lifted. Beat in the vanilla.

6. In another, grease-free, bowl of the stand-up electric mixer, beat the egg whites at low speed until they start to foam. Add the salt and gradually increase the speed to medium high. Continue beating for about 1 minute or until the whites form stiff, shiny peaks.

7. Fold the chocolate mixture into the egg yolk mixture. Lighten by folding in one third of the beaten egg whites. Fold in the remaining whites. Divide the batter between the two cake pans and spread evenly. Bake for 20 minutes or until a cake tester or toothpick inserted in the center of each layer comes out clean. Cool the cake layers in the pans on wire racks for 10 minutes.

8. Run a knife around the edges of the cake layers to loosen them. Remove the sides of the springform pans. Invert the cake layers onto two 9- or 10-inch cardboard cake circles and carefully lift off the bottoms of the springforms. Carefully peel off the papers. Invert the layers again onto two more cardboard circles, so that the layers are right side up. Cool completely.

Make the apricot filling:

9. In a small bowl, stir together the apricot preserves and the cognac.

Assemble the torte:

10. Using a long serrated knife, trim the tops of the cake layers so that they are level. Spread the apricot filling evenly over the top of each cake layer. Put one of the cake layers in the freezer for 20 minutes or until firm enough to handle easily. Wrap the sides of a 9-inch springform cake pan around the other cake layer. Gently press down on the cake so that the outer edge of the cake and the pan sides fit together snugly. Spoon the whipped ganache over the apricot-coated layer and spread it evenly. Invert the chilled, firm layer on top of the

ganache so that the apricot glaze is face down. Remove the top cardboard circle and gently press the cake layer into place. Cover the torte with plastic wrap and refrigerate for 2 hours, until firm.

Make the chocolate glazes:

11. In a food processor fitted with the metal chopping blade, process the milk chocolate for 20 seconds or until it is finely chopped. With the machine still running, pour the boiling water through the feed tube and process for 20 seconds or until smooth. Scrape the mixture into a metal mixing bowl and set it over a saucepan of hot, not simmering, water to keep it warm.

12. In a small saucepan, bring the 1½ table-spoons of water for the dark chocolate glaze to a boil. Remove the pan from the heat and stir in the bittersweet chocolate. Blend until smooth. Trans-fer the mixture to a small metal bowl and set it over a saucepan of hot, not simmering, water to keep it warm.

Decorate the torte:

13. Using a hot knife, cut around the edge of the torte to loosen the sides from the springform pan.

Invert the cake onto a wire rack and carefully remove the bottom of the springform. Set the torte on its rack over a jelly-roll pan. Smooth the sides of the torte with a narrow metal cake spatula.

14. Pour the warm milk chocolate glaze over the torte and spread it evenly over the top and sides. Fill a small paper cone with the dark chocolate glaze and cut a 1/16-inch opening at the tip (for instructions on making a paper cone, see page 187). Pipe several thin straight parallel lines across the top of the cake about ½ inch apart. Using a wooden or metal skewer, draw the tip completely across the cake perpendicular to the piped lines to create a feathered effect. Pull the skewer back across the cake, reversing the direction, in ½-inch intervals. Wipe the skewer clean after each pull. Keep moving the skewer back and forth across the cake until the entire surface has been covered.

15. Refrigerate the torte on its rack over the jelly-roll pan for 20 minutes, until the glaze is firm. Transfer the cake to a serving plate. Allow the torte to sit at room temperature for 1 hour before serving. Slice the cake with a clean, hot knife, warmed in hot water and then dried.

Chocolate Fig Cake with Gianduja Glaze

This is a European-style cake with an American flair for the unconventional. Gianduja, a very smooth mixture of chocolate and hazelnuts, is sold to confectioners throughout Europe and, increasingly, in the United States. For more information, see chapter 1. You can usually buy a block from a professional chocolatier, or if not, you can mail order it (see the listings in the back of the book). Here, gianduja is combined with the flavor of figs in an intriguing double-glazed cake designed to satisfy cravings for subtle chocolate flavor yet meet a desire for a dessert with a gentle difference.

YIELD: 8 servings

DIFFICULTY: ◼◼

PREPARATION TIME: 1½ hours plus roasting (the nuts), baking, and cooling times, and 3 hours setting time for the cake

SPECIAL EQUIPMENT: stand-up electric mixer

Cake:

½ cup dried figs, finely chopped
¼ cup Armagnac or cognac
4 ounces bittersweet chocolate, coarsely chopped
1¼ cups roasted hazelnuts (for roasting instructions,
*   see page 20)*
¼ cup dried bread crumbs
8 tablespoons (1 stick) unsalted butter, softened
⅔ cup granulated sugar
Pinch of salt
3 large eggs, at room temperature, lightly beaten

Gianduja glaze:

4 ounces bittersweet chocolate, coarsely chopped
3 ounces gianduja or 1 3-ounce chocolate-praline bar, such as
*   Lindt's Swiss Milk Chocolate Praline-Filled Bar*
¾ cup plus 1 tablespoon heavy (whipping) cream

48 blanched sliced almonds, for decoration

Make the cake:

1. Position a rack in the center of the oven and preheat to 375°F. Lightly butter the bottom and sides of an 8-by-2-inch round cake pan. Line the bottom with a circle of baking parchment or waxed paper. Dust the sides of the pan with flour and tap out the excess.

2. In a small saucepan over medium heat, bring the figs and Armagnac to a gentle simmer. Remove the pan from the heat and cool.

3. In the top of a double boiler over hot, not simmering, water, melt the chocolate, stirring until smooth. Remove the pan from the heat and cool to lukewarm.

4. Reserve 8 of the best-looking hazelnuts for decorating the cake. In a food processor fitted with the metal chopping blade, process the remaining hazelnuts and the bread crumbs for 20 seconds or until the mixture is finely ground.

5. In a large bowl of a stand-up electric mixer, beat the butter for 1 minute at high speed until creamy. Gradually add the sugar and salt and continue beating for 2 minutes or until light. Add the eggs in a thin stream (the batter will look separated). Remove the bowl from the mixer and fold in the melted chocolate (the batter will become smooth again). Gently fold in the hazelnut-bread crumb mixture and the figs. Transfer the batter to the prepared cake pan and spread evenly. Bake for 30 minutes or until a cake tester or toothpick inserted 1 inch from the sides of the pan comes out clean. (The center of the cake will be very moist.) Cool the cake in the pan on a wire rack for 10 minutes. Run a knife around the edge of the cake to loosen, and invert it onto a rack. Carefully peel off the paper. Invert the cake again onto another rack and cool completely.

Make the gianduja glaze:

6. Using a food processor fitted with the metal chopping blade, process the chocolate and gianduja for 20 seconds or until finely chopped.

7. In a small saucepan over medium heat, bring the cream to a gentle boil. With the processor running, gradually pour the hot cream through the feed tube. Blend for 20 seconds, until smooth.

Assemble the cake:

8. Set the cake on its rack on a jelly-roll pan.

(continued)

Pour a little less than half of the glaze over the top of the cake and using a narrow metal cake spatula, smooth the glaze over the top and sides. Refrigerate the cake for 20 minutes, until the glaze is firm. Keep the bowl with the remaining glaze warm over a saucepan of hot water. Pour the reserved glaze over the top of the chilled cake and carefully spread it over the top and sides. Let the second coating set at room temperature for 2 hours. Position the hazelnuts around the top of the cake. Insert 6 sliced almonds around each hazelnut to form a nut "flower." With two narrow metal spatulas, carefully lift the cake off the rack and onto a serving plate.

⟶ *Incredible Chocolate Cake* ⟶

If it's time for a good, chocolate layer cake, it's time for this one. Two layers of tender chocolate cake are sandwiched together with classic ganache and flavored with a bit of raspberry preserves. The entire cake is frosted with chocolate buttercream— no fancy decorations or garnishes. Just a good plain cake. Take care when cooling the ganache over ice water not to let it thicken too much, or it will be impossible to spread.

YIELD: 12 servings

DIFFICULTY: ▬▬

PREPARATION TIME: 1 hour plus baking and chilling times

SPECIAL EQUIPMENT: stand-up electric mixer

Cake:

4 ounces unsweetened chocolate, coarsely chopped

8 tablespoons (1 stick) unsalted butter

1 cup hot water

1 teaspoon instant coffee powder

2 cups granulated sugar

2 large eggs, at room temperature

½ cup sour cream, at room temperature

1½ cups all-purpose flour

1½ teaspoons baking soda

½ teaspoon double-acting baking powder

⅛ teaspoon salt

Ganache:

¾ cup heavy (whipping) cream

6 tablespoons unsalted butter

9 ounces semisweet chocolate, coarsely chopped

Chocolate buttercream:

1 ounce unsweetened chocolate

1 ounce semisweet chocolate

1 large egg white

¼ cup granulated sugar

*7 tablespoons unsalted butter, softened until shiny and cut into
   tablespoons*

1 teaspoon dark rum

To assemble:

2 tablespoons seedless raspberry preserves

Make the cake:

1. Position a rack in the center of the oven and preheat to 350°F. Lightly butter two 9-by-2-inch round cake pans and flour them. Tap out the excess flour.

2. In the top of a double boiler over hot, not simmering, water, combine the chocolate, butter, water, and coffee powder. Stir until the chocolate and butter are melted and the mixture is smooth. Transfer to a large bowl and stir in the sugar.

3. In a small bowl, stir together the eggs and sour cream until well blended. In another small bowl, combine the flour, baking soda, baking powder, and salt.

4. Using a whisk, stir the dry ingredients into the chocolate-sugar mixture alternately with the egg-sour cream mixture. Stir until the batter is smooth.

5. Divide the batter evenly between the two prepared pans. Bake for 30 minutes or until the cake layers spring back when lightly touched in the center. Cool the cakes in their pans for 10 minutes. Run a knife around the edges of the cake layers to loosen them, and turn them out onto wire racks to cool completely.

Make the ganache:

6. In a small saucepan, combine the heavy cream and butter. Stir over medium heat until the butter melts and the mixture comes to a gentle boil. Remove from the heat.

7. In a food processor fitted with a metal chopping blade, finely chop the chocolate. With the motor running, pour the hot cream mixture through the feed tube. Process for 20 seconds or until the ganache is smooth. Transfer to a metal mixing bowl and let stand until cool, stirring occasionally.

Make the buttercream:

8. In the top of a double boiler over hot, not simmering, water, melt the chocolates. Stir until smooth. Remove the top part of the double boiler from the bottom and cool for 5 to 10 minutes until tepid.

9. In the small bowl of a stand-up electric mixer, combine the egg white and sugar. Set the bowl over hot, not simmering, water. The water should touch the bottom of the bowl. Whisk until white and creamy and the egg feels hot to the touch (110°F). Rub a small amount between your thumb and forefinger to be sure the sugar has dissolved. Transfer the bowl to the stand-up electric mixer. Beat the mixture at medium speed about 5 minutes or until it is cool and it has formed a thick meringue.

10. Add the butter 1 tablespoon at a time, beating well after each addition until all the butter is incorporated. Add the melted chocolate and the rum. Continue beating for a few seconds, until the buttercream is thick and smooth.

Assemble the cake:

11. Put one cake layer onto a 9-inch cardboard cake circle or a serving plate. Spread the top with the raspberry preserves. Cover the preserves with the chocolate buttercream. Top with the second layer of cake.

12. If the ganache has not cooled to a spreadable consistency, put the bowl over another bowl of ice water. Gently stir until it starts to thicken, about 30 seconds. Remove the bowl from the ice water. Do not let it get too thick.

13. Using a metal cake spatula, spread the ganache evenly over the top and sides of the cake. Cover and refrigerate the cake until 20 minutes before serving time.

Kathy Fleegler's Chocolate ∾ Strawberry Patch ∾

Choose the brightest, most perfectly formed strawberries you can find to top this show-stopping cake—although the apricot glaze, brushed over the berries shortly before serving, will hide some imperfections. Because the cake, filled with a luscious chocolate buttercream, must chill for hours, this is a good cake to make ahead of time. Several hours before serving, all you need do is pour the chocolate glaze over it, arrange the strawberries, . . . and wait for the compliments.

YIELD: 16 servings	
DIFFICULTY: ▰▰▰	
PREPARATION TIME: 1 hour plus baking and chilling times	
SPECIAL EQUIPMENT: 12-by-3-inch round springform pan	

Genoise:

8 large eggs, at room temperature

1⅓ cups sugar

1 teaspoon vanilla extract

1 cup sifted cake flour (not self-rising)

½ cup sifted unsweetened alkalized cocoa powder

¼ teaspoon salt

8 tablespoons (1 stick) unsalted butter, melted and cooled

Chocolate buttercream:

6 ounces bittersweet or semisweet chocolate, coarsely chopped

1 tablespoon instant espresso coffee powder

1 tablespoon hot water

4 large egg yolks

1 cup sifted confectioners' sugar

¼ teaspoon salt

1½ cups (3 sticks) unsalted butter, at room temperature, cut into tablespoons

⅓ cup dark rum

1 cup red raspberry jam

Bittersweet cocoa glaze:

8 tablespoons (1 stick) unsalted butter

1 cup unsweetened alkalized cocoa powder

1 teaspoon instant espresso coffee powder

1 cup granulated sugar

⅔ cup heavy (whipping) cream

½ cup red currant jelly

3 pints fresh strawberries, rinsed and hulled

Make the genoise:

1. Position a rack in the center of the oven and preheat to 350°F. Butter the springform pan. Dust with flour and shake out the excess.

2. In a large heatproof bowl set over and touching a pan of hot, not simmering water, beat the eggs with a whisk or hand-held electric mixer for 1 minute. Beat in the sugar and vanilla. Continue beating until the sugar has dissolved and the mixture is just barely warm to the touch. Remove from the water and beat at high speed for 8 to 10 minutes until tripled in volume and a ribbon forms when the beaters are lifted.

3. Stir together the flour, cocoa, and salt. Sift the mixture twice. Quickly fold the flour mixture a third at a time into the egg mixture. Fold in the butter and immediately spread the batter into the prepared pan. Bake for 30 to 35 minutes until the top springs back when lightly touched, the edges begin to pull away from the pan, and a cake tester or toothpick inserted in the center comes out clean. Cool in the pan for 10 minutes and remove the sides of the springform. Cool the cake on a wire rack.

Make the chocolate buttercream:

4. In the top of a double boiler over hot, not simmering, water, melt the chocolate, stirring frequently, until smooth. Remove the top of the double boiler from the bottom and cool for 5 to 10 minutes or until tepid. Dissolve the espresso powder in the tablespoon of hot water.

5. In a medium mixing bowl, using a hand-held electric mixer set at medium-high speed, beat together the egg yolks, confectioners' sugar, and salt until very light and the mixture forms a thick ribbon when the beaters are lifted. Beat in the melted chocolate and the dissolved espresso. Beat in the butter, 2 tablespoons at a time, until smooth and fluffy.

6. Using a long, serrated knife, cut the cake in half horizontally to make two even layers. Put the layers, cut side up, on a work surface. Brush the layers evenly with the rum. Spread the raspberry jam over one layer. Spread the chocolate buttercream over the raspberry jam so that it is about ½ inch thick. Cover with the top cake layer, cut side down. Cover with plastic wrap and chill for several hours or overnight until the buttercream has set.

Make the glaze:

7. In a small saucepan, combine the butter, cocoa, coffee, sugar, and cream. Cook over low heat, stirring constantly, until smooth, about 5 minutes. Remove from the heat and let cool for 3 to 5 minutes.

8. In a small saucepan over low heat, warm the red currant jelly. Set the cake on a rack sitting on a jelly-roll pan and pour the warm glaze over the top and sides. Spread the glaze evenly with a small metal cake spatula. Using the largest strawberries first, arrange them along the outside edge and continue in concentric circles until the entire cake is covered. Brush the strawberries with the warm red currant jelly. Refrigerate until set and serve chilled.

～ *Chocolate Orange Marble Cake* ～

This cake, sent to us several years ago by a reader, has long been one of our favorites. It's baked in square pans and combines the delicious combination of chocolate and orange in a simple, appealing marble cake with an easy chocolate frosting—just right for dessert after a casual dinner or with a cup of hot tea at the end of the afternoon.

YIELD: 8 servings

DIFFICULTY: ▬

PREPARATION TIME: 40 minutes plus baking and cooling times

Cake:

1 ounce unsweetened chocolate, coarsely chopped
2 cups sifted cake flour (not self-rising)
2½ teaspoons double-acting baking powder
½ teaspoon salt
8 tablespoons (1 stick) unsalted butter, softened
1⅓ cups granulated sugar
2 large eggs, at room temperature
1½ teaspoons vanilla extract
¾ cup milk, chilled
2 teaspoons finely grated orange zest

Frosting:

4 ounces unsweetened chocolate, finely chopped
8 tablespoons (1 stick) unsalted butter, at room temperature
3½ cups sifted confectioners' sugar
¼ cup milk, chilled
1 teaspoon vanilla extract

Make the cake:

1. Position a rack in the center of the oven and preheat to 350°F. Butter two 8-inch square baking pans and line them with baking parchment or waxed paper. Dust the pans with flour. Tap out the excess.

2. In a double boiler over hot, not simmering, water, melt the chocolate, stirring frequently until smooth. Remove the top part of the double boiler from the bottom and cool the chocolate for 5 minutes or until tepid.

3. Stir together the flour, baking powder, and salt, and sift the mixture over a piece of waxed paper. In a large bowl, using a hand-held electric mixer set at medium speed, beat the butter and sugar for 1 to 1½ minutes or until well combined. Beat in the eggs one at a time, beating well after each addition. Beat in the vanilla. In three additions each, beat in the dry ingredients and the milk, beginning with the flour mixture and beating well after each addition.

4. Pour half of the batter into a medium bowl. Whisk the orange zest into one bowl of batter and the cooled chocolate into the other. Spoon the chocolate batter into the four corners and center of one of the prepared pans. Spoon the orange batter into the unfilled spaces, making a checkerboard

pattern. Fill the other cake pan by spooning the orange batter into the four corners and the center and using the chocolate batter to fill in the spaces. Tap the pans on a work surface to level the batter. Swirl a knife through each cake pan to marbleize it, and tap it on a work surface again.

5. Bake the cake layers for 35 to 45 minutes or until the edges begin to pull away from the sides of the pans and the tops spring back when lightly touched. Cool the cake layers in their pans on a rack for 20 minutes. Run a thin knife around the edges of the pans to loosen, and invert the layers onto wire racks. Carefully peel off the papers and leave them loosely set on the bottoms of the layers. Invert the layers onto other wire racks, so they are right side up. Cool completely.

Make the frosting:

6. In the top of a double boiler over hot, not simmering, water, melt the chocolate, stirring frequently until smooth. Remove the top part of the double boiler from the bottom part and cool the chocolate for 5 minutes or until tepid.

7. In a large bowl, using a hand-held electric mixer set at medium speed, beat the butter for about 30 seconds or until creamy. Increase the speed to medium high and gradually beat in half of the confectioners' sugar until the frosting becomes very stiff. Add the chocolate, milk, and vanilla, alternating with the remaining confectioners' sugar to make a fluffy frosting of spreading consistency.

Assemble the cake:

8. Remove the waxed paper from the layers. Put one cake layer on a serving plate. If necessary, use a long, serrated knife to trim the tops of the cake layers so that they are level. Using a metal cake spatula, spread about 1 cup of the frosting over the cake layer on the serving plate. Put the second cake layer on top and cover the top and sides of the cake with the remaining frosting. Using a small metal cake spatula, gently swirl the frosting to make a decorative pattern.

4

Gary Perweiler

Puddings, Custards, and Mousses

Baked Chocolate Mousse with Rum Sauce
Chocolate Hazelnut Terrine
Chocolate Tulips with Raspberry Bavarian Cream
Chocolate Cream Puffs with Cappuccino Cream
City Chocolate with Espresso Crème Anglaise
Chocolate Timbales with Warm Cherry Compote
Cherry Bread Pudding with Chocolate Sauce
Chocolate Custard with Raspberries
Belgian Chocolate Mousse Parfaits
Mocha Pudding
Mohr Im Hemd
Classic Chocolate Mousse
White Chocolate Mousse
Milk Chocolate Mousse
Dark Chocolate Raspberry Mousse
Orange White Chocolate Mousse with Fresh Strawberry
Sauce

ere are the creamy, smooth, satiny chocolate desserts we often find ourselves dreaming about when we want something rich and satisfying but with no complicated textures to interfere with our pleasure. We assembled this chapter with luxury and homey comfort in mind—which may sound like a contradiction but really is not. Few desserts are more luxurious than a classic chocolate mousse, and few are as comforting as chocolate custard. And yet these two desserts share many characteristics: both are smooth, soft, chocolaty, and go down ever so easily.

Puddings and custards are sometimes called nursery foods simply because small children, weaned on them owing to their soft consistency, yearn for them even as they grow into adults. These become the comfort foods of our childhood, which when eaten, for instance, as we snuggle under a warm quilt in our favorite chair, make us feel secure and safe, just as we felt as children. Perhaps this is why even the most sophisticated adult is thrilled when a satiny, creamy mousse is placed before him or her after the most cosmopolitan of meals—the mousse, in all its glory, feels right in the mouth and tastes wonderful on the tongue. Whatever the reason, these lovely desserts, none of them particularly hard to make, are among everyone's favorites—including ours.

Baked Chocolate Mousse with ~ Rum Sauce ~

If you try the chilled mousse by itself, you may be tempted to eat it without the sauce, spooning it directly from the bowl into your mouth. But don't. Take the extra time to make the rum sauce and the two ganaches, and arrange the mousse on individual plates, as we suggest. The combination of flavors and smooth textures is wonderful; the visual effect is spectacular.

YIELD: 8 servings

DIFFICULTY: ■

PREPARATION TIME: 1 hour and 15 minutes plus baking and cooling times, and 8 to 12 hours chilling time

SPECIAL EQUIPMENT: pastry bag fitted with a small writing tip (such as Ateco #1) or paper cones

Chocolate mousse:

9 ounces semisweet chocolate, coarsely chopped
4 tablespoons (½ stick) unsalted butter, cut into tablespoons
5 large eggs, at room temperature, lightly beaten
1 tablespoon vanilla extract
1½ tablespoons dark rum
1½ cups heavy (whipping) cream
⅓ cup superfine sugar

Rum sauce:

1 cup granulated sugar

½ cup water

¾ cup heavy (whipping) cream

5 tablespoons unsalted butter, cut into ½-inch cubes

¼ cup dark rum

Dark chocolate ganache:

1 ounce semisweet chocolate, coarsely chopped

2 tablespoons heavy (whipping) cream

White chocolate ganache:

1½ ounces white chocolate, coarsely chopped

2 tablespoons heavy (whipping cream)

White chocolate curls, for garnish (optional; for instructions on making chocolate curls, see page 21)

Make the chocolate mousse:

1. Position a rack in the center of the oven and preheat to 350°F. Put a wire rack inside a 12-by-15½-inch roasting pan. Butter a 9-by-2-inch round cake pan and put it on the wire rack.

2. In the top of a double boiler over hot, not simmering, water, melt the chocolate and the butter, stirring occasionally until smooth. Remove the top part of the double boiler from the bottom and cool the chocolate mixture for 5 to 10 minutes or until tepid. In a large bowl, whisk together the eggs, vanilla, rum, and cooled chocolate mixture until well combined.

3. In a chilled large bowl, using a hand-held electric mixer set at medium speed, beat the cream and sugar until soft peaks start to form.

4. Using a rubber spatula, fold the cream mixture into the chocolate-egg mixture a third at a time. Scrape the mousse into the prepared pan. Hold a towel or pot holder over the mousse to protect it and then pour hot water into the roasting pan until the water comes halfway up the sides of the cake pan. Bake the mousse in the water bath for 40 to 45 minutes or until set. Remove the pan from the water bath and set it on a wire rack. Cool completely. Cover the surface of the mousse with plastic wrap and refrigerate for 8 to 12 hours to chill thoroughly.

Make the rum sauce:

5. In a heavy, high-sided 2-quart saucepan set over medium-high heat, stir together the sugar and water until the sugar dissolves. Increase the heat to medium high and bring the syrup to a boil. Continue cooking without stirring for 10 to 12 minutes or until the syrup caramelizes and turns amber in color.

6. Remove the caramel from the heat. Using a wooden spoon, stir in the heavy cream, taking great care so that the caramel does not spatter. Continue stirring until the bubbles subside. Put the pan of caramel mixture back on medium heat and bring to a boil, stirring constantly. Remove the pan from the heat and stir in the butter until melted. Stir in the rum and cool the sauce to tepid.

Make the dark chocolate ganache:

7. In the top of a double boiler over hot, not simmering, water, melt the semisweet chocolate, stirring occasionally until smooth.

8. In a small saucepan over medium heat, heat the cream until bubbles begin to form around the edges. Remove the saucepan from the heat and whisk in the melted chocolate. Cover the surface of the dark chocolate ganache with plastic wrap and keep it warm until ready to use.

(continued)

Make the white chocolate ganache:

9. In the top of a double boiler over hot, not simmering, water, melt the white chocolate, stirring frequently until smooth.

10. In a small saucepan over medium heat, heat the cream until bubbles begin to form around the edges. Remove the saucepan from the heat and whisk in the white chocolate. Cover the surface of the white chocolate ganache with plastic wrap and keep it warm until ready to use.

Assemble the mousse:

11. Spoon about 3 tablespoons of the rum sauce onto each of eight dessert plates so that it covers the plate. Using an ice cream scoop or a large spoon, put one rounded scoopful of chilled mousse in the top portion of each plate, on top of the rum sauce.

12. Fill two separate paper cones or pastry bags fitted with plain writing tips (such as Ateco #1) with the dark and white chocolate ganaches. (For instructions on making a paper cone, see page 187.) Pipe alternating circles of the dark and white chocolate ganaches about ¼ inch apart on the plate near the mousse. Draw the tip of a small knife through the piped ganache circles at ¾-inch intervals to create a feathered effect. If desired, garnish with white chocolate curls. Serve immediately.

⟿ *Chocolate Hazelnut Terrine* ⟿

Make room in your freezer for this terrine. It's darkly chocolate, frozen solid, and covered with a glossy glaze. At serving time, each slice is sweetly kissed with caramel sauce. The terrine must have 4 hours to freeze, but if you like to plan ahead, it can be made up to 2 weeks in advance, wrapped well in plastic and foil, and frozen. It should be glazed, however, the day of serving. The caramel sauce can be made 2 days ahead of time and kept in the refrigerator. This terrine is perfect for a good-sized dinner party when you want to be well prepared in advance.

YIELD: 14 servings	
DIFFICULTY: ▰▰	
PREPARATION TIME: 45 minutes plus 4 hours freezing time	
SPECIAL EQUIPMENT: 4½-by-12-by-3-inch metal loaf pan	

Chocolate hazelnut terrine:

9 ounces bittersweet chocolate, finely chopped

11 tablespoons (1 stick plus 3 tablespoons) unsalted butter

6 large eggs, at room temperature, separated

2 tablespoons unsweetened nonalkalized cocoa powder

½ cup granulated sugar

1 cup heavy (whipping) cream

1 cup roasted hazelnuts, coarsely chopped (for roasting instructions, see page 20)

Chocolate ganache glaze:

1 cup heavy (whipping) cream

12 ounces bittersweet chocolate, finely chopped

Caramel sauce:

2½ cups heavy (whipping) cream
1 cup granulated sugar
Chocolate leaves, for garnish (optional)

Make the chocolate hazelnut terrine:

1. Line the loaf pan with aluminum foil, being careful not to tear the foil.

2. In the top of a double boiler over hot, not simmering, water, melt the chocolate with the butter, stirring occasionally, until smooth. Remove the top part of the double boiler from the bottom and immediately whisk in the egg yolks one at a time into the warm chocolate mixture. Sift the cocoa over the mixture and whisk until smooth.

3. In a large, grease-free bowl, using a hand-held electric mixer set at low speed, beat the egg whites until foamy. Gradually increase the speed to medium high. Continue beating the egg whites until they start to form soft peaks. Continue beating and gradually add the sugar, beating just until the egg whites are glossy and form stiff peaks. Fold one fourth of the egg whites into the chocolate mixture to lighten it. Fold in the remaining egg whites.

4. In a chilled medium bowl, using a hand-held electric mixer set at medium speed, beat the cream just until soft peaks begin to form. Fold the whipped cream into the chocolate mixture. Fold in the hazelnuts.

5. Use a rubber spatula to transfer the chocolate-nut mixture to the prepared pan and smooth the top. Wrap the terrine tightly in plastic wrap. Freeze the terrine for at least 4 hours, or overnight, until firm.

Make the chocolate ganache glaze:

6. In a medium saucepan, bring the cream to a gentle boil over medium-low heat. Take the pan off

the heat and add the chocolate to the hot cream, stirring constantly until smooth. Cool the ganache glaze until tepid but still pourable.

7. Remove the plastic wrap from the top of the terrine. Invert the terrine onto a wire rack set over a baking sheet. Pour the ganache glaze over the terrine, using a metal spatula to help spread it evenly. Freeze the terrine on the rack for 5 to 10 minutes or until the glaze has set. Using two long metal cake spatulas, remove the terrine from the wire rack and transfer it to a 4½-by-12-inch piece of cardboard. Keep the terrine frozen until ready to serve.

Make the caramel sauce:

8. In a medium saucepan over medium heat, bring the cream just to a simmer. In a heavy, medium saucepan over high heat, stir the sugar with a wooden spoon for 4 to 6 minutes, until the sugar melts and turns amber colored. Take the pan off the heat. Slowly and carefully stir the warm cream into the caramel taking care that the caramel does not splatter. Reduce the heat to low and return the pan to the heat. Cook the caramel sauce, stirring constantly, for 1 to 2 minutes or until the caramel is completely melted. Cool the sauce completely, cover tightly, and refrigerate for at least 1 hour or until chilled.

Assemble the terrine:

9. Using a sharp, thin knife, cut the terrine into fourteen slices. Transfer the slices to large dinner plates. Pour a scant ¼ cup of the caramel sauce around each slice. Serve immediately or thaw in the refrigerator for 15 to 30 minutes or until softened slightly. If desired, garnish with chocolate leaves.

Chocolate Tulips with Raspberry
～Bavarian Cream ～

Fragile, crispy tulip cookies are one of the loveliest edible containers, perfect for filling with airy creams and soft puddings. They can be stored in an airtight container for up to a week and may even be frozen for a month but should never be filled until right before serving, since they so easily absorb moisture.

<table>
<tr><td>YIELD: 10 servings</td></tr>
<tr><td>DIFFICULTY: ▰▰</td></tr>
<tr><td>PREPARATION TIME: 1 hour plus chilling, baking, and setting times</td></tr>
</table>

Chocolate tulips:

⅔ *cup sifted cake flour (not self-rising)*

3 tablespoons unsweetened nonalkalized cocoa powder

¼ *teaspoon salt*

4 tablespoons (½ stick) unsalted butter, softened

½ *cup sifted granulated sugar*

½ *teaspoon vanilla extract*

1 large egg white, at room temperature

Raspberry Bavarian cream:

½ *cup cold water*

2½ *teaspoons (1 package) unflavored gelatin*

4 10-ounce packages frozen raspberries in light syrup, thawed and drained

⅓ *cup plus 2 tablespoons granulated sugar, divided*

1 tablespoon orange liqueur

½ *cup heavy (whipping) cream*

3 large egg whites, at room temperature

Pinch of cream of tartar

To serve:
1 recipe D and D Chocolate Sauce (optional; see page 281)

Make the chocolate tulips:

1. Position a rack in the center of the oven and preheat to 425°F. Butter five baking sheets and refrigerate until ready to use. (You may use fewer baking sheets by reusing them after you have baked the first batch of tulips, but they must be buttered and chilled again.)

2. In a medium bowl, stir together the flour, cocoa, and salt. Sift the mixture onto a piece of waxed paper. In a large bowl, use a wooden spoon to stir together the butter and sugar for 1 to 2 minutes or until creamy. Mix in the vanilla and egg white. Incorporate the flour-cocoa mixture and stir quickly until well blended.

3. Cut a 6-inch square from a thin sheet of cardboard, and, keeping the square intact, cut a 5-inch circle from it to make a stencil. Put the stencil to one side of a prepared baking sheet. Drop 1½ level tablespoons of the dough into the center of the circle. Using a small offset metal cake spatula, spread the dough evenly just to the edges of the circle. Lift the cardboard stencil and repeat on the

other half of the baking sheet. Refrigerate for 5 minutes or until the dough is firm. Continue to spread the dough onto the prepared baking sheets until all is used.

4.   On a work surface, invert two 4-ounce custard cups and lightly butter their bottoms and sides.

5.   Bake the cookies, one sheet at a time, for 5 to 6 minutes or until the edges start to look brown. Cool the cookies on the baking sheet set on a wire rack for no longer than 1 minute. Working quickly, use a wide metal spatula to loosen the cookies from the baking sheet. Carefully drape the cookies, one at a time, over the inverted buttered custard cups. Using your forefinger and thumb, gently pinch the sides of the cookie to form a tulip shape. If the cookie hardens before shaping, put it back on the baking sheet and heat it in the oven for a few seconds until softened. The center of the cookie will be the base of the tulip. Let the tulips cool on the custard cups for 3 to 4 minutes or until firm. Gently lift them from the custard cups and set them aside. Bake the remaining circles of dough one baking sheet at a time. Shape these cookies into tulips and cool completely. Store the tulips in an airtight container until ready to fill.

Make the raspberry Bavarian cream:

6.   Put the ½ cup of water in a small saucepan. Sprinkle the gelatin over the water and let it soften for 1 minute. Cook over low heat, stirring constantly, until the gelatin has dissolved and the mixture is transparent. Remove the pan from the heat.

7.   In a food processor fitted with the metal chopping blade, or a blender, puree the raspberries. Strain the puree through a fine sieve into a large nonaluminum bowl. There should be about 1½ cups of seedless raspberry puree. Stir in ⅓ cup of the sugar, the orange liqueur, and the hot gelatin. Put the bowl over a larger bowl filled with ice water. Stir the mixture frequently for 10 to 15 minutes or until it just begins to thicken. (It should be about the consistency of raw egg whites.) Remove the bowl from the ice water.

8.   In a chilled, medium bowl and using a wire whisk, whip the cream until soft peaks start to form. Fold the whipped cream into the raspberry mixture.

9.   In a large bowl, using a hand-held electric mixer set at low speed, beat the egg whites until frothy. Add the cream of tartar and gradually increase the speed to medium high. Slowly beat in the remaining 2 tablespoons of sugar, a teaspoon at a time. Continue beating the whites until stiff, shiny peaks start to form.

10.   Fold one third of the beaten whites into the raspberry-cream mixture to lighten. Fold in the remaining whites.

11.   Cover the Bavarian cream with plastic wrap and refrigerate for 2 to 4 hours or until firm. Spoon into the tulip cups just before serving. If desired, drizzle with D and D Chocolate Sauce.

Chocolate Cream Puffs with ⁓ *Cappuccino Cream* ⁓

When was the last time you had a cream puff? Try these light-as-air chocolate puffs filled with a seductive coffee-flavored cream and you won't wait as long for your *next* cream puff! Cream puffs are made from choux paste, the same dough that is used for eclairs and other French pastries. We think this chocolate-flavored version is wonderful.

YIELD: 10 servings

DIFFICULTY: ▬▬

PREPARATION TIME: 50 minutes plus baking, drying, cooling, and setting times

Chocolate cream puffs:

1 cup water

4 tablespoons (½ stick) unsalted butter, cut into tablespoons

2 ounces German sweet chocolate, finely chopped

¼ teaspoon salt

1 cup all-purpose flour

4 large eggs, at room temperature, lightly beaten

Cappuccino cream:

1 cup water, divided

2 teaspoons unflavored powdered gelatin

2½ teaspoons instant espresso coffee powder

2 tablespoons coffee liqueur

1 teaspoon vanilla extract

½ cup heavy (whipping) cream

3 large egg whites, at room temperature

Pinch of cream of tartar

⅓ cup granulated sugar

Confectioners' sugar, for dusting (optional)

Make the chocolate cream puffs:

1. Position a rack in the center of the oven and preheat to 450°F. Lightly butter a baking sheet. Dust with flour and tap off the excess.

2. In a medium saucepan, combine the water, butter, chocolate, and salt. Cook the mixture over medium-low heat, stirring constantly until the butter and chocolate are completely melted. Increase the heat to high and bring the mixture to a boil. Remove the pan from the heat and stir in the flour to make a smooth paste.

3. Return the pan to the stove and stir vigorously over medium heat for 1 to 2 minutes or until the paste forms a solid mass that comes away cleanly from the sides of the pan. Transfer the paste to a large bowl.

4. Using a hand-held electric mixer set at low speed, gradually beat in all but 2 teaspoons of the beaten eggs. The dough should be thick and smooth when the last bit of egg has been added.

5. Drop ten heaping spoonfuls 2 inches apart on the prepared baking sheet. Lightly brush the cream

puffs with the reserved beaten eggs. Bake for 15 minutes, reduce the heat to 375°F, and continue baking for an additional 20 to 25 minutes or until the tops of the cream puffs have browned and they feel firm to the touch. As soon as the puffs are done, turn off the oven and open the oven door. Using a cake tester or toothpick, pierce each puff in a couple of places. Dry the puffs in the hot oven with the door slightly ajar for 20 minutes. Transfer the puffs to a wire rack and cool completely.

Make the cappuccino cream:

6. Put ½ cup of the water in a small saucepan. Sprinkle the gelatin over the water and let it soften for 1 minute. Cook, stirring constantly over low heat, until the gelatin is dissolved and the mixture is transparent. Remove the pan from the heat.

7. In a large metal bowl, combine ½ cup of boiling water with the espresso powder. Add the hot gelatin, coffee liqueur, and vanilla. Put the bowl over a larger bowl filled with ice water. Stir the mixture frequently for 10 to 15 minutes or until it just begins to thicken. It should be about the consistency of raw egg whites. Remove the bowl from the ice water.

8. In a medium bowl, whip the cream with a wire whisk until soft peaks start to form. Fold the whipped cream into the coffee mixture.

9. In a large bowl, using a hand-held electric mixer set at low speed, beat the egg whites until frothy. Add the cream of tartar and gradually increase the speed to medium high. Slowly beat in the sugar, 1 teaspoon at a time. Continue beating the whites until they form stiff, shiny peaks.

10. Fold one third of the beaten egg whites into the coffee-cream mixture to lighten it. Fold in the remaining egg whites. Cover the bowl of cappuccino cream and refrigerate for 2 to 4 hours or until firm.

Assemble the cream puffs:

11. Remove the top third of each cream puff and fill with the cappuccino cream. Replace the top and lightly sprinkle with confectioners' sugar.

City Chocolate with Espresso ∽ Crème Anglaise ∽

Studded with raisins and flavored with brandy, this simple chocolate terrine sits pretty atop a pool of coffee-flavored crème anglaise—an attractively sleek dessert from Los Angeles' City Restaurant. The custard can be made 2 days ahead of time, covered with plastic, and refrigerated until serving time. Be sure to allow at least 4 hours for chilling the terrine.

YIELD: 12 servings

DIFFICULTY: ▰▰

PREPARATION TIME: 50 minutes plus chilling time

City chocolate:

⅔ cup golden raisins

¼ cup brandy

12 ounces bittersweet chocolate, finely chopped

1¼ cups (2½ sticks) unsalted butter, softened, cut into tablespoons

7 large eggs, at room temperature, separated

Espresso crème anglaise:

8 large egg yolks

¾ cup granulated sugar

2 cups half-and-half

1 tablespoon instant espresso coffee powder, dissolved in 2 teaspoons boiling water

1 teaspoon vanilla extract

Make the City chocolate:

1. Line the inside of a 5-by-9-by-2½-inch loaf pan with plastic wrap, leaving a 2-inch overhang over the sides of the pan.

2. In a small saucepan over very low heat, combine the raisins with the brandy. Cook, stirring, for about 30 seconds or until the brandy is warm. Remove the pan from the heat and allow the raisins to soak in the brandy.

3. In the top of a double boiler over hot, not simmering, water, melt the chocolate with the butter, stirring occasionally, until smooth. The chocolate should be warm, not hot. Remove the top part of the double boiler from the bottom and immediately whisk the egg yolks into the warm chocolate mixture. Stir in the brandy-soaked raisins and any brandy still in the pan.

4. In a large, grease-free bowl, using a hand-held electric mixer set at low speed, beat the egg whites until frothy. Gradually increase the speed to medium high. Continue beating the egg whites until they start to form soft peaks. Fold one fourth of the egg whites into the chocolate mixture to lighten it. Fold in the remaining egg whites.

5. Using a rubber spatula, transfer the mixture to the prepared loaf pan and smooth the top. Fold the overhanging plastic wrap over the top of the chocolate mixture. It should cover the terrine, but if not, use more plastic. Refrigerate for at least 4 hours or overnight or until firm.

Make the espresso crème anglaise:

6. In a large bowl, using a hand-held electric mixer set at medium speed, beat the egg yolks with the sugar for 3 to 4 minutes or until a thin ribbon forms when the beaters are lifted.

7. In a heavy, large, nonaluminum saucepan, bring the half-and-half to a gentle boil over medium heat. Gradually stir ½ cup of the hot half-and-half into the egg yolk mixture. When blended, pour this mixture back into the saucepan. Continue cooking over medium-low heat, stirring constantly with a wooden spoon for 2 to 4 minutes or until the custard has thickened slightly. It is done when you can run your finger down the back of a custard-coated spoon and a path remains in the custard for several seconds. Do not let the custard boil.

8. Remove the pan from the heat and immediately strain the custard into a nonaluminum metal bowl. Put the bowl over a larger bowl filled with ice water and stir in the dissolved espresso powder and the vanilla. Stir the custard for 5 to 10 minutes or until cool. Remove the bowl from the ice, cover with plastic wrap, and refrigerate.

Assemble the terrine:

9. Peel back the plastic wrap from the top of the chocolate terrine. Invert the chocolate terrine onto a platter and lift off the loaf pan. Peel off the plastic wrap. Using a sharp knife, slice the terrine into 12 slices, dipping the knife into hot water before slicing each piece.

10. Spoon about 3 tablespoons of the crème anglaise onto the center of a dessert plate and twirl the plate to cover. Place a slice of the City Chocolate in the center of the sauce and serve.

Chocolate Timbales with Warm
⌢⌣ Cherry Compote ⌢⌣

The bright, tangy compote that accompanies these cherry-flavored chocolate timbales can be made a couple of days ahead of time and refrigerated. Reheat it gently before serving. The timbales look especially pretty with rosettes of whipped cream piped on top, but if you prefer, spoon dollops of cream on them instead.

> YIELD: 8 timbales
>
> DIFFICULTY: ◼◼
>
> PREPARATION TIME: 45 minutes plus baking and cooling times
>
> SPECIAL EQUIPMENT: 8 6-ounce metal timbale molds, custard cups, or ramekins; pastry bag fitted with a medium star tip (such as Ateco #5)

Timbales:

3 ounces unsweetened chocolate, coarsely chopped
3 ounces semisweet chocolate, coarsely chopped
8 tablespoons (1 stick) unsalted butter, softened
⅔ cup plus 2 tablespoons granulated sugar, divided
4 large eggs, at room temperature, separated
½ cup cherry preserves
2 tablespoons kirsch (cherry brandy)
Pinch of salt
⅔ cup sifted all-purpose flour

Cherry compote:

2 tablespoons cornstarch
1 tablespoon kirsch (cherry brandy)
1 16-ounce can pitted tart red cherries, packed in water, drained (reserve ¾ cup of the juice)
⅓ cup freshly squeezed orange juice
¼ teaspoon finely grated orange zest
¼ cup granulated sugar

To assemble:

1 cup heavy (whipping) cream
1 tablespoon granulated sugar
Strips of orange zest, for garnish (optional)

Make the chocolate timbales:

1. Position a rack in the center of the oven and preheat to 325°F. Butter the bottoms and sides of eight 6-ounce metal timbale molds, custard cups, or ramekins. Line the bottom of each mold with a small circle of baking parchment or waxed paper. Dust the sides of the molds with flour and tap out the excess.

2. In the top of a double boiler over hot, not simmering, water, melt the chocolates, stirring frequently until smooth. Remove the top part of the double boiler from the bottom and cool the chocolate for 5 to 10 minutes or until tepid.

3. In a large bowl, using a hand-held electric mixer set at medium-high speed, beat the butter with ⅔ cup of the sugar for 1 to 2 minutes or until creamy. Beat in the egg yolks one at a time. Blend in the cherry preserves, kirsch, and melted chocolate.

4. In a large, grease-free bowl, using a hand-held electric mixer set at low speed, beat the egg whites until frothy. Add the salt and gradually increase the speed to medium high. Continue beating until the whites form soft peaks. Add the remaining 2 tablespoons of sugar a teaspoon at a time. Continue beating the whites until they form stiff, shiny peaks when the beaters are lifted.

5. Fold a quarter of the egg whites into the chocolate mixture to lighten it. In two additions, alternately fold in the remaining egg whites with the flour. Spoon the batter into the prepared molds, filling them three-quarters full. Smooth the tops of each one with a spatula.

6. Put the molds into a large, shallow roasting pan and pour an inch of hot water into the pan around the molds. Put the pan in the oven and bake the timbales for 40 to 45 minutes or until a cake tester or toothpick inserted into the center of each pudding comes out slightly moist. Do not overbake.

Remove the timbales from the hot water bath and cool on a wire rack for 20 to 30 minutes.

Make the warm cherry compote:

7. In a small bowl, stir together the cornstarch and kirsch to make a smooth paste. In a heavy, medium, nonaluminum saucepan, combine the cherry juice, orange juice, orange zest, and sugar. Set the saucepan over medium heat and stir constantly to dissolve the sugar until the mixture is hot. Remove the pan from the heat and whisk in the cornstarch mixture. Return the pan to the heat and continue whisking for 1 minute, until the mixture comes to a boil and thickens enough to coat the back of a spoon. Remove the pan from the heat and gently stir in the cherries.

Assemble the timbales:

8. In a chilled large bowl, using a hand-held electric mixer set at medium speed, beat the cream with the sugar until it forms stiff peaks when the beaters are lifted. Fit a pastry bag with a medium star tip (such as Ateco #5) and fill with the whipped cream.

9. Unmold the timbales by running a small knife around the sides to loosen them. Turn the timbales out onto eight dessert plates. Spoon some of the warm cherry compote around the base of each timbale. Pipe a large, swirled rosette on top of each dessert and garnish with strips of orange zest, if desired.

Cherry Bread Pudding with ⟶ Chocolate Sauce ⟶

As warm and comforting as any sweet, soft bread pudding is, this one, gently flavored with cherries, is warmer and comfier than most . . . perhaps because it is served with plenty of whipped cream and dark, smooth chocolate sauce.

YIELD: 6 to 8 servings

DIFFICULTY: ◾

PREPARATION TIME: 55 minutes plus baking and cooling times

Bread pudding:

10 ounces Italian bread, trimmed of crust and cut into
  ½-inch thick slices
10 tablespoons (1 stick plus 2 tablespoons) unsalted butter,
  melted
2 cups milk
½ cup heavy (whipping) cream
1½ cups granulated sugar, divided
2 large egg yolks
1 12-ounce package frozen pitted dark sweet cherries, thawed
  and drained (about 1 cup)
2 tablespoons kirsch (cherry brandy)
½ teaspoon finely grated orange zest

Chocolate sauce:

2½ tablespoons unsalted butter, cut into ½-inch pieces
2 tablespoons milk, at room temperature
2 tablespoons heavy (whipping) cream, at room temperature
1 tablespoon granulated sugar
4 ounces semisweet chocolate, finely chopped
1 tablespoon dark rum

Whipped cream:

1 cup heavy (whipping) cream
1 tablespoon confectioners' sugar

Make the bread pudding:

1. Position a rack in the center of the oven and preheat to 350°F.

2. Cut the bread slices into triangles. Brush the slices on both sides with the melted butter.

3. In a heavy, medium saucepan, combine the milk, cream, and ½ cup of the sugar. Put the pan over medium-low heat and stir for 5 minutes or until the sugar dissolves.

4. In a large bowl, lightly whisk the egg yolks. Slowly stir in the hot cream mixture.

5. Arrange half of the bread triangles over the bottom of a heatproof 6-cup oval or rectangular dish—it should be 2½ to 3 inches deep. Spoon about one third of the custard, or enough to moisten the bread triangles, into the dish.

6. In a medium bowl, combine the cherries with the remaining 1 cup of sugar, the kirsch, and orange zest. Spoon the mixture over the bread in the dish.

7. Arrange the remaining bread triangles on top of the cherries. Pour the remaining custard over the top and let the pudding stand for 20 minutes. Bake about 40 minutes or until firm and lightly browned. Cool on a rack.

Make the chocolate sauce:

8. In a small saucepan, combine the butter, milk, heavy cream, and sugar. Bring to a gentle boil over medium-low heat. Remove the pan from the heat and stir in the chocolate and rum until smooth.

Make the whipped cream:

9. In a chilled, large bowl, using a hand-held electric mixer set at medium-high speed, beat the cream with the sugar until stiff peaks form.

10. Serve the bread pudding slightly warm or at room temperature with a dollop of whipped cream on the top. Spoon some of the chocolate sauce next to each piece.

Chocolate Custard with ⌒ *Raspberries* ⌒

Here's an easy custard that is simply dressed up with fresh raspberries and a dusting of confectioners' sugar. It looks especially nice when chilled in elegant champagne flutes, but you may choose another shape dish.

YIELD: 6 servings

DIFFICULTY: ◣

PREPARATION TIME: 20 minutes plus chilling time

7 tablespoons superfine sugar
1/4 cup unsweetened nonalkalized cocoa powder
2 tablespoons cornstarch
1 teaspoon unflavored powdered gelatin
Pinch of salt
1 cup half-and-half
1 cup low-fat (2 percent) milk
2/3 cup plus 1 tablespoon whole milk
2 large eggs, lightly beaten
2 tablespoons vanilla extract
1 cup fresh raspberries
1 teaspoon confectioners' sugar

1. In a heavy, medium, nonaluminum saucepan, sift together the sugar, cocoa, cornstarch, gelatin, and salt. Whisk in the half-and-half, low-fat milk, whole milk, and eggs. Cook over medium heat, stirring constantly, for 3 to 5 minutes or until the mixture thickens and comes to a boil. Remove from the heat and strain into a medium bowl. Stir in the vanilla.

2. Spoon the custard into six 5-ounce champagne flutes. Cover the surface of the custards with plastic wrap and refrigerate for 1 hour or until firm.

3. Top the chilled custards with raspberries and dust with confectioners' sugar.

Belgian Chocolate Mousse
⌒◯ Parfaits ◯⌒

Everyone will be delighted with these tri-layered parfaits—quick and easy to make and so pretty, too.

YIELD: 4 to 6 servings

DIFFICULTY: ▰▰

PREPARATION TIME: 40 minutes plus cooling and setting times

SPECIAL EQUIPMENT: pastry bag fitted with a large star tip (such as Ateco #5)

Chocolate mousse:

6 ounces bittersweet chocolate, coarsely chopped

4 tablespoons (½ stick) unsalted butter

6 large eggs, at room temperature, separated

1 teaspoon vanilla extract

3 tablespoons granulated sugar, divided

¾ cup heavy (whipping) cream

Decoration:

¼ cup heavy (whipping) cream

Make the mousse:

1. In the top of a double boiler over hot, not simmering, water, melt the chocolate, stirring frequently until smooth. Remove the top part of the double boiler from the bottom.

2. In a small saucepan over low heat, melt the butter. Transfer the melted butter to a large bowl. Whisk in the melted chocolate. Let the mixture cool 5 to 10 minutes or until tepid.

3. In a medium bowl, using a hand-held electric mixer set at medium-high speed, beat the egg yolks for 3 to 5 minutes or until a thick yellow ribbon forms when the beaters are lifted. Beat in the vanilla. Fold the beaten yolks into the chocolate mixture.

4. In a large, grease-free bowl, using a hand-held electric mixer, beat the egg whites at low speed until frothy. Gradually increase the speed to medium high and continue beating the whites until they start to form soft peaks. While continuing to beat the egg whites, gradually add 2 tablespoons of the sugar, a teaspoon at a time. Beat the egg whites until they form stiff, shiny peaks.

5. Fold one third of the egg whites into the chocolate-egg yolk mixture to lighten it. Fold in the remaining egg whites.

6. In a chilled bowl, whip the cream with the remaining tablespoon of sugar until stiff peaks form.

Assemble the parfaits:

7. Spoon the mousse into tall parfait glasses, filling the glasses two-thirds full. Spoon a layer of the whipped cream over the mousse layer. Top the cream with more mousse. Whether you are filling four or six glasses, you should have enough mousse for a generous top layer in each glass. Cover the glasses with plastic wrap and refrigerate for 2 or 3 hours or until set.

Decorate the parfaits:

8. In a chilled, medium bowl, whip the cream until stiff peaks start to form. Spoon the whipped cream into a pastry bag fitted with a large star tip (such as Ateco #5) and pipe a large rosette on top of each parfait.

⌒ *Mocha Pudding* ⌒

A sprinkling of cinnamon brightens the smooth flavor of this easy creamy pudding. If you are not planning to eat the pudding soon after chilling, cover each dish with plastic wrap.

YIELD: 6 servings
DIFFICULTY: ◼
PREPARATION TIME: 30 minutes plus chilling time

⅓ cup plus 2 teaspoons granulated sugar, divided
2 tablespoons cornstarch
1 large egg plus 1 egg yolk
2½ cups milk
1½ tablespoons fresh coarsely ground coffee
A few grains of salt
6 ounces bittersweet chocolate, finely chopped
2 teaspoons vanilla extract
¾ cup heavy (whipping) cream
Ground cinnamon, for garnish

1. In a heavy, medium saucepan, stir together the ⅓ cup sugar, the cornstarch, egg, and egg yolk until creamy.

2. In a medium saucepan, combine the milk, coffee, and salt. Bring to a gentle boil over medium heat. Remove the pan from the heat and strain the mixture through a fine sieve into the pan containing the sugar and eggs. Stir in the chocolate. Cook over medium-high heat, stirring constantly with a whisk, for about 6 minutes or until the pudding thickens and starts to boil. Continue stirring the boiling mixture for 2 minutes. Remove the pan from the heat and quickly strain the mixture into a medium bowl. Stir in the vanilla. Divide the pudding among six small serving bowls. Refrigerate for 1 hour, until chilled. (Cover the puddings with plastic wrap if not serving immediately after chilling.)

3. In a chilled large bowl, using an electric mixer set at medium speed, beat the heavy cream with the remaining 2 teaspoons of sugar until soft peaks start to form. Spoon the cream on top of the puddings. Sprinkle the whipped cream with a small pinch of cinnamon.

∽ *Mohr Im Hemd* ∾

These little molded chocolate puddings are a great favorite in Austria. They get their name from the fluffy white ring of whipped cream piped around them as they sit on individual serving plates. Translated, it means "Moor in a shirt."

> YIELD: 6 servings
>
> DIFFICULTY: ◢◣
>
> PREPARATION TIME: 45 minutes plus baking and assembly times
>
> SPECIAL EQUIPMENT: 6 6-ounce custard cups; pastry bag fitted with a small star tip (such as Ateco #2)

Pudding:

Butter and sugar, for custard cups
3 ounces semisweet chocolate, coarsely chopped
5 tablespoons unsalted butter, at room temperature
¼ cup plus 1 tablespoon confectioners' sugar
1 teaspoon vanilla extract
3 large egg yolks, at room temperature
4 large egg whites, at room temperature
Pinch of salt
2 tablespoons granulated sugar
½ cup finely chopped walnuts
1 cup fresh bread crumbs

Chocolate glaze:

9 ounces semisweet chocolate, coarsely chopped
⅓ cup hot water

To assemble:

¾ cup heavy (whipping) cream
2 teaspoons granulated sugar
Candied violets, for garnish (optional)

Make the pudding:

1. Position a rack in the center of the oven and preheat to 325°F. Lightly butter and sugar 6 6-ounce custard cups. Put the cups in a roasting pan large enough to hold them easily.

2. In the top of a double boiler over hot, not simmering, water, melt the chocolate. Stir until smooth. Remove the top part of the double boiler from the bottom and cool the chocolate for 5 to 10 minutes or until tepid.

3. In a large mixing bowl, combine the cooled chocolate, butter, confectioners' sugar, and vanilla. With a hand-held electric mixer set at medium-high speed, beat the mixture until creamy. Add the egg yolks one at a time, beating well after each addition.

4. In a large, grease-free bowl, beat the egg whites at low speed until foamy. Add the salt and increase the speed to medium. Continue beating until the whites form soft peaks. One teaspoon at a time, gradually add the granulated sugar and beat

until stiff, shiny peaks start to form. Fold one third of the whites into the chocolate mixture. Fold in the remaining whites with the walnuts and bread crumbs.

5. Spoon the pudding mixture into the prepared cups, filling each one three-quarters full. Remove one of the cups from the roasting pan and carefully pour in enough boiling water, without splashing, to come one third of the way up the sides of the cups. Replace the custard cup. Bake for 25 to 30 minutes or until a cake tester or toothpick inserted in the center of each pudding comes out clean.

Make the chocolate glaze:

6. In the top of a double boiler over hot, not simmering, water, melt the chocolate with the water. Stir until smooth.

7. Unmold the puddings and place them on a wire rack set over a jelly-roll pan. Using a ladle, pour the glaze over the tops of the puddings, letting it spill over the sides. Lift the puddings with a metal spatula and set them on individual dessert plates.

8. In a chilled bowl, whip the cream with the sugar until it holds stiff peaks. Using a pastry bag fitted with a small star tip (such as Ateco #2), pipe the cream into a shell border around the base of each pudding. Pipe a small rosette on top of each. Nestle a small candied violet on top of each rosette, if desired. Serve immediately.

⌒ *Classic Chocolate Mousse* ⌒

Once you have mastered the recipe for this deep, dark chocolate mousse, you can easily concoct the white and milk chocolate variations that follow, which (along with the raspberry and orange white chocolate mousse recipes that follow these) were developed for us a number of years ago by Chef Michael McLaughlin. We think this is just the sort of mousse you'd expect to find in a restaurant tucked away on a cobbled street in Paris, one that is bathed with dim rosy light and where each table is set with a starched white tablecloth. This is truly a mousse that stands the tests of time and tradition.

YIELD: 6 to 8 servings
DIFFICULTY: ◼
PREPARATION TIME: 25 minutes plus chilling time (allow 2 to 5 hours for the mousse to set)

10 ounces bittersweet or semisweet chocolate, coarsely chopped
4 tablespoons (½ stick) unsalted butter, cut into tablespoons
3 jumbo eggs, at room temperature, separated
2 tablespoons granulated sugar
1½ teaspoons vanilla extract
1 cup heavy (whipping) cream

1. In a heatproof bowl over a saucepan of hot, not simmering, water, melt the chocolate with the butter, stirring occasionally until smooth. Remove the saucepan from the heat, keeping the bowl over the pan of hot water.

2. In a small bowl, whisk together the egg yolks and sugar until smooth. Stir in the vanilla.

3. In a large, grease-free bowl, using a hand-held electric mixer set at low speed, beat the egg whites until frothy. Increase the speed to medium high

and continue to beat the whites until they form stiff, shiny peaks.

4. Remove the bowl from the pan of hot water. Stir the egg yolk mixture into the chocolate mixture until well combined.

5. With a large rubber spatula, fold one third of the egg whites into the chocolate mixture to lighten it. Fold in the remaining egg whites.

6. In a chilled medium bowl, using a hand-held electric mixer set at medium-high speed, whip the cream until soft peaks start to form when the beaters are lifted. Do not overbeat the cream. Using a large rubber spatula, fold the whipped cream into the chocolate mixture. A few white streaks may remain.

7. Scrape the mousse into a large serving bowl or individual dishes. Chill for about 30 minutes or until set. Cover and chill until firm—about 2 hours for individual portions, 5 hours for a large bowl of mousse.

White Chocolate Mousse

Follow the instructions for Classic Chocolate Mousse (see page 133) using these ingredients:

15 ounces white chocolate, coursely chopped
4 tablespoons (½ stick) unsalted butter
2 jumbo eggs, at room temperature, separated
1½ teaspoons vanilla extract
¾ cup heavy (whipping) cream

Milk Chocolate Mousse

Follow the instructions for Classic Chocolate Mousse (see page 133) using these ingredients:

12 ounces Swiss milk chocolate, finely chopped
4 tablespoons (½ stick) unsalted butter
2 jumbo eggs, at room temperature, separated
1½ teaspoons vanilla extract
¾ cup heavy (whipping) cream

Dark Chocolate Raspberry
⌒ Mousse ⌒

The dark intense red flavor of raspberries blends perfectly with the dark chocolate in a wickedly dense, smooth mousse of indescribable richness.

YIELD: 6 to 8 servings
DIFFICULTY: ◼
PREPARATION TIME: 25 to 30 minutes plus standing and chilling times

1½ cups fresh raspberries
¼ cup granulated sugar
2 tablespoons Framboise (raspberry brandy) (optional)
10 ounces bittersweet chocolate, finely chopped
4 tablespoons (½ stick) unsalted butter, cut into tablespoons
3 jumbo eggs, at room temperature, separated
1 cup heavy (whipping) cream
¾ cup heavy cream, (whipping) for garnish
½ pint fresh raspberries, for garnish

1. In a small bowl, crush the raspberries roughly with a fork. Stir in the sugar and the Framboise. Let the mixture stand at room temperature for 30 minutes.

2. In a heatproof bowl over a pan of hot, not simmering, water, melt the chocolate and the butter, stirring occasionally until smooth. Remove the pan from the heat, keeping the bowl of chocolate over the pan of hot water.

3. In a large, grease-free bowl, using a hand-held electric mixer set at low speed, beat the egg whites until frothy. Increase the speed to medium high and continue to beat the whites until they form stiff, shiny peaks.

4. Take the bowl containing the chocolate mixture from over the hot water. Stir in the egg yolks and then stir in the crushed berries. Using a large rubber spatula, fold one third of the egg whites into the mixture to lighten it. Fold in the remaining egg whites.

5. In a chilled medium bowl, using a hand-held electric mixer set at medium-high speed, whip the cream until soft peaks start to form when the beaters are lifted. Do not overbeat the cream. Using a large rubber spatula, fold the whipped cream into the chocolate-egg yolk mixture. A few white streaks may remain.

6. Scrape the mousse into a serving bowl or individual dishes. Chill the mousse for about 30 minutes or until set. Cover the mousse with plastic wrap and chill until firm, about 2 hours for individual portions, 5 hours for a large bowl of mousse.

7. Garnish each serving with a dollop of softly whipped cream and 1 or 2 fresh raspberries.

Orange White Chocolate Mousse
with Fresh Strawberry Sauce

Let the fresh flavors of oranges and a chunky strawberry sauce offset the sweetness of the white chocolate in this delectable, satiny mousse.

```
YIELD: 6 to 8 servings

DIFFICULTY: ◣

PREPARATION TIME: 30 to 35 minutes
    plus chilling time
```

Mousse:

14 ounces white chocolate, finely chopped
4 tablespoons (½ stick) unsalted butter, cut into tablespoons
2 jumbo eggs, at room temperature, separated
1½ tablespoons freshly grated orange zest
3 tablespoons Triple Sec (orange liqueur)
¾ cup heavy cream, chilled

Strawberry sauce:

2 pints fresh strawberries, plus 8 whole strawberries for garnish
2 tablespoons Triple Sec (orange liqueur)
⅓ cup granulated sugar

Make the mousse:

1. In a heatproof bowl set over a pan of hot, not simmering, water, melt the chocolate and the butter, stirring occasionally until smooth. Remove the pan from the heat, keeping the bowl over the pan of hot water.

2. In a small bowl, whisk together the egg yolks, orange zest, and liqueur.

3. In a large, grease-free bowl, using a hand-held electric mixer set at low speed, beat the egg whites until frothy. Increase the speed to medium high and continue to beat the whites until they form stiff, shiny peaks.

4. Remove the bowl of melted chocolate from the pan of hot water. Stir the egg yolk mixture into the chocolate mixture until well combined. With a large rubber spatula, fold one third of the egg whites into the chocolate mixture to lighten it. Fold in the remaining egg whites.

5. In a chilled medium bowl, using a hand-held electric mixer set at medium-high speed, beat the cream until soft peaks start to form when the beaters are lifted. Do not overbeat the cream. Using a large rubber spatula, fold the whipped cream into the chocolate-egg white mixture. A few white streaks may remain.

6. Scrape the mousse into a large serving bowl. Chill the mousse for about 30 minutes, until set. Cover the mousse with plastic wrap and chill until firm, about 2 hours for individual portions and 5 hours for a large bowl.

Make the sauce:

7. Rinse and hull the strawberries. Put the strawberries, orange liqueur, and sugar in a food processor fitted with a metal chopping blade. Pulse the berries 10 to 12 times or until they are coarsely chopped. Do not overprocess—the strawberries should not be pureed, just chopped. Cover and chill, stirring once or twice, until ready to serve.

8. To serve, spoon a pool of strawberry sauce onto each dessert plate. Put a dollop of mousse in the center of each plate on top of the sauce. Garnish each serving with a whole fresh strawberry.

5

Pies and Tarts

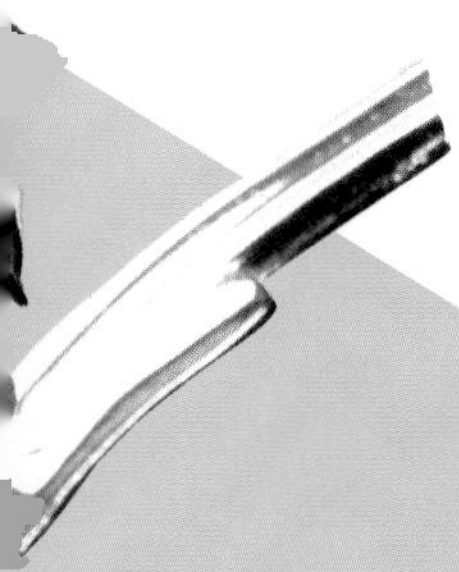

Aloha Peanut Pie

Chocolate Cream Pie

Choclava

Double Chocolate Raspberry Tart

California Linzertorte

Chocolate Mousse Tart

Basic Pie Shell

Chocolate Chess Pie

Double Fudge Pie

Chocolate Bourbon Pecan Pie
    with Bourbon Butter Crust

Chocolate Banana Cream Pie

Chocolate Angel Pie

White Chocolate and Coconut Pie

Mocha Mousse Pie

he image of a just-baked pie cooling on the windowsill is an American classic. We have long been known for our wonderful pies, whether they are baked in a home kitchen or the kitchen of a diner or coffee shop, where they are proudly displayed on the counter under a dome of polished glass. In this chapter we have collected some of the best chocolate pies and tarts to which you will ever take a fork—from a traditional Chocolate Cream Pie to an updated California Linzertorte and a jazzy Double Chocolate Raspberry Tart.

Many of the pies and tarts are chilled. These are usually filled with a pudding or mousse that is spooned into a baked crust and left to set in the refrigerator. Others are baked after they are assembled and served warm or at room temperature. Some of the crusts are traditional pastry; others are simpler crumb crusts, which often taste best with chilled fillings. We explain how to bake a crust "blind"—or without filling—as well as the best methods to use to blend the ingredients for a light and flaky pastry crust. Whether you serve these pies as a mid-afternoon snack with a cup of freshly brewed coffee or as dessert after dinner, you will find them seductively soothing, deliciously rich, and ultimately satisfying.

⁓ Aloha Peanut Pie ⁓

What a sweet way to say "Aloha" to your guests—with a slice of this sumptuously rich chilled pie. It takes a while to make, since the chocolate layer must chill for an hour before the frothy peanut butter mousse is smoothed over it. And then the mousse must chill for another couple of hours. The taste is well worth the wait.

YIELD: 8 servings

DIFFICULTY: ◼

PREPARATION TIME: 45 minutes plus chilling times

Crust:

1½ cups graham cracker crumbs
6 tablespoons (¾ stick) unsalted butter, melted
2 tablespoons granulated sugar

Chocolate layer:

1 cup heavy (whipping) cream
9 ounces bittersweet chocolate, finely chopped

Peanut butter mousse:

4 cups heavy (whipping) cream, divided
12 ounces (about 2 cups) peanut butter chips
¼ cup granulated sugar

⅓ cup coarsely chopped unsalted roasted macadamia nuts or peanuts (for roasting instructions, see page 20), for garnish

Make the crust:

1. Position a rack in the center of the oven and preheat to 350°F. Lightly butter a 9-inch pie pan.

2. In a medium bowl, mix together the graham cracker crumbs, butter, and sugar. Using your fingers, firmly and evenly press the crumb mixture into the bottom and sides of the prepared pie pan. Bake for 10 to 12 minutes or until set and just beginning to brown. Cool the crust completely on a wire rack.

Make the chocolate layer:

3. In a medium saucepan over medium-low heat, slowly bring the cream to a gentle boil. Remove the pan from the heat and add the chocolate. Let the mixture sit for 1 to 2 minutes and then whisk until smooth. Pour the chocolate mixture into the crumb crust and smooth the top with a metal spatula. Chill the filled crust for 1 hour or until the chocolate layer is set.

Make the peanut butter mousse:

4. In a medium saucepan over medium-low heat, slowly bring 1 cup of the cream to a gentle boil.

Remove the pan from the heat and add the peanut butter chips. Let the mixture sit for 1 to 2 minutes and then whisk until smooth. Transfer the peanut butter mixture to a medium bowl. Let the peanut butter mixture stand for 10 to 15 minutes or until cool.

5. In a chilled large bowl, using a hand-held electric mixer set at medium speed, beat the remaining 3 cups of cream with the sugar for about 2 minutes or just until it begins to form soft peaks. Do not overbeat the cream. Using a rubber spatula, fold about 1 cup of the whipped cream into the peanut butter mixture. Using a hand-held electric mixer set at low speed, beat this mixture back into the rest of the whipped cream just until smooth and thickened. (The whipped cream will deflate.)

6. Spoon the peanut butter mousse on top of the chocolate layer. Using a metal spatula, smooth the top of the peanut butter mousse so that it mounds high in the center. Sprinkle the surface of the mousse with the chopped nuts and press them lightly into the mousse. Cover the pie loosely with plastic wrap and refrigerate for at least 2 hours or until the mousse is firm.

∾ *Chocolate Cream Pie* ∾

Topped with a snowy cloud of whipped cream, this tastes the way good old-fashioned American Chocolate Cream Pie should. It's important to line the unbaked pie shell with weighted aluminum foil before baking it. The foil prevents it from browning too much and the weights keep the pastry flat. The buttered foil is easy to peel off the baked crust. Be sure the crust is completely cool before filling.

YIELD: 6 to 8 servings

DIFFICULTY: ▰▰

PREPARATION TIME: 1½ hours plus chilling, baking, and cooling times

SPECIAL EQUIPMENT: 2 cups of pie weights or enough dry rice or beans to weight a 9-inch pie crust

Pie shell:

1½ cups sifted all-purpose flour
1½ teaspoons granulated sugar
¼ teaspoon salt
4 tablespoons (½ stick) unsalted butter, chilled and cut into
  ½-inch cubes
4 tablespoons solid vegetable shortening, chilled and cut into
  ½-inch pieces
3 to 4 tablespoons ice water

Chocolate filling:

¾ cup plus 3 tablespoons granulated sugar
⅓ cup plus 2 tablespoons cornstarch
⅛ teaspoon salt
5 large egg yolks, lightly beaten
2¾ cups milk
1 cup half-and-half
1 vanilla bean or ¾ teaspoon vanilla extract
4 ounces bittersweet chocolate, finely chopped
2½ ounces unsweetened chocolate, finely chopped

Whipped-cream topping:

1 cup heavy (whipping) cream
1 tablespoon granulated sugar
1 teaspoon vanilla extract

Garnish (*optional*):

Chocolate curls (for instructions on making chocolate curls, see
  page 21)

Make the pie shell:

1. In a medium bowl, stir together the flour, sugar, and salt. Distribute the butter and shortening evenly over the flour mixture. Using your fingertips, quickly rub the butter and shortening into the flour mixture until the butter flakes.

2. Make a well in the center of the mixture and add 3 tablespoons of the ice water. Using your fingers, toss the mixture until the dough clings together. Add the remaining tablespoon of water only if the dough is still dry and crumbly. Form the dough into a ball, flatten to a 5-inch disk, and wrap in waxed paper. Refrigerate the dough for 30 to 45 minutes or until firm enough to roll.

3. On a floured work surface or between two sheets of lightly floured waxed paper, roll the chilled dough into a 12-inch circle with a lightly floured rolling pin. Remove the sheets of waxed paper and brush off any flour clinging to the surface of the dough. Carefully roll the dough onto the rolling pin and transfer it to a 9-inch glass pie plate. Unroll the dough and gently ease it onto the bottom and sides of the pie plate. Tuck the dough underneath itself and flute the edge. Using the tines of a fork, prick the bottom and sides of the pie shell in several places. Refrigerate the pie shell for 15 to 20 minutes or until firm.

4. Position a rack in the center of the oven and preheat to 350°F. Lightly butter a large sheet of aluminum foil. Line the pie shell with the aluminum foil, buttered side facing down, and fill with dried beans, rice, or pie weights. Bake the pie shell for 25 to 30 minutes or until the edges start to turn golden brown. Remove the foil and beans from the pie shell and continue baking for 10 to 12 more minutes or until evenly browned. Transfer the pie shell still in the pie plate to a wire rack and cool completely.

Make the chocolate filling:

5. In a heavy, large saucepan, stir together the sugar, cornstarch, and salt. Slowly whisk in the egg yolks until creamy. Stir in the milk and half-and-half. Using a small, sharp knife, split the vanilla bean in half and scrape the tiny black seeds from the inside of the vanilla bean into the milk mixture. Add the scraped vanilla bean to the milk mixture.

6. Cook the mixture over medium-low heat, stirring constantly with a whisk, for 8 to 10 minutes or until the mixture thickens and comes to a boil. Remove the pan from the heat and add the chocolates, stirring until smooth. Quickly strain the mixture through a sieve into a bowl. Scrape the chocolate filling into the pie shell and spread evenly. Cover the surface of the filling with a piece of plastic wrap to prevent a skin from forming. Cool to room temperature. Refrigerate the cooled pie for several hours or overnight.

Make the whipped-cream topping:

7. In a chilled large bowl, using a hand-held electric mixer set at medium speed, beat the cream and sugar until soft peaks form. Add the vanilla and continue beating until stiff peaks form. Cover the pie filling with the whipped-cream topping. If desired, garnish with chocolate curls. Keep the pie refrigerated until ready to serve.

～ *Choclava* ～

Flaky layers of buttery phyllo encase a chocolate and nut filling to make a dessert reminiscent of classic baklava. Be sure to keep the phyllo covered with a damp cloth when not working with it, to keep it from drying out.

YIELD: Approximately 60 diamonds

DIFFICULTY: ▰▰

PREPARATION TIME: 45 minutes plus baking and cooling times

Chocolate nut filling:

4 cups pecan halves, finely chopped
6 ounces (about 1 cup) semisweet chocolate chips
⅔ cup granulated sugar
1 teaspoon ground cinnamon

To assemble:

1 1-pound package phyllo dough, unrolled and covered with a damp towel
10 tablespoons (1 stick plus 2 tablespoons) unsalted butter, melted

Syrup:

½ cup plus 1 tablespoon water
½ cup honey
½ cup granulated sugar
½ cup orange juice
3 tablespoons lemon juice
Pinch of salt
½ teaspoon vanilla extract

Chocolate glaze:

2 ounces (about ⅓ cup) semisweet chocolate chips
2 tablespoons water

Orange slices, for garnish (optional)

Make the filling:

1. In a large bowl, combine the pecans, chocolate chips, sugar, and cinnamon.

Assemble the choclava:

2. Position a rack in the center of the oven and preheat to 325°F. Lightly butter the bottom and sides of a 11-by-15-by-2-inch rectangular pan.

3. Cut six sheets of phyllo to fit the pan. The scrap pieces of phyllo may be pieced together to form a layer. Keep the phyllo covered with a damp cloth when not working with it. Put one sheet of phyllo in the pan and brush it with melted butter, using a pastry brush. Continue layering and buttering the five remaining sheets of cut phyllo. After buttering the last layer, sprinkle it with 2 cups of the chocolate-nut filling. Cut four more sheets of phyllo to fit the pan. Layer and butter each one in

the same manner. Sprinkle the top layer with 2 cups of the chocolate nut filling. Cut four more sheets of phyllo to fit the pan and layer and butter each one as before. Sprinkle the top layer with the remaining filling. Cut six more sheets of phyllo. Layer and butter each one as before. Be sure not to piece the final layer together from scrap dough. It must be a whole piece of phyllo. Brush the final layer with the remaining butter.

4. Being careful not to cut through the bottom six layers of the phyllo, cut the choclava into diamonds. Bake for 55 to 60 minutes or until golden brown. Transfer the choclava in the pan to a wire rack. While the choclava is baking, make the syrup.

Make the syrup:

5. In a medium saucepan, combine the water, honey, sugar, orange and lemon juices, and salt. Cook over medium heat, stirring with a wooden spoon until the sugar dissolves. Bring the syrup to a boil. Reduce the heat and simmer for 20 minutes.

Remove the pan from the heat and stir in the vanilla.

6. Pour the hot syrup evenly over the hot choclava. Cool completely to room temperature. With a sharp knife, cut along the pre-made cuts and cut through the bottom layer.

Make the chocolate glaze:

7. In a small, heavy saucepan, combine the chocolate chips and water. Cook over low heat, stirring constantly with a wooden spoon until the chocolate melts and the mixture is smooth.

8. Drizzle the chocolate glaze in a random pattern over the choclava. Let the chocolate set. Remove the choclava diamonds from the pan. Serve with orange slices, if desired. Store the choclava in an airtight container in a single layer for up to 5 days.

Double Chocolate Raspberry ⌒〜 Tart ⌒〜

Entered as a surefire crowd-pleaser at a chocolate festival in Akron, Ohio, this pretty fluted tart is made of three layers: a smooth raspberry filling, a white chocolate buttercream, and a shiny chocolate glaze.

> YIELD: 10 servings
>
> DIFFICULTY: ▰▰▰
>
> PREPARATION TIME: 1 hour plus chilling, baking, cooling, and setting times (allow 1 hour for the tart pastry to chill)
>
> SPECIAL EQUIPMENT: 11-inch fluted tart pan with a removable bottom; 2 cups of pie weights, dry rice, or beans; pastry bag fitted with a star tip (such as Ateco #4)

Tart pastry:

1½ cups all-purpose flour
1 tablespoon granulated sugar
¼ teaspoon salt
1 large egg yolk
3 to 4 tablespoons ice water
10 tablespoons (1 stick plus 2 tablespoons) unsalted butter, chilled and cut into ½-inch cubes

Raspberry filling:

1 10-ounce package frozen raspberries in light syrup, thawed
2 tablespoons granulated sugar
1½ tablespoons cornstarch

White chocolate buttercream:

4 ounces white chocolate, coarsely chopped
8 tablespoons (1 stick) unsalted butter, softened
¼ cup superfine sugar
2 large eggs, at room temperature
½ teaspoon vanilla extract

Chocolate glaze:

4 ounces bittersweet chocolate, coarsely chopped
4 tablespoons (½ stick) unsalted butter, softened

Decoration:
10 fresh raspberries

Make the tart pastry:

1. In a medium bowl, stir together the flour, sugar, and salt. In a glass measuring cup, stir together the egg yolk and 3 tablespoons of ice water.

2. Put the butter cubes on top of the flour mixture. Using your fingertips, quickly rub the butter into the flour until the mixture is the texture of oatmeal flakes.

3. Make a well in the center of the flour-butter mixture and add 2 tablespoons of the egg yolk-water mixture. Using your fingertips, toss the flour mixture and continue adding the liquid until the dough just clings together. Add the remaining 1 tablespoon of ice water only if necessary.

4. Using the heel of your hand, smear half the dough across about 3 inches of a smooth work surface until the dough is thoroughly blended. Repeat with the other half of the dough. Using a pastry scraper, gather all the dough into a ball. Pat the dough into a small flat disk and wrap it in waxed paper. Refrigerate for 45 to 60 minutes or until firm.

Prepare the tart shell:

5. Butter the bottom and sides of the tart pan with a removable bottom.

6. Lightly dust a work surface and rolling pin with flour and roll the pastry into a 14-inch circle. Using a pastry brush, brush the excess flour from the surface of the dough. Carefully roll the dough onto the rolling pin and transfer it to the prepared tart pan. Gently ease the dough into the fluted edges. Fold in the edges of the dough to make a double layer of dough against the inside rim of the pan. Press the dough against the sides of the pan, making sure that there are no air pockets. Using your thumb, trim the excess dough by pressing it against the fluted edge. Refrigerate the tart shell for 30 minutes.

7. Position a rack in the center of the oven and preheat to 375°F. Lightly butter one side of a 14-inch piece of aluminum foil. Set the foil but-

tered side down into the pastry shell. Using the tines of a fork, prick through both the foil and the pastry shell in eight different places at least 1 inch apart. Fill the foil with 2 cups of pie weights, raw beans or rice to help the pastry shell keep its shape.

8. Bake the pastry shell for 20 to 25 minutes, until the edges are slightly puffed and brown. Carefully remove the foil and its contents. Continue baking the shell for 8 to 12 minutes or until the bottom and sides are golden brown. Cool the pastry shell completely on a wire rack. Remove the shell from the tart pan.

Make the raspberry filling:

9. In a food processor fitted with the metal chopping blade, puree the raspberries with the syrup. Strain the puree through a fine sieve into a bowl to remove the seeds.

10. In a small, nonaluminum saucepan, stir together the sugar and the cornstarch. Stir in the raspberry puree until smooth. Cook over medium heat, stirring constantly, until the mixture comes to a full boil. Remove the pan from the heat. Transfer the mixture to a metal bowl. Set the bowl over a bowl of ice water and stir the raspberry filling frequently for 5 to 10 minutes or until cold. Remove the bowl from the ice water. Cover the surface of the raspberry filling with plastic wrap and refrigerate.

Make the white chocolate buttercream:

11. In the top of a double boiler over hot, not simmering, water, melt the white chocolate, stirring constantly until smooth. Remove the top part of the double boiler and cool the chocolate for 5 to 10 minutes or until tepid.

12. In a medium bowl, using a hand-held electric mixer set at medium speed, beat the butter and the sugar for 1 to 2 minutes or until creamy. Gradually mix in the white chocolate. Add the eggs, one at a time, beating well after each addition until light and fluffy. Beat in the vanilla.

(continued)

Assemble the tart:

13. Put the tart shell on a serving plate. Reserve ½ cup of the buttercream to pipe rosettes on the top of the tart. Using a small offset metal cake spatula, spread the chilled raspberry filling in the bottom of the tart in a thin, even layer. Spread the white chocolate buttercream in an even layer over the raspberry filling. Refrigerate the tart for 20 to 30 minutes or until the buttercream is firm.

Prepare the chocolate glaze:

14. In the top of a double boiler over hot, not simmering, water, melt the chocolate and butter, stirring frequently until smooth. Using a small offset metal cake spatula, carefully spread the glaze in a thin, even layer over the white chocolate buttercream. Refrigerate the tart for 5 to 10 minutes to set the glaze.

Decorate the tart:

15. Fill a pastry bag fitted with a star tip (such as Ateco #4) with the reserved buttercream. Pipe 10 rosettes, evenly spaced, around the edge of the tart. Top each rosette with a raspberry. Keep the tart refrigerated until 30 minutes before serving.

~ *California Linzertorte* ~

A new twist on a classic dessert, Flo Braker's torte is filled with a sweetened apricot mixture and topped with chocolate dough—rather than the traditional raspberry filling topped with spicy yellow dough. Called California Linzertorte because it takes advantage of the wonderful apricot crop from that sun-filled state, it tastes good anywhere from coast to coast.

YIELD: 8 servings
DIFFICULTY: ▬▬
PREPARATION TIME: 55 minutes plus baking and cooling times
SPECIAL EQUIPMENT: 8-by-3-inch round springform pan

Filling:
⅓ cup dried apricots
⅓ cup fresh orange juice
2 tablespoons almond paste
1 tablespoon granulated sugar
1 large egg white, at room temperature

Chocolate dough:
¾ cup all-purpose flour
2 tablespoons unsweetened alkalized cocoa powder
½ teaspoon ground cinnamon
⅛ teaspoon double-acting baking powder
10 tablespoons (1 stick plus 2 tablespoons) unsalted butter, softened
½ cup plus 2 tablespoons granulated sugar
1 large egg yolk, at room temperature
½ teaspoon almond extract
2 cups finely ground unblanched almonds

Decoration:
3 tablespoons apricot jam
Dried apricots, cut into slivers (optional)

Make the filling:

1. In a small saucepan, combine the apricots and orange juice and let stand for 5 minutes. Cook the mixture over medium heat for 6 to 8 minutes or until the apricots are soft and only 1 tablespoon of orange juice is left. Cool for 5 to 10 minutes or until tepid.

2. Scrape the apricot mixture into a food processor fitted with the metal chopping blade. Add the almond paste, sugar, and egg white, and process for 15 to 20 seconds or until a smooth, sticky paste forms.

Make the chocolate dough:

3. Position a rack in the lower third of the oven and preheat to 350°F. Lightly butter the bottom and sides of the springform pan. Dust the bottom and sides of the pan with flour and tap out the excess.

4. In a medium bowl, stir together the flour, cocoa, cinnamon, and baking powder. Sift the mixture.

5. In a large bowl, using a hand-held electric mixer set at low speed, beat the butter for 30 to 60 seconds until creamy. Gradually add the sugar and beat at medium speed for 1 to 2 minutes or until light. Beat in the egg yolk and almond extract. With the mixer on low speed, mix in the ground almonds. Gradually beat in the dry ingredients until just combined and the ingredients form a soft dough.

Assemble the linzertorte:

6. Using lightly floured fingertips, press half of the dough evenly into the bottom of the prepared pan.

7. Using a rubber spatula, spread the apricot filling evenly over the dough, stopping ½ inch from the edge of the pan.

8. Divide the remaining dough into nine equal pieces. On a lightly floured work surface, roll each piece into a 7- to 8-inch long rope. Beginning in the center of the torte, wind one rope of dough into a spiral. Continue winding the dough around the surface of the torte, leaving ⅛ inch between each coil, until all the dough has been used. Lightly press the outer edges of the dough against the sides of the pan to seal. Bake the torte for 35 to 45 minutes or until the edges start to brown and the dough looks set and dull. The torte will puff up during baking and collapse a little as it cools. Cool the torte on a wire rack for 5 minutes. Gently run a knife around the edges of the torte to loosen, and remove the sides of the springform pan.

Decorate the linzertorte:

9. In a small saucepan set over low heat, gently warm the apricot jam until melted. Press the jam through a small sieve to remove any pulp or lumps. Using a small pastry brush, lightly coat the warm torte with the warm jam. Cool completely before serving and garnish, if desired, with slivers of dried apricots.

∼ *Chocolate Mousse Tart* ∼

The coffee-scented, satiny chocolate mousse contrasts deliciously with a crunchy nut-chocolate crust to produce a tart that is rich and incredibly chocolaty—just as you would hope a mousse tart would be.

YIELD: 10 servings

DIFFICULTY: ▬▬

PREPARATION TIME: 1 hour plus baking, cooling, and chilling times (allow at least 4 hours for the mousse to chill)

SPECIAL EQUIPMENT: 10-inch fluted tart pan with a removable bottom

Chocolate nut crust:

4 ounces semisweet chocolate, finely ground
⅓ cup finely ground walnuts
2 cups finely ground vanilla wafers
6 tablespoons (¾ stick) unsalted butter, melted

Mousse:

1 tablespoon cold freshly brewed coffee
1 teaspoon instant coffee powder
1 teaspoon brandy or cognac
1 teaspoon vanilla extract
3 large eggs, at room temperature, separated
3 ounces unsweetened chocolate, coarsely chopped
3 ounces semisweet chocolate, coarsely chopped
6 tablespoons water, divided
12 tablespoons granulated sugar, divided
Pinch of cream of tartar
⅓ cup heavy (whipping) cream

Decoration:

1 cup heavy (whipping) cream
1½ tablespoons granulated sugar
½ teaspoon vanilla extract
10 chocolate-dipped orange slices, for garnish (optional)

Make the chocolate nut crust:

1. Position a rack in the center of the oven and preheat to 375°F. Butter the bottom and sides of a the tart pan with a removable bottom.

2. In a large bowl, whisk together the chocolate, walnuts, and cookie crumbs. Whisk in the butter until well combined. Press the crumb mixture evenly into the sides and bottom of the tart pan.

Bake for 8 to 10 minutes or until set. Place the tart shell on a wire rack to cool completely.

Make the mousse:

3. In a small bowl, combine the coffee, coffee powder, brandy, vanilla, and egg yolks.

4. In a food processor fitted with the metal chopping blade, process the chocolates for 20 to 25 seconds or until they are finely ground.

5. In a small saucepan, combine 4 tablespoons of the water and 6 tablespoons of the sugar. Over medium heat, stir the mixture with a wooden spoon until the sugar dissolves. Stop stirring and increase the heat to high. As soon as the syrup simmers, take it from the heat.

6. With the motor running, pour the sugar syrup through the feed tube of the food processor. Turn off the processor and scrape down the sides of the work bowl with a rubber spatula. Add the remaining 2 tablespoons of water. Process the mixture for 10 seconds longer and scrape the sides of the container again. Add the egg yolk mixture and process for 15 to 20 seconds or until the batter is smooth. Transfer the batter to a large bowl.

7. In a medium, grease-free bowl, using a hand-held electric mixer set at low speed, beat the egg whites and the cream of tartar until foamy. Gradually increase the speed to medium high and beat until soft peaks form. Add the remaining 6 tablespoons of sugar a tablespoon at a time, and continue beating until stiff, shiny peaks form. Using a rubber spatula, fold one quarter of the egg whites into the chocolate batter to lighten it. Gently fold in the remaining egg whites.

8. In a large bowl, beat the cream with a whisk until soft peaks form. Gently fold the cream into the chocolate egg mixture.

9. Scrape the mousse into the prepared crust and smooth evenly with a rubber spatula. Chill for 4 to 5 hours, or overnight.

Decorate the tart:

10. Remove the tart from the refrigerator. Using a small, sharp knife, loosen the sides of the tart from the pan. Place the center of the bottom of the tart pan over the top of a bottle and gently press down to loosen the bottom of the tart from the pan. Using two metal cake spatulas, lift the tart off the bottom of the tart pan and transfer it to a serving platter.

11. In a large bowl, whisk together the cream, sugar, and vanilla until soft peaks form. Serve wedges of the tart with a dollop of whipped cream and garnish with a chocolate-dipped orange slice, if desired.

〜 *Basic Pie Shell* 〜

Use this recipe for all sorts of pies, as well as the pies specified in this chapter. It is just what it promises to be: a good basic pastry.

> YIELD: crust for one 9-inch pie shell
>
> DIFFICULTY: ◼
>
> PREPARATION TIME: 15 minutes plus chilling time (allow at least 1 hour and 20 minutes to chill the pie dough and pie shell)
>
> SPECIAL EQUIPMENT: 2 cups of pie weights, dried beans or uncooked rice

1 cup all-purpose flour
2 teaspoons granulated sugar
2 tablespoons plus 1 teaspoon ice water
¼ teaspoon salt
2 tablespoons plus 2 teaspoons unsalted butter, chilled and cut
*   into ½-inch cubes*
3 tablespoons solid vegetable shortening, chilled and cut
*   into ½-inch pieces*

(continued)

1. In a small bowl, stir together the flour and sugar. In another small bowl or cup, stir the ice water and salt together.

2. Mound the dry ingredients on a work surface. Distribute the butter and shortening evenly over the flour. Using your fingertips, quickly rub the butter and shortening into the flour until the mixture is the size of small peas.

3. Make a well in the center of the mixture and add the salt water. Using your fingers, toss the mixture until the dough just clings together.

4. Using the heel of your hand, smear half the dough across about 3 inches of the work surface until the butter is almost thoroughly blended. Repeat with the rest of the dough. Using a pastry scraper, gather the dough together. Form the dough into a small flat disk and wrap it in plastic. Refrigerate for 1 hour or until firm.

5. Butter the inside bottom and sides of a 9-inch pie plate. On a lightly floured work surface with a lightly floured rolling pin, roll the chilled pastry into a 12-inch circle. Brush off any flour on the surface of the dough. Carefully roll the dough onto a rolling pin. Transfer the pastry onto the pie plate and unroll. Gently ease it into the bottom and sides of the pie plate. Using scissors or a small knife, trim the edge of the pastry so that it is even with the edge of the pie plate, or fold the overhanging dough under and pinch it to form a high edge. Flute or crimp as desired for a decorative rim. Refrigerate the pie shell for 20 minutes or until firm.

6. To bake the pie shell without filling (to "blind bake" it), position a rack in the center of the oven and preheat to 450°F. Using the tines of a fork, prick the dough around the edges and on the bottom of the pie shell. Lightly butter a sheet of aluminum foil and put the buttered side against the crust. Fill the foil-lined shell with pie weights, dried beans, or uncooked rice until they come to the top of the pie. Bake the pie shell for 8 minutes or until the crust is golden brown. Take the pie shell from the oven and remove the aluminum foil and pie weights. Return the crust to the oven for another 3 minutes. Cool on a wire rack.

7. To bake the pie shell after it has been filled, follow the instructions in the specific recipe. Some fillings require more or less time than others.

Freezing Pie Shells

Pie shells made from pastry are easy to freeze and nice to have on hand when you want to make a pie in a hurry. Press the pastry into the pie plate (choose one that is freezer resistant), trim the sides, and crimp the edges to make it pretty. Wrap the unbaked pie shell first in plastic and then in a double layer of foil. Freeze it for up to a month. When you are ready to bake it, take it from the freezer and unwrap it carefully. By the time you fill the shell, it will be thawed sufficiently so that you need not adjust the baking time, but, nevertheless, judge its doneness more by visual checks than time.

⌒ *Chocolate Chess Pie* ⌒

The tale of how chess pie, an old Southern favorite, got its name is as likely as any explanation. The simple pie was made with what every farm wife had in her larder: eggs, cream, and butter. When a guest asked what kind of pie was being served, the inevitable answer was "Jes pie." We have added chocolate (of course!) to this good, homey dessert and probably would never refer to it is "Jes pie"— you won't either, once you taste it.

YIELD: 8 servings
DIFFICULTY: ◼
PREPARATION TIME: 20 minutes plus baking and cooling times

1 recipe 9-inch Basic Pie Shell (see page 151), unbaked
1 cup packed light brown sugar
½ cup plus 1 tablespoon granulated sugar, divided
1 teaspoon all-purpose flour
2 large eggs, at room temperature
¼ cup milk, at room temperature
1 teaspoon vanilla extract
8 tablespoons (1 stick) unsalted butter, cut into tablespoons
1½ ounces unsweetened chocolate, coarsely chopped
1 cup heavy (whipping) cream, chilled
Grated chocolate, for garnish (optional)

1. Make the Basic Pie Shell.

2. Position a rack in the center of the oven and preheat to 325°F. In a medium bowl, combine the brown sugar, ½ cup of the granulated sugar, and the flour.

3. In another bowl, combine the eggs, milk, and vanilla.

4. In a small saucepan over low heat, melt the butter and chocolate, stirring frequently until smooth. Gradually beat in the egg mixture until combined. Stir this mixture into the dry ingredients until smooth. Pour the batter into the pie shell and bake for 35 to 40 minutes or until just set.

5. In a chilled bowl, whip the cream and the remaining 1 tablespoon of sugar just until it forms soft peaks. Serve the pie warm. Top each wedge with a dollop of whipped cream and sprinkle with grated chocolate, if desired.

⌣◯ Double Fudge Pie ◯⌣

A smooth, creamy pie with a nice chocolaty filling enhanced by melted chocolate chips, this pie couldn't be easier to make. If the pie shell is already made and waiting in the freezer, you will be able to set a warm pie on the table in a twinkling—the perfect complement to icy-cold vanilla (or your favorite flavor) ice cream.

YIELD: 8 servings

DIFFICULTY: ◼

PREPARATION TIME: 20 minutes plus baking and cooling times

1 recipe 9-inch Basic Pie Shell (see page 151), unbaked
1 cup granulated sugar
3 large eggs, at room temperature
½ cup light corn syrup
½ cup heavy (whipping) cream
½ cup unsweetened nonalkalized cocoa powder
3 tablespoons unsalted butter, melted and cooled
1 teaspoon vanilla extract
¼ teaspoon salt
3 ounces (about ½ cup) semisweet chocolate chips
Vanilla ice cream (optional)

1. Make the Basic Pie Shell.

2. Position a rack in the center of the oven and preheat to 325°F.

3. In a large bowl, combine the sugar, eggs, corn syrup, cream, cocoa, butter, vanilla, and salt. Pour the mixture into the pie shell and scatter the chocolate chips over the top.

4. Bake for 40 to 45 minutes or until a knife inserted in the center of the pie comes out clean. Serve warm with ice cream, if desired.

Chocolate Bourbon Pecan Pie ⌣◯ *with Bourbon Butter Crust* ◯⌣

In this recipe, a sweet egg-based, bourbon-flavored filling is poured over a good handful or two of nuts and chocolate chips scattered in the bottom of the crust. The crust, we're happy to report, is also spiked with a pleasant amount of bourbon. As the pie bakes and the filling sets, the chocolate chips melt and mingle with the nuts, and the bourbon flavors everything.

YIELD: 8 servings

DIFFICULTY: ◼

PREPARATION TIME: 30 minutes plus chilling, baking, and cooling times

Bourbon butter crust:

1 cup all-purpose flour

¼ teaspoon salt

*6 tablespoons (¾ stick) unsalted butter, chilled and cut into
    ½-inch cubes*

2 tablespoons plus 1 teaspoon bourbon, chilled

Filling:

6 tablespoons (¾ stick) unsalted butter, melted and cooled

¾ cup packed light brown sugar

¾ cup light corn syrup

3 large eggs, at room temperature

1 tablespoon bourbon

1½ teaspoons vanilla extract

4 ounces (about ¾ cup) semisweet chocolate chips

1 cup pecan halves

Make the pie crust:

1. In a small bowl, stir together the flour and salt.

2. Mound the dry ingredients on a work surface. Distribute the butter evenly over the flour. Using your fingertips, quickly rub the butter into the flour until the butter is the size of small peas.

3. Make a well in the center of the mixture and add the bourbon. Using your fingers, toss the mixture until the dough just clings together.

4. Using the heel of your hand, smear half the dough across about 3 inches of the work surface until the butter is almost thoroughly blended. Repeat with the rest of the dough. Using a pastry scraper, gather the dough together. Form the dough into a small flat disk and wrap it in plastic. Refrigerate for 1 hour or until firm.

Make the filling:

5. In a large bowl, combine the butter, sugar, and corn syrup. Using a hand-held electric mixer

set at medium speed, beat in the eggs one at a time until combined. Beat in the bourbon and vanilla.

Assemble the pie:

6. Position a rack in the center of the oven and preheat to 350°F. Butter the bottom and sides of a 9-inch pie plate. On a lightly floured work surface with a lightly floured rolling pin, roll the chilled pastry into a 12-inch circle. Brush off any flour clinging to the surface of the dough. Carefully roll the dough onto a rolling pin. Transfer the dough to the pie plate and unroll. Gently ease it into the bottom and sides of the plate. Using scissors or a small knife, trim the edge of the pastry so that it is even with the edge of the pie plate, or fold the overhanging dough under and pinch to form a high edge. Flute or crimp as desired to make a decorative rim. Refrigerate the pie shell for 20 minutes.

7. Sprinkle the chocolate chips over the bottom of the chilled crust. Sprinkle the pecans over the chocolate chips. Pour in the filling and bake for 45 to 50 minutes or until the pie filling is set.

∽ *Chocolate Banana Cream Pie* ∾

For a double dose of sweetness, try chocolate and banana together. In this recipe, the two flavors are married when banana puree is combined with sweetened whipped cream, which is then spread over the chilled chocolaty filling. Easy and oh-so-delicious—here's a lovely twist on classic banana cream pie.

YIELD: 8 servings
DIFFICULTY: ▰
PREPARATION TIME: 45 minutes plus chilling time (allow time to make the pie shell)

1 recipe 9-inch Basic Pie Shell (see page 151), baked
¾ cup granulated sugar
2 tablespoons cornstarch
¼ teaspoon salt
2 large eggs, lightly beaten
1½ cups milk
2 ounces unsweetened chocolate, finely chopped
2 tablespoons unsalted butter, chilled and cut into ½-inch cubes
½ teaspoon vanilla extract
1½ cups chilled heavy (whipping) cream, divided
1 tablespoon confectioners' sugar
½ cup pureed ripe banana
Chocolate shavings, for garnish (optional)
Sliced banana, for garnish (optional)

1. Make the Basic Pie Shell and bake it.

2. In a medium bowl, combine the sugar, cornstarch, and salt. Stir in the eggs with a wooden spoon. In a medium, heavy saucepan, bring the milk to a gentle boil. Remove the pan from the heat and gradually whisk the hot milk into the egg mixture. Return the mixture to the saucepan and cook over medium-high heat. Stirring constantly, bring the mixture to a boil, remove the pan from the heat, and stir in the chocolate.

3. Using a fine sieve, strain the mixture into a bowl. Stir in the butter, piece by piece. Stir in the vanilla. Let the filling cool completely.

4. In a chilled bowl, using a hand-held electric mixer set at high speed, whip ½ cup of the heavy cream until it holds soft peaks. Gently fold the whipped cream into the cooled filling, pour it into the baked pie shell, and refrigerate.

5. In the same chilled bowl, whip the remaining 1 cup of cream with the confectioners' sugar until it holds soft peaks. Fold in the banana puree and whip until stiff. Spread the banana cream decoratively over the top of the pie. Refrigerate for 1 hour before serving. Garnish with chocolate shavings and banana slices, if desired.

⌒ *Chocolate Angel Pie* ∽

Nestled in a cloud of sweet meringue, the chocolate filling for this version of an American classic is about as close to heaven as we can get. Bert Greene, who provided us with this treasured recipe, admonished readers never to make the pie on a rainy day. Humidity may turn the meringue soggy—as can waiting too long to eat the assembled pie. But who would want to wait?

YIELD: 6 to 8 servings
DIFFICULTY: ▰▰
PREPARATION TIME: 30 minutes plus baking, cooling, and chilling times

Meringue shell:

3 large egg whites, at room temperature
¼ teaspoon cream of tartar
Pinch of salt
⅔ cup sifted granulated sugar
½ teaspoon vanilla extract
⅓ cup finely chopped walnuts or pecans

Chocolate cream filling:

5 ounces semisweet chocolate, coarsely chopped
¼ cup milk
1 teaspoon vanilla extract
Pinch of salt
1 cup heavy (whipping) cream

To assemble:

¾ cup heavy (whipping) cream
2 tablespoons confectioners' sugar
Chocolate curls (optional; for instructions on making chocolate
*   curls, see page 21)*

Make the meringue shell:

1. Position a rack in the center of the oven and preheat to 275°F. Generously butter the bottom and sides of a 10-inch glass pie plate.

2. In a medium, grease-free bowl, using a hand-held electric mixer set at low speed, beat the egg whites until frothy. Add the cream of tartar and salt and increase the speed to medium high. Continue beating until the whites start to form soft peaks. Gradually add the granulated sugar and continue beating until the whites form a glossy, stiff meringue. Beat in the vanilla.

3. Using a metal cake spatula, spread the meringue over the bottom and sides of the plate, building up the sides as high as possible. Sprinkle the chopped nuts over the surface. Bake for 1 hour or until the meringue shell is dry and light brown in color. If the sides of the meringue fall, press them back into position with the spatula. Turn off the oven and let the meringue stay in the oven for 30 minutes. Cool the meringue shell completely on a wire rack.

(continued)

Make the chocolate cream filling:

4. In the top of a double boiler over hot, not simmering, water, melt the chocolate, stirring frequently until smooth. Remove the pan from the heat. In a small saucepan, heat the milk until hot. Pour the milk into a heatproof medium bowl. Stir in the vanilla and salt. Stir in the chocolate until smooth. Let stand for 30 minutes until cool.

5. In a chilled, medium bowl, beat the heavy cream until soft peaks start to form. Fold the cream into the cooled chocolate mixture. Spread the filling evenly in the cooled meringue shell. Cover with plastic wrap and chill for at least 2 hours, until firm.

Assemble the pie:

6. In a chilled small bowl, beat the heavy cream with the confectioners' sugar until stiff peaks start to form. No more than 1½ hours before serving, remove the plastic wrap and spread the whipped cream evenly over the filling. Refrigerate until ready to serve. Decorate the pie with chocolate curls, if desired, and serve it on the day it is made.

White Chocolate and Coconut ⁓ Pie ⁓

White chocolate and coconut are a stunning combination. Here the coconut-flecked custard is topped with billows of whipped cream and decorative curls of white chocolate. The unfilled pie crust is baked upside down—a rather unusual procedure that, Chef Jim Dodge says, ensures that the crust does not shrink from the top of the pie plate as it bakes.

YIELD: 8 servings

DIFFICULTY: ◼◼

PREPARATION TIME: 1 hour plus chilling and cooling times

Pie crust:

1 cup all-purpose flour

1½ teaspoons granulated sugar

¼ teaspoon salt

4 to 5 teaspoons ice water

8 tablespoons (1 stick) cold unsalted butter, cut into ½-inch cubes

Coconut filling:

2 cups unsweetened coconut flakes

2 cups milk

1 vanilla bean, split in half lengthwise

½ cup granulated sugar

2 tablespoons all-purpose flour

2 large eggs

4 tablespoons (½ stick) unsalted butter, cut into 4 pieces

Topping:

1½ cups heavy (whipping) cream
Freshly grated nutmeg, for garnish (optional)
2 ounces white chocolate, for curls (for instructions on making
Chocolate Curls, see page 21)

Make the pie crust:

1. In a small bowl, stir together the flour and sugar. In another small bowl or a cup, stir the salt into the ice water.

2. Mound the dry ingredients on the work surface. Distribute the butter cubes evenly over the flour. Using your fingertips, quickly rub the butter into the flour until the butter is the size of small peas.

3. Make a well in the center of the mixture and add 2 tablespoons of the salt water. Using your fingers, toss the flour-butter mixture and continue adding enough water until the dough just clings together.

4. Using the heel of your hand, smear half the dough across about 3 inches of the work surface until the butter is almost thoroughly blended. Repeat with the rest of the dough. Using a pastry scraper, gather the dough together. Form the dough into a small flat disk and wrap it in plastic. Refrigerate for 1 hour or until firm.

Make the filling:

5. Put the coconut in a food processor fitted with the metal chopping blade. Pulse the motor on and off for 20 seconds or until the coconut flakes are about half of their original size.

6. In a medium, heavy, noncorrosive saucepan, combine the milk and coconut. Scrape the tiny black seeds from the inside of the vanilla bean and add them to the milk mixture. Add the scraped bean pod.

7. Over medium heat, bring the milk-coconut mixture to a slow boil. Reduce the heat to medium low and simmer for 5 minutes. Meanwhile, in a medium bowl, combine the sugar, flour, and eggs. Whisk until creamy.

8. Stir in ¼ cup of the milk-coconut mixture into the egg mixture and then pour this back into the saucepan of hot milk and coconut. Raise the heat to medium high and, stirring constantly with a wooden spoon, cook for 1 minute or until the mixture comes to a boil and is very thick. Remove from the heat and stir in the butter. Remove the vanilla pod. Set the bowl of filling over a bowl of ice water. Stir the filling for 5 minutes or until cold. Cover the surface with plastic wrap and refrigerate the mixture until ready to use.

Assemble the pie crust:

9. Butter the inside bottom and sides of a 9-inch pie plate. Butter the outside bottom and sides of another 9-inch pie plate. On a lightly floured work surface with a lightly floured rolling pin, roll the chilled pastry into a 12-inch circle. Brush off any flour clinging to the surface of the rolled circle. Carefully roll the dough onto the rolling pin and transfer the dough to the pie plate that has been buttered on the inside. Line the pie plate with the dough, using your fingers to gently press it into place. With scissors or a small knife, trim the edge of the pastry so that it is even with the edge of the pie plate. Refrigerate the pie shell for 20 minutes or until firm.

10. Position a rack in the center of the oven and preheat to 400°F. Put an empty baking sheet in the oven.

11. Set the second pie plate in the chilled pie shell. Invert the two pie plates and set them upside down on the preheated baking sheet. Bake for 20 minutes or until the pastry is puffy around the edge. Turn the pie plates right side up and remove the top pan. Bake for 5 minutes longer or until the pie crust is golden brown. Cool for 20 minutes on a wire rack.

(continued)

Assemble the pie:

12. Transfer the chilled filling to the pie crust and spread evenly.

13. In a chilled, large mixing bowl, using a hand-held electric mixer set at medium speed, whip the cream until it forms soft peaks. Using a metal cake spatula, spread the whipped cream over the coconut filling. Sprinkle with the nutmeg, if desired. With a vegetable peeler, scrape the edge of the white chocolate to make curls and scatter them over the top of the whipped cream. Serve immediately or refrigerate until ready to serve.

⟶ Mocha Mousse Pie ⟶

This fudgy mocha pie is made from mixes found in any supermarket, one for the brownie "crust" and the other for the mousse filling. You add the coffee and other flavorings for a dessert with homemade panache that is nearly as easy as whipping up a mix.

YIELD: 8 servings

DIFFICULTY: ◼

PREPARATION TIME: 45 minutes plus baking, cooling, and freezing times

SPECIAL EQUIPMENT: pastry bag fitted with a star tip (such as Ateco #4)

Brownie crust:

¼ cup water
2 teaspoons instant espresso coffee powder
1 14.1-ounce box fudge brownie mix
¼ cup vegetable oil
1 large egg, at room temperature
½ cup pecans, coarsely chopped

Mousse:

1 cup milk
1 tablespoon coffee liqueur
1 teaspoon instant espresso coffee powder
1 3.5-ounce box chocolate fudge mousse mix

Garnish:

½ cup heavy (whipping) cream, chilled
2 teaspoons confectioners' sugar
1 teaspoon coffee-flavored liqueur
Chocolate curls (optional; for instructions on making chocolate curls, see page 21)

Make the brownie crust:

1. Position a rack in the center of the oven and preheat to 350°F. Lightly butter the bottom of a 9-inch pie plate. In a small glass measuring cup, stir together the water and espresso powder until the powder dissolves. In a large bowl, combine the brownie mix, oil, egg, and coffee mixture with a large spoon and stir for 1 minute or until combined. Stir in the pecans.

2. Scrape the batter into the prepared pie plate and spread evenly. Bake for 28 to 32 minutes or until a cake tester or toothpick inserted into the center comes out clean. Do not overbake.

3. Cool the brownie crust completely in the plate on a wire rack for 1½ hours. Run a spatula around the edges of the crust to loosen.

Make the mousse:

4. In a medium bowl, stir together the milk, coffee liqueur, and espresso powder. When the powder is nearly dissolved, add the mousse mix. Using a hand-held electric mixer set at low speed, beat just until blended. Increase the mixer speed to high and beat for 3 to 3½ minutes or until the mixture thickens.

5. Put both the cooled brownie crust and the mousse in the freezer for 15 to 20 minutes or until the mousse is firm enough to mound.

6. Spread the mousse over the brownie crust, mounding it slightly in the center. Return the pie to the freezer for 15 minutes or until firm enough to slice.

Make the garnish:

7. In a chilled small bowl, using a hand-held electric mixer set at medium-high speed, whip together the cream, sugar, and coffee liqueur until soft peaks form. Store the whipped cream in an airtight container in the refrigerator until ready to serve the pie. Store the pie in an airtight container in the refrigerator, too. Let the pie stand for a few minutes at room temperature before serving. With a pastry bag fitted with a star tip (such as Ateco #4) and filled with the flavored whipped cream, decorate the top of the pie and sprinkle with chocolate curls, if desired. Or serve each wedge with a dollop of whipped cream.

6

Chocolate
Masterpieces

*T*his is the chapter to turn to when you want to mark a very special occasion. Perhaps you have decided to bake your own wedding cake, or your daughter's or sister's (truly a loving gift to the bride). Here you will find glorious cakes for small and large weddings, as well as explicit instructions for assembling them. Or you may want to create some incredible chocolate delight for Valentine's Day or Easter. Try our Chocolate Valentine Box or Marbleized Chocolate Easter Egg. If it is Christmas and you feel in the mood to bake cookies that are a little different from the usual, you are in luck with Two-Tone Cutout Cookies. Whatever the occasion—wedding, shower, important birthday, holiday, or large party of any sort—you will surely find a dessert in the following pages that will inspire you to new culinary heights.

As might be expected by the chapter's title, none of the recipes are easy. Masterpieces, after all, take time and effort. But our recipes are constructed so that you cannot fail if you follow them carefully and allow yourself plenty of time. Some of the cakes need several days to bake and assemble; other desserts require long freezing or setting times. We have indicated in the note or preparation information preceding each recipe exactly how much time you will need and what special equipment and/or techniques you are likely to need or encounter. We have made every one of these recipes several times (at least!) in our test kitchens and have been extremely excited by the results. You will be, too, we're sure.

Allen Leiberman

Chocolate Almond Wedding Cake

When chocolate is to be an honored guest at a small wedding, consider pastry chef Nicholas Malgieri's splendid carnation-bedecked creation. The delectably almond-flavored chocolate cake layers can be baked and frozen, well wrapped in plastic, for up to a month. Or they can be refrigerated for up to 5 days. The marzipan decorations add just enough extra almond flavor, which is offset to a tee by a rich chocolate ganache flavored with dark rum.

YIELD: 30 to 40 servings
DIFFICULTY: ▰▰▰
PREPARATION TIME: Allow 2 days to make this cake
SPECIAL EQUIPMENT: 1 6-by-2-inch and 1 12-by-2-inch round cake pan; triangular metal or plastic pastry comb; five plastic straws; pastry bag fitted with a star tip (such as Ateco #1)

Chocolate almond cake (make the cake in two batches,
using half of the listed ingredients each time):

18 ounces semisweet chocolate, coarsely chopped
4 ounces unsweetened chocolate, coarsely chopped
3 cups whole almonds
2 cups dry bread crumbs
1½ teaspoons ground cinnamon
2 cups (4 sticks) unsalted butter, softened
2 cups granulated sugar
2 tablespoons vanilla extract
24 large eggs, at room temperature, separated
A pinch of salt

Ganache (make the ganache in two batches, using half of
the listed ingredients each time):

3 pounds bittersweet chocolate, finely chopped
4 cups heavy (whipping) cream
½ cup dark rum (optional)

Chocolate and white marzipans:
1 8-ounce can almond paste
4 cups confectioners' sugar
⅓ cup light corn syrup
6 tablespoons sifted unsweetened nonalkalized cocoa powder
¾ teaspoon water

Day 1
Make the chocolate almond cake:

1. Position one rack in the top third and another rack in the bottom third of the oven and preheat to 350°F. Lightly butter the bottoms and sides of cake pans. Line the bottom of each pan with a circle of baking parchment or waxed paper.

2. In the top of a double boiler over hot, not simmering, water, melt 9 ounces of the semisweet chocolate with 2 ounces of the unsweetened chocolate, stirring frequently until smooth. Remove the top part of the double boiler from the bottom and let the chocolate cool 5 to 10 minutes or until tepid.

3. In a food processor fitted with the metal chopping blade, combine ¾ cup of the almonds with ½ cup of the dry bread crumbs. Process for 35 to 45 seconds or until finely ground. Transfer the almond mixture to a bowl. Process another ¾ cup of the almonds with another ½ cup of bread

crumbs in the same manner and add the mixture to the bowl of ground almonds and bread crumbs. Stir in ¾ teaspoon of the ground cinnamon.

4. In a large bowl, using a hand-held electric mixer set at medium-high speed, beat 1 cup of the butter for 1 to 2 minutes or until creamy. Gradually beat in ¾ cup of the sugar and continue beating for 3 to 4 minutes or until the mixture whitens. Beat in 1 tablespoon of the vanilla and the cooled melted chocolate. Scrape down the sides of the bowl. One at a time, beat in 12 of the egg yolks. Continue beating for 1 or 2 minutes or until the mixture is light and fluffy and looks like chocolate buttercream. Using a rubber spatula, fold the almond-bread crumb mixture into the butter-chocolate mixture.

5. In a large, grease-free bowl, using a hand-held electric mixer set at low speed, beat 12 of the egg whites until frothy. Add a pinch of salt and

gradually increase the speed to medium high and continue beating the whites until they start to form soft peaks. While continuing to beat, add ¼ cup of the sugar a tablespoon at a time. Beat the whites until they form stiff, shiny peaks.

6.　Using a rubber spatula, fold one fourth of the beaten egg whites into the chocolate batter. Scrape the remaining egg whites over the batter and fold in gently until no streaks of white remain. Fill the prepared 6-inch cake pan with 2 cups of the batter and spread it evenly with a spatula. Scrape the remaining batter into the 12-inch pan and spread it evenly with a spatula.

7.　Bake the 6-inch layer for 30 to 35 minutes or until a cake tester or toothpick inserted in the center of the cake comes out clean. Bake the 12-inch layer for 40 to 45 minutes or until a cake tester or toothpick inserted in the center comes out clean. Halfway through baking, switch positions of the cake layers for even browning.

8.　Cool the cake layers in their pans on wire racks for 10 minutes. Run a thin knife or spatula around the edges of the cake layers to loosen, and invert them onto wire racks. Peel off the papers and leave them loosely set on the bottoms of the layers. Invert the layers onto other racks, so that they are right side up. Cool the layers completely. Wrap the layers in plastic and let them stand at room temperature overnight. Using the remaining half of the cake ingredients, make two more cake layers following the instructions.

Make the ganache:

9.　Put 1½ pounds of the chocolate in a large bowl. In a medium saucepan over medium heat, bring 2 cups of the cream to a gentle boil. Pour the cream over the chocolate and let it sit for 3 to 4 minutes to melt the chocolate. Whisk the ganache until smooth and stir in ¼ cup of the rum, if desired.

10.　Line a large bowl with plastic wrap. Scrape the ganache into the lined bowl and cover the surface with plastic wrap. Refrigerate the ganache. Using the remaining half of the ganache ingredients, make the second batch of ganache, following the instructions.

Make the white marzipan:

11.　Separate the almond paste into sixteen pieces and put them in a food processor fitted with the metal chopping blade. Add 2 cups of the confectioners' sugar and process for 10 to 15 seconds or until the mixture forms fine crumbs. Add the remaining 2 cups of the confectioners' sugar and pulse 8 to 10 times or until the mixture resembles cornmeal. Add the corn syrup and pulse 4 to 6 times or until the mixture is reduced to a fine powder.

12.　Scrape the mixture onto a smooth, clean work surface and divide it into four sections. Vigorously knead the first section for 2 to 3 minutes or until the marzipan becomes smooth and soft. Put the first section aside and knead the remaining three sections one at a time. Combine the pieces of marzipan into one ball and knead the ball for 1 to 2 minutes or until evenly mixed and smooth. Roll the marzipan into a 12-inch long cylinder that is 2 inches in diameter. Score the cylinder into five sections and break off two fifths of the cylinder to make the chocolate marzipan. Wrap the remaining white marzipan in plastic to prevent it from drying out before you are ready to use it.

Make the chocolate marzipan:

13.　Pat the piece of marzipan for the chocolate marzipan into a 4-inch disk. Put the cocoa powder in the center of the disk. Fold in the edges of the marzipan. Knead the cocoa into the marzipan until it is thoroughly blended. If the marzipan seems dry and crumbly, sprinkle up to ¾ teaspoon of water over it and continue kneading until it is soft and smooth. Roll the marzipan into a 6-inch long log that is about 2 inches in diameter. Wrap the chocolate marzipan in plastic to prevent it from drying out.

14.　Cut a ½-inch piece off both the white and chocolate marzipan logs. (Keep the unused sections of the marzipan logs wrapped in plastic at all times to prevent them from drying out.) Roll the ½-inch pieces into two 6-inch long logs. Twist the two logs together by attaching them along their sides and twisting the ends simultaneously in opposite directions. Roll the twisted marzipan into a 12-inch long log. Break the log in half and squeeze it together two more times, finishing with a short, fat piece of marzipan. Reroll the marzipan into a 12-inch long log. Using the heel of your hand, flatten the log into a strip. With the back of a soup spoon, flatten and smooth the strip until the strip measures 14 inches long and is 2 inches wide. Run a metal cake spatula under the strip to release it from the work surface. Cut the strip diagonally into smaller ¼-inch wide strips. Make a carnation leaf by first pinching a point at one end of a small strip. Then hold each end of the strip and twist the ends in opposite directions. Make a total of 22 leaves and let them dry at room temperature overnight. Wrap the variegated leaf scraps in plastic and reserve for making bows.

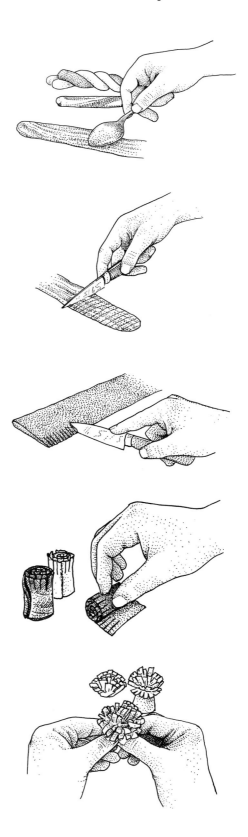

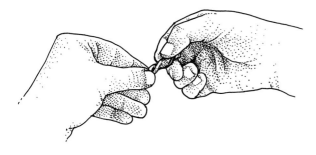

Make the chocolate carnation:

15. Cut off a 1-inch piece from the chocolate marzipan cylinder and roll it into a 12-inch long log. Using the heel of your hand, flatten the log into a strip. With the back of a soup spoon, flatten and smooth the strip until it measures 14 inches long and is 2 inches wide. Flatten the long edge that is directly in front of you so that it is quite a bit thinner than the rest of the strip. Run a metal cake spatula underneath the strip to loosen it from the work surface. Using a small, sharp knife, slash the long, thin edge of the strip at ⅛-inch intervals, making ½-inch deep slashes. Roll up the strip, making sure that the slashed edge is straight and about ¼ inch below the slashes to open the flower. Stand the flower in a tiny cup or in an egg carton lined with aluminum foil. Let the flower dry overnight at room temperature. Reserve the scraps wrapped in plastic.

(continued)

Make the white carnations:

16.   Cut off a 1-inch piece from the white marzipan cylinder and roll it into a 12-inch long log. Repeat the procedure used to make the chocolate carnation. Make 5 more white carnations. Let the flowers dry overnight at room temperature. Reserve the scraps in plastic wrap.

Make the variegated carnations:

17.   Cut a ½-inch piece off of both the white and chocolate marzipan cylinders. Roll the ½-inch pieces into two 6-inch long logs. Twist the two logs together by attaching them along their sides and twisting the ends simultaneously in opposite directions. Roll the twisted marzipan into a 12-inch long log. Break the log in half and squeeze it together to make one short, fat log. Do this two more times and roll the marzipan again into a 12-inch long log. Repeat the procedure used for the chocolate and white carnations. Make 7 more variegated carnations. Let the flowers dry overnight at room temperature. Reserve the scraps with the other variegated scraps for the bows.

Make the bows:

18.   Squeeze together all the variegated scraps and roll them into a cylinder that is about 6 inches long and 2 inches in diameter. Cut off a 1-inch piece. (Keep the cylinder wrapped in plastic.) Roll the 1-inch piece of marzipan into a 12-inch long log. Using the heel of your hand, flatten the log into a strip. With the back of a soup spoon, flatten and smooth the strip until the strip measures 14 inches long and is 2 inches wide. Run a metal cake spatula under the strip to release it from the work surface. Using a small, sharp knife, cut the strip into ¼-inch wide, 2-inch long strips. For each bow you will use four and a half of the ¼-inch wide strips. Shape two of the strips into two loops. Use half of a strip to attach the two loops together to make a bow. Make two ribbons from the remaining two strips and attach them to the back of the center of the bow by pinching them gently. Make more bows with the remaining strips. Roll three more logs to

make more strips, enough to make 16 bows. Let the bows dry overnight at room temperature.

Day 2
Frost the cake:

19.   Unwrap the cake layers. Remove the papers from the bottoms of the layers. Using a long, serrated knife, trim the tops of the cake layers so that they are level. Invert the layers so that the smooth, untrimmed bottoms become the tops of the finished tiers.

20.   Remove the bowls of ganache from the refrigerator. Unmold the ganache and peel off the plastic wrap. Keeping the two batches of ganache separate, cut each one into 1-inch chunks. Put the chunks into two large bowls. Set one of the bowls of ganache over a pot of hot, not simmering, water. (The bottom of the bowl should touch the hot water.) Heat the ganache until about ⅓ to ½ is melted. Remove the bowl of ganache from the heat. Using a rubber spatula, stir the ganache until it is an even, creamy consistency.

21.   Using a hand-held electric mixer set at medium-high speed, beat the bowl of melted ganache for 1 to 2 minutes or until soft peaks start to form when the beaters are lifted. Do not overbeat, or it will become grainy.

22.   Put one of the 12-inch layers on a 12-inch cardboard cake circle. Using a metal cake spatula, spread 2 cups of the whipped ganache over the top of the 12-inch layer. Put the second 12-inch layer with the smooth, untrimmed bottom right side up on top of the ganache. Gently press it into place.

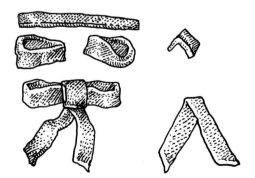

23. Put one of the 6-inch layers on a 6-inch cardboard cake circle. Spread ½ cup of the ganache over the top of the 6-inch layer. Put the second 6-inch layer with the smooth, untrimmed bottom right side up on top of the ganache and gently press it into place.

24. Using a metal cake spatula, spread the remaining ganache to cover the sides of the 6-inch cake, filling in the space between the edge of the cardboard and the sides of the cake. Frost the top of the cake and smooth the sides. Finish the top of the cake by holding the metal cake spatula at a slight angle and, with several strokes, smooth the raised lip of ganache around the edge toward the center of the cake until the top is completely smooth.

25. Using a triangular metal or plastic pastry comb, comb the sides of the 6-inch tier before the ganache has a chance to set. Hold the comb at a slight angle at the base of the cake. While lightly pressing, slowly pull up on the ganache with a zigzag motion to make a vertical zigzag pattern. Wipe the excess frosting from the comb and continue combing all around the cake. Comb the top of the cake, starting from the edge and pulling inward toward the center of the cake.

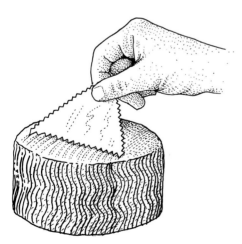

26. Set a second bowl of ganache over a pot of hot, not simmering, water. (The bottom of the bowl should touch the hot water.) Heat the ga-

nache as before and remove the bowl from the heat. Using a rubber spatula, stir the ganache until it is an even, creamy consistency.

27. Using a hand-held electric mixer set at medium-high speed, beat the second bowl of ganache for 1 to 2 minutes, until soft peaks start to form when the beaters are lifted.

28. Reserve 1½ cups of the ganache for decorating the cake and ½ cup for adhering the flowers and bows to the cake. Use the remaining ganache to frost the 12-inch tier in the same manner as the 6-inch tier. Comb the sides and the top of the tier with the same zigzag pattern.

Tier the cakes:

29. Making sure that the circle is centered, trace a 5½-inch circle on top of the 12-inch tier. Insert four plastic straws, evenly spaced, around the edge of the traced circle. Insert a straw into the center of the circle. Using scissors, cut the straws so that they are level with the surface of the cake. (The straws will support the weight of the 6-inch tier.) Cut a 5½-inch circle of aluminum foil. Put the foil circle over the traced circle. Put the 6-inch cake on the cardboard circle over the circle of foil.

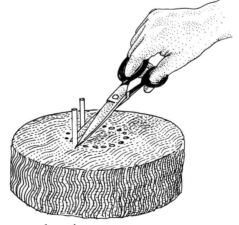

Decorate the cake:

30. Fit a pastry bag with a star tip (such as Ateco #1) and fill it with 1½ cups of the ganache. Pipe a flat shell border around the top edges and bases of the 6-inch and 12-inch tiers.

(continued)

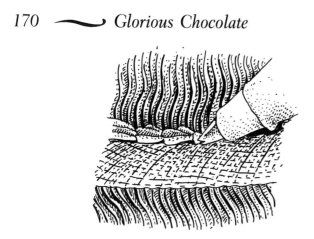

31. Fill the pastry bag with the remaining ½ cup of ganache. Pipe a small dab of ganache at the base of each white carnation. Arrange the white carnations in a tight circle on top of the 6-inch tier. Pinch off a tablespoon of leftover marzipan and roll it into a ball. Put it in the center of the circle of white carnations. Pipe a small dab of ganache on the base of the chocolate carnation and place it on top of the marzipan ball that is in the center of the white carnations. Pipe a small dab of ganache on the base of each variegated carnation. Put the variegated carnations evenly around the top of the 12-inch tier. Put 1 leaf between each of the white carnations. Put 1 leaf on both sides of each variegated carnation. Pipe a small dab of ganache on the back of each bow. Attach 8 of the bows, evenly spaced, around the middle of the outside of the 6-inch tier. Attach the remaining 8 bows around the middle of the 12-inch tier. Keep the cake at cool room temperature (65° to 70°F) or refrigerate for up to 24 hours. The cake should be removed from the refrigerator and kept at cool room temperature for 3 hours before serving. even. Squeeze the carnation with your fingertips

⟿ White Chocolate Nostalgia Cake ⟿

Here is a cake with such old-fashioned grace and charm it would be perfect for a small wedding, a very special birthday, or a christening. Rose Levy Beranbaum, author of *The Cake Bible*, guides you with a sure hand as you re-create her pretty masterpiece, originally designed for the pages of our magazine. The luscious white chocolate cake layers can be made and frozen a month before the event, which saves time, and the fondant and violets made a day or two before. Because it is rather difficult to handle, we suggest that you make the fondant in two batches, one right after the other. Otherwise, you will have trouble kneading it. The cake layers are sandwiched with a pretty pink raspberry cream, so that once the satiny sheath of fondant is cut, the inside of the cake is as delightful to look at as the outside—and wonderful to taste.

YIELD: 30 to 40 servings

DIFFICULTY: ■■■

PREPARATION TIME: Allow 3 days to make this cake

SPECIAL EQUIPMENT: several disposable pastry bags fitted with small writing tips (such as Ateco #1 and #2); ½-inch 5-petaled gum paste cutter (see Ingredient Note); pizza cutter; piece of soft foam; chopstick, crochet needle or cotton swab

Allen Leiberman

Rolled fondant (Make the rolled fondant in two batches, using half of the listed ingredients each time):

4 tablespoons freshly squeezed lemon juice

2 tablespoons water

2 tablespoons unflavored powdered gelatin

4 tablespoons solid vegetable shortening

1 cup light corn syrup

2 tablespoons glycerine (see Ingredient Note)

16 cups (about 4 pounds) confectioners' sugar

White chocolate layer cake:

10 ounces white chocolate, coarsely chopped

1 cup egg whites (7 or 8 large eggs), at room temperature
   (reserve 6 egg yolks for the buttercream)

1⅓ cups milk, at room temperature, divided

2½ teaspoons vanilla extract

(ingredients continued)

5 cups sifted cake flour (not self-rising)
2 cups granulated sugar
2 tablespoons plus ½ teaspoon double-acting baking powder
1¼ teaspoons salt
15 tablespoons (1 stick plus 7 tablespoons) unsalted butter, cut into tablespoons and softened

Raspberry puree:

1 12-ounce bag frozen unsweetened raspberries, thawed
1 teaspoon freshly squeezed lemon juice
⅓ cup granulated sugar

Raspberry neoclassic buttercream:

6 large egg yolks, at room temperature (reserved from the cake)
¾ cup granulated sugar
½ cup light corn syrup
2 cups (4 sticks) unsalted butter, softened and cut into tablespoons
4 to 6 drops red liquid food color
2 tablespoons Framboise (raspberry liqueur) (optional)

Forget-me-nots:

Violet paste food color (see Ingredient Note)
Blue liquid food color
Nonstick vegetable cooking spray
½-inch 5-petaled gum paste cutter (see Ingredient Note)
Silver dragées (see Ingredient Note)

Royal icing:

2 large egg whites
2⅔ cups confectioners' sugar
Moss green paste food color (see Ingredient Note)
Red and yellow liquid food color
Disposable pastry bags (see Ingredient Note)

INGREDIENT NOTE: Glycerine can be purchased at most pharmacies. Paste food color, gum paste cutters, silver dragées, and disposable pastry bags are available at professional baking stores and by mail from Maid of Scandinavia, 3244 Raleigh Avenue, Minneapolis, MN 55416, (800) 328-6722. Write or call for a catalog.

Day 1
Make the rolled fondant:

1. In a 2-cup glass measuring cup, combine 2 tablespoons of the lemon juice with 1 tablespoon of the water. Sprinkle 1 tablespoon of the gelatin over the top of the liquid and let it soften for 3 minutes. Put the glass measuring cup in a small saucepan of simmering water and stir for 2 to 3 minutes or until the gelatin is completely dissolved. Stir in 2 tablespoons of the shortening until melted. Blend in ½ cup of the corn syrup and 1 tablespoon of the glycerine. Remove the measuring cup from the pan of water.

2. Put 8 cups of the confectioners' sugar in a large mixing bowl and make a well in the center of it. Pour the gelatin mixture into the well and stir with a wooden spoon until blended. Vigorously knead the mixture with your hands until smooth. If the mixture seems very dry, add a few drops of water and knead well. If the mixture seems too sticky, knead in more confectioners' sugar. The fondant should be malleable, like modeling clay.

3. Rub one side of a disposable cloth towel with enough shortening to coat it well, and wrap the fondant in it. Wrap the bundle in plastic and put it in an airtight container. Let the fondant "ripen" overnight before using. Make the second batch of fondant with the remaining half of the ingredients, following the instructions.

Make the white chocolate layer cake:

4. Position one rack in the top third and another in the bottom third of the oven and preheat to 350°F. Lightly butter the bottoms and sides of two 10-by-2-inch round cake pans. Line the bottom of each cake pan with a circle of baking parchment or waxed paper. Dust the sides of the pan with flour and tap out the excess.

5. In the top of a double boiler over hot, not simmering, water, melt the white chocolate, stirring constantly. Remove the top part of the double boiler from the bottom and cool the chocolate to tepid.

6. In a medium bowl, lightly stir together the egg whites, ⅓ cup of the milk, and the vanilla.

7. In a large mixing bowl, combine the flour, sugar, baking powder, and salt. Using a hand-held electric mixer set at low speed, mix the dry ingredients for 20 to 30 seconds or until blended. Add the remaining 1 cup of milk and the butter. Continue mixing at low speed for 20 to 30 seconds or until the dry ingredients are moistened. Raise the speed to medium high and beat for 1½ to 2 minutes to aerate and develop the cake's structure. Scrape down the sides of the bowl. Gradually add the egg white mixture in three parts to the batter, beating at the same speed for 20 seconds after each addition. Scrape down and stir in any batter clinging to the sides of the bowl. Add the cooled melted white chocolate and beat for 10 to 15 seconds or until the batter is smooth.

8. Scrape the batter into the prepared pans and smooth the surfaces with a spatula. Bake the layers for 40 to 45 minutes. Halfway through baking, switch each cake layer from one rack to the other for even browning. The cake is done when a cake tester or toothpick inserted into the center of each layer comes out clean and the layers spring back when gently pressed.

9. Cool the cake layers in the pans set on wire racks for 10 minutes. Run a thin knife or spatula around the edges of the cake layers to loosen, and then invert them onto wire racks. Peel off the papers and leave them loosely attached to the bottoms of the layers. Invert the layers onto other racks, so that they are right side up. Cool the layers completely and then wrap them in plastic and let them stand at room temperature overnight or freeze them for up to 1 month.

Make the raspberry puree:

10. In a fine sieve that is suspended over a deep bowl, allow the raspberries to thaw completely. Using a rubber spatula, lightly press the berries to force out the juice. Transfer the raspberry juice to a glass measuring cup. There should be at least ½ cup of juice. Press the crushed raspberries through the sieve into the bowl to remove the seeds. There should be at least ½ cup of raspberry puree.

11. In a high-sided, medium saucepan set over medium heat, boil down the ½ cup of raspberry juice until only 2 tablespoons remain. Stir the reduced raspberry syrup and lemon juice into the ½ cup of raspberry puree. Stir in the sugar. Transfer the raspberry puree to a small bowl, cover with plastic wrap, and refrigerate.

Day 2
Make the raspberry neoclassic buttercream:

12. Remove the raspberry puree from the refrigerator. In a large bowl, using a hand-held electric mixer set at medium-high speed, beat the egg yolks for 3 to 4 minutes, until they form a thin pale-yellow ribbon when the beaters are lifted.

13. In a medium saucepan, combine the sugar and corn syrup. Using a wooden spoon, stir the mixture over medium heat until the sugar dissolves. Continue stirring and bring the mixture to a full rolling boil. Remove the pan from the heat. With the mixer set at medium speed, immediately beat the hot syrup in a thin, steady stream into the yolks. Raise the speed to medium high and continue beating for 5 to 8 minutes or until the mixture is cool and forms a thick pale-yellow ribbon when the beaters are lifted. Reduce the speed to medium and beat in the butter a tablespoon at a time, beating well after each addition, until each piece is incorporated and the buttercream is thick and smooth. Beat in the ½ cup of raspberry puree. Freeze any leftover puree for up to two months. Beat in the red food coloring and the raspberry liqueur, if desired.

Assemble the cake:

14. Unwrap the cake layers and remove the papers from the bottoms of the layers. If necessary, using a long, serrated knife, trim the tops of the cake layers so that they are level. Horizontally slice each cake layer into two equal layers, so that there are four layers. Using a metal cake spatula, spread a small amount of buttercream in the center of a 10-inch cardboard circle and set the bottom layer of

one of the original layers on it. The buttercream will hold the cake in place. Spread 1¼ cups of the buttercream on the layer. Put the second cake layer on top of the filling. Spread 1¼ cups of the buttercream on the second cake layer. Put the third cake layer on top of the filling. Spread 1¼ cups of the buttercream on the third cake layer and top with the fourth cake layer. Press the layer gently into place.

15. Using a serrated knife, trim the top edge of the cake all the way around so that it is slightly beveled. This will prevent a sharp edge from piercing the rolled fondant.

16. Cover the top and sides of the cake with a thin layer of the remaining buttercream. Finish the top of the cake by holding the metal cake spatula at a slight angle and, with several strokes, smooth the raised rim of buttercream around the edge toward the center of the cake until the top is completely smooth. Refrigerate the cake for 20 minutes while preparing the rolled fondant.

Cover the cake with the rolled fondant (Do not wear rings when you work with fondant):

17. Unwrap the two packages of fondant. Reserve a quarter of one of the pieces of fondant for making the forget-me-not flowers. Wrap the reserved piece in a disposable cloth towel that has been rubbed with enough shortening to coat it well, and wrap this in plastic. Knead the two remaining pieces of fondant together into a ball. Continue to knead the fondant until it is malleable enough to roll. Spray a smooth, clean work surface and a large, heavy rolling pin with nonstick vegetable cooking spray. Form the piece of fondant into a flat disk and roll it into an 18-by-¼-inch circle. Lift up and rotate the circle every two or three rolls to ensure that it does not stick. If necessary, respray the work surface. Work quickly to prevent the fondant from drying out. If it is taking more than 3 to 4 minutes to roll out, cover the fondant with three or four pieces of plastic wrap to prevent it from drying out.

18. Remove the cake from the refrigerator. Slip your fist, palm side down, under the fondant, being careful not to stretch or tear it. Lift the fondant onto the cake, covering it as evenly as possible. Using the palm of your hand, smooth the top and the sides of the cake until it is evenly covered and

the fondant is smooth. Use a pizza cutter to trim excess fondant from the bottom edge of the cake. Form the trimmings into a ball and wrap them in plastic.

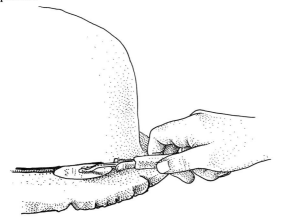

19. Transfer the cake to a serving plate. Using the palms of your hands, roll about ⅔ cup of the remaining fondant scraps into two 16-inch coils that are about ½ inch thick. Wrap the coils around the base of the cake and pinch the ends together with your fingers. Let the cake stand at room temperature in a cool, dry place overnight.

Make the forget-me-nots:

20. Unwrap the reserved piece of fondant. Put it on a fresh piece of plastic wrap and using the tip of a toothpick, put a small amount of the violet paste food color and squeeze a little liquid blue food color on the fondant. With the plastic wrap to protect your fingers from staining from the food colors, knead the colors into the fondant. Add more paste or blue liquid food color if necessary to make the fondant a deep violet-blue color.

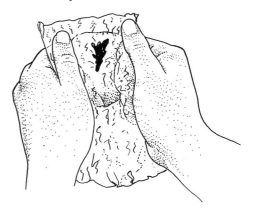

21. Lightly spray a smooth, clean work surface with nonstick vegetable cooking spray. Roll the piece of colored fondant into a 7-by-8-inch rectangle, 1/16 inch thick. Using a ½-inch 5-petaled gum

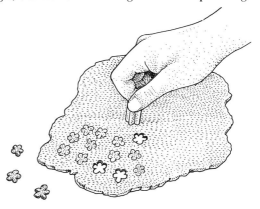

paste cutter, cut out 30 flowers. Using the pointed tip of a chopstick or a knitting needle, widen the flower petals by lightly pressing the center of each one.

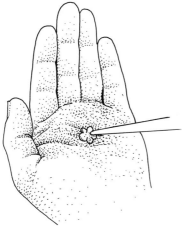

22. One at a time, put the flowers on a piece of soft foam or a clean pot holder. Using the rounded end of a chopstick, crochet needle, or cotton swab, gently press each flower in the center so the petals curve up. Put a silver dragée in the center of each flower. Let the forget-me-nots dry overnight in a cool, dry place.

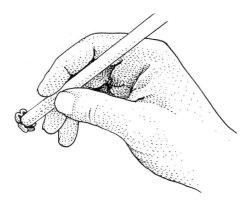

Day 3
Make the royal icing:

23. In a large, grease-free bowl, using a hand-held electric mixer set at low speed, beat the egg whites and confectioners' sugar for 30 to 45 seconds or until the confectioners' sugar is moistened. Increase the speed to medium high and continue

beating for 5 to 8 minutes or until the icing forms stiff glossy peaks when the beaters are lifted. The tips of the peaks should curve slightly. Divide the icing among four small, grease-free bowls. Cover the bowls with damp cloths to prevent the icing from drying out.

24. Reserve one bowl of icing for the white dots. Using the tip of a toothpick, put a small amount of the moss green paste food color into the second bowl of royal icing. Using a small metal cake spatula, stir until the color is evenly blended to create a pale green icing. Squeeze a couple of drops of the red liquid food coloring into the third bowl of icing. Stir until the color is evenly blended to create a pale-pink icing. Squeeze a couple of drops of the yellow liquid food coloring into the fourth bowl of icing. Stir until the color is evenly blended to create a pale-yellow icing. Keep the bowls of icing covered with damp cloths so that the icing does not dry out, and let the icing sit for 2 hours before using. If it darkens a little, add a little white icing to restore it to the correct color.

Decorate the cake:

25. Using the tip of a toothpick, outline an evenly spaced dotted scroll pattern on the top and sides of the cake. Work out your own pattern before you start to mark the cake.

26. Fit a disposable pastry bag with a coupling and a small writing tip (such as Ateco #2). Using a small metal cake spatula, fill the bag with the white icing. Pipe tiny white dots onto the marked outline of the scroll design.

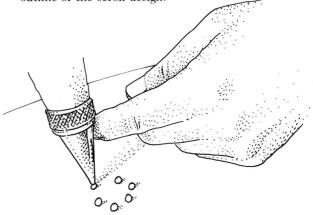

27. Pipe a small dot of the white icing on the back of the forget-me-nots and affix them inside the scrolled areas of the cake. Put 10 forget-me-nots evenly spaced around the bottom edge of the cake.

28. Fit a disposable pastry bag with a coupling and a small writing tip (such as Ateco #1). Using a small metal cake spatula, fill the bag with the green icing. Pipe green stems starting at the base of each forget-me-not.

29. Fit two disposable pastry bags with small writing tips (such as Ateco #2). Using a small metal cake spatula, fill one bag with yellow icing and one bag with pink icing. Pipe tiny 5-petaled flowers on the top and sides of the cake. Store the cake in a cool, dry place, not the refrigerator, and serve it within 24 hours.

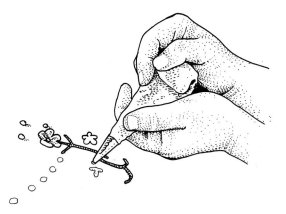

∽ *Charlotte Royale* ∾

Frozen desserts are wonderful for entertaining, in cool weather as well as in warm. They can be made well ahead of the party and served straight from the freezer with no fuss. This elegant charlotte, filled with raspberry mousse and orange-scented chocolate ice cream (an outrageously decadent combination!) is pretty enough for the most sophisticated party. The hazelnut sponge cake, rolled around a delicious raspberry-truffle filling, which handsomely decorates the outside of the charlotte, can be made and frozen for up to a month before assembly. Or, if you prefer, the entire dessert can be made, unmolded, and kept in the freezer for up to a month. Decorate it with whipped cream and

fresh raspberries minutes before serving, if you so desire.

YIELD: 8 servings

DIFFICULTY: ▰▰▰

PREPARATION TIME: Allow 3 days to prepare and assemble this dessert

---

SPECIAL EQUIPMENT: 10½-by-15½-inch jelly-roll pan; 6½-cup charlotte mold; candy thermometer; hair dryer; pastry bag fitted with a star tip (such as Ateco #5); ice cream maker

---

Raspberry truffle filling:

3 tablespoons heavy (whipping) cream
1 tablespoon unsalted butter
3 ounces bittersweet chocolate, finely chopped
1½ tablespoons black raspberry liqueur

Hazelnut sponge cake:

¼ cup plus 2 tablespoons sifted cake flour
¼ cup roasted hazelnuts (for roasting instructions, see page 20)
3 large eggs, at room temperature, separated
6 tablespoons granulated sugar, divided
½ teaspoon vanilla extract
Confectioners' sugar

Chocolate hazelnut orange ice cream:

¼ *cup water*

5 *tablespoons granulated sugar, divided*

6 *ounces bittersweet chocolate, coarsely chopped*

2 *tablespoons unsalted butter*

3 *large egg yolks, at room temperature*

2 *teaspoons finely grated orange zest*

1½ *cups heavy (whipping) cream*

1½ *tablespoons orange liqueur, such as Grand Marnier*

½ *cup roasted hazelnuts, coarsely chopped (for roasting instructions, see page 20)*

Raspberry mousse:

1 *10-ounce package frozen raspberries in light syrup, thawed and syrup reserved*

7 *tablespoons granulated sugar, divided*

4 *large egg yolks, at room temperature*

¼ *cup water*

⅔ *cup heavy (whipping) cream*

Red food coloring (optional)

Decoration (*optional*):

¾ *cup heavy (whipping) cream*

8 *fresh raspberries or hazelnuts*

Day 1
Make the raspberry truffle filling:

1. In a small saucepan, combine the cream and butter. Over medium-low heat, slowly heat the mixture until tiny bubbles form around the sides of the pan. Remove the pan from the heat. Add the chocolate to the cream and let the mixture stand 1 to 2 minutes. Whisk until smooth. Stir in the raspberry liqueur. Cover the surface of the truffle filling with plastic wrap and let it cool to room temperature.

Make the hazelnut sponge cake:

2. Position a rack in the center of the oven and preheat to 350°F. Line a 10½-by-15½-inch jelly-roll pan with aluminum foil, leaving a 2-inch overhang on the short ends. Fold the overhang underneath the pan. Butter the bottom of the foil-lined pan. Do not butter the sides of the pan. Lightly dust the bottom of the pan with flour and tap out the excess.

3. In a food processor fitted with the metal chopping blade, combine the flour and hazelnuts. Process for 15 to 20 seconds or until the mixture is powdery. Transfer the flour-nut mixture to a small bowl.

4. In a large bowl, using a hand-held electric mixer set at medium-high speed, beat the egg yolks with 3 tablespoons of the sugar and the vanilla for 6 to 8 minutes or until the mixture forms a thick, very pale, almost white ribbon when the beaters are lifted. Beat in the vanilla.

5. In a large, grease-free bowl, using a hand-held electric mixer set at low speed, beat the egg whites until frothy. Gradually increase the speed to medium high and continue to beat the whites until they start to form soft peaks. Slowly add the remaining 3 tablespoons of sugar and continue beating until the whites form stiff, shiny peaks.

6. Scrape the beaten egg yolks on top of the beaten egg whites. Sprinkle half of the flour-nut mixture over the egg mixture and gently fold it in. Fold in the remaining flour-nut mixture. Scrape the batter into the prepared pan and spread evenly. Bake for 10 to 15 minutes or until lightly browned and the center of the cake springs back when gently pressed.

7. While the sponge cake is baking, sprinkle a clean dish towel (at least 11½ inches by 16½ inches) heavily with confectioners' sugar. When the sponge cake has finished baking, release the sides of the cake with a metal spatula and immediately turn the cake out onto the towel. Carefully peel off the aluminum foil. Using the towel as a guide and beginning at a long end, roll the sponge cake lengthwise into a tight cylinder. Cool the rolled sponge cake on a wire rack.

8. Unroll the sponge cake carefully but do not flatten. Using a metal cake spatula, spread the truffle filling evenly over the cake. Roll the cake into a tight cylinder again. Wrap the roll in plastic and then in aluminum foil. Freeze the roll overnight or up to 1 month.

Make the chocolate hazelnut orange ice cream:

9. In a small saucepan, combine the water and 2½ tablespoons of the sugar. Cook over medium heat, stirring with a wooden spoon until the sugar dissolves. Increase the heat to high and bring the syrup to a boil. Remove the pan from the heat and add the chocolate and butter. Cover the saucepan with a lid. Let the mixture stand for 3 to 4 minutes. Remove the lid and whisk until smooth.

10. In a medium bowl, using a hand-held electric mixer set at medium-high speed, beat the egg yolks with the remaining 2½ tablespoons of sugar and the orange zest for 6 to 8 minutes or until a thick, very pale, almost white ribbon forms when the beaters are lifted. Beat in the chocolate mixture.

11. In a medium saucepan over medium heat, heat the cream until tiny bubbles start to form around the edges of the pan. Remove the pan from the heat. Slowly beat the hot cream into the egg yolk-chocolate mixture. Blend the orange liqueur into the custard.

12. Put the bowl containing the custard over a bowl of ice water. Stir frequently for 10 to 15 minutes or until cold. Pour the custard into an ice cream maker, add the chopped hazelnuts, and follow the manufacturer's instructions for making ice cream. Freeze the ice cream for 8 hours or overnight. Let the ice cream soften slightly before assembling the charlotte.

Day 2
Assemble the charlotte:

13. Remove the hazelnut jelly roll from the freezer. Using a serrated knife and with a sawing motion, cut the roll into ¼-inch slices. To prevent smearing, keep the knife clean by wiping it on a damp paper towel after cutting each slice. If the roll starts to soften, return it to the freezer until firm.

14. Line the bottom of a 6½-cup charlotte mold with eight jelly-roll slices placed tightly around the bottom edge of the mold and one in the center. Line the sides of the mold with two rows of jelly-roll slices placed tightly together. Use leftover slices, separating the sponge cake from the filling, to fill in any small gaps.

15. Spread the ice cream in an even layer over the jelly-roll slices. Put the mold in the freezer while preparing the raspberry mousse.

Make the raspberry mousse:

16. Press the raspberries with the juice through a fine sieve to remove the seeds. Put the puree in a medium, high-sided saucepan. Stir in 2 tablespoons of the sugar. Cook the mixture over medium-low heat, stirring constantly, until the sugar dissolves. Increase the heat to medium and bring the raspberries to a boil. Continue to boil the raspberries for 10 to 15 minutes or until they reduce to ½ cup. Transfer the raspberries to a medium bowl and set the bowl over a bowl of ice water. Stir frequently for 5 to 10 minutes or until cold. Remove the raspberries from the bowl of ice water.

17. In a medium bowl, using a hand-held electric mixer set at medium-high speed, beat the egg yolks for 6 to 8 minutes or until a thick, very pale, almost white ribbon forms when the beaters are lifted.

18. In a small saucepan, combine the water and the remaining 5 tablespoons of sugar. Cook over medium-low heat, stirring constantly with a wooden spoon, until the sugar dissolves. Increase the heat to high and bring the syrup to a boil. Wipe down the sides of the pan with a clean pastry brush to dissolve any sugar crystals. Attach a candy thermometer to the pan and continue cooking the syrup for 4 to 5 minutes or until the thermometer registers 240°F (soft-ball stage). Immediately pour the hot syrup in a thin, steady stream into the egg yolks while beating constantly with a hand-held electric mixer set at medium speed. Continue beating for 5 to 8 minutes or until the mixture is cool and thick. Beat in the raspberry puree. The mixture will become quite thin.

19. In a large bowl, using a hand-held electric mixer set at medium-high speed, beat the cream until stiff peaks start to form. Fold the cream into the egg yolk raspberry mixture. Add a drop of red food coloring if you desire more vibrant color. Pour the raspberry mousse into the prepared charlotte mold. Cover the top of the mold tightly with plastic wrap and freeze for 8 hours or overnight.

Day 3
Unmold the charlotte:

20. Invert the charlotte mold onto a serving plate. With a portable hair dryer set on high and held about ⅛ inch from the mold, slowly circle the sides and top of the mold several times to warm it and help release the mold. Hold the mold against the plate and with a sharp downward motion, release the charlotte from the mold. If it does not release, repeat warming the mold with the hair dryer. Keep the unmolded charlotte in the freezer if not serving immediately.

Decorate the charlotte (*optional*):

21. In a large bowl, using a hand-held electric mixer set at medium speed, beat the heavy cream until it starts to form stiff peaks. Keep the whipped cream refrigerated until ready to use.

22. Just before serving, fill a pastry bag fitted with a star tip (such as Ateco #5) with the whipped cream. Pipe 8 rosettes evenly spaced on the top edge of the charlotte. Put a fresh raspberry or hazelnut on top of each rosette. Pipe a shell border around the base of the charlotte.

⁓ *Chocolate Valentine Box* ⁓

Swiss-trained pastry chef Hans Bussinger created this enchanting box for a Valentine's Day issue of the magazine. We filled it with twice-dipped strawberries, but you could tuck any tiny treat inside for a gift of love any time of year. It would also be a delightful centerpiece for a tea table or dessert party. Make it up to a month beforehand and store it in an airtight container in a cool, dry place.

YIELD: 1 chocolate box

DIFFICULTY: ■■■

PREPARATION TIME: 5 hours (allow time for the white chocolate and milk chocolate plastics to set overnight)

SPECIAL EQUIPMENT: small paper cone (for instructions on making a paper cone, see page 187)

White chocolate plastic:

4 ounces Swiss white chocolate, coarsely chopped
2 tablespoons light corn syrup, at room temperature

Milk chocolate plastic:

1 ounce Swiss milk chocolate, coarsely chopped
1 tablespoon light corn syrup, at room temperature

Milk chocolate hearts:

1¼ pounds milk chocolate couverture, tempered (for tempering instructions, see page 22)

Chocolate box:

2½ pounds bittersweet couverture chocolate, tempered
1¼ pounds white chocolate couverture, tempered
1½ cups medium strawberries, washed and dried, at room temperature

Day 1
Make the white chocolate plastic:

1. In the top of a double boiler over 125°F water, melt the white chocolate. (The water should touch the bottom of the top part of the double boiler.) Stir the chocolate constantly until smooth. Remove the pan from the heat and transfer the chocolate to a bowl. Cool 10 to 15 minutes or until the chocolate is at room temperature.

2. Using a rubber spatula, blend in the corn syrup and mix for 5 to 10 seconds or until the mixture thickens and starts to lose its shine. Form the "plastic" into a ball and wrap it in plastic wrap. Let the white chocolate plastic set overnight at room temperature.

Make the milk chocolate plastic:

3. In the top of a double boiler over 125°F water, melt the milk chocolate. (The water should touch the bottom of the top part of the double boiler.) Stir the chocolate frequently until smooth. Remove the pan from the heat and transfer the chocolate to a bowl. Cool 5 to 10 minutes or until the chocolate is room temperature.

4. Using a rubber spatula, blend in the corn syrup and mix for 5 to 10 seconds or until the mixture thickens and starts to lose its shine. Form the "plastic" into a ball and wrap it in plastic wrap. Let it set overnight at room temperature.

Day 2
Make the white chocolate roses:

5. Unwrap the white chocolate plastic and knead it on a smooth work surface, such as marble or Formica, until soft and smooth. Divide it in half and roll it into two 7- to 8-inch long logs that are about ¾ inch thick. Cut a 3-inch piece from one of the logs and form it into a ball. Form the ball into a cone. Cut the remaining logs into twenty-one or more ½-inch slices that will become the rose petals.

6. Put a large piece of plastic wrap on the work surface. Arrange the slices for the rose petals 2 inches apart on the plastic. Put a 3-inch square of plastic wrap on top of one slice. Use your thumb to press the top section of the slice to flatten and elongate it so that it resembles a petal. The bottom edge should be as thick as it was when you started. Shape the remaining slices into petals in the same manner.

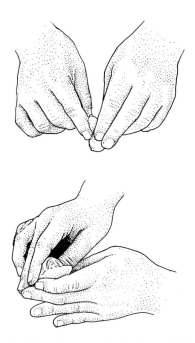

8. Cup both hands around the base of the rose and roll gently. The rolling action will open up the petals of the rose slightly, making it appear more real. Separate the rose from the cone by pinching the base of the rose with your fingers. Using your thumb, gently roll the tops of the rose petals back to open them up a little. Make 2 more roses using the same method. Let the roses set at room temperature.

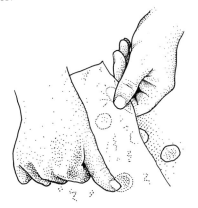

7. Starting at the top of the cone, wrap the thick end of one of the petals around it. Press firmly but gently so that the petal adheres to the cone. Continue adding 6 more petals, overlapping each one slightly, to make a rose.

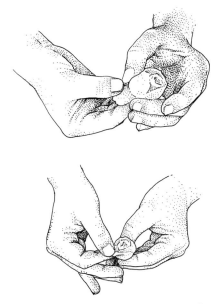

(continued)

Make the milk chocolate leaves:

9.   Unwrap the milk chocolate plastic and knead it on a smooth work surface until it is soft and smooth. Roll it into a 6- to 7-inch long log that is about ½ inch thick. Cut the log into ¼-inch slices. Using your thumb and forefinger, gently form each slice into an oval.

10.   Put a piece of plastic wrap on the work surface. Arrange the ovals 2 inches apart on the plastic. Put a 3-inch square of plastic wrap on top of an oval and using your forefinger, press the oval into a 1½-inch long leaf. Shape the remaining leaves in the same way. Remove the plastic. With the tip of a small knife, score a vein pattern on each leaf. Twist the tip and pinch the stem end of each to form a curved leaf. Let the leaves set at room temperature.

Make the milk chocolate hearts:

11.   Trace the heart pattern given on page 186. Put a large piece of baking parchment on the work surface. Pour the tempered milk chocolate onto the center of the paper. Using a clean, dry, offset metal cake spatula, spread the chocolate into a 9-inch square that is ¼ inch thick. Lift two diagonally opposite corners of the paper and tap the paper on the work surface to remove any air bubbles from the chocolate. Slide a flat baking sheet underneath the paper. Refrigerate the chocolate square for 2 to 4 minutes or until the chocolate starts to set. (Do not overchill the chocolate, or it will be too difficult to cut.)

12.   With a small, sharp knife, cut out 2 chocolate hearts using the heart pattern as a guide. Let the hearts set completely at room temperature on the baking parchment until ready to use.

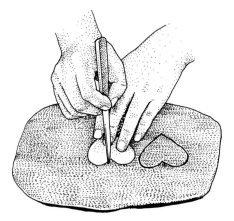

Make the chocolate box:

13.   Put a large sheet of baking parchment on the work surface. Pour approximately two thirds of the chocolate onto the center of the paper. (Keep the remaining tempered chocolate warm on the heating pad—see tempering instructions.) Using a clean, dry, offset metal cake spatula, spread the chocolate into a 12-by-16-inch rectangle that is ⅛ inch thick. Lift two diagonally opposite corners of the paper and tap it on the work surface to remove any air bubbles from the chocolate. Slide a large, flat

baking sheet or piece of cardboard underneath the paper. Refrigerate the chocolate rectangle for 4 to 6 minutes or until it begins to set. (Do not overchill the chocolate, or it will be difficult to cut.)

14. Invert the chocolate rectangle onto the work surface and peel off the paper. Using a ruler and a sharp knife, trim the edges of the rectangle so they are straight. Mark two 7-inch squares to form the base and the lid of the box. Mark four 6-by-1¼-inch strips to form the sides of the box. Cut out the chocolate squares and strips with the knife, reserving trimmings for a later use.

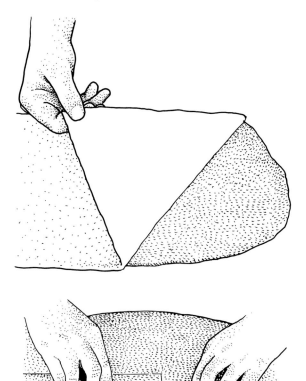

Assemble the chocolate box:

15. Dip the bottom edge and the two short ends of one of the chocolate strips into the reserved tempered bittersweet chocolate. Set the strip, bottom edge down, ¾ inch in from the edge of one of

the 7-inch squares, which will be the base of the box. Hold the strip in place for a few moments until the tempered chocolate begins to set and glues one side of the box into place. Set the base of the box on a baking sheet or piece of cardboard. Glue the remaining three sides of the box in place with tempered chocolate, as well. Refrigerate the box for 2 to 3 minutes to set the chocolate.

16. With a clean, dry pastry brush, paint the inside and outside of the box with tempered chocolate, using long, sweeping strokes. Paint the top of the box lid in the same manner and then create a

slightly textured pattern on it by dabbing it with the brush. Keep the tempered chocolate warm, and refrigerate the box and its lid for 2 to 3 minutes to set the chocolate.

(continued)

Decorate the box lid:

17. Remove the hearts from the paper. Save the milk chocolate trimmings for another use. Using a small amount of the dark tempered chocolate, glue the hearts to the top of the box lid. Glue the 3 roses to the top right-hand corner of the lid. Glue 4 of the most attractive leaves around the base of the roses. Continue to keep the dark tempered chocolate warm.

18. Fill a small paper cone with some of the white chocolate and pipe a filigree pattern on the box lid and on the bottom edge of the box. Pipe a delicate white chocolate border around the edges of the hearts. Refrigerate the box for 2 to 3 minutes to set the white chocolate.

Make the chocolate-dipped strawberries:

19. Line a baking sheet with aluminum foil. Dip each strawberry in the tempered white chocolate, covering three quarters of the berry. Put the dipped strawberry on the foil-lined baking sheet. When all are dipped, refrigerate them for 3 to 5 minutes to set the white chocolate.

20. Line the baking sheet with more aluminum foil. Dip the strawberries a second time in the tempered dark chocolate, leaving a narrow border of white chocolate visible on each berry. Refrigerate the strawberries on the foil-lined baking sheet for 3 to 5 minutes to set the dark chocolate.

21. Line two baking sheets with aluminum foil. Pour the left over white and dark tempered chocolate onto separate foil-lined baking sheets and spread evenly. Refrigerate the chocolate for 5 to 10 minutes or until firm. Let the chocolate stand at room temperature for 30 minutes. Break the chocolate into small pieces and store to use again in other candy-making or baking projects.

22. Fill the chocolate Valentine box with the chocolate-dipped strawberries. The strawberries will keep for up to 5 hours.

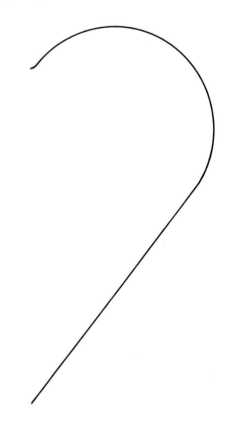

How to Make a Paper Cone

1. Cut an 15-by-18-inch rectangle of baking parchment and fold it diagonally along the dotted line.

2. Using a long, sharp knife, slit the paper along the fold to form two triangles, each with two pointed corners and one snipped corner.

3. Place the triangle on a work surface with the long side at the top and the snipped corner at the upper right.

4. Fold the snipped corner into a loose curl, forming a point at A.

5. Continue rolling the curl into a cone, bringing B up so that it protrudes above the front rim of the cone and a sharp point forms at the bottom.

6. Fold B over the rim of the cone to secure the bottom point.

7. Fill the cone three-fourths full and press the front of the rim against the back so that the cone is closed and the filling is pressed down toward the point.

8. Fold C down over the front of the cone.

9. Fold D and E to the center.

10. Fold down the new point.

11. Fold down the top of the cone as far as it will go.

12. Use your forefinger to guide the point of the cone and your thumb to hold the fold. If desired, use your other hand to steady your piping hand.

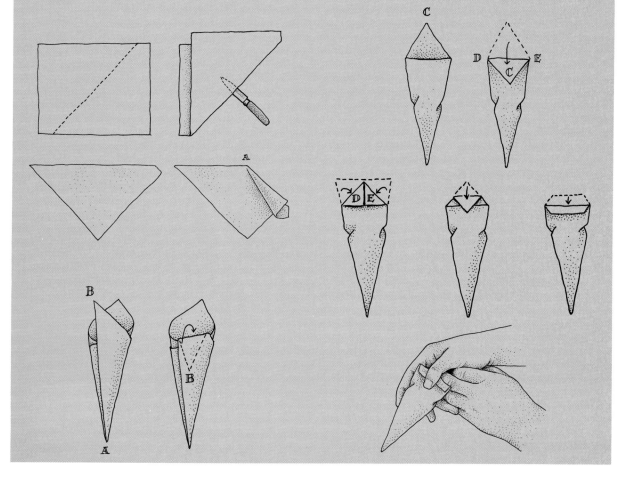

Two-Tone Cutout Cookies

Our editor, Barbara Albright, developed these cookies for Christmas one year, although there is no reason why you shouldn't make them other times as well. The cookies are mirror images of each other; one with insets of dark cookie dough, the other with insets of white cookie dough. When Barbara made the cookies, she used large, star cookie cutters and small aspic cutters shaped like diamonds, ovals, stars, and crescents. You might decide to use larger or smaller cookie cutters, in which case you will have to adjust the baking time accordingly. Deduct or add a minute or two to the suggested time and, more importantly, watch for browning to detect when the cookies are done.

YIELD: Approximately 25 3-inch cookies, but yield varies depending on the size of the cookies

DIFFICULTY: ◣◼

PREPARATION TIME: 2 hours plus chilling, baking, and cooling times

SPECIAL EQUIPMENT: large cookie cutters; aspic cutters or smaller-sized cookie cutters

4½ cups all-purpose flour
¼ teaspoon salt
1½ cups (3 sticks) unsalted butter, softened
¾ cup granulated sugar
¼ cup confectioners' sugar
1 large egg, lightly beaten
2 teaspoons vanilla extract
2 ounces unsweetened chocolate, melted and cooled

Make the doughs:

1. In a large bowl, stir together the flour and salt. In another large bowl, using a hand-held electric mixer set at medium-high speed, beat together the butter and the two sugars for 1 to 2 minutes or until combined. Add the egg and vanilla and beat 1 to 2 minutes or until light. Beat in the flour mixture until thoroughly mixed.

2. Divide the dough in half. Wrap one half of the dough in plastic. Beat the melted chocolate into the remaining dough until thoroughly combined, and wrap the dough in plastic. Refrigerate both doughs for at least 2 hours.

Make the cookies:

3. Position a rack in the center of the oven and preheat to 350°F. Cover two flat baking sheets with aluminum foil and dust lightly with flour. Break off one third of each kind of dough. Refrigerate the remaining dough until ready to use. If the dough is hard, let it soften for 20 to 30 minutes. Or, soften

the dough in the microwave using the defrost setting for 20 to 30 seconds until it is soft enough to roll. You can also work the dough with your hands. On the baking sheets, using a lightly floured rolling pin, roll each dough to about 3/16 inch thickness.

4. Using large cookie cutters of any shape you choose, cut out the cookies. Using aspic cutters or smaller-sized cutters, cut out shapes from the cookies. Be sure you cut out the same number of the same shapes from both kinds of cookies, light and dark. Pick up the tiny shapes of dough with a small offset spatula or your fingers and transfer them to the cookies of the opposing color. Insert the proper shape into the appropriately shaped cutout,

so that the dark cookies are decorated with white shapes and vice versa. If the doughs become too soft, refrigerate them on their sheets for a few minutes to make them easier to work with. Gather together the leftover scraps of dough, wrap in plastic, and refrigerate.

5. Bake the cookies, one sheet at a time, for 8 to 10 minutes or until the cookies start to brown slightly. Put the baking sheet on a wire rack and cool for about 5 minutes. Using a metal spatula, carefully transfer the cookies to a wire rack to cool completely. Repeat cookie making and baking with the remaining dough.

∾ White Chocolate Citrus Roulade ∾

Adrift in a swirl of white chocolate curls, this white chocolate genoise roll, snugly wrapped around a sweet ganache tempered with refreshing hints of lemon and orange, makes a smashing winter dessert—which tastes awfully good in the summer, too. The curls are easy to make if the chocolate is correctly softened: too firm, and the curls will be tight corkscrews; too soft, and the chocolate will barely curl.

YIELD: 12 servings

DIFFICULTY: ▪▪▪

PREPARATION TIME: 1½ hours plus baking, cooling, and chilling times

White chocolate citrus ganache:

2¼ cups heavy (whipping) cream
3 ¾-by-2-inch strips lemon zest
3 ¾-by-2-inch strips orange zest
10 ounces Swiss white chocolate, coarsely chopped

Citrus sugar syrup:

½ cup freshly squeezed orange juice
1 tablespoon freshly squeezed lemon juice
3 tablespoons granulated sugar
1 tablespoon Grand Marnier

(ingredients continued)

White chocolate genoise:

3 ounces Swiss white chocolate, coarsely chopped
2 tablespoons hot water
½ cup plus 2 tablespoons sifted cake flour (not self-rising)
1 tablespoon cornstarch
⅓ cup plus 3 tablespoons granulated sugar, divided
5 large eggs
A pinch of salt
1 teaspoon vanilla extract

White chocolate curls:

1 4-ounce chunk white chocolate, at least ¾ inch thick

Make the white chocolate citrus ganache:

1. In a medium, nonaluminum saucepan, combine the cream and zests. Over medium-low heat, slowly heat the mixture until tiny bubbles form around the edge of the pan. Remove the pan from the heat and let the zests infuse the cream for 30 minutes. Gently reheat the mixture until tiny bubbles form around the edge of the pan. Take the pan off the heat and strain into a 1-quart measuring cup.

2. In a food processor fitted with the metal chopping blade, pulse the white chocolate for 10 to 15 seconds or until finely chopped. With the machine running, pour the hot cream mixture through the feed tube of the food processor. Process for 10 to 15 seconds or until the mixture is smooth. Scrape the ganache into a medium bowl and cover the surface with plastic wrap. Refrigerate the ganache for at least 3 hours or overnight.

Make the citrus sugar syrup:

3. In a small saucepan, combine the juices and sugar. Cook over medium heat, stirring constantly, until the sugar dissolves. Increase the heat to high and bring the syrup to a simmer. Remove the pan from the heat and let the syrup cool to room temperature. Stir in the Grand Marnier.

Make the white chocolate genoise:

4. Position a rack in the center of the oven and preheat to 350°F. Line the bottom of a 10½-by-15½-inch jelly-roll pan with aluminum foil, leaving a 2-inch overhang on the short ends. Fold the overhang underneath the pan. Butter the aluminum foil and the sides of the pan. Lightly dust the bottom and the sides of the pan with sifted cake flour and tap out the excess.

5. In the top of a double boiler over hot, not simmering, water, melt the white chocolate, stirring constantly, until smooth. Remove the top part of the double boiler from the bottom.

6. Put the 2 tablespoons of hot water in a medium bowl. Slowly whisk in the melted chocolate until smooth, stirring constantly. Let the mixture cool until tepid.

7. Stir together the cake flour, cornstarch, and 1 tablespoon of the sugar. Sift the mixture onto a sheet of waxed paper.

8. In a heatproof bowl, whisk the eggs until the yolks and whites are blended. While continuing to whisk, add the remaining ⅓ cup plus 2 tablespoons of sugar in a steady stream. Add the salt. Set the bowl over a pot of hot, not simmering, water so that the bottom of the bowl touches the water. Continue whisking the egg mixture for 3 to 4 minutes or until the sugar crystals have dissolved and the mixture is hot to the touch (120°F). Remove the bowl from the hot water.

9. Using a hand-held electric mixer set at medium-high speed, beat the egg mixture for 5 to 7 minutes or until it has tripled in volume, is a pale

yellow, and forms a thick ribbon when the beaters are lifted. Beat in the vanilla. Sift one third of the flour mixture over the batter. Fold in the remaining flour in two additions. Remove 1 cup of the batter and carefully fold it into the chocolate. Gently fold this mixture back into the batter. Scrape the batter into the prepared pan and spread it evenly with a spatula. Tap the pan on a flat work surface to release any large air bubbles.

10. Bake the genoise for 15 to 17 minutes or until the center of the cake springs back when gently pressed. Cool the genoise in the pan on a wire rack for 10 minutes. Using the aluminum foil ends as handles, transfer the cake to a large wire rack. Let the cake cool completely. Cover the genoise with an inverted baking sheet and invert the cake. Gently peel off the aluminum foil. Cover the genoise with a new piece of aluminum foil and top the foil with an inverted baking sheet. Invert the genoise so that it is right side up.

Assemble the roulade:

11. Use a pastry brush to paint the citrus-sugar syrup evenly over the top of the genoise.

12. Transfer 1 cup of the chilled ganache to a medium bowl. Cover and refrigerate.

13. Using a hand-held electric mixer set at medium speed, beat the remaining ganache for 45 to 75 seconds or until it starts to form soft peaks. Do not overbeat, or the ganache will become too stiff and the texture will be grainy.

14. Using a metal cake spatula, quickly spread the whipped ganache in an even layer over the top of the genoise. Using the aluminum foil as a guide, roll the roulade, starting at one of the two long sides, into a tight cylinder. Wrap the roulade in the foil. Twist the ends of the foil to secure the round shape of the roulade. Refrigerate the roulade for 1 to 2 hours or until firm.

Decorate the roulade:

15. Unwrap the chilled roulade and put it seam side down on a rectangular serving dish. Cover the border of the dish with strips of waxed paper to keep the plate clean while decorating the roulade.

16. Using a hand-held electric mixer set at medium speed, beat the reserved ganache for 10 to 45 seconds or until it starts to form soft peaks. Again, do not overbeat the ganache.

17. Using a metal cake spatula, frost the roulade with a smooth coating of ganache.

18. Warm the chunk of white chocolate by putting it in the microwave for 25 seconds at medium (50 percent) power or until it starts to soften. Or, warm the chocolate by putting it about 6 inches from a lamp for 5 to 10 minutes, turning it every couple of minutes until it starts to soften.

19. Grip the chunk of white chocolate with a paper towel, so that your hand does not melt it. Use a vegetable peeler to scrape the long edge of the chocolate chunk in a downward motion and form loose curls. As you make the curls, let them fall onto the roulade. Using tweezers or a toothpick, pick up any curls that don't adhere and gently press them onto the roulade so that the top and sides are completely covered. Remove the waxed paper strips and refrigerate the roulade for 20 minutes before serving.

John Paul Endress

Cile's Daisy Chocolate Wedding Cake

When you want a deeply delicious chocolate wedding cake covered with sparkling white frosting, consider this extravaganza from cake decorator Cile Bellefleur-Burbidge. The glorious tumble of brightly colored daisies and grape clusters takes several days to make, but a bride fortunate enough to find a friend to make it will be assured of a cake her guests will talk about long after the rice is tossed. The chocolate cake layers can be baked well ahead of time, as they will keep in the freezer for 2 months if well wrapped in plastic. The classic royal icing used to form the daisies and clusters can be made up to 3 weeks ahead of time and stored at room temperature in a perfectly clean glass jar (no grease!) covered with a piece of waxed paper and a screw-on lid. The basic frosting will keep for 2 weeks if stored at room temperature in an airtight container.

YIELD: 75 servings

DIFFICULTY: ▬▬▬

PREPARATION TIME: Allow 3 days to prepare this cake

SPECIAL EQUIPMENT: stand-up electric mixer; 5 new pastry bags; decorator couplings and tips (such as Ateco #61, #60, #59, #4, #68, #20, #22); several #7 rose nails; 25 egg cartons; 4-inch plastic-foam ball; pastry comb; round wooden toothpicks; 10 plastic straws; wire cutters

---

Royal icing (You will need three times the amount of the royal icing ingredients to make the flowers, grape clusters, and leaves for this two-tiered cake. The following icing must be made three times. You will need at least three new pastry bags for piping the royal icing. Do not use the same pastry bags for the basic frosting):

5 cups confectioners' sugar, divided
5 tablespoons fine meringue powder (see Ingredient Note)
½ teaspoon cream of tartar
½ cup less 1 tablespoon water
Few drops clear flavoring, such as mint, vanilla, or almond

Daisies and leaves:

> *Yellow, pink, and green paste food color (see Ingredient Note)*
> *¼ cup granulated sugar*
> *1 teaspoon water*

Chocolate cake (You will need three times the amount of the chocolate cake layer ingredients to make this two-tiered cake. The following batter must be made three times to make three 8-inch and three 12-inch cake layers):

> *2 cups all-purpose flour*
> *⅔ cup unsweetened nonalkalized cocoa powder*
> *1 teaspoon baking soda*
> *¾ teaspoon double-acting baking powder*
> *¼ teaspoon salt*
> *8 tablespoons (1 stick) unsalted butter, softened*
> *¼ cup solid vegetable shortening*
> *2 cups granulated sugar*
> *3 large eggs, at room temperature*
> *2 teaspoons vanilla extract*
> *1¼ cups milk, at room temperature*

Basic frosting (You will need to make five times the amount of the basic frosting to ice this two-tiered cake, which means that the following frosting must be made five times. To pipe the frosting, you'll need at least two new pastry bags. Do not use the same pastry bags for the royal icing):

> *6 cups sifted confectioners' sugar, divided*
> *1 cup solid vegetable shortening*
> *⅓ cup water*
> *½ teaspoon salt*
> *½ to 1 teaspoon clear flavoring, such as almond, vanilla, or*
>   *lemon*

INGREDIENT NOTE: Meringue powder, paste food colors, disposable pastry bags, decorating tips, and rose nails are available in professional cake-decorating stores, many gourmet cookware shops, and by mail. (See mail order information at the back of the book.)

Day 1
Make the royal icing:

1. In a large, grease-free bowl of a stand-up electric mixer, combine 4½ cups of the confectioners' sugar, the meringue powder, cream of tartar, water, and flavoring. Mix at low speed for 1 to 2 minutes or until creamy. Using a rubber spatula, scrape the bottom and sides of the bowl. Add the remaining ½ cup of confectioners' sugar and mix thoroughly. Increase the speed to high and continue mixing for 4 or 5 minutes or until the icing is stiff and creamy.

2. Remove the bowl from the mixer and immediately cover the bowl with a damp cloth to prevent the icing from drying out. Make two more batches of the royal icing, using the same formula.

Make the large colored daisies:

3. Tear off four strips of waxed paper, each one 2 inches wide. Fold the strips in half and cut on the crease. Then, with all the halved strips held together, fold the strips in thirds and cut on the creases with scissors. The resulting squares should measure 2 inches by 2 inches. Holding a stack of squares, cut a 1-inch slit from the midpoint of one side into the center of the squares. Use more waxed paper to make more squares until you have 75 of them.

4. Put ½ cup of royal icing into each of three small bowls. Using the tip of a toothpick, put a small amount of the yellow paste food color into the

first bowl of icing. Do not blend in the color completely; the icing should be streaked. Put a small amount of pink paste food color in the second bowl of icing. Mix in the color in the same manner. Do not color the third bowl of icing. Cover the bowls of royal icing with damp towels to prevent it from drying out.

5. Fit a pastry bag with a coupling and a curved rose tip (such as Ateco #61). Using a small metal cake spatula, fill the bag alternately with small, equal amounts of the yellow, white, and pink royal icing, in that order.

6. Pipe a small dot of icing on a #7 rose nail. Affix one of the waxed paper squares to the nail, with the slit in the twelve o'clock position. Holding

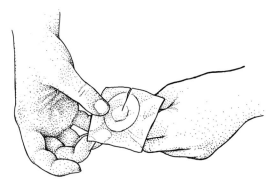

the pastry bag at a 25° angle, put the widest part of the tip at the center of the nail. Apply pressure and move the tip in an upward, rounded motion to the edge of the nail and then bring it back down. As you come down, stop squeezing at the center of the nail and the icing will break. Pipe 4 more petals in

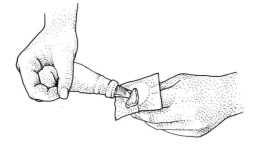

the same way, leaving an empty space on the paper square about the size of another petal. Each petal should measure approximately 1¼ inches long. If icing collects in the center of the flower, you are applying too much pressure. Pipe a small dot of icing over the empty space and remove the paper from the nail. Using the slit, overlap the paper so that the petals meet and the paper forms a shallow

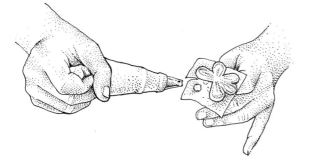

cup with the daisy inside. Gently press against the dot of icing to make the paper stick. You now have a cupped daisy. Put the daisy in the grooves of an inverted egg carton. Continue to pipe 59 more large daisies. Let the daisies stand in a warm, dry place for 24 hours. Color more icing and fill the pastry bag as necessary.

Make the large white daisies:

7. Fit a pastry bag with a coupling and a curved

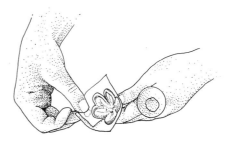

rose tip (such as Ateco #61) and fill the bag with the white royal icing. Pipe 15 large white daisies as explained in step 6. Put the daisies in the grooves of inverted egg cartons to dry.

Make the medium colored daisies:

8. Cut 30 1½-inch waxed paper squares using the method explained in step 3. Prepare yellow, pink, and white royal icing in three bowls as explained in step 4. Fit a pastry bag with a coupling and a curved rose tip (such as Ateco #60 or #61) and fill with the colored royal icing as explained in step 5. Make 50 medium daisies as explained in step 6 with petals that are approximately ¾ inch long. Put the daisies in the grooves of inverted egg cartons to dry.

Make the small white daisies:

9. Cut 30 1½-inch waxed paper squares as explained in step 3. Fit a pastry bag with a coupling and a curved rose tip (such as Ateco #59) and fill with white royal icing. Make 30 small white daisies as explained in step 6. Pipe only 4 petals instead of 5 and make each petal only ¼ inch long. Set them on a baking sheet to dry.

Make the small and large grape clusters:

10. On a piece of heavy paper, draw a line ¼ inch from the top across the width of the paper. Draw a second line ¾ inch from the first line. Draw a third line ¼ inch from the second line. Continue drawing lines at intervals alternating between ¾ and ¼ inch until the end of the paper is reached. Lay a sheet of waxed paper over the piece of lined paper.

(continued)

11. Fit a pastry bag with a coupling and a plain tip (such as Ateco #4) and fill with white royal icing. To make the small clusters, hold the bag at a 45° angle over the top of the first ¾-inch-wide space. Apply pressure to make a small rounded mound. Release the pressure and pull back. Make a second mound to the left; release the pressure and pull back. Make a third mound to the right of the first and a fourth between the second and third. Pipe seven more mounds back and forth in the same pattern until you have a cluster. Continue to pipe more clusters across the width of the paper.

12. To make slightly larger grape clusters, pipe slightly larger mounds and fill in the 1-inch space created by combining the ¾-inch and ¼-inch spaces on the paper.

13. Continue to make grape clusters, alternating rows of smaller and larger clusters, until you have made 30 small grape clusters and 24 large ones. Let the grape clusters dry overnight until firm.

Make the leaves:

14. Put ½ cup of the royal icing in a small bowl. Using the tip of a toothpick, add a small amount of the green paste food color to the icing, and mix just until blended. Fit a pastry bag with a coupling and a medium leaf tip (such as Ateco #68) and fill with the green royal icing. Put a sheet of waxed paper on a baking sheet. Holding the pastry bag at a 45° angle with the tip touching the paper, apply pressure and draw out to 1¾ inches. Stop squeezing just before pulling away to make a point. Make 50 leaves. Color additional icing and refill the pastry bag as necessary. Let the leaves dry overnight.

Day 2
Finish the daisies:

15. Peel off the waxed paper from the large and medium colored daisies. Put the granulated sugar in a small bowl. Fit a pastry bag with a coupling and a small plain tip (such as Ateco #4) and fill with white royal icing. Pipe a small mound of icing in the center of a daisy. Spoon some sugar over the mound and invert the daisy over the bowl to remove the excess sugar. Using your finger, flatten the point. Pipe centers into all of the colored daisies, coat with sugar, and flatten the points.

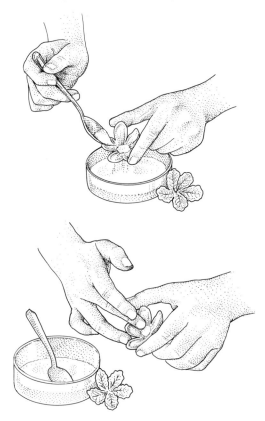

16. Peel off the waxed paper from the large white daisies. Put ½ cup of royal icing in a small bowl. Using the end of a toothpick, add a small dab of yellow paste food color and mix in just until blended. Fit a pastry bag with a coupling and a small plain tip (such as Ateco #4) and fill with the yellow royal icing. Pipe centers into the large white daisies using the same procedure as for the colored daisies.

17. In a small, shallow dish, combine the water with a small amount of green paste food color. Add 10 toothpicks and soak for 1 to 2 minutes or until dyed green. With a fork, remove the toothpicks and dry them on paper towels.

18. Put ¼ cup of royal icing in a small bowl. Using the tip of an ordinary toothpick, add a small amount of green paste food color to the icing and mix just until blended. Fit a pastry bag with a coupling and a small plain tip (such as Ateco #4) and fill with the green icing. Turn 10 medium colored daisies upside down. Put the tip of the pastry bag against the center bottom of one flower. Apply pressure slowly and pull up slowly so that the icing forms a ball. To form a stem, gently push a green toothpick into the center of the ball. Continue piping and attaching the toothpicks. These daisies will be used to make the ornament on top of the cake. Let the flowers dry overnight.

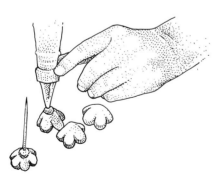

Make the chocolate cake:

19. Position one rack in the top third and one rack in the bottom third of the oven and preheat to 350°F. Lightly butter the bottoms and sides of one 8-by-2-inch round and one 12-by-2-inch round cake pan. Line the bottom of each pan with a circle of baking parchment or waxed paper. Dust the sides of the pans with flour and tap out the excess.

20. In a medium bowl, stir together the flour, cocoa, baking soda, baking powder, and salt. Sift the mixture onto a piece of waxed paper.

21. In a large bowl of a stand-up electric mixer set at medium-high speed, beat the butter and the shortening until creamy. Gradually add the sugar and continue beating for 5 to 7 minutes or until light, scraping down the sides of the bowl occasionally. Add the eggs one at a time, beating well after each addition. Beat in the vanilla. Reduce the speed to low, and in three additions, alternately mix in the flour mixture and the milk, scraping down the sides of the bowl after each addition.

22. Measure 2 cups of the batter and scrape it into the 8-inch pan and spread it evenly. Scrape the remaining batter into the 12-inch pan and spread it evenly. Bake the layers for 30 to 40 minutes or until a cake tester or toothpick inserted into the center comes out clean. Halfway through baking, switch the positions of the cake layers for even browning.

23. Cool the cake layers in the pans set on wire racks for 10 minutes. Run a knife around the edges of the layers to loosen, and invert them onto wire racks. Peel off the papers and leave them loosely set on the bottoms of the layers. Invert the layers onto other racks, so that they are right side up. Cool the layers completely. Wrap the layers in plastic and let stand at room temperature overnight. Make the cake layers two more times, using the same formula. In the end, you will have three 8-inch and three 12-inch layers.

Make the basic frosting:

24. In the large bowl of a stand-up electric mixer, combine 4 cups of the confectioners' sugar with the shortening, water, salt, and flavoring. Beat at low speed for 1 to 2 minutes or until creamy. Using a rubber spatula, scrape down the sides of the bowl. Add the remaining 2 cups of

confectioners' sugar and continue to mix for 4 to 5 minutes or until smooth. Remove the bowl from the mixer and transfer the frosting to an airtight container.

Make the top ornament:

25. Using a sharp serrated knife, cut the 4-inch plastic-foam ball in half. Cut out 2 circles of aluminum foil, one 5 inches in diameter, the other 4 inches. Set aside the 4-inch circle.

26. Fit a new pastry bag with a coupling and a star tip (such as Ateco #20) and fill with basic frosting. Pipe a circle of basic frosting on the 5-inch foil circle 1 inch from the edge. Put a plastic-foam half-sphere, cut side down, on top of the foil circle. With your fingers, fold the ½-inch border of aluminum foil up against the sides of the dome. Put the dome, flat side down, on a baking sheet lined with waxed paper. Using the pastry bag, pipe a zigzag border along the base of the dome and continue piping four or five rows of frosting until the dome is completely covered.

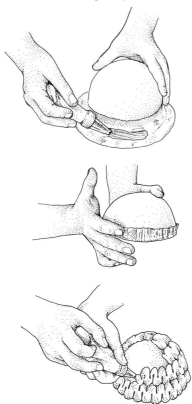

27. Starting at the base, attach large colored daisies alternating with large white daisies and medium colored daisies. Work quickly so that the frosting does not have time to harden. Continue to add three or four more rows of daisies until the dome is covered. Insert leaves in the empty spaces. Using a pair of wire cutters, cut the ends off the green toothpicks attached to the 10 daisies. Cut the toothpicks at an angle to make points. Spear these toothpicked daisies into the empty spaces in the dome 2 at a time so that the ornament doesn't slide. Let the ornament dry.

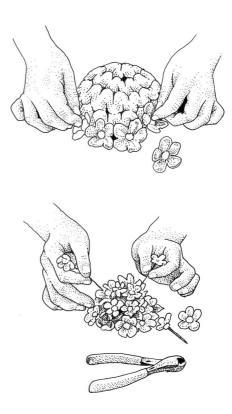

Day 3
Assemble the cake layers:

28. Unwrap the cake layers and remove the papers. Using a long, serrated knife, trim the tops of the cake layers so that they are level. Put a 14- or 16-inch round cake platter on a cake stand and set one of the 12-inch cake layers on top. Using a metal cake spatula, evenly spread the cake layer with 2 cups of the frosting. Put the second 12-inch cake layer on top of the frosting. Spread 2 cups of the frosting evenly on top of the second cake layer. Put the third 12-inch cake layer on top of the frosting and gently press into place.

29. Cut out an 8-inch circle of aluminum foil. Wrap one side of a 7½-inch cardboard cake circle with the foil circle. Spread a small dab of frosting in the center of the foil-covered circle and set one of the 8-inch cake layers on top. Spread the cake layer with ¾ cup of frosting. Put the second 8-inch cake layer on top of the frosting. Spread ¾ cup of frosting evenly over the second layer. Put the third 8-inch layer on top of the frosting and gently press into place.

Crumb-coat the tiers:

30. Put 4½ cups of the frosting in a medium bowl. Mix in ½ to 2 teaspoons of cold water to thin the frosting.

31. With a pastry brush, brush any loose crumbs from the surface of the tiers. Put the 8-inch tier on a second revolving cake stand or use an inverted cake pan of an appropriate size.

32. Using a metal cake spatula, frost the sides and top of the 8-inch tier with a thin, even layer of the thinned frosting. Frost the 12-inch tier in the same manner. Let the frosting set for 30 to 40 minutes or until dry to the touch.

Comb the tiers:

33. Put 6 cups of frosting in a medium bowl. Mix in 1½ to 4 teaspoons of water to thin the frosting for combing.

34. Using a metal cake spatula, frost the top of the 8-inch tier with a second, thicker, even layer of frosting, using long, straight strokes. When the top of the tier is completely frosted, dip the spatula in a glass of hot water and go over the top of the tier. The hot, wet blade will melt the frosting to give it a shiny, smooth appearance.

35. Frost a small section at the base of the 8-inch tier. Dip a metal or plastic pastry comb in hot water and slowly pull the frosting up, making vertical stripes and spreading the frosting up the side of the tier. Wipe the excess frosting from the comb and continue frosting small sections at the base of the tier and combing it up the sides, being careful to make the lines straight. Frost and comb the 12-inch tier in the same way.

Tier the cake:

36. Trace a 7½-inch circle on top of the 12-inch tier, making sure that the circle is centered. Insert 10 sturdy plastic straws, evenly spaced, around the inner circumference of the circle. Using scissors, cut the straws so that they are even with the surface of the tier. (The straws will support the weight of the tiered cake.) Cut out a 7½-inch circle of aluminum foil. Put the foil circle over the traced circle. Put the 8-inch tier on the cardboard circle over the foil circle.

Pipe the decorations on the cake:

37. Fit a pastry bag with a coupling a coupling and a plain tip (such as Ateco #4) and fill with white royal icing. Pipe stems and leaves around the sides of each tier. Pipe small mounds of icing and attach the small grape clusters and small white daisies to the sides of the tiers.

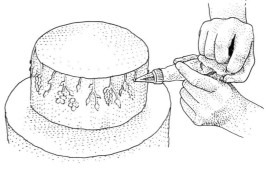

Attach the daisies and leaves to the cake:

38. Fit a new pastry bag with a coupling and a star tip (such as Ateco #22) and fill with basic frosting. Hold the pastry bag at a 45° angle at the base of the 12-inch tier. Apply pressure and pipe a wavy line around the base. Release the pressure and remove the tip. Put the tip under the raised

mound of the wavy line and pipe an "S" shape over it to make a rope border. Continue piping "S"-shaped ropes in this manner all the way around the base of the cake.

39. Put 6 equally spaced clusters made up of 2 medium colored daisies and 1 large colored daisy around the base of the 12-inch tier. Insert 4 leaves in each cluster. Put a large grape cluster on either side of the daisy clusters.

40. Fit another pastry bag with a coupling and a smaller star tip (such as Ateco #20) and fill with frosting. Pipe a slightly smaller rope border around the base of the 8-inch tier.

41. Using the pastry bag with the larger star tip, pipe about 6 inches of the rope border on the top edge of the 12-inch tier. Attach a border of daisies on top of the piped rope, using daisies of assorted colors and sizes. Continue to pipe about 6 inches of the rope pattern at a time and attach flowers until the border is complete. Insert leaves in the empty spaces.

42. Using the pastry bag with the smaller star tip, pipe a rope border on the top edge of the 8-inch tier. Put 6 equally spaced clusters of 2 medium colored daisies on the rope border. Insert 2 leaves in each cluster.

Put the daisy ornament on top of the cake:

43. Put the reserved 4-inch foil circle on top of the 8-inch cake, making sure that it is centered. Carefully lift the daisy ornament and put it on the circle of foil. (The circle of foil is used so that the ornament can be removed easily when the cake is cut.) Store the cake in a cool, dry place until ready to serve.

Cupid's Delight Wedding Cake

Swirls and twirls of ivory-colored white chocolate adorn this graceful wedding cake, providing the perfect backdrop for lacy nosegays of pink sweetheart roses and baby's breath—or for any combination of flowers. Beneath the richly textured frosting are chocolaty layers of cake filled with a creamy chocolate mousse. Surely any bride would be thrilled to have this glorious creation as the centerpiece of her wedding. The cake needs 2 days for baking and assembly, and to mix the large amounts of batter, frosting, and mousse, you will need a heavy-duty electric mixer with both the paddle and whip attachments.

YIELD: About 60 servings

DIFFICULTY: ▄▄▄

PREPARATION TIME: 7 hours plus baking, cooling, and chilling times (allow 2 days to make this cake)

SPECIAL EQUIPMENT: 5-quart heavy-duty mixer; 1 8-inch and 1 6-inch Plexiglas separator tier, available at specialty baking shops and through the mail

Rudy Muller

8- and 12-inch cake layers:

5½ cups plus 1 tablespoon all-purpose flour

3¾ teaspoons baking soda

1 teaspoon double-acting baking powder

⅛ teaspoon salt

1¾ cups plus 2 tablespoons unsweetened nonalkalized cocoa powder

3¾ cups cold water

1¾ cups (3½ sticks) plus 2 tablespoons unsalted butter, softened

4¼ cups plus 3 tablespoons granulated sugar

8 large eggs, at room temperature, lightly beaten

(ingredients continued)

10-inch cake layer:

2¼ cups all-purpose flour
1½ teaspoons baking soda
⅜ teaspoon double-acting baking powder
Pinch of salt
¾ cup unsweetened nonalkalized cocoa powder
1½ cups cold water
¾ cup (1½ sticks) unsalted butter, softened
1¾ cups plus 1 tablespoon granulated sugar
3 large eggs, at room temperature, lightly beaten

Sugar syrup:

2½ cups water
1⅛ cups granulated sugar
3 tablespoons orange liquer, such as Grand Marnier

Chocolate mousse filling:

21 ounces bittersweet chocolate, coarsely chopped
½ ounce (2 envelopes) unflavored powdered gelatin
¼ cup plus 2 tablespoons cold water
4½ cups heavy (whipping) cream
¾ cup plus 1½ teaspoons unflavored sugar syrup (see preceding
   sugar syrup ingredient list and step 7 of instructions)

Buttercream:

1⅓ cups egg whites (from about 12 large eggs)
2⅔ cups granulated sugar
2¼ pounds (9 sticks) unsalted butter, softened
1 to 3 teaspoons vanilla extract

Decoration:

1½ pounds white chocolate, for curls (see Ingredient Note)
Fresh miniature roses, for garnish (optional)
Baby's breath, for garnish (optional)

INGREDIENT NOTE: 5.5-pound blocks of Carma's chocolate couverture (ivory), which are well-suited for making white chocolate curls, are available from Albert Uster (see back of book for mail order information).

Day 1
Make the 8-inch and 12-inch cake layers:

1. Position a rack in the center of the oven and preheat to 350°F. Lightly butter the bottoms and sides of an 8-by-3-inch round cake pan and a 12-by-3-inch round cake pan. Line the bottom of each pan with a circle of baking parchment or waxed paper. Dust the sides of the pans with flour and tap out the excess.

2. In a large bowl, stir together the flour, baking soda, baking powder, and salt. Sift onto a piece of waxed paper.

3. In a medium bowl, combine the cocoa powder and cold water and stir until smooth.

4. In a 5-quart bowl of a heavy-duty electric mixer fitted with the paddle attachment, beat the butter for 30 to 60 seconds at low speed or until light and creamy. Increase the mixer speed to medium and gradually add the sugar. Continue beating for 2 to 3 minutes or until the batter is light. Scrape down the sides of the bowl. Slowly add the eggs in five small parts, mixing well after each addition. Beat for 1 minute or until the batter is smooth and creamy. Transfer the batter to a large bowl.

5. Using a wooden spoon, in six parts, alternately stir the flour mixture and the cocoa mixture into the batter. Do not overmix. Scrape the batter into the prepared pans, filling each pan a little more than half full. Using a spatula, spread the batter evenly and tap the cake pans a couple of times on the counter to release any large air bubbles. Bake the 8-inch cake layer for 60 to 65 minutes or until a cake tester or toothpick inserted in the center of the cake comes out clean. Continue baking the 12-inch layer for a total of 1 hour and 10 to 15 minutes or until a toothpick or cake tester inserted in the center of the cake comes out clean. Cool the cake layers in the pans set on wire racks for 15 minutes. Run a knife around the edges of the cake layers to loosen them. Invert the cake layers onto wire racks and carefully peel off the papers. Invert again so that the cake layers are right side up, and let them cool completely. Wrap the cake layers in plastic and refrigerate overnight.

Make the 10-inch cake layer:

6. Prepare a 10-by-3-inch round cake pan as directed in step 1. Make the batter using the same method as described in steps 2 through 5. Bake this layer for 50 to 60 minutes or until a cake tester or toothpick inserted in the center comes out clean. Cool in the same manner as the 8-inch and 12-inch layers. Wrap the cake layer in plastic and refrigerate overnight.

Make the sugar syrup:

7. In a large saucepan, combine the water and sugar. Stir over medium heat until the sugar dissolves. Bring the syrup to a gentle boil and then pour it into a medium bowl to cool. Measure ¾ cup

plus 1½ teaspoons of the syrup and set aside in a separate bowl to use in the mousse filling. Add the orange liquer to the remaining syrup. Cover both bowls and store at room temperature.

Day 2
Make the chocolate mousse filling:

8. In the top of a double boiler over hot, not simmering, water, melt the bittersweet chocolate, stirring until smooth. Remove the double boiler from the heat.

9. In a large, heatproof bowl, sprinkle the gelatin over the cold water and stir to soften. Put the bowl over a saucepan of hot, not simmering, water and stir constantly to dissolve. Remove the bowl from the heat.

10. In a 5-quart bowl of a heavy-duty electric mixer fitted with the whip attachment, whip the heavy cream at high speed just until soft peaks start to form.

11. In a small saucepan, heat the ¾ cup plus 1½ teaspoons unflavored sugar syrup to 100°F.

12. Stir the warm syrup into the warm dissolved gelatin. Quickly mix in the warm chocolate and then stir gently until the mixture is completely combined and smooth.

13. Gently fold 3 cups of the whipped cream a cup at a time into the chocolate mixture to lighten it. Put the bowl of the electric mixer back onto the machine fitted with the whip attachment and with the mixer running at low speed, quickly pour the lightened chocolate mixture back into the bowl of whipped cream. Whip for 20 seconds, just until combined. Using a rubber spatula, scrape down the sides and bottom of the bowl to make sure the mixture is well combined. Cover the bowl with plastic wrap and refrigerate the mousse for 20 to 30 minutes or until set.

Assemble the cake layers:

14. Remove the cake layers from the refrigerator. Using a long, serrated knife, trim each one so that the tops are level. Horizontally slice each cake layer into three layers of equal thickness. Spread a small amount of chocolate mousse on the center of a 7½-inch cardboard circle and set the bottom layer of the 8-inch cake on top. Using a pastry brush, brush the layer with the sugar syrup. Spread 1 cup of the chocolate mousse over the layer and position the second 8-inch cake layer on top of the filling. Brush this layer with sugar syrup and spread it with 1 cup of the chocolate mousse. Brush the bottom surface of the third layer with the sugar syrup. Put the third cake layer on the second, soaked side down on the filling. Press the layer gently into place. Spread a small amount of chocolate mousse in the center of a 9½-inch cardboard circle and put the bottom layer of the 10-inch cake on top. Assemble this tier in the same manner, brushing with syrup and using 2 cups of mousse for each layer. Spread a small amount of chocolate mousse in the center of an 11½-inch cardboard circle and set the bottom layer of the 12-inch cake on top. Assemble this tier in the same manner, brushing with the syrup and using 2½ cups of mousse for each layer. Refrigerate the 3 assembled cake tiers for at least 2 hours or overnight, until the filling is firm.

Make the buttercream:

15. In a 5-quart bowl of a heavy-duty electric mixer, combine the egg whites and sugar. Set the bowl over hot, not simmering, water. Whisk the egg white mixture constantly until it is white and creamy and hot to the touch (110°F). Rub a small dab of the mixture between your thumb and forefinger to make sure the sugar crystals are completely dissolved.

16. Transfer the bowl to the electric mixer. Beat the mixture with the whip attachment at medium-high speed for 15 to 20 minutes or until it is cool and has formed a thick meringue. Add the butter 1 tablespoon at a time, beating after each addition until each piece is incorporated and the buttercream is thick and smooth. Beat in 1 to 3 tablespoons of vanilla to taste.

Frost the tiers:

17. Remove the cake tiers from the refrigerator. With a pastry brush, brush off any loose crumbs

from the surface of the tiers. Put the first tier to be frosted on an inverted cake pan of an appropriate size or use a revolving cake-decorating stand. Using a metal cake spatula, frost the top and the sides of each tier with two layers of buttercream. The first layer, or crumb coating, should be very thin, as it is meant to seal the cake. The second layer of buttercream should be thicker and applied so that it is very smooth and even and so no dark chocolate cake shows through. Smooth the top of each tier by holding the cake spatula at a slight angle, sweeping it from the edge of the tier inward. Frost all three cake tiers this way.

Decorate the tiers:

18. Wrap the blade of a paring knife with paper towels so that only ½ inch of the point is exposed. Firmly grasp the blade of the knife so that the cutting edge is facing upward toward your hand. The paper towel will prevent you from cutting yourself. Form shavings by pushing the dull side of the blade across the surface of a block of chocolate with quick, flicking motions. Hold the block of chocolate over the cake tier so that the shavings fall directly onto it, covering the tops and sides completely. Cover all three tiers with chocolate shavings.

Tier the cake:

19. Put the 12-inch cake tier on a 14-inch round serving plate. Assemble the 8-inch Plexiglas separator tier and insert the legs into the 12-inch cake tier. Spread a little buttercream on the plate and set the 10-inch cake tier on top. Assemble the 6-inch Plexiglas separator tier and insert the legs into the middle cake tier. Spread a little buttercream on this plate and set the 8-inch cake tier on top. If you disturb some of the shavings, simply make a few more and gently press them into the cake where they are needed.

Decorate the cake:

20. Decorate the cake with miniature roses and baby's breath, if desired.

Chocolate Alpine Cake

Inspired by the lofty peaks and pitched-roofed mountain chalets of Switzerland, this triangular, multilayered cake with its nutty chocolate glaze is a charming—and wonderfully tasty—centerpiece. Erecting the cake may sound tricky, but if you take it a step at a time and let logic rule, you will have no trouble at all. Because the cake is assembled while it is frozen, remember to allow at least 3 hours for freezing. A note about the ingredients: we like the full, rich flavor provided by the vanilla bean, but if you prefer to use extract, substitute 1½ teaspoons of pure vanilla extract for the bean and add it to the ganache with the cognac.

Allen Leiberman

YIELD: 12 servings
DIFFICULTY: ▬▬▬
PREPARATION TIME: 2½ hours plus baking, roasting (the nuts), cooling, freezing, and chilling times

Ganache:

1⅓ cups heavy (whipping) cream
8 tablespoons (1 stick) unsalted butter, cut into tablespoons
A few grains of salt
2 vanilla beans, split in half lengthwise
9 ounces bittersweet chocolate, coarsely chopped
3 ounces Swiss milk chocolate, coarsely chopped
2 large egg yolks, at room temperature
1 tablespoon cognac

Sponge cake:

4 large eggs
3 large egg yolks
½ cup plus 2 tablespoons granulated sugar
Pinch of salt
1½ teaspoons vanilla extract
½ cup sifted cake flour (not self-rising)

To assemble:

½ cup seedless raspberry preserves
2 tablespoons cognac

(ingredients continued)

Almond croquant:

½ cup finely chopped slivered almonds

1 teaspoon lightly beaten egg white

1 tablespoon granulated sugar

Chocolate glaze:

¾ cup heavy (whipping) cream

2 tablespoons light corn syrup

A few grains of salt

5 ounces bittersweet chocolate, finely chopped

2½ ounces Swiss milk chocolate, finely chopped

1½ teaspoons cognac

Garnish (optional):

½ pint fresh raspberries

Make the ganache:

1. In a medium saucepan, combine the cream, butter, and salt. Scrape the tiny black seeds from the vanilla beans into the saucepan. Add the scraped bean pods and slowly bring the mixture to a gentle boil over medium-low heat. Take the pan off the heat and remove the vanilla pods.

2. In a food processor fitted with the metal chopping blade, process the chocolates for 15 to 20 seconds or until finely chopped. Add the egg yolks and pulse twice. With the machine running, pour the hot cream mixture through the feed tube and blend for 10 to 15 seconds, until smooth. Add the cognac and process briefly to blend. Scrape the ganache into a medium bowl and cover the surface with plastic wrap. Refrigerate for no longer than 1½ hours, until the ganache has thickened to the consistency of chocolate pudding.

Make the sponge cake:

3. Position a rack in the center of the oven and preheat to 350°F. Line the bottom of an 11-by-17-inch jelly-roll pan with aluminum foil, leaving a 2-inch overhang on the short ends. Fold the overhang underneath the pan. Butter the aluminum foil and the sides of the pan, and lightly dust the bottom and sides with flour and tap out the excess.

4. In a large, heatproof bowl, whisk together the eggs, egg yolks, sugar, and salt. Set the bowl over a pot of hot, not simmering, water so that the bottom of the bowl touches the water. Continue whisking the mixture for 3 to 4 minutes or until the sugar crystals have dissolved and the mixture is warm to the touch. Remove the bowl from the hot water.

5. Using a hand-held electric mixer set at medium-high speed, beat the mixture for 5 to 7 minutes or until it has tripled in volume and the batter is a pale yellow and forms a thick ribbon when the beaters are lifted. Beat in the vanilla. Sift one fourth of the flour over the batter and fold it in briskly but gently. Fold in the remaining flour in three additions. Scrape the batter into the prepared pan and spread it evenly. Tap the pan on a work surface to remove any large air bubbles.

6. Bake for 15 to 17 minutes or until the center of the cake springs back when lightly pressed. Cool the cake in the pan on a wire rack for 10 minutes. Unfold the aluminum foil ends and use them as handles to transfer the sponge cake to a large wire rack. Let the cake cool completely. Using your fingers or a small knife, carefully peel off the soft brown, paper-thin layer from the surface of the sponge cake. Removing this layer produces a more defined pattern when the cake is cut into slices.

7. Using the aluminum foil handles, transfer the sponge cake to a large work surface. With a long, serrated knife, trim ¼ inch off all four edges of the cake. Carefully invert the cake onto a work surface and gently peel off the aluminum foil.

8. Cut three 3¾-by-10-inch thin cardboard strips. Using the cardboard strips as guides, cut the sponge cake into four equal strips with the long, serrated knife. Wrap the three cardboard strips separately in aluminum foil.

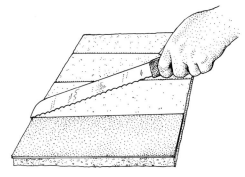

Assemble the cake:

9. In a small bowl, stir together the raspberry preserves and cognac.

10. Set aside 1¼ cups of the ganache and hold at room temperature. Using a hand-held electric mixer set at medium speed, beat the remaining 1¾ cups of ganache for 5 to 10 seconds, until its color lightens and it forms stiff peaks when the beaters are lifted. (Do not overbeat or the ganache will become grainy.)

11. Put one of the cake strips onto one of the foil-covered cardboard strips. Using a small offset metal cake spatula, coat the strip with 2 tablespoons of the raspberry mixture. Spread ½ cup of the whipped ganache over the raspberry layer. Put a

second strip of sponge cake on top of the filling, coat with 2 tablespoons of the raspberry mixture, and spread with ½ cup of the ganache. Put a third strip of sponge cake on top of the filling and repeat the process. Put the fourth strip of the sponge cake on top of the filling. Cover the assembled cake with plastic wrap and freeze for 2 to 3 hours, until firm.

12. Position the frozen cake along the front edge of a work surface so that its long side is facing you. Using a long, serrated knife and leaning it against the table edge to guide it, slice the cake at a diagonal between the upper rear and the lower front corners. Remove the front half of the sliced cake with a long metal cake spatula and lay it lengthwise, cut side down, on the second foil-covered cardboard strip.

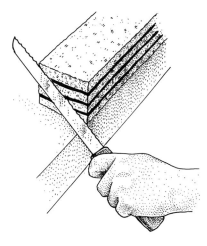

13. Using a hand-held electric mixer set at medium speed, beat the remaining ganache until it lightens in color and forms stiff peaks when the beaters are lifted. Spread ½ cup of the ganache onto the unlayered surface of the cake half that is lying on the second foil-covered strip. Using the

foil-covered strip for support, lift the cake half and stand it on the third foil-covered strip. Put the second cake half, cut side facing outward, alongside it. Gently press the two halves together to form a pyramid. Coat the sides of the cake with the remaining ganache. Put a piece of plastic wrap over the top and sides of the cake and gently press so that it adheres to the ganache. Using a plastic scraper, smooth the sloping sides of the cake by running the scraper over the plastic. Refrigerate the cake for 30 minutes, until the ganache is firm.

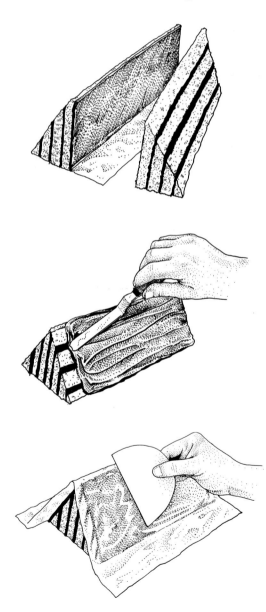

Make the almond croquant:

14. Position a rack in the center of the oven and preheat to 300°F. On a baking sheet, mix together the almonds and egg white until the mixture is moist. Add the sugar and toss until the almonds are evenly coated. Spread the almonds in a single layer and roast them for 12 to 15 minutes, stirring three or four times, until the sugar starts to caramelize and the almonds are golden. Transfer the almond croquant to another baking sheet to stop the cooking process. Let the croquant cool completely.

Make the chocolate glaze:

15. In a medium saucepan over medium heat, slowly bring the cream, corn syrup, and salt to a gentle boil. Remove the pan from the heat and add the chocolates. Let the mixture sit for 1 to 2 minutes and gently whisk until smooth. Stir in the cognac. Strain the glaze into a bowl. Let the glaze cool to 88° to 90°F, stirring frequently so that it cools evenly.

16. Put the chilled cake on a large wire rack set over a baking sheet. Remove the plastic wrap. Gently stir the almond croquant into the chocolate glaze. Ladle the warm chocolate glaze over the cake, using a metal cake spatula to help spread it evenly. Chill the cake on the rack for 5 to 10 minutes or until the glaze has set. Using two long metal cake spatulas, remove the cake from the wire

rack and transfer it to a cutting surface. Cut the cake into twelve slices using a hot, clean knife for each cut. Arrange the slices on a serving plate. If

desired, garnish with fresh raspberries. Let the slices sit at room temperature for 15 minutes before serving.

⌒ *Chocolate Cashew Dacquoise* ⌒

Two kinds of buttercream—one gently flavored with cashews—are sandwiched between layers of crunchy chocolate meringue. To top it all off, the dacquoise is frosted with a rich ganache.

YIELD: 8 to 10 servings

DIFFICULTY: ▰▰▰

PREPARATION TIME: 1½ hours plus baking, cooling, and chilling times

SPECIAL EQUIPMENT: 2 pastry bags, each fitted with a ⅜-inch plain tip (such as Ateco #1)

Meringue layers:

1 tablespoon plus 1 teaspoon unsweetened alkalized cocoa powder
1 tablespoon cornstarch
6 large egg whites, at room temperature
¼ teaspoon cream of tartar
Pinch of salt
1 cup granulated sugar

Chocolate buttercream:

4 ounces German's sweet chocolate, coarsely chopped
¼ cup hot strong coffee
1½ cups (3 sticks) unsalted butter, softened
¾ cup confectioners' sugar
3 large egg yolks

Cashew buttercream:

1 cup (2 sticks) unsalted butter, softened
¾ cup confectioners' sugar
2 large egg yolks, at room temperature
¾ teaspoon vanilla extract
½ cup unsalted dry-roasted cashews, finely ground

Chocolate ganache:

8 ounces German's sweet chocolate, finely chopped
⅔ cup heavy (whipping) cream
4 teaspoons unsalted butter

(ingredients continued)

Decoration:

¾ cup unsalted dry-roasted cashews, finely chopped
Chocolate curls, for garnish (optional; for instructions on
making chocolate curls, see page 21)

Make the meringue layers:

1.   Position one rack in the top third and another rack in the bottom third of the oven and preheat to 300°F. Line two heavy baking sheets with baking parchment. Trace two 8-inch circles on one of the sheets of parchment, making sure that there is a 1-inch space between them. Trace one 8-inch circle in the middle of the second sheet of parchment paper. Turn the paper over.

2.   In a small bowl, sift together the cocoa and cornstarch.

3.   In a large, grease-free bowl, using a hand-held electric mixer set at low speed, beat the egg whites until they start to foam. Add the cream of tartar and salt. Gradually increase the speed to medium high and beat until soft peaks start to form. Slowly add the sugar and continue beating for 3 to 5 minutes or until the whites form glossy, stiff peaks. Fold in the cocoa-cornstarch mixture.

4.   Spoon some of the meringue mixture into a pastry bag fitted with a large ⅜-inch plain tip (such as Ateco #1). Affix the parchment paper to the baking sheet by piping a dot of meringue under all four corners of the paper. Pipe the meringue into the 8-inch circles, starting at the center of each traced circle and working your way out in a spiral.

5.   Put the baking sheets in the oven and bake for 30 minutes. Reduce the oven temperature to 200°F and bake for 1 hour longer or until the meringue layers are stiff and dry. Cool the layers on the baking sheets set on wire racks for 30 minutes. Carefully remove the meringue layers from the paper.

Make the chocolate buttercream:

6.   In the top of a double boiler over hot, not simmering, water, combine the chocolate and hot coffee. Stir frequently until smooth and remove the pan from the heat. Let the chocolate-coffee mixture cool 5 to 10 minutes or until tepid.

7.   In a large bowl, using a hand-held electric mixer set at medium-high speed, beat the butter and confectioners' sugar for 5 minutes or until very light. Beat in the egg yolks and the melted chocolate-coffee mixture.

Make the cashew buttercream:

8.   In a large bowl, using a hand-held electric mixer set at medium-high speed, beat the butter with the confectioners' sugar for about 5 minutes or until very light. Beat in the egg yolks, vanilla, and cashews.

Assemble the dacquoise:

9.   Using an 8-inch cardboard circle or cake pan as a guide and a small knife, trim any uneven edges off each meringue layer.

10.   Fill a pastry bag fitted with a ⅜-inch plain tip (such as Ateco #1) with the chocolate buttercream. Fill a second pastry bag fitted with the same size tip with the cashew buttercream.

11.   To secure the dacquoise during assembly, dab the center of an 8-inch cardboard circle or an inverted 8-inch cake pan with a teaspoon of buttercream. Put one meringue layer on top of the dab of buttercream. Pipe a circle of the cashew buttercream along the outer edge of the meringue layer. Pipe a circle of the chocolate buttercream inside and immediately adjacent to the circle of cashew buttercream. Continue to pipe alternate concentric circles of cashew and chocolate buttercream into the center of the meringue layer. Put the second meringue layer on top of the piped buttercream and repeat the procedure, piping alternating circles of buttercream. Turn the third meringue layer flat side up and gently press it into the second layer of buttercream. Using a metal cake spatula, spread the remaining cashew buttercream around the sides of the dacquoise to fill in any gaps. Refrigerate the dacquoise for 45 minutes or until firm.

Make the chocolate ganache:

12. Put the chocolate in a medium bowl. In a small saucepan, combine the cream and butter. Cook over medium heat until the mixture comes to a gentle boil. Remove the pan from the heat, pour the hot cream mixture over the chocolate, and stir until completely smooth. Cover the surface of the ganache with plastic wrap and refrigerate for 20 to 30 minutes or until it is spreadable.

Decorate the dacquoise:

13. Using a metal cake spatula, frost the top and then the sides of the dacquoise with the ganache. Smooth the top of the cake by holding the spatula at a slight angle and sweeping it from the edges of the cake inward. Sweep the spatula back and forth over the top of the dacquoise to produce a simple design. Coat the sides of the cake with the cashews. Garnish with chocolate curls, if desired. Transfer the dacquoise to a cake stand. Serve the dacquoise at room temperature.

⟋⟍ *Chocolate Lovers' Wedding Cake* ⟋⟍

The pristine elegance of this white wedding cake is relieved by clusters of dark chocolate roses nestled on the tiers. Marzipan roses and sprigs of baby's breath crown the cake. Inside, the white cake layers are generously studded with chunks of bittersweet chocolate and layered with raspberry preserves and a luscious raspberry filling. This is a grand cake, big enough for a large wedding with as many as 100 guests. You will need a couple of days to make it—but none of the steps is difficult.

> YIELD: 100 servings
>
> DIFFICULTY: ▰▰▰
>
> PREPARATION TIME: 8 hours plus cooling, baking, and chilling times (allow 2 days to make this cake)
>
> SPECIAL EQUIPMENT: 5-quart heavy-duty stand-up electric mixer; plastic straws; pastry bag fitted with assorted tips (such as Ateco #104, #18, #101, #65S, #5, #2)

Cake layers (you will need four times the amount of ingredients listed here to make the four-tiered cake, which means the batter will have to be mixed up four times):

4 cups sifted all-purpose flour
1 tablespoon plus 1 teaspoon double-acting baking powder
¾ teaspoon salt
1¼ cups (2½ sticks) unsalted butter, softened
2½ cups granulated sugar, divided
1 teaspoon vanilla extract
1⅓ cups milk, at room temperature
8 large egg whites, at room temperature (reserve yolks for filling)
8 ounces bittersweet chocolate, chopped into ¼-inch chunks

Raspberry filling:

18 large egg yolks, at room temperature
1½ cups granulated sugar

(ingredients continued)

1¾ cups half-and-half

1 tablespoon vanilla extract

7 10-ounce packages frozen raspberries in light syrup, thawed and drained

3 pounds (12 sticks) unsalted butter, softened

2 tablespoons Chambord liqueur, divided

Sugar syrup:

3 cups water

1½ cups granulated sugar

Milk chocolate plastic:

8 ounces Swiss milk chocolate, finely chopped

¼ cup corn syrup, at room temperature

White chocolate buttercream:

3 cups granulated sugar, divided

½ cup cornstarch

3 cups heavy (whipping) cream

1 pound white chocolate, finely chopped

2 tablespoons vanilla extract

4 pounds (16 sticks) unsalted butter, cut into tablespoons and softened

To assemble:

3½ cups seedless raspberry preserves

Decoration:

Small and medium marzipan roses (see Ingredient Note)
Sprigs of baby's breath, for garnish (optional)

INGREDIENT NOTE: The marzipan roses used to decorate the top of the wedding cake are ¾ inch and 1 inch wide. They are available in white, yellow, peach, pink, and red from Albert Uster (see the back of the book for mail order information).

Day 1
Make the cake layers:

1. Position one rack in the top third and another in the bottom third of the oven and preheat to 325°F. Lightly butter the bottoms and sides of one 6-by-2-inch round cake pan, one 8-by-2-inch round cake pan, and one 10-inch round cake pan. Line the bottom of each pan with a circle of baking parchment or waxed paper. Dust the sides of the pans with flour and tap out the excess.

2. In a large bowl, stir together the flour, baking powder, and salt. Sift onto a piece of waxed paper.

3. In a 5-quart bowl of a heavy-duty electric mixer fitted with the paddle attachment and set at medium speed, cream the butter for 30 seconds or until light. Gradually add 2¼ cups of the sugar and continue beating for 4 minutes or until the mixture is light and fluffy. Beat in the vanilla. With the mixer at low speed, add the flour mixture and milk together, a quarter of each at a time, scraping down the sides of the bowl after each addition. Mix for about 30 seconds or until the batter is smooth and well blended. Remove the bowl from the mixer.

4. In another large, grease-free bowl of the electric mixer, beat the egg whites at low speed until they start to foam. Gradually increase the speed to medium high and continue beating until the whites start to form soft peaks. Add the remaining ¼ cup of sugar 1 tablespoon at a time and continue beating until the whites form stiff, shiny peaks.

5. Lighten the cake batter by folding in one fourth of the beaten egg whites. Gently fold in the remaining whites, one fourth at a time. Carefully fold in the chocolate chunks. Transfer the batter to the prepared cake pans, filling each pan a little more than half full. Use a spatula to spread the batter evenly. Bake the 6-inch cake layer for 45 to 50 minutes or until a cake tester or toothpick inserted in the center of the cake comes out clean. Halfway through baking, switch positions of the cake pans for even browning. Bake the 8-inch and 10-inch cake layers for 55 to 60 minutes or until a cake tester or toothpick inserted in the centers of the cakes comes out clean. Cool the cakes in their pans set on wire racks for 15 minutes. Run a knife around the edges of the layers to loosen, and invert them onto a rack. Carefully peel off the papers and invert the layers again so that they are right side up, and cool completely. Wrap the cake layers in plastic and let them sit at room temperature overnight.

6. Prepare a 12-by-2-inch round cake pan as directed in step 1. Make the cake batter using the same procedure as before. Bake this layer at 325°F for 55 to 60 minutes or until tested for doneness. Cool in the same manner as the other cake layers. Wrap the layer in plastic and let sit overnight at room temperature.

7. Make a second batch of 6-inch, 8-inch, and 10-inch cake layers. Prepare the cake pans as directed in step 1. Make the cake batter using the same procedure as before. Bake these layers as directed in step 5. Cool in the same manner as the other cake layers. Wrap the cake layers in plastic and let sit overnight at room temperature.

8. Make a second 12-inch cake layer. Prepare the 12-inch cake pan as directed in step 1. Make the cake batter using the same procedure as before. Bake this layer at 325°F for 55 to 60 minutes or until tested for doneness. Cool in the same manner

as the other layers. Wrap the cake layer in plastic and let it sit overnight at room temperature.

Make the raspberry filling:

9. In a large bowl, whisk together the egg yolks and sugar until creamy. In a large saucepan, bring the half-and-half to a gentle boil over medium heat. Remove the saucepan from the heat. Gradually stir 1 cup of the hot half-and-half into the egg yolk mixture until well blended. Pour this mixture back into the pan of half-and-half. Continue cooking over medium-low heat, stirring constantly with a wooden spoon for 2 to 3 minutes or until the yolk mixture has thickened enough to coat the back of the spoon. Do not let the custard come to a boil. Immediately strain the custard into a bowl and put the bowl over a bowl of ice water. Stir the custard for 8 minutes or until cool, and remove the bowl from the ice water. Stir in the vanilla extract. Cover the bowl with plastic wrap and refrigerate overnight.

10. In a food processor fitted with the metal chopping blade, puree the raspberries. Strain, cover, and refrigerate.

Make the sugar syrup:

11. In a large saucepan, combine the water and sugar. Stir over medium heat until the sugar dissolves. Bring the syrup to a gentle boil. Pour into a medium bowl, cool, and cover.

Make the milk chocolate plastic:

12. In the top of a double boiler over 125°F water, melt the chocolate. (The water should touch the bottom of the top part of the double boiler.) Stir the chocolate constantly until smooth. Remove the pan from the heat and transfer the chocolate to a bowl. Cool for 10 to 15 minutes or until tepid.

13. Stir in the corn syrup and mix for 20 seconds or until the mixture thickens and starts to lose its shine. Wrap in plastic and let stand at room temperature overnight.

Day 2
Finish the raspberry filling:

14. Remove the custard and the raspberry puree

from the refrigerator. Pour half of the custard (about 1¾ cups) into a 5-quart bowl of a heavy-duty electric mixer. Beat at medium-high speed for 5 to 7 minutes or until the custard forms a thick ribbon when the beaters are lifted. Reduce the speed to medium and slowly beat in 1 cup plus 2 tablespoons of the raspberry puree. Add 1½ pounds of the butter 1 tablespoon at a time, beating after each addition until each piece is incorporated and the mixture is very fluffy and smooth. Beat in 1 tablespoon of the Chambord. (If the filling separates, heat the outside of the bowl by putting it over a saucepan of hot water for 1 minute or until hot. Return the bowl to the electric mixer and continue beating the filling at medium speed for 30 to 60 seconds or until smooth. The warmth of the bowl will heat the filling just enough to emulsify it.) Transfer the filling to a large mixing bowl.

15. Prepare a second batch of raspberry filling, using the remaining custard, raspberry puree, butter, and Chambord, and add it to the first batch of filling.

Assemble the cake layers:

16. Using a long, serrated knife, trim each cake layer so that the tops are level. Horizontally slice each cake into two layers of equal thickness. Spread a small dab of raspberry preserves in the center of a 5½-inch cardboard circle and set the bottom layer of a 6-inch cake on top. Using a pastry brush, brush the layer with sugar syrup. Coat the soaked layer with 1 tablespoon of raspberry preserves and spread with ½ cup of the raspberry filling. Put the second 6-inch cake layer on top of the filling, brush with sugar syrup, coat with raspberry preserves, and spread with ½ cup of the filling. Put the third 6-inch cake layer on top of the filling, brush with sugar syrup, coat with raspberry preserves, and spread with ½ cup of the filling. Brush the bottom of the fourth cake layer with the sugar syrup. Invert the cake layer and put it soaked side down against the filling. Press the layer gently into place. Put the bottom layer of an 8-inch cake on a 7½-inch cardboard circle. Assemble the tier in the same manner with the sugar

syrup, using ¼ cup of the raspberry preserves and 1 cup of the raspberry filling for each layer. Put the bottom layer of a 10-inch cake on a 9½-inch cardboard circle. Assemble the tier in the same manner with the sugar syrup, using ⅓ cup of the raspberry preserves and 1½ cups of the raspberry filling for each layer. Put the bottom of a 12-inch cake on an 11½-inch cardboard circle. Assemble the tier in the same manner with the sugar syrup, using ½ cup of the raspberry preserves and 2 cups of the raspberry filling for each layer. Refrigerate the tiers for 1 hour or until the filling is firm.

Make the white chocolate buttercream:

17. In a medium bowl, stir together ½ cup of the sugar and the cornstarch. In a large saucepan, combine the remaining sugar and the cream. Stir over medium heat until the sugar dissolves. Bring the mixture to a gentle boil and remove the pan from the heat. Gradually stir 1 cup of the hot cream mixture into the sugar-cornstarch mixture. Pour this back into the pan of cream. Continue cooking over medium heat, stirring constantly for 1 minute or until the mixture thickens and comes to a boil. Remove the pan from the heat and stir in the chocolate until smooth. Transfer the chocolate mixture to a medium bowl. Set the bowl over a bowl of ice water and stir the mixture for 10 minutes or until cold. Remove the bowl from the ice water. Transfer half of the chocolate mixture (about 2½ cups) to the 5-quart bowl of a heavy-duty electric mixer. Beat at medium-high speed for 4 minutes or until the mixture is light colored and soft peaks start to form. Beat in 1 tablespoon of vanilla. Add 2 pounds of the butter 1 tablespoon at a time, beating after each addition until each piece is incorporated and the buttercream is thick and smooth. Transfer the buttercream to a large bowl.

18. Prepare a second batch of buttercream, using the remaining chocolate mixture, vanilla, and butter. Combine with the first batch of buttercream.

Frost the tiers:

19. With a pastry brush, brush off any loose crumbs from the surface of the tiers. Put the first

tier to be frosted on an inverted cake pan of an appropriate size or use a revolving cake-decorating stand. Using a metal cake spatula, frost the top and then the sides of each tier with two layers of buttercream. The first layer of buttercream, the crumb coat, should be very thin to seal the cake. The second layer of buttercream should be a bit thicker and applied so that it is very smooth and even. Smooth the top of each tier by holding the spatula at a slight angle, sweeping it from the edge of the tier inward. Refrigerate the cake tiers for 30 minutes or until the frosting is firm. Keep the leftover frosting in a cool place and use to decorate the cake.

Tier the cake:

20. Put the 12-inch tier on a 14-inch serving plate. Trace a 9½-inch circle on top of the cake, making sure that the circle is centered. Insert 10 plastic straws evenly spaced around the circle. Cut the straws so that they are even with the surface of the cake. (The straws will support the weight of the tiered cake.) Put a small dab of frosting on top of the tier in the center of the circle. Put the 10-inch tier over the traced circle and press gently. Repeat the procedure with the 10-inch tier using 9 straws. Repeat with the 8-inch tier using 7 straws, and top with the 6-inch tier. Refrigerate until you are ready to decorate.

Pipe the decorations on the cake:

21. Using a pastry bag fitted with a rose tip (such as Ateco #104), pipe ruffles along the edges of each cake tier. Using a pastry bag fitted with a star tip (such as Ateco #18), pipe evenly spaced curls on the top edge and on the sides of each tier.

Using a pastry bag fitted with a smaller rose tip (such as Ateco #101), pipe buds between each curl. Using a pastry bag fitted with a leaf tip (such as Ateco #65S), pipe leaves around each bud. Using a pastry bag fitted with a plain tip (such as Ateco #5), pipe the fleurs-de-lis and the large dots. Using a pastry bag fitted with a plain tip (such as Ateco #2), pipe the filigree and the small dots. Refrigerate the cake.

Make the milk chocolate plastic roses:

22. Pinch off three small pieces of the milk chocolate plastic and form into 1-inch balls. Form each ball into a cone shape.

23. Using a rolling pin, roll the remaining chocolate plastic into a ¹⁄₁₆-inch thick circle. With the base of a #4 pastry tip, cut out 15 1-inch circles. These will become the rose petals. Leaving the bottom edge of each petal thick, roll out the tops of the circles to make them thinner and longer and more petal shaped. If the chocolate plastic becomes too soft, let it stand a few minutes to firm up.

24. Starting at the top of one of the cones, begin wrapping the thick end of a petal around the cone, overlapping and adding 8 more petals around the cone until you reach the bottom. Make 2 rosebuds using the remaining 2 cones and petals. Form the rosebuds using 3 petals per flower.

Decorate the cake:

25. Using buttercream, secure the marzipan roses to the top of the cake. Insert sprigs of baby's breath. With buttercream, secure the chocolate roses to the cake.

⌒ *Chocolate Toffee Torte* ⌒

Four layers of different flavors and textures make up this delectable torte. It was submitted by a reader for one of our recipe contests, and we're sure that with the first bite you will discover why we call it a winner.

YIELD: 12 servings

DIFFICULTY: ▰▰▰

PREPARATION TIME: 2 hours plus chilling, baking, and assembly times (allow at least 4 hours for chilling and freezing)

SPECIAL EQUIPMENT: 10-by-3-inch round springform pan; pastry bag fitted with a large star tip (such as Ateco #4)

Pecan layer:

2½ cups pecan pieces
½ cup granulated sugar
¼ teaspoon salt
8 tablespoons (1 stick) unsalted butter, melted and cooled

Chocolate fudge layer:

½ pound semisweet chocolate, finely chopped
1 cup heavy (whipping) cream
4 tablespoons (½ stick) unsalted butter, softened
2 tablespoons light corn syrup

Toffee layer:

2 ounces unsweetened chocolate, finely chopped
2 teaspoons instant coffee powder
4 large eggs, at room temperature
1½ cups packed light brown sugar
1 cup (2 sticks) unsalted butter, softened

Frosting:

3 cups heavy (whipping) cream, divided
2 tablespoons instant coffee powder
¾ cup confectioners' sugar

Garnish:

2 ounces semisweet chocolate, finely grated
Candied chocolate coffee beans

Make the pecan layer:

1. Position a rack in the top of the oven and preheat to 350°F. Lightly butter the bottom and sides of the springform pan. Line the bottom of the pan with a circle of baking parchment. Generously butter the baking parchment.

2. In a food processor fitted with the metal chopping blade, process the pecans, sugar, and salt until finely chopped.

3. In a medium bowl, combine the pecan mixture with the melted butter. Press the mixture firmly and evenly into the bottom of the prepared pan. Freeze the pecan layer for 10 minutes or until very cold. Bake the layer for 15 minutes or until the edges begin to brown. Cool completely in the pan on a wire rack. Cover the pan tightly with plastic wrap and refrigerate for about 1 hour or until cold and firm.

Make the chocolate fudge layer:

4. In the top of a double boiler over hot, not simmering, water, melt the chocolate with the heavy cream, stirring often, until smooth. Remove the pan from the heat. Stir in the butter until melted and well combined. Stir in the corn syrup.

5. Transfer the mixture to a medium bowl. Put the bowl in a larger bowl filled with ice water. Stir the fudge until cool and it begins to thicken. Remove the plastic wrap from the springform pan. Using a flexible metal spatula, spread the chocolate fudge evenly over the pecan layer. Cover the pan loosely with plastic wrap and refrigerate for 1 hour or until cold and firm.

Make the toffee layer:

6. In the top of a double boiler over hot, not simmering, water, melt the chocolate with the instant coffee, stirring often, until smooth. Remove the pan from the heat.

7. Using a hand-held electric mixer set at medium-high speed, beat in the eggs one at a time, beating well after each addition. Gradually beat in the brown sugar. Mix for 1 minute or until the mixture is light and fluffy. While continuing to beat, gradually add the butter and mix until smooth.

8. Remove the plastic wrap from the springform pan. Using a flexible metal spatula, spread the toffee layer evenly over the fudge layer. Cover the surface of the toffee layer with plastic wrap and freeze for 1 to 2 hours or until very firm.

Make the frosting:

9. In a small saucepan over low heat, warm ⅓ cup of the heavy cream with the instant coffee, stirring until the coffee is dissolved. Transfer the warm cream to a small bowl. Put the bowl in a larger bowl filled with ice water and stir the cream mixture until it is very cold.

10. In a chilled bowl, beat the remaining 2⅔ cups of cream with the coffee-cream mixture and confectioners' sugar until the mixture is stiff and holds its shape when cut into with a knife.

Assemble the torte:

11. Remove the torte from the freezer and uncover it. Using a thin knife, cut around the edges to loosen the sides from the springform pan. Remove the sides of the springform pan. Rest the frozen torte gently on its side. Using a sharp knife, separate the torte from the pan bottom. Peel the baking parchment from the bottom of the torte. Put the torte, pecan layer down, on an inverted 10-inch round cake pan.

12. Reserve ¾ cup of the whipped-cream mixture for garnish. Using a metal cake spatula, spread about two thirds of the remaining whipped cream in a thick, even layer on the top of the torte. Frost the sides of the torte with the remaining one third of the whipped-cream mixture. Lightly sprinkle the edges and sides of the torte with the grated chocolate. Fit a pastry bag with a large star tip (such as Ateco #4) and fill it with the reserved whipped-cream mixture. Pipe 12 swirled rosettes evenly spaced around the top edge of the torte and pipe a thin border around the bottom edge of the torte. Put a chocolate coffee bean or two in the center of each rosette. Serve chilled.

⌢ *Gâteau Charlene Blanche* ⌢

Pretty in red and white, this genoise layer cake makes a perfect dessert on a spring day when temptingly plump, juicy strawberries are in season. Of course, the beribboned cake would be just right for Valentine's Day, too, or for any occasion when light layers of genoise filled with airy white chocolate mousse would taste good. The classic genoise is leavened by the air beaten into the eggs in the warm batter. Be sure to beat the batter long enough after you remove it from the hot water so that it turns into a voluminous, light-colored foam. For just the right texture, we have found that a stand-up electric mixer works better than a hand-held electric mixer, as the larger, more powerful machine incorporates more air. For the ladyfingers ringing the cake, use store-bought confections unless you have a favorite recipe for homemade.

YIELD: 12 servings

DIFFICULTY: ▬▬▬

PREPARATION TIME: 1 hour and 15 minutes, plus baking and chilling times

---

SPECIAL EQUIPMENT: stand-up electric mixer; 3½-feet-by-½-inch red ribbon; pastry bag fitted with a large star tip (such as Ateco #4)

Genoise:

5 large eggs plus 6 large egg yolks
Pinch of salt
1 cup granulated sugar
1½ cups cake flour (not self-rising)
3 tablespoons unsalted butter, melted and cooled

Orange syrup:

⅓ cup granulated sugar
½ cup water
⅓ cup orange liquer, such as Grand Marnier

White chocolate mousse:

3 cups heavy (whipping) cream
1 pound Swiss white chocolate, coarsely chopped

To assemble:

1 cup sliced strawberries
20 to 24 ladyfingers, store-bought or homemade
1 3½-feet-by-½-inch red ribbon
8 ounces Swiss white chocolate, coarsely chopped
8 medium strawberries, washed and hulled

Make the genoise:

1. Position a rack in the center of the oven and preheat to 350°F. Lightly butter and flour two 9-by-2-inch round cake pans.

2. In a large, heatproof bowl of a stand-up electric mixer, whisk together the eggs, yolks, salt, and sugar. Set the bowl over a pot of simmering water. Do not let the bottom of the bowl touch the

water. Continue whisking the mixture until it is frothy and very hot (130°F). Transfer the bowl to the electric mixer. Beat at medium speed for 5 minutes or until the mixture has tripled in volume and the batter forms a thick, pale-yellow ribbon when the beaters are lifted.

3. Remove the mixing bowl from the mixer. Sift one third of the flour over the batter. Using a large rubber spatula, briskly but gently fold in the flour. Sift and then fold in the remaining flour in two additions until well combined. Fold in the cooled butter. Divide the batter evenly between the two prepared pans and spread evenly.

4. Bake for about 30 minutes or until the genoise springs back when lightly touched and the edges have pulled away from the sides of the pans. Invert the layers onto a wire rack and cool completely.

Make the Orange syrup:

5. In a small saucepan, combine the sugar and water. Stir over medium heat until the sugar dissolves. Bring the syrup to a boil. Pour into a small bowl and let it cool. Stir in the orange liquer.

Make the white chocolate mousse:

6. In a small saucepan, bring 1 cup of the heavy cream to a boil. Remove from the heat.

7. Put the white chocolate in a food processor fitted with the metal chopping blade and process until finely chopped. With the motor still running, pour the hot cream through the feed tube. Process the mixture for about 20 seconds or until smooth.

8. Pour the mixture into a large metal mixing bowl. Cover and refrigerate, stirring occasionally, for about 45 minutes or until it is completely cold and has started to thicken.

9. In a chilled mixing bowl, whip the remaining 2 cups of heavy cream until it begins to thicken.

Stir one third of the whipped cream into the chilled white chocolate mixture. Fold in the remaining whipped cream until blended.

Assemble the cake:

10. With a long, serrated knife, trim the tops of the two genoise layers to make them flat.

11. Put one genoise layer onto a 9-inch cardboard circle or serving plate. Using a pastry brush, brush half of the Grand Marnier syrup over the cake layer.

12. Spread a ¼-inch layer of white chocolate mousse over the soaked layer. Arrange the strawberry slices on top of the mousse. Spread a thin layer of the mousse over the berries.

13. Put the second genoise layer on top of the filling. Brush this layer with the remaining syrup.

14. Reserving 1 cup of the mousse for piping, use a metal spatula to smooth the remaining mousse over the top and sides of the cake.

15. Press the ladyfingers upright into the sides of the cake. Tie the ribbon in a bow around the ladyfingers.

16. Fit a pastry bag with a large star tip (such as Ateco #4) and fill with the reserved mousse. Pipe 8 rosettes around the top edge of the cake.

17. In the top of a double boiler over hot, not simmering, water, melt the white chocolate, stirring constantly until smooth. Remove the top part of the double boiler from the bottom.

18. One at a time, dip the point of each strawberry halfway into the white chocolate. Let the excess chocolate drip off, and put the berries directly on the cake, between each rosette. Refrigerate the cake until ready to serve.

⌒ *Hazelnut-Praline Ganache Cake* ⌒

This majestic cake, filled with a rich hazelnut ganache and frosted with mounds of sweetened whipped cream, is the perfect choice when you are planning a party for your chocolate-loving friends. The whipped ganache—mousse-like in texture and generously spread between thin layers of airy chocolate cake—renders every bite absolutely sublime. Make the chilled cake well ahead of time and then frost and decorate it shortly before serving. We think it is one of our most luscious creations. You will, too!

YIELD: 24 servings

DIFFICULTY: ▰▰▰

PREPARATION: 4½ hours plus baking, cooling, and chilling times, (allow 2 days to make this cake)

SPECIAL EQUIPMENT: it is necessary to use a large food processor with a work bowl that measures 7 inches across and 4⅞ inches deep to make the cake batter, hazelnut praline, and the ganache, and to use a 4½-quart heavy-duty stand-up mixer to whip the ganache; 10-by-3-inch round springform cake pan

Chocolate cake:

2 cups sifted cake flour (not self-rising)
1½ cups granulated sugar, divided
1½ teaspoons baking soda
¾ teaspoon double-acting baking powder
¼ teaspoon salt
⅓ cup packed light brown sugar
6 ounces unsweetened chocolate, coarsely chopped
1 cup water
12 tablespoons (1½ sticks) unsalted butter, cut into tablespoons
¾ cup sour cream, chilled
2 large eggs plus 1 large egg yolk, chilled
1 tablespoon vanilla extract

Hazelnut praline:

1 cup granulated sugar
¾ teaspoon lemon juice
1¼ cups roasted hazelnuts, coarsely chopped (for roasting instructions, see page 20)

Hazelnut-praline ganache (The following mixture must be made twice to fill the chocolate layers. You will need two times the amount of ingredients listed):

12 ounces bittersweet chocolate, coarsely chopped
2 large egg yolks
2 cups heavy (whipping) cream

12 tablespoons (1½ sticks) unsalted butter, cut into tablespoons
A few grains of salt
¼ cup hazelnut liqueur, such as Capella or Frangelico
2 teaspoons vanilla extract

To assemble:

6 tablespoons hazelnut liqueur, such as Capella or Frangelico

Chocolate shavings:

2 3-ounce bars bittersweet chocolate, about ¼ inch thick
1 8-ounce chunk bittersweet chocolate, about 1 inch thick

Whipped-cream frosting:

2 cups heavy (whipping) cream
2 tablespoons granulated sugar
1½ teaspoons vanilla extract

Day 1
Make the chocolate cake:

1. Position a rack in the center of the oven and preheat to 350°F. Lightly butter the bottom and side of the springform cake pan. Line the bottom of the pan with a circle of baking parchment or waxed paper. Dust the sides of the pan with flour and tap out the excess.

2. In a food processor fitted with the metal chopping blade, combine the flour, 1 tablespoon of the granulated sugar, the baking soda, baking powder, and salt. Pulse 3 or 4 times until blended and transfer the flour mixture to a medium bowl.

3. Without washing the container of the food processor, combine the remaining 1¼ cups plus 3 tablespoons of the granulated sugar, brown sugar, and chocolate. Process for 20 to 30 seconds or until the mixture is finely ground.

4. In a medium saucepan, combine the water and butter. Cook over medium heat, stirring frequently, until the mixture comes to a boil and the butter melts. Remove the pan from the heat. With the motor running, pour the hot butter mixture through the feed tube of the food processor into the ground chocolate mixture. Process for 15 to 25 seconds or until the chocolate mixture is smooth.

5. Add the sour cream, eggs, egg yolk, and vanilla. Process for no longer than 20 second or

until the mixture is smooth. Add half of the flour mixture and pulse no more than 6 times, until there is barely a trace of flour left. Add the remaining flour mixture and pulse no more than 6 times, until there is barely a trace of flour left in the batter.

6. Scrape the batter into the prepared pan and bake for 45 to 55 minutes or until a cake tester or toothpick inserted into the center of the cake comes out clean. Cool the cake in the pan set on a wire rack for 10 minutes. Run the tip of a sharp knife around the edges of the cake to loosen it from the sides of the pan. Remove the side of the springform pan. Invert the cake onto another wire rack and carefully remove the bottom of the springform pan. Peel off the paper and leave it loosely set on the bottom of the cake. Invert the cake onto another rack so that it is right side up. Cool the cake completely. (If desired, the cake may be wrapped in plastic and left to sit overnight or frozen for up to 1 month. It will be easier to slice the cake if it is chilled.)

Make the hazelnut praline:

7. Lightly butter a 6-inch square on a marble slab or baking sheet.

8. In a heavy 10-inch nonstick skillet, using a wooden spoon, stir together the sugar and lemon juice until thoroughly blended. Over medium heat,

cook the sugar mixture for 4 to 8 minutes, stirring frequently, or until it liquefies and then turns to an amber-colored caramel. Remove the pan from the heat and stir in the hazelnuts. Quickly spread the hazelnut praline onto the prepared surface and cool for 20 to 30 minutes or until firm.

9. Transfer the praline to a cutting board. Coarsely chop the praline with a large knife and then put it in a food processor fitted with the metal chopping blade. Process one half of the praline at a time for 40 to 50 seconds or until finely ground. Transfer the ground praline to a small bowl.

Make the hazelnut-praline ganache:

10. In a food processor fitted with the metal chopping blade, process the chocolate for 30 to 40 seconds or until finely chopped. Add the egg yolks and pulse 3 or 4 times or until blended.

11. In a medium saucepan, combine the cream, butter, half of the hazelnut praline (about 1 cup plus 1 tablespoon), and the salt. Bring the mixture to a gentle boil over medium heat, stirring constantly with a wooden spoon to dissolve the praline.

12. Pour the hot cream mixture through the feed tube of the food processor while the motor is running. Process for 30 to 40 seconds or until the mixture is smooth. Scrape down the side of the bowl once and add the hazelnut liqueur and vanilla. Process for 5 to 10 seconds or until smooth. Transfer the mixture to a metal bowl and cover the surface with plastic wrap. Make a second batch of ganache in the same manner using the remaining ground hazelnut praline. Transfer it to a separate metal bowl and cover the surface of the ganache with plastic wrap. Refrigerate the two bowls of ganache for no longer than 4 hours or until the ganache has thickened to the consistency of chocolate pudding.

13. Scrape the contents of one of the chilled bowls of ganache into a 4½-quart bowl of a heavy-duty mixer. Using the wire whip attachment, beat the ganache at medium speed for 45 to 60 seconds or until it lightens in color and forms soft peaks

when the beaters are lifted. (Do not overwhip the ganache or it will set too quickly.) Transfer the whipped ganache to a large mixing bowl. Scrape the contents of the second bowl of chilled ganache into the 4½-quart mixer and whip in the same manner. Scrape the whipped ganache into the large mixing bowl and, using a large rubber spatula, fold the two batches of ganache together. (Use the ganache as quickly as possible before it starts to set.)

Assemble the cake:

14. Remove the paper circle from the bottom of the chocolate cake. Using a long serrated knife, trim the top of the cake so that it is flat and level. Horizontally slice the cake into three layers of equal thickness. Place the bottom cake layer in the bottom of a 10-inch springform pan. Brush the cake layer with 2 tablespoons of the hazelnut liqueur. Scoop 3 cups of the whipped ganache into the springform pan. Using a small offset metal cake spatula, spread the ganache in an even layer. (Make sure that the ganache is evenly distributed between the side of the springform pan and the edge of the cake layer.) Place the second cake layer on top of the ganache filling. Brush the second cake layer with 2 tablespoons of the hazelnut liqueur and spread with another 3 cups of the ganache. Place the third cake layer on top of the ganache filling. Brush the cake layer with the remaining 2 tablespoons of hazelnut liqueur. Mound the remaining ganache on top of the cake layer, so that the top of the cake is dome-shaped. Carefully cover the surface of the cake with plastic wrap and refrigerate for at least 4 hours or overnight.

Make the chocolate shavings:

15. To make the smaller chocolate shavings, hold one of the 3-ounce chocolate bars in one hand (grip the bar with a folded paper towel so as not to melt the chocolate) over a waxed paper-lined baking sheet. (To get shavings rather than curls, warm the chocolate slightly by placing it on a piece of waxed paper in a microwave set on medium (50 percent) power for 10-second intervals, or by placing it

about 6 inches from a desk lamp for 2 to 5 minutes or until it begins to soften.) Using a sharp vegetable peeler, scrape the long edge of the bar to produce small paper-thin shavings. Make more small shavings using the second bar of chocolate. Over a second waxed paper-lined baking sheet, make the larger shavings in the same manner, using the 8-ounce chocolate chunk with a wider edge. Refrigerate the shavings until ready to decorate the cake.

Day 2
Make the whipped-cream frosting:

16. Place the 4½-quart bowl of a heavy-duty mixer in the freezer for 3 to 5 minutes, until chilled. Using the wire whip attachment, whip the cream with the sugar and vanilla until it starts to form stiff peaks.

Decorate the cake:

17. Using a portable hair dryer or a hot, wet towel, heat the side of the springform pan. Run a thin-bladed knife or metal spatula around the edge of the cake to release it from the side of the springform pan. Remove the side of the springform pan. Using two large metal cake spatulas, remove the cake from the bottom of the springform pan and transfer it to a 10-inch cardboard cake circle.

18. Lift up the cake, supporting the bottom of the cake in one hand. With the other hand, using a metal cake spatula, spread whipped cream over the top of the cake, accenting the shape of the mounded ganache. Then spread whipped cream around the side of the cake, filling in the space between the edge of the cardboard and the side of the cake. Set the cake down onto a revolving cake-decorating stand or lazy Susan. Finish the top of the cake by holding the spatula at a slight angle and with several strokes, smooth the raised lip of ganache around the edge toward the center of the cake until the top is completely smooth.

19. Using a baker's scraper or metal pancake spatula, scoop up some of the small shavings and gently press them against the side of the frosted cake. Coat the entire side of the cake with the small shavings.

20. Fill a pastry bag fitted with a star tip (such as Ateco #4) with the remaining whipped cream. Pipe a shell border around the top edge of the cake. Sprinkle the large chocolate shavings over the top of the cake within the piped border. Pipe a large rosette in the center of the shavings. Refrigerate the cake until 30 minutes before serving.

7

Allen Leiberman

*Chocolate in
the Morning
and in the Afternoon*

Banana Chocolate Chip Pancakes
Chocolate Chip Granola
Coconut Chocolate Streusel Coffee Cake
Chocolate-Speckled Banana Loaves
Deborah's Chocolate Brunch Cake
Karen's Chocolate Sin-amon Bundt Cake
Macadamia Chocolate Chip Streusel Coffee Cake
Chocolate Almond Shortbread
Chocolate Chip Banana Bran Muffins
Scones with Chocolate and Ginger
Chocolate Chunk Sour Cream Coffee Cake
Chocolate Chip Banana Muffins
Whole Wheat Tea Scones with Chocolate Butter
Chocolate Muffins with White Chocolate Chunks
Chocolate Kugelhupf
Chocolate Coffee Cake
Chocolate Doughnuts
Chocolate Stollen
Chocolate Coffee Twist

*W*e have never believed anyone should have to wait until the sun is high in the heavens to begin enjoying chocolate. A bit of chocolate baked into the morning muffin or coffee cake can brighten up a dull dawn and soothe the spirit as few other ingredients can. If the day is bright and sunny and holds great promise, a taste of chocolate only makes the morning that much better. In this chapter we have recipes for quick breads, coffee cakes, doughnuts, and muffins, which, with their tantalizing aromas and satisfying flavors, will ensure that you start the day on a sweet note. We also have a recipe for chocolate chip pancakes that will surely become a Sunday morning favorite in any chocolate-loving household. And our recipe for chocolate chip granola will have your children begging for spoonfuls to sprinkle on their hot cereal on cold, snowy mornings.

These recipes go hand in hand, we think, with recipes that are appropriate for afternoon tea. Certainly most muffins and quick breads are as welcome on the tea table as on the breakfast table. Afternoon tea, that most gracious of customs, is happily coming back into style. It's later than lunch, earlier than cocktails, and many hosts and hostesses are discovering that the end of the afternoon, when the light is fading and the evening is gently beckoning, is the perfect time to gather a few friends together for a simple tea party where everyone can indulge in some wonderful baked treats. We doubt any tea table would be as tempting if it lacked chocolate and therefore suggest serving chocolate shortbread, scones, cakes, muffins, and breads with the pot of Earl Grey.

Banana Chocolate Chip ⟳ Pancakes ⟲

Start the day out right with sweet banana pancakes generously studded with chocolate chips. Terrific with no embellishment, their goodness reaches new heights of sweet pleasure when they are drenched with maple syrup. As with all hot cakes, these are best served right off the griddle, but you may, if it is easier, make them in batches and keep them warm in a low oven.

YIELD: 8 pancakes

DIFFICULTY: ◼

PREPARATION TIME: 30 minutes

1 cup all-purpose flour
2 tablespoons packed light brown sugar
1½ teaspoons double-acting baking powder
⅛ teaspoon salt
½ cup mashed very ripe banana (about 1 large banana)
⅔ cup milk
1 large egg, lightly beaten
1 teaspoon vegetable oil
¼ teaspoon vanilla extract
2 ounces (about ¼ cup) miniature chocolate chips
Sliced bananas, maple syrup, and butter, for serving (optional)

1. In a very large measuring cup or a medium bowl, stir together the flour, brown sugar, baking power, and salt.

2. In a medium bowl, stir together the banana, milk, egg, oil, and vanilla until well combined. Using a wooden spoon, stir the banana mixture into the dry ingredients just until blended. Stir in the chocolate chips. Do not overmix the batter.

3. Over high heat, heat a nonstick griddle or two large nonstick skillets until very hot. The griddle is ready when a drop of water sprinkled on the surface immediately forms a ball and begins to sputter. Using ¼ cup of batter for each pancake, pour 8 pancakes onto the hot griddle. Cook the pancakes for about 1 minute or until small bubbles appear on the uncooked surface of the pancakes. Using a large metal spatula, turn the pancakes and continue cooking for about 1 minute or until the undersides are golden brown. Adjust the heat as necessary to avoid burning. Serve the pancakes immediately with the sliced bananas, maple syrup, and butter, if desired. The pancakes may also be made in batches, if necessary. Keep the prepared pancakes warm in a single layer on a baking sheet in a preheated 200°F oven.

∽ Chocolate Chip Granola ∾

Granola never tasted like this! Already crunchy and tasty before any additions, the high-energy snack can be tossed with dried papaya and white chocolate chips *or* with dates and miniature semisweet chocolate chips. Whichever you select, sprinkle some of the granola on hot cereal on a chilly day or pack some in the kids' lunch boxes.

YIELD: about 3¾ cups

DIFFICULTY: ◣

PREPARATION TIME: 25 minutes plus baking and cooling times

1½ cups uncooked old-fashioned rolled oats
¼ cup lightly salted shelled sunflower seeds
¼ cup sweetened flaked coconut
¼ cup lightly salted macadamia nuts, very coarsely chopped
¼ cup unsalted roasted cashews, very coarsely chopped
2 tablespoons toasted wheat germ
¼ cup honey
3 tablespoons vegetable oil
1 tablespoon unsalted butter
¼ teaspoon vanilla extract

Additions:

½ cup chopped dried papaya
2 ounces (about ⅓ cup) white chocolate chips or 2 ounces white chocolate, chopped

or:

½ cup pitted dates, chopped
2 ounces (about ⅓ cup) miniature semisweet chocolate chips

(continued)

1. Position a rack in the center of the oven and preheat to 350°F. Lightly oil a 10-by-15-inch jelly-roll pan.

2. In a large bowl, combine the oats, sunflower seeds, coconut, nuts, and wheat germ.

3. In a 3-quart saucepan, combine the honey, oil, and butter. Cook over medium heat, stirring often with a wooden spoon, until the butter is melted. Remove the pan from the heat and stir in the vanilla.

4. Add the dry ingredients to the saucepan and stir to coat. Spread the mixture in an even layer in the prepared pan. Bake for 13 to 18 minutes, stirring the mixture twice during the baking for even browning, until the mixture is lightly toasted and golden brown. Cool the granola in the pan on a wire rack for about 5 minutes. Transfer the granola to a large bowl and cool for about 30 minutes, stirring occasionally, until it reaches room temperature. Stir in your choice of papaya and white chocolate or dates and semisweet chocolate.

Coconut Chocolate Streusel
〜 Coffee Cake 〜

Coconut and chocolate have long made a good pair. Here they are matched in a sweet, moist coffee cake and have never tasted better. Be sure you buy sweetened coconut flakes; the unsweetened will not be sweet enough for the topping and filling.

YIELD: 9 servings

DIFFICULTY: ▬

PREPARATION TIME: 30 minutes plus baking and cooling times

Streusel topping/filling:

½ cup granulated sugar
½ cup all-purpose flour
1 tablespoon nonalkalized unsweetened cocoa powder
½ teaspoon ground cinnamon
4 tablespoons (½ stick) unsalted butter, chilled and cut into ½-inch cubes
½ cup pecans, finely chopped
½ cup sweetened flaked coconut

Coffee cake:

1 cup sweetened flaked coconut
2 cups all-purpose flour
1 teaspoon double-acting baking powder
½ teaspoon baking soda
½ teaspoon salt
¾ cup granulated sugar
8 tablespoons (1 stick) unsalted butter, softened

2 large eggs, at room temperature
1 teaspoon vanilla extract
1 cup sour cream, at room temperature
3½ ounces (about ⅓ cup plus ¼ cup) miniature semisweet
    chocolate chips, divided

Prepare the streusel topping/filling:

1. Combine the sugar, flour, cocoa, and cinnamon in a food processor and process for 5 to 10 seconds, until blended. Distribute the butter cubes evenly over the flour mixture and process for 10 to 20 seconds, until the mixture resembles coarse crumbs. Add the nuts and coconut and pulse 3 to 6 times, just until combined.

Make the coffee cake:

2. Position a rack in the center of the oven and preheat to 350°F. Line a 9-inch square baking pan with aluminum foil so that the foil extends 2 inches beyond opposite sides of the pan. Lightly butter the bottom and sides of the foil-lined pan.

3. Put the coconut in a food processor fitted with the metal chopping blade. Pulse the motor on and off for 45 to 50 seconds, until the coconut is very finely chopped.

4. In a medium bowl, stir together the flour, baking powder, baking soda, and salt. Stir in the chopped coconut.

5. In a large bowl, using a hand-held electric mixer set at medium-high speed, beat the sugar and butter for 2 to 3 minutes or until light. Add the eggs one at a time, beating well after each addition. (The mixture may look a little curdled.) Beat in the vanilla.

6. At low speed, in two additions each, add the flour-coconut mixture and the sour cream alternately, beating after each addition. Beat the mixture just until smooth.

7. Scrape half of the batter into the prepared pan and spread evenly with a spatula. Sprinkle with 1¼ cups of the streusel mixture. Sprinkle with ⅓ cup of the chocolate chips. Top with the remaining batter and spread evenly. Sprinkle with the remaining streusel mixture.

8. Bake for 45 to 55 minutes or until a cake tester or toothpick inserted in the center of the cake comes out clean. Immediately sprinkle with the remaining ¼ cup of chocolate chips. Cool the cake in the pan on a wire rack for 10 minutes. Using the two ends of the aluminum foil as handles, transfer the cake to a wire rack. Cool for approximately 45 minutes before slicing. Serve warm or at room temperature.

Chocolate-Speckled Banana Loaves

These quick-from-a-mix loaves of chocolaty banana bread are so good in the morning you may not be able to save them for later in the day. If you want to dress them up for a tea or coffee party, top them with a creamy chocolate glaze. Unglazed and completely cool, they may be wrapped in foil and frozen for up to a month.

YIELD: 2 loaves

DIFFICULTY: ■

PREPARATION TIME: 30 minutes plus baking, cooling, and setting times

Banana loaves:

1 cup pecans, finely chopped
3 ounces bittersweet chocolate, finely chopped
2 tablespoons all-purpose flour
1 18½-ounce box yellow cake mix with pudding in the mix
1½ cups mashed ripe banana (about 4 medium bananas)
¾ cup water
3 large eggs, at room temperature
¼ cup vegetable oil
2 teaspoons vanilla extract

Glaze (optional):

⅔ cup heavy (whipping) cream
6 ounces bittersweet chocolate, finely chopped
2 teaspoons vanilla extract
½ cup pecans, coarsely chopped, for garnish (optional)

Make the banana loaves:

1. Position a rack in the center of the oven and preheat to 350°F. Lightly butter the bottoms and sides of two 4½-by-8½-by-2¾-inch loaf pans. Dust the bottoms and sides of the pans with flour and tap out the excess.

2. In a small bowl, toss together the pecans, chocolate, and flour.

3. In a large bowl, using a hand-held electric mixer set at medium speed, beat together the cake mix, banana, water, eggs, oil, and vanilla until moist. Increase the speed to high and beat 1½ to 2 minutes or until the batter forms a thin ribbon when the beaters are lifted.

4. Using a rubber spatula, fold in the chocolate-nut mixture. Evenly divide the batter between the prepared pans. Bake for 40 to 50 minutes, until the loaves are golden brown and a cake tester or toothpick inserted into the center of each loaf comes out clean.

5. Cool the loaves in their pans on wire racks for 10 minutes. Run a knife around the edges of the loaves to loosen, and invert them onto a wire rack. Turn them over so they are right side up and cool completely.

Make the glaze:

6. In a medium saucepan over medium-low heat, bring the cream to a gentle boil. Take the pan off the heat and add the chocolate. Let sit for 2

minutes. Using a wire whisk, stir the chocolate and cream until smooth. Stir in the vanilla. Strain the glaze through a fine sieve into a small bowl to remove any air bubbles.

7.   Put the cooled loaves at least 2 inches apart on a wire rack set on a baking sheet. Pour the warm glaze evenly over the loaves, spreading it over the tops with a spatula. Allow the glaze to drip down the sides onto the baking sheet. Sprinkle chopped pecans in a line lengthwise down the center of each loaf, if desired. Refrigerate the glazed loaves for 10 minutes to set the glaze. To serve, slice the loaves with a sharp knife. Store in an airtight container for up to 3 days.

Deborah's Chocolate Brunch ⌒ *Cake* ⌒

This coffee-flavored chocolate cake is extra moist because, after baking, holes are poked in it and a sweet coffee syrup is poured into the holes.

YIELD: 12 to 14 servings

DIFFICULTY: ◣

PREPARATION TIME: 40 minutes plus baking and cooling times

SPECIAL EQUIPMENT: 12-cup fluted Bundt cake pan

Cake:

3 ounces unsweetened chocolate, coarsely chopped

2 cups all-purpose flour

1½ teaspoons baking soda

½ teaspoon double-acting baking powder

½ teaspoon salt

8 tablespoons (1 stick) unsalted butter, softened

1½ cups granulated sugar

3 large eggs, at room temperature

¾ cup coffee liqueur

1 teaspoon instant espresso coffee powder dissolved in
    1 tablespoon hot water

1¼ cups sour cream, at room temperature

Coffee syrup:

8 tablespoons (1 stick) unsalted butter, cut into tablespoons

¾ cup granulated sugar

¼ cup water

¾ cup coffee liqueur

(continued)

Make the cake:

1. Position a rack in the center of the oven and preheat to 350°F. Lightly butter the bottom and sides of a 12-cup fluted Bundt cake pan. Dust the pan with flour and tap out the excess.

2. In the top of a double boiler over hot, not simmering, water, melt the chocolate, stirring frequently until smooth. Remove the top part of the double boiler from the bottom part and cool the chocolate for 5 to 10 minutes or until tepid.

3. In a medium bowl, stir together the flour, baking soda, baking powder, and salt. Sift the mixture.

4. In a large bowl, using a hand-held electric mixer set at medium speed, beat the butter for 30 to 45 seconds or until creamy. Gradually add the sugar and beat at medium speed for 1 to 2 minutes or until light in color and texture. Add the eggs one at a time, beating well after each addition. At low speed, beat in the melted chocolate, coffee liqueur, and dissolved espresso powder. In three additions each, beat in the flour mixture alternating with the sour cream.

5. Scrape the batter into the prepared pan and bake for 45 to 50 minutes or until a cake tester or tookpick inserted into the center comes out clean. While the cake is baking, make the syrup.

Make the coffee syrup:

6. In a medium saucepan over low heat, melt the butter. Add the sugar and water and stir constantly for 1 to 2 minutes or until the sugar dissolves. Increase the heat to medium and bring the syrup to a boil. Remove the pan from the heat and stir in the coffee liqueur. Transfer the hot syrup to a glass measuring cup.

Soak the cake:

7. Using a wooden skewer or long fork, gently poke ¾-inch holes in the top of the hot cake while it is still in the pan.

8. Slowly pour the coffee syrup over the cake and around the edges so that it soaks into the cake. Let the cake stand for 15 minutes. Gently run a knife around the edges of the cake to loosen it. Invert the cake onto a serving plate and cool completely.

Karen's Chocolate Sin-amon ～ Bundt Cake ～

A high-standing Bundt cake looks handsome indeed on the breakfast or brunch table. This one, filled with cinnamon-scented nuts and fruit, and glazed with a cinnamon-flavored chocolate topping, is especially appealing.

YIELD: 12 to 14 servings

DIFFICULTY: ◾

PREPARATION TIME: 45 minutes plus baking and cooling times

SPECIAL EQUIPMENT: 12-cup fluted Bundt cake pan

Filling:

6 ounces (about 1 cup) semisweet chocolate chips
1 cup walnuts, coarsely chopped
½ cup packed light brown sugar
3 tablespoons dried currants
1 tablespoon ground cinnamon

Cake:

3 *cups sifted all-purpose flour*
1½ *teaspoons double-acting baking powder*
1½ *teaspoons baking soda*
½ *teaspoon salt*
¾ *cup (1½ sticks) unsalted butter, softened*
1½ *cups granulated sugar*
2 *teaspoons vanilla extract*
3 *large eggs, at room temperature*
2 *cups sour cream, at room temperature*

Glaze (optional):

2 *cups confectioners' sugar, sifted*
1 *tablespoon unsweetened nonalkalized cocoa powder*
¼ *teaspoon ground cinnamon*
Pinch of salt
3 *tablespoons hot milk*
¼ *teaspoon vanilla extract*

½ *cup coarsely chopped walnuts*

Make the filling:

1. In a small bowl, combine the chocolate chips, walnuts, brown sugar, currants, and cinnamon.

Make the cake:

2. Position a rack in the center of the oven and preheat to 350°F. Lightly butter the bottom and sides of a 12-cup fluted Bundt cake pan. Dust the pan with flour and tap out the excess.

3. In a medium bowl, stir and then sift together the flour, baking powder, baking soda, and salt.

4. In a large bowl, using a hand-held electric mixer set at medium speed, beat the butter 30 to 45 seconds or until creamy. Gradually add the sugar and beat at medium speed for 1 to 2 minutes or until light in color and texture. Beat in the vanilla. Add the eggs one at a time, beating well after each addition. At low speed, in three additions each, beat in the flour mixture alternating with the sour cream.

5. Scrape one third of the batter into the prepared pan. Using a small spatula, spread the batter evenly. Cover with half of the filling. Scrape in another third of the batter, followed by the remaining filling, and finish with the remaining batter. Bake the cake for 55 to 65 minutes or until a cake tester or toothpick inserted into the center comes out clean. Cool the cake in its pan on a wire rack for 15 minutes. If you are not glazing the cake, gently run a knife around its edge to loosen it, and invert it onto a wire rack. Cool completely. If you plan to glaze the cake, the glaze should be made after the cake has cooled for 15 minutes and then used immediately.

Make the glaze:

6. In a medium bowl, combine the confectioners' sugar, cocoa, cinnamon, and salt. Whisk in the hot milk and vanilla to make a smooth glaze.

Glaze the cake:

7. Gently run a knife around the edge of the cake to loosen it, and invert it onto a wire rack. Set the wire rack with the cake over a baking sheet. Pour the glaze over the warm cake, spreading it evenly with a spatula. Sprinkle the chopped walnuts on top of the cake. Cool completely.

Macadamia Chocolate Chip
⁓ Streusel Coffee Cake ⁓

An easy way to make a simple coffee cake special is to layer the batter with a fair share of macadamia nut and chocolate chip streusel.

YIELD: 12 servings
DIFFICULTY: ◼
PREPARATION TIME: 30 minutes plus baking and cooling times
SPECIAL EQUIPMENT: 12-cup fluted Bundt cake pan

Streusel:

½ cup light brown sugar
½ cup all-purpose flour
Pinch of salt
3 tablespoons unsalted butter, chilled and cut into ½-inch cubes
1 cup macadamia nuts, coarsely chopped
8 ounces (about 1⅓ cups) semisweet chocolate chips

Cake:

4 cups all-purpose flour
2 teaspoons double-acting baking powder
1 teaspoon baking soda
1 teaspoon salt
1 cup (2 sticks) unsalted butter, melted and cooled
2 cups granulated sugar
2 cups sour cream, at room temperature
2 extra-large eggs, at room temperature
2 tablespoons vanilla extract
Confectioners' sugar, for sifting over the finished cake

Make the streusel:

1. In a medium bowl, stir together the brown sugar, flour, and salt. Distribute the butter cubes evenly over the sugar-flour mixture. Using your fingertips, quickly rub the butter into the dry ingredients until the mixture resembles coarse meal. Stir in the nuts and chocolate chips.

Make the cake:

2. Position a rack in the center of the oven and preheat to 350°F. Butter a 12-cup fluted Bundt cake pan.

3. In a large bowl, stir together the flour, baking powder, baking soda, and salt. Sift the mixture.

4. In another large bowl, whisk together the butter, sugar, sour cream, eggs, and vanilla until creamy.

5. Make a well in the center of the flour mixture and whisk in the butter mixture just until smooth.

6. Spread one third of the batter over the bottom of the prepared Bundt pan. Sprinkle half of the streusel evenly over the batter. Top with another third of the batter and sprinkle with the remaining streusel. Top with the remaining batter and spread evenly. Bake for 60 to 70 minutes or until a cake tester or toothpick inserted into the center of the cake comes out clean. Cool the cake in the pan on a wire rack for 10 minutes. Invert the cake onto the rack and cool for at least 20 minutes. Sift confectioners' sugar lightly over the top of the cake. Serve warm or at room temperature. Store in an airtight container for up to 4 days.

〜 Chocolate Almond Shortbread 〜

Try this easy, buttery chocolate shortbread the next time you pour yourself a cup of tea in the late afternoon. Chocolate shortbread is a pleasant surprise to anyone who has never tried it but loves the texture and taste of conventional shortbread—and also likes chocolate. This recipe was developed by California innkeeper Rachel Binah to remind her of living in Wales.

YIELD: 16 servings
DIFFICULTY: ▰
PREPARATION TIME: 20 minutes plus baking and cooling times
SPECIAL EQUIPMENT: 8-by-3-inch round springform pan

1 cup all-purpose flour
⅓ cup unsweetened nonalkalized cocoa powder
⅔ cup granulated sugar
½ cup roasted slivered almonds (for roasting instructions, see page 20)
8 tablespoons (1 stick) unsalted butter, chilled and cut into tablespoons
1 tablespoon confectioners' sugar

1. Position a rack in the center of the oven and preheat to 350°F. Butter the bottom of the springform pan.

2. Using a food processor fitted with the metal chopping blade, blend the flour, cocoa, and sugar by pulsing several times. Add the almonds and butter and pulse about 16 times or until the mixture is a crumbly meal.

3. Pat the mixture into the bottom of the prepared pan. Bake for 25 to 30 minutes or until firm to the touch and then cool the shortbread on a wire rack.

4. Remove the sides of the springform pan while the shortbread is still warm. Cut it into 16 wedges. Cool the shortbread thoroughly before removing the bottom of the pan. Sprinkle with the confectioners' sugar. Store in an airtight container.

Chocolate Chip Banana Bran
～ *Muffins* ～

Freshly baked muffins, with their characteristically homely cracked crust, entice even the busiest, most harried member of the family to sit down at the breakfast table. Here, the classic bran muffin is enhanced by the addition of bananas and chocolate chips—and yet each healthy muffin has only 175 calories.

YIELD: 12 muffins

DIFFICULTY: ◼

PREPARATION TIME: 15 minutes plus baking and cooling times

---

1 cup shredded bran cereal (such as Kellogg's All-Bran)
½ cup plus 2 tablespoons low-fat (2 percent) milk, at room temperature
1½ cups all-purpose flour
¼ cup granulated sugar
2 ounces (about ¼ cup) miniature semisweet chocolate chips
1 tablespoon double-acting baking powder
¼ teaspoon salt
1 cup mashed ripe banana (about 2 large bananas)
1 large egg, at room temperature
¼ cup vegetable oil

1. Position a rack in the center of the oven and preheat to 400°F. Lightly butter twelve 1¼-by-2¾-inch (3-ounce) muffin cups.

2. In a medium bowl, combine the bran and milk. Let stand for 3 to 4 minutes or until the bran is softened.

3. In a large bowl, stir together the flour, sugar, chocolate chips, baking powder, and salt. In another bowl, stir together the banana, egg, oil, and softened bran mixture until blended.

4. Make a well in the center of the dry ingredients. Add the liquid ingredients and stir with a wooden spoon just to combine.

5. Spoon the batter into the prepared muffin cups, making each three-fourths full. Bake for 20 to 25 minutes or until the muffins are golden brown and a cake tester or toothpick inserted into the center of one comes out clean. Cool the muffins in the pan set on a wire rack for 5 minutes. Remove the muffins from the cups and finish cooling on the rack. Serve warm or cool completely. You may store the muffins in an airtight container at room temperature for up to 2 days.

Scones with Chocolate and ⌒ Ginger ⌒

Scones are rather like baking powder biscuits—only heavier. These are dropped onto the baking sheet, not stamped out of rolled dough as biscuits. When baked, they are warm and tender inside, a little rough outside. Flavored with crystallized ginger and dark chocolate as these are, they are a splendid addition to the afternoon tea table.

YIELD: 9 to 12 scones
DIFFICULTY: ◼
PREPARATION TIME: 40 minutes plus baking and cooling times

5 ounces bittersweet chocolate, chopped into ¼-inch pieces
¼ cup crystallized ginger, finely chopped
2 cups all-purpose flour
¼ cup granulated sugar
¼ cup packed light brown sugar
1½ teaspoons double-acting baking powder
1 teaspoon baking soda
1 teaspoon salt
6 tablespoons (¾ stick) unsalted butter, chilled and cut into
    ¼-inch cubes
½ cup buttermilk
1 large egg, lightly beaten
2 teaspoons vanilla extract
⅛ teaspoon grated orange zest

1. Position a rack in the center of the oven and preheat to 375°F.

2. In a small bowl, combine the chocolate and ginger.

3. Into a large bowl, press the flour, sugars, baking powder, baking soda, and salt through a sieve. Distribute the butter cubes over the flour mixture. Using your fingertips, quickly rub the butter into the flour mixture until the mixture resembles coarse meal.

4. In a medium bowl, stir together the buttermilk, egg, vanilla, and orange zest.

5. Add the liquid ingredients to the flour mix-

ture. With a large rubber spatula, using as few strokes as possible, stir gently until the dough is moistened and begins to cling together. Add the chocolate and ginger. Handling the dough as little as possible, stir until all the ingredients are completely combined.

6. Using a ⅓-cup measuring cup, drop the dough onto an ungreased baking sheet, leaving at least 1 inch between scones. Bake for 16 to 18 minutes or until the scones are golden brown. Cool the scones on the baking sheet on a wire rack for 5 minutes. Using a metal spatula, transfer the scones to the wire rack and cool completely. Serve warm or store completely cooled scones in an airtight container at room temperature.

Chocolate Chunk Sour Cream
⌒ Coffee Cake ⌒

Here's an easy, filled coffee cake gently perfumed with cinnamon and flavored with chopped chocolate and walnuts.

YIELD: 12 to 14 servings

DIFFICULTY: ◼

PREPARATION TIME: 35 minutes plus baking and cooling times

SPECIAL EQUIPMENT: 10-by-4-inch round tube pan

Filling:

¾ cup granulated sugar
2 teaspoons ground cinnamon
12 ounces (about 2 cups) semisweet chocolate, coarsely chopped
1 cup walnuts, coarsely chopped

Coffee cake:

2¾ cups all-purpose flour
2 teaspoons double-acting baking powder
½ teaspoon baking soda
1 cup (2 sticks) unsalted butter, softened
1 cup granulated sugar
3 large eggs, at room temperature
1½ teaspoons vanilla extract
1 cup sour cream, at room temperature

Make the filling:

1. In a small bowl, combine the sugar and cinnamon. Add the semisweet chocolate and walnuts and stir to combine.

Make the coffee cake:

2. Position a rack in the center of the oven and preheat to 350°F. Lightly butter the bottom, sides, and center tube of the tube pan. Lightly dust the bottom and sides of the pan with flour and tap out the excess.

3. In a medium bowl, stir together the flour, baking powder, and baking soda. Sift the mixture.

4. In a large bowl, using a hand-held electric mixer set at low speed, beat the butter for 30 seconds or until creamy. Gradually add the sugar and beat at medium speed for 1 to 2 minutes or until light and fluffy. Add the eggs one at a time, beating well after each addition. Beat in the vanilla. In three additions, beating at low speed, mix in the dry ingredients alternating with the sour cream.

5. Scrape one third of the batter into the prepared pan. Using a small, offset spatula, spread the batter evenly. Cover the batter with one third of the filling. Scrape half of the remaining batter over the filling and spread evenly. Cover the batter with half of the remaining filling. Scrape the remaining

batter into the pan, spread evenly, and cover with the remaining filling. Bake for 55 to 65 minutes or until a cake tester or toothpick inserted into the cake comes out clean. Cool the cake in the pan on a wire rack for 15 minutes or until the chocolate on

top starts to harden. Run a knife around the edge of the pan to loosen, and invert the cake onto a wire rack. Quickly invert the cake again onto another wire rack and cool completely.

⌒ *Chocolate Chip Banana Muffins* ⌒

These banana muffins livened up with chocolate chips—in fact, they're *chock-full* of chocolate chips—would be good on the breakfast table or tucked into a lunch box or briefcase for a mid-morning snack.

YIELD: 12 muffins

DIFFICULTY: ◢

PREPARATION TIME: 20 minutes plus baking time

2 cups all-purpose flour
1½ teaspoons double-acting baking powder
¼ teaspoon baking soda
¼ teaspoon salt
8 tablespoons (1 stick) unsalted butter, softened
½ cup packed light brown sugar
2 large eggs, at room temperature, lightly beaten
1 cup mashed ripe banana (about 2 large bananas)
⅓ cup milk, at room temperature
1 teaspoon vanilla extract
¾ cup walnuts, coarsely broken
4½ ounces (about ¾ cup) semisweet chocolate chips

1. Position a rack in the center of the oven and preheat to 375°F. Lightly butter twelve 1⅛-by-2¾-inch (3-ounce) muffin cups and the edges surrounding the cups.

2. In a large bowl, stir together the flour, baking powder, baking soda, and salt. In another bowl, using a hand-held electric mixer set at medium speed, cream the butter and the brown sugar for 2 minutes or until light. Beat in the eggs. Stir in the banana, milk, and vanilla. (The mixture will look curdled.) Add the flour mixture and stir just to combine. Reserve 2 tablespoons each of the walnuts

and chocolate chips and stir in the remaining walnuts and chocolate chips.

3. Spoon the batter into the prepared muffin cups. Sprinkle the tops with the reserved walnuts and chocolate chips. Bake for 25 to 30 minutes or until a cake tester or toothpick inserted into the center of one muffin comes out clean.

4. Cool the muffins in their pans on a wire rack for 5 minutes. Remove the muffins from the cups and finish cooling on the rack. Serve warm, or cool completely and store the muffins in an airtight container.

Whole Wheat Tea Scones with ∽ *Chocolate Butter* ∾

Break open a hot whole wheat scone and spread it with softened chocolate butter—exquisite. Try the chocolate butter on toast, English muffins, or anything toasted, or just baked and in need of a very special spread.

YIELD: Approximately 16 scones

DIFFICULTY: ▄▄

PREPARATION TIME: 40 minutes plus baking time

SPECIAL EQUIPMENT: 2-inch crinkled biscuit cutter

Chocolate butter:

2 tablespoons unsweetened cocoa powder
¼ cup confectioners' sugar
8 tablespoons (1 stick) unsalted butter, softened
⅛ teaspoon vanilla extract

Whole wheat tea scones:

1¾ cups all-purpose flour
½ cup whole wheat flour
¼ cup packed light brown sugar
2 teaspoons double-acting baking powder
1 teaspoon baking soda
¼ teaspoon salt
8 tablespoons (1 stick) unsalted butter, chilled and cut into ½-inch cubes
About ¾ cup buttermilk

Make the chocolate butter:

1. Stir together the cocoa powder and confectioners' sugar. Sift the mixture over a piece of waxed paper.

2. In a medium bowl, using a hand-held electric mixer set at medium speed, beat the butter until creamy. Add the cocoa-sugar mixture and vanilla. Continue beating for 1 minute or until the mixture is smooth. Pack into a small crock. Serve or cover and refrigerate until ready to serve. If refrigerated, let the butter stand at room temperature for about 15 minutes to soften slightly before serving.

Make the scones:

3. Position a rack in the center of the oven and preheat to 400°F.

4. In a medium bowl, stir together the flours, brown sugar, baking powder, baking soda, and salt.

5. Mound the dry ingredients on a work surface. Distribute the butter cubes evenly over the flour mixture. Using your fingertips, quickly rub the butter into the dry ingredients until the mixture resembles coarse meal.

6. Make a well in the center of the mound and

add ¼ cup of the buttermilk. Using your fingers, toss the flour-butter mixture and continue adding the buttermilk until the mixture starts to clump together and forms a soft dough. Gather the dough into a ball and knead gently 3 or 4 times. Clean the work surface and lightly sprinkle with the flour.

7.   Pat the dough into a 7-inch circle that is ¾ inch thick. Using a floured 2-inch crinkled biscuit cutter, cut rounds from the circle of dough. Put the scones 1 inch apart on an ungreased baking sheet. Gather the scraps together and reroll to make more scones. With a pastry brush, lightly brush the tops of the scones with buttermilk. Bake for about 15 minutes or until the tops are lightly browned. Serve warm with the chocolate butter.

Chocolate Muffins with White *Chocolate Chunks*

Try something different in the muffin basket with these dark chocolate muffins filled with melting chunks of sweet white chocolate.

YIELD: 12 muffins

DIFFICULTY: ▬

PREPARATION TIME: 20 minutes plus baking time

1¾ cups all-purpose flour
¾ cup granulated sugar
½ cup unsweetened nonalkalized cocoa powder
2 teaspoons double-acting baking powder
½ teaspoon salt
¼ teaspoon baking soda
1 cup milk, at room temperature
8 tablespoons (1 stick) unsalted butter, melted and cooled
1 large egg, at room temperature, lightly beaten
1 teaspoon vanilla extract
6 ounces white chocolate, cut into ¾-inch chunks

1.   Position a rack in the center of the oven and preheat to 375°F. Lightly butter twelve 1⅛-by-2¾-inch (3-ounce) muffin cups and the edges surrounding the cups.

2.   In a large bowl, stir together the flour, sugar, cocoa, baking powder, salt, and baking soda. In another bowl, stir together the milk, butter, egg, and vanilla until blended. Make a well in the center of the dry ingredients. Add the liquid ingredients and stir just to combine. Stir in half of the white chocolate chunks.

3.   Spoon the batter into the prepared muffin cups. Sprinkle the tops with the remaining white chocolate chunks. Bake for 20 to 25 minutes or until a cake tester or toothpick inserted in the center of one of the muffins comes out clean.

4.   Cool the muffins in their pans set on a wire rack for 5 minutes. Remove the muffins from the cups and finish cooling on the wire rack. Serve warm, or cool completely and store the muffins in an airtight container at room temperature.

⌒ *Chocolate Kugelhupf* ⌒

Baked in a traditional Kugelhupf pan, this sweet yeast bread is bursting with chocolate, raisins, and nuts. If you decide to make the bread in very humid weather, you may have to add as many as 2 extra tablespoons of flour when kneading the dough (step 4). Be sure to allow 5 hours for rising, as well as 3 hours for chilling the Kugelhupf.

YIELD: 12 servings

DIFFICULTY: ◼◼

PREPARATION TIME: 30 minutes plus baking and cooling times (allow at least 8 hours for rising)

SPECIAL EQUIPMENT: 11-cup Kugelhupf pan or similar fluted tube pan

---

¾ cup warm milk (105° to 115°F)

1 teaspoon granulated sugar

3½ teaspoons (about 1½ packages) active dry yeast

1 cup bread flour

About 3¾ cups all-purpose flour

½ cup packed light brown sugar

2 large eggs plus 2 large egg yolks

12 tablespoons (1½ sticks) unsalted butter, softened and cut into 12 pieces

2 teaspoons vanilla extract

1½ teaspoons salt

2 teaspoons grated orange zest

4 ounces bittersweet chocolate, finely chopped

4 ounces milk chocolate, finely chopped

¾ cup golden raisins

1¼ cups pecans, coarsely chopped

¾ teaspoon ground cinnamon

1 tablespoon confectioners' sugar, for dusting

1. In a food processor fitted with the dough blade, combine the warm milk and sugar. Sprinkle the yeast over the top of the milk and let it stand for 10 minutes or until the yeast foams.

2. Sprinkle the bread flour over the top of the milk. Process for 5 seconds. Scrape down the sides of the bowl and process for 20 seconds or until a smooth batter forms. Leave on the top of the processor and let the batter sit for 30 minutes or until it has doubled in volume.

3. Distribute 1 cup of the all-purpose flour, the brown sugar, eggs, egg yolks, butter, vanilla, salt, and orange zest in the food processor with the risen batter. Process for 20 seconds or until the batter is smooth. Add 2½ cups of the remaining all-purpose flour and process for another 20 seconds or until a soft, sticky dough starts to form. It will not pull away from the sides of the bowl the way a normal bread dough does.

4. Scrape the dough out onto a smooth work surface. Sprinkle 2 tablespoons of the remaining flour over the dough and knead for 1 minute. The dough will still be soft and slightly sticky. If the weather is humid, you may have to add the extra 2

tablespoons of flour. Form the dough into a ball and transfer to a large ungreased bowl. Cover tightly with plastic wrap and let rise in a warm, draft-free place for about 2 hours or until doubled in volume.

5. In a medium bowl, combine both chocolates, the raisins, pecans, and cinnamon. Punch down the dough and turn out onto a work surface. Roll the dough into a 12-inch circle. Sprinkle half of the chocolate mixture over the circle of dough and press it into the dough. Fold the outside edge of the circle of dough into the center to form a round package. Pinch the seams together and turn the package over. Roll once more into a circle and sprinkle the remaining chocolate mixture over the circle. Press the chocolate into the dough and repeat the folding process. Put the package seam-side down into a clean mixing bowl. Cover and refrigerate for at least 3 hours or overnight.

6. Generously butter an 11-cup Kugelhupf mold or similar fluted tube pan. Punch the dough down and turn out onto a work surface. Press into an 8-inch disk and poke a hole in the center of the dough as if making a large doughnut. Put the dough ring into the prepared pan. Cover and let rise for about 3 hours or until double in volume.

7. Position a rack in the center of the oven and preheat to 375°F.

8. Bake the Kugelhupf for about 50 minutes or until the top is a dark brown. With a small sharp knife, carefully loosen the edges of the Kugelhupf from the mold and turn it out onto a wire rack. Cool completely before dusting lightly with confectioners' sugar, or wrap in aluminum foil, let it sit overnight, and dust with the confectioners' sugar before serving.

⁓ Chocolate Coffee Cake ⁓

At the Cafe Beaujolais in Mendocino, California, chef/owner Margaret Fox serves this chocolate coffee cake mostly because it represents everything she likes in a morning bread: the crumb is cakelike, the yogurt provides a bit of tang, and the chocolate is simply, as she says, luscious. We agree.

YIELD: 16 servings

DIFFICULTY: ◼

PREPARATION TIME: 35 minutes plus baking and cooling times

SPECIAL EQUIPMENT: 12-cup fluted Bundt cake pan

Filling:

¾ cup packed light brown sugar
½ cup finely chopped dried apricots
½ cup coarsely chopped walnuts
2 ounces (about ⅓ cup) semisweet chocolate chips
2 tablespoons unsweetened nonalkalized cocoa powder
1 tablespoon instant coffee powder
2 teaspoons ground cinnamon

Cake batter:

2¾ cups all-purpose flour
1½ teaspoons double-acting baking powder

(ingredients continued)

1½ teaspoons baking soda
¾ teaspoon salt
12 tablespoons (1½ sticks) unsalted butter, at room temperature
1½ cups granulated sugar
1 teaspoon vanilla extract
3 large eggs, at room temperature
2 cups plain yogurt, at room temperature
Confectioners' sugar, for dusting

Make the filling:

1. In a medium bowl, combine all the filling ingredients.

Make the cake batter:

2. Position a rack in the center of the oven and preheat to 350°F. Generously butter the inside of a 12-cup (10-inch) round Bundt cake pan and lightly dust with flour. Tap out the excess.

3. In a medium bowl, stir together the flour, baking powder, baking soda, and salt. Sift the mixture onto a large sheet of waxed paper.

4. In a large bowl of an electric mixer, cream the butter, sugar, and vanilla at medium-high speed for 3 minutes or until light and fluffy. Add the eggs one at a time, beating well after each addition. Beat just until the mixture is smooth.

5. With the mixer set at low, add the sifted flour mixture a third at a time, alternating with the yogurt and beating after each addition.

6. Spread one third of the batter over the bottom of the Bundt pan. Sprinkle half of the filling evenly over the batter. Top with another third of the batter and sprinkle with the remaining filling. Top with the remaining batter and spread evenly.

7. Bake for 55 to 60 minutes or until a cake tester or toothpick inserted in the center of the cake comes out clean. Cool the cake in the pan on a wire rack for 10 minutes. Invert the cake onto a rack and cool for at least 10 minutes before slicing. Sift confectioners' sugar lightly over the top of the cake. Serve warm or at room temperature. Store in an airtight container.

⌒ *Chocolate Doughnuts* ⌒

These glossy chocolate doughnuts go far beyond the chocolate-glazed doughnuts available in doughnut shops. Not only are they dipped in a smooth chocolate glaze so that they are completely covered, but inside they're chocolate, too. And we have not forgotten about the holes—they're dipped in glaze too, and just the right size for a mouthful of chocolate delight. Be sure to let the oil regain its heat between frying batches of doughnuts and holes.

YIELD: Aproximately 14 doughnuts and 14 doughnut holes
DIFFICULTY: ▬▬
PREPARATION TIME: 1 hour plus frying, cooling, and setting times
SPECIAL EQUIPMENT: 2¾-inch biscuit cutter

Doughnuts:

3¼ cups plus 3 tablespoons all-purpose flour
1 teaspoon double-acting baking powder
1 teaspoon baking soda
¾ teaspoon salt
3 ounces bittersweet chocolate, finely chopped
3 ounces milk chocolate, finely chopped
1 large egg plus 1 large egg white, at room temperature
¾ cup plus 3 tablespoons granulated sugar
¾ cup buttermilk, at room temperature
3 tablespoons vegetable oil
2 teaspoons vanilla extract
6 cups vegetable oil, for frying the doughnuts

Chocolate glaze:

1 pound plus 2 ounces bittersweet chocolate, coarsely chopped, divided
¾ cup plus 2 tablespoons water
¼ cup granulated sugar
2 tablespoons light corn syrup
½ teaspoon vanilla extract

Decoration:

½ cup walnuts, finely chopped (optional)
Sifted confectioners' sugar

Make the doughnuts:

1. In a large bowl, stir together the flour, baking powder, baking soda, and salt. Stir in the finely chopped chocolates.

2. In a medium bowl, using a hand-held electric mixer set at medium-high speed, beat the egg and egg white with the sugar for about 2 minutes or until the mixture forms a thin yellow ribbon when the beaters are lifted. Beat in the buttermilk, vegetable oil, and vanilla.

3. Make a well in the center of the dry ingredients. Add the egg-sugar mixture. Using a wooden

spoon, stir the mixture into a soft dough. Scrape the dough onto a work surface. Gather the dough into a ball and knead it gently 3 or 4 times. Clean the work surface and lightly sprinkle the dough with flour.

4. Pat the dough into a circle 12 inches in diameter and about ½ inch thick. Using a floured 2¾-inch biscuit cutter, cut rounds from the circle of dough. With a floured 1-inch biscuit cutter, cut doughnut holes from the centers of the cut rounds of dough. Roll the doughnut holes into small balls. Transfer the doughnuts and the doughnut holes to a baking sheet. Gather the scraps of dough together and reroll to make more doughnuts. Let the doughnuts sit for 10 minutes before frying.

5. In a deep-fat fryer or a 2½-quart saucepan, heat the oil to 360°F. Fry the doughnuts, 3 at a time, for 1 minute on each side or until golden brown. Using a slotted spoon, remove the doughnuts from the hot oil to paper towels to drain. Set the doughnuts on a wire rack to cool completely. Fry the doughnut holes in the same manner, 6 at a time.

Make the chocolate glaze:

6. In the top of a double boiler over hot, not simmering, water, melt 8 ounces of the chocolate.

Gradually add the remaining 10 ounces of chocolate, stirring frequently until smooth. Remove the pan from the heat.

7. In a small saucepan, combine the water, sugar, and corn syrup. Cook over medium heat, stirring with a wooden spoon until the sugar dissolves. Do not let the mixture boil. Remove the pan from the heat. Transfer the sugar syrup to a medium bowl. Whisk the melted chocolate into the sugar syrup, blending until smooth. Stir in the vanilla extract. Keep the glaze warm by setting the bowl over a pot of warm water so that the water touches the bottom of the bowl. Tilt the bowl so that it leans against the edge of the pot and creates a deep pool of glaze for dipping.

8. Dip each doughnut into the glaze. Using a fork, turn the doughnut over so that it is fully coated in chocolate. Lift the doughnut out of the glaze, scraping the excess off the fork. Put each doughnut onto a wire rack set over a baking sheet and carefully remove the fork. Coat the doughnut holes in the chocolate glaze using the same procedure. Sprinkle the doughnuts with chopped walnuts before the glaze sets, if desired. Refrigerate for 5 minutes to harden the glaze and lightly dust the doughnuts with confectioners' sugar.

～ *Chocolate Stollen* ～

Generously filled with rum-soaked raisins, pistachios, and *both* dark and milk chocolate pieces, this traditionally shaped German Christmas bread is slathered with rum butter while still hot from the oven. The butter seals in the bread's moisture before it is wrapped and set aside to ripen for a day or two. Chocolate Stollen is a festive addition to your holiday table as well as a good choice for gift giving—wrap it in plastic and tie it with a bright bow. You can make it well ahead of time, as it

keeps for up to 2 weeks if well wrapped in foil and can also be frozen for up to 2 months. The rum butter can be frozen right alongside the stollen.

YIELD: 24 servings
DIFFICULTY: ▬▬
PREPARATION TIME: 30 minutes plus baking and cooling times (allow at least 7 hours for rising)

Stollen:

½ cup milk plus 2 tablespoons warm milk (105° to 115°F)

1 tablespoon plus 1 teaspoon granulated sugar, divided

6¼ teaspoons (2½ envelopes) active dry yeast

¾ cup bread flour

About 2½ cups all-purpose flour, divided

1 7-ounce roll almond paste, such as Odense

1 large egg plus 1 large egg yolk

6 tablespoons unsalted butter, softened and cut into tablespoons

2 teaspoons vanilla extract

1 teaspoon almond extract

¾ teaspoon salt

¼ teaspoon grated orange zest

¼ teaspoon grated lemon zest

¾ cup golden raisins

¼ cup dark rum

⅔ cup shelled unsalted pistachio nuts

3 ounces bittersweet chocolate, finely chopped

3 ounces milk chocolate, finely chopped

Egg wash:

1 large egg

1 teaspoon water

Rum butter:

1 cup (2 sticks) unsalted butter, softened

3 tablespoons dark rum

2 teaspoons vanilla extract

Confectioners' sugar, for dusting

1. In a food processor fitted with the metal chopping blade, combine the warm milk and 1 teaspoon of the sugar. Sprinkle the yeast on top of the milk. Let the mixture stand 10 minutes or until the yeast foams.

2. Sprinkle the bread flour over the top of the yeast mixture. Process for 5 seconds. Scrape down the sides of the bowl and process for another 45 to 60 seconds or until the batter looks stringy. Sprinkle 1 cup of the all-purpose flour over the batter. Leave the top on the processor and let the sponge sit for 30 minutes, until doubled in volume and the surface of the flour layer is cracked.

3. Add the remaining tablespoon of sugar, the almond paste, egg, egg yolk, butter, vanilla and almond extracts, salt, and orange and lemon zests to the risen sponge. Process for 15 to 20 seconds or until creamy. Add 1¼ cups of the remaining all-purpose flour and process for another 15 to 20 seconds or until a soft, sticky dough starts to form. It will not pull away from the sides of the bowl, as a regular bread dough does.

4. Scrape the dough out onto a smooth work surface. Sprinkle half of the remaining ¼ cup of flour over the dough and knead for 1 minute. The dough will still be soft and slightly sticky. In humid weather you may have to add an extra 1 to 2 tablespoons of flour. Form the dough into a ball and transfer it to a large, ungreased bowl. Cover the bowl tightly with plastic wrap and let the dough rise in a warm, draft-free place for 2 to 3 hours or until doubled in volume.

5. In a small saucepan, combine the raisins and rum. Cook over medium heat and bring the mixture to a boil. Remove the pan from the heat and cover. Let the raisins soak for 2 hours and then drain the excess rum. Save any excess rum for the rum butter.

6. In a small bowl, combine the pistachio nuts, soaked raisins, and the chocolates. Punch the dough down and turn it out onto a lightly floured work surface. Roll the dough into a 12-inch circle. Sprinkle half of the chocolate mixture over the circle of dough and press the pieces of chocolate, nuts, and raisins into the dough. Fold the outside of the circle into the center to form a round package. Pinch the seams together and turn the package over. Roll the dough once more into a circle and sprinkle the remaining chocolate mixture over the dough. Press the pieces of chocolate, nuts, and raisins into the dough and repeat the folding process. Put the package seam-side down into a clean mixing bowl, cover tightly with plastic wrap, and let the dough rise once more in a warm, draft-free place for 1 to 2 hours or until doubled in volume.

7. Line a heavy baking sheet with aluminum foil. Punch the dough down and turn it out onto a work surface. Form the dough into a ball. Using a rolling pin, roll the dough into a 7-by-11-inch rectangle, 1 inch thick. Start at the center of the rectangle and, with the rolling pin, roll toward the ends of the rectangle to form thick, raised borders on each of the long ends. The rectangle will now measure 8½ by 11 inches. The raised edge prevents the rich stollen dough from spreading out too much during the rising and baking. Fold each of the short ends to create a 1-inch border to keep the width of the stollen uniform during rising and baking. Fold the dough lengthwise (as if folding a book) so that the

two raised borders are parallel to one another. Transfer the stollen to the foil-lined baking sheet. Cover with plastic wrap and let rise for 1 to 2 hours or until the stollen has increased in size by half. To test if the stollen is sufficiently risen, gently press a finger into the dough and lift it up right away. If an indentation remains, the stollen is ready for baking. If the dough bounces back, the stollen needs more rising time.

Make the egg wash:

8. In a small bowl, beat the egg and water until the mixture is frothy.

Make the rum butter:

9. In a medium bowl, using a hand-held electric mixer set at medium speed, cream the butter for 30 seconds. Gradually beat in the rum and vanilla. Pack all but 3 tablespoons of the rum butter into a crock. Cover with plastic wrap and refrigerate. Reserve the remaining 3 tablespoons at room temperature to brush onto the stollen after it has baked.

Bake the stollen:

10. Position a rack in the center of the oven and preheat to 400°F, about 30 minutes before the stollen is ready for baking.

11. Lightly brush the stollen with the egg wash. Bake the stollen for 15 minutes. Lower the temperature to 350°F and continue baking for 35 to 40 minutes or until the top is a dark brown and a cake tester or toothpick inserted into the stollen comes out clean with no dough clinging to it. Put the stollen on the baking sheet set on a wire rack. Brush the top and bottom of the hot stollen repeatedly with the 3 tablespoons of the rum butter until it is all used. Cool completely and wrap the stollen tightly in aluminum foil. Let the stollen ripen for 1 to 2 days at room temperature. Before serving, lightly dust with confectioners' sugar. Cut into thin slices and serve with the chilled rum butter.

~ *Chocolate Coffee Twist* ~

The almond-paste–pastry-cream filling gives this yeast-risen, rolled coffee cake European flair. The good chocolate flavor has universal appeal. If you make it in humid weather, you may have to add as much as a quarter cup of flour when kneading the dough to get the right consistency. Because the recipe is rather involved and time consuming, we have made it large enough to make 2 twists—just right for a large breakfast, brunch party, or holiday celebration.

YIELD: 2 14-inch coffee twists (20 servings)
DIFFICULTY: ▄▄▄
PREPARATION TIME: 1 hour plus rising, chilling, and baking times

Dough:

10 tablespoons (1 stick plus 2 tablespoons) unsalted butter, melted
1 tablespoon sour cream
½ cup hot milk (105° to 115°F)
¼ cup plus 1 teaspoon granulated sugar, divided
1 package active dry yeast
½ cup unbleached bread flour
2 large eggs plus 1 large egg yolk, at room temperature
½ teaspoon salt
About 2¾ cups all-purpose flour

Pastry cream:

½ cup plus 1 tablespoon milk
1 tablespoon granulated sugar
1 tablespoon cornstarch
1 large egg yolk (reserve white for almond filling)
¼ teaspoon vanilla extract

Almond filling:

5 ounces (about ½ cup) almond paste
1 tablespoon reserved egg white
1 tablespoon granulated sugar
4 tablespoons (½ stick) unsalted butter, softened

Streusel topping:

1 cup all-purpose flour
¼ cup granulated sugar
Pinch of salt
5 tablespoons unsalted butter

(ingredients continued)

To assemble:

5 ounces semisweet chocolate, coarsely chopped
4 tablespoons (½ stick) unsalted butter, melted

Garnish:

¼ cup confectioners' sugar
4 ounces semisweet chocolate, coarsely chopped

Make the dough:

1. In a small bowl, combine the melted butter and sour cream. Cool.

2. In another small bowl, combine the hot milk and 1 teaspoon of the sugar. Sprinkle the yeast over the top of the milk and let stand for about 10 minutes or until the yeast foams.

3. Transfer the yeast mixture to a food processor fitted with the dough blade. Sprinkle the bread flour over the yeast mixture. Process for 30 seconds, scrape down the sides of the bowl, and process for another 10 seconds or until smooth. Leave the top on the food processor and let the sponge sit for 30 minutes or until doubled in volume.

4. Add the butter-sour cream mixture, eggs, egg yolk, the remaining ¼ cup of sugar, salt, and 1¾ cups of the all-purpose flour to the risen dough. Process for 10 seconds. Add ¾ cup of the remaining flour and process for another 10 seconds or until the mixture forms a ball. The dough will be soft and elastic and slightly sticky. In humid weather, you may have to add up to ¼ cup additional flour.

5. Turn the dough out onto a smooth work surface that is dusted lightly with flour. Knead the dough for 30 seconds, shape into a ball, and put into an ungreased bowl. Cover and let rise in a warm, draft-free place for 1½ hours, until doubled.

6. Punch the dough down and turn it over. Cover and refrigerate for 1½ hours.

Make the pastry cream:

7. Bring the milk almost to a boil and remove the sauce pan from the heat. In another small, heavy saucepan, combine the sugar and cornstarch. Stir in the egg volk to make a thick paste. Gradually whisk in the hot milk. Stirring constantly, cook the pastry cream over medium heat for 2 minutes, until it comes to a boil. Remove from the heat and strain. Stir in the vanilla. Cover and refrigerate.

Make the almond filling:

8. In a food processor fitted with the metal chopping blade, combine all the ingredients for the almond filling. Blend for 45 seconds.

Make the streusel topping:

9. In a food processor fitted with the metal chopping blade, combine the streusel ingredients. Blend for 45 seconds.

Assemble the chocolate coffee twist:

10. In a food processor fitted with the metal chopping blade, process the chocolate for 30 seconds.

11. Lightly butter two heavy baking sheets. Punch down the chilled dough and form into a rectangle. Cut the dough in half and return one half to the refrigerator.

12. Roll the first half into a 9-by-17-inch rectangle. Spread half of the almond filling over the rectangle leaving a ½-inch border. Stir the chilled pastry cream and spread half over the almond filling. Sprinkle half of the chocolate over the cream.

13. Starting with the long edge, tightly roll up the rectangle in jelly-roll fashion. Pinch the edges to seal in the filling. Transfer the cylinder seam-side down to one of the prepared baking sheets. Position the baking sheet so that the cylinder of dough is vertical to you. Using a baker's scraper or a sharp knife, cut the cylinder completely in half lengthwise. Starting at the center and working away from yourself, tightly twist the top portion of

the two strands around each other and pinch the two ends together to seal. Return to the center and, working toward yourself, tightly twist the lower portion of the two strands around each other and pinch the ends together. Cover loosely with a piece of plastic wrap. Let rise for about 45 minutes, until almost doubled.

14. Repeat with the second half of dough and the remaining fillings. Position one rack in the top third and one rack in the bottom third of the oven and preheat to 350°F.

15. Brush the risen twists with the melted butter, sprinkle with the streusel, and bake for 30 minutes or until evenly browned, rotating the baking sheets midway through baking. Cool the twists on baking sheets.

Garnish:

16. Sift the confectioners' sugar over the cooled chocolate coffee twists.

17. In the top of a double boiler over hot, not simmering water, melt the chocolate stirring frequently until smooth.

18. Make a small parchment paper cone and fill with chocolate. (For instructions on making a paper cone, see page 187.) Cut off the tip of the cone to form a $\frac{1}{16}$-inch opening. Drizzle chocolate over the coffee twists and transfer to serving boards.

8

Allen Leiberman

Frozen Chocolate

White Chocolate Almond Ice Cream
Chocolate Peanut Butter Pudding Pops
Jack Daniels Chocolate Ice Cream
Brownie Ice Cream Sandwiches
Chocolate Mint Ice Cream Pie
Frozen Chocolate Mint Soufflé
Crème de Menthe Ice Cream
Vanilla Ice Cream with Chocolate Chunks
Chocolate Ice Cream with White Chocolate
    Chunks
Crispy Sugar Cones
Charleston Cobblestone Ice Cream
Milk Chocolate Ice Cream
Bailey's Irish Cream Chocolate Chip
    Ice Cream
Peanut Butter Chocolate Chunk
    Ice Cream
Chocolate Ginger Ice Cream
Swiss Chocolate Cherries Jubilee
Mocha Chocolate Chip Ice Cream
    Sandwiches
Mile High Ice Cream Pie
Raspberry Sauce
Chocolate Caramel-Praline Ice Cream
    Terrine with Warm Caramel Sauce
Chocolate Sherbet with Pistachio Sauce
D and D (Dark and Delicious) Chocolate
    Sauce

or many of us, chocolate ice cream—in any of its many incarnations—is about as good as it gets. Or perhaps it's chocolate-coated ice cream on a stick or a gooey sundae with a cherry on top that satisfies your chocolate appetite. If your preferences run to ice cold chocolate, the recipes that follow will surely entice you into making all sorts of frozen deserts.

The most important piece of equipment you will need for these recipes is a good freezer. In most instances, a tiny ice chest will not do, but a standard freezer either above or below the refrigerator is fine. To maintain an even, frigid temperature, keep the freezer well filled but not chock-full, and before you begin, be sure there is ample room for the dessert you are making.

If you plan to make your own ice cream you will have to buy an ice cream machine. Happily, there are several different kinds to choose from. Unless you plan to make a lot of ice cream very often, buying an expensive machine may not be worth the money or the counter space it occupies. Other models, either electric ones that require ice and salt or hand-cranked ones chilled by a pre-frozen freon-filled jacket, make very good ice cream and are easy to use and handy to store. Whatever you decide, once you begin making your own ice cream and discover how good it is and how easy to make, you will become a quick convert.

On the other hand, there are times when buying ice cream makes more sense than making it. The variety of high-quality brands available, which are very good indeed and can be used in many of our recipes, is growing all the time. It is also possible to add ingredients to commercial ice cream to customize it.

Whatever your preference, it is interesting (although not surprising) to note that ice cream occupies a special place in the hearts of most Americans. According to the National Dairy Board, our favorite flavor is vanilla, which comprises 32 percent of all the ice cream consumed in the United States. The four runners-up are chocolate (9 percent), Neapolitan (6.4 percent), vanilla-fudge (4.1 percent), and cookies 'n' cream (3.8 percent). The most popular ice cream toppings are, in order, chocolate fudge, hot fudge, butterscotch, caramel, and strawberry sauce. Ice cream is eaten in more than 98 percent of the households in the United States and 86 percent of these households purchase ice cream at least once a month. Most folks seem to indulge on Sundays, and overall consumption is generally higher on weekends. The peak hours for eating ice cream—weekend or not—are between 9:00 and 11:00 P.M. It's no surprise that more ice cream is eaten in June and July than other months.

Whether the weather is balmy or nippy, we hope you will never forgo the pleasure of a frozen chocolate dessert simply because you may not have the time or the equipment to make your own ice cream. These desserts are too good for that sort of stubbornness!

White Chocolate Almond Ice
⌒ *Cream* ⌒

Try this seductively sweet ice cream with the White Chocolate Pound Cake in chapter 3. Its custard base makes it especially rich and creamy, and the almonds offset the sweetness of the chocolate. It's good without the nuts, too.

YIELD: Approximately 2 quarts

DIFFICULTY: ▰▰

PREPARATION TIME: 30 minutes plus chilling and freezing times (allow at least 10 hours for the ice cream to stand)

SPECIAL EQUIPMENT: ice cream maker

---

6 ounces white chocolate, finely chopped

4 large egg yolks, at room temperature

3 cups heavy (whipping) cream

1 cup milk

¾ cup granulated sugar

1¼ cups roasted slivered almonds, coarsely chopped (for roasting instructions, see page 20)

1. In the top of a double boiler over hot, not simmering, water, melt the white chocolate, stirring constantly, until smooth. Remove the pan from the heat.

2. In a large bowl, whisk the egg yolks for 1 minute or until they are slightly thickened. In a medium, heavy, noncorrosive saucepan over medium heat, bring the cream, milk, and sugar to a gentle boil, stirring the mixture constantly to dissolve the sugar. Remove the pan from the heat and gradually stir about 1 cup of the hot cream mixture into the egg yolks until well blended. Pour the egg mixture back into the saucepan of cream. Slowly pour about 1 cup of the hot cream mixture into the melted chocolate, whisking constantly until well blended. Slowly pour this mixture back into the saucepan, whisking constantly. Cook over medium-low heat, stirring constantly with a wooden spoon, for about 2 minutes or until the custard is thick enough to coat the back of the spoon. Do not allow the custard to boil. Remove the pan from the heat. Strain the custard into a large bowl. Cool the custard for about 30 minutes, stirring it occasionally. Cover the surface of the custard with plastic wrap and refrigerate overnight or for at least 4 hours.

3. Pour the ice cream mixture into the container of an ice cream maker and freeze according to the manufacturer's directions. Add the roasted almonds to the container and process briefly until they are evenly distributed in the ice cream.

4. Transfer the ice cream to a freezer container. Cover and freeze the ice cream overnight or for at least 6 hours before serving.

Chocolate Peanut Butter Pudding
⌒ Pops ⌒

There is hardly a child alive who can resist these chocolate-on-a-stick frozen pops, particularly since they are flavored with peanut butter, an all-time kids' favorite. If you are out of time or ingredients, substitute instant vanilla or chocolate pudding mixed with smooth peanut butter for the chocolate peanut butter pudding (see the recipe Note).

YIELD: 10 pops

DIFFICULTY: ▬▬

PREPARATION TIME: 45 minutes plus freezing time (allow at least 2 hours for the pops to freeze)

SPECIAL EQUIPMENT: 10 3-ounce paper cups; 10 lollipop or popsicle sticks

Chocolate filling and coating:

1 cup milk

3 tablespoons light corn syrup

12 ounces (about 2 cups) semisweet chocolate chips

1 teaspoon vanilla extract

Chocolate peanut butter pudding:

⅓ cup granulated sugar

2 tablespoons cornstarch

2 large eggs

2½ cups milk

Few grains of salt

6 ounces milk chocolate, coarsely chopped

⅓ cup creamy peanut butter

2 teaspoons vanilla extract

1 cup finely chopped unsalted peanuts (optional)

Make the chocolate filling and coating:

1. In a medium saucepan over medium-high heat, bring the milk and corn syrup to a gentle boil. Remove the pan from the heat and add the chocolate chips. Cover the saucepan and set aside for 2 minutes to allow the chocolate chips to melt. Remove the lid and use a whisk to stir the mixture until smooth. Stir in the vanilla. Set aside or refrigerate until the chocolate mixture is cool and slightly thicker. Stir occasionally.

Make the chocolate peanut butter pudding:

2. In a medium saucepan, stir together the sugar, cornstarch, and eggs until creamy. In another medium saucepan, over medium heat, bring the milk and salt to a gentle boil. Remove the pan from the heat and whisk the milk mixture into the sugar-egg mixture. Stir in the chocolate and peanut butter. Cook the mixture over medium-high heat, stirring constantly with a whisk, for about 6 minutes or until the pudding thickens and starts to boil. Remove the pan from the heat and pour the mixture into a medium bowl. Stir in the vanilla. Cover the surface of the pudding with plastic wrap until ready to spoon it into the cups.

3. Put the 10 paper cups on a small baking sheet. Spoon about 2 tablespoons of the pudding mixture into the bottom of each of the cups. One by one, tap

the bottom of each cup on a flat surface to level the pudding mixture. Top each portion with about 2 teaspoons of the chocolate filling and then add about 2 more tablespoons of the pudding mixture. Tap again to level them. Reserve the remaining chocolate filling for dipping. Insert a lollipop stick into the center of each filled cup. Freeze the pops until firm.

Dip the frozen pops:

4. Put the pan of chocolate filling over medium heat and stir for 2 to 3 minutes or until it melts and liquefies.

5. Line a baking sheet with aluminum foil. One at a time, peel the paper cups from the frozen pops and dip each pop into the melted chocolate. Dip the pops in chopped peanuts, if desired. Put the dipped pops on the baking sheet and freeze for at least 10 minutes longer, until the coating has set. Let the pops stand at room temperature for 5 minutes before serving.

NOTE: If desired, you can substitute 1 3½-ounce package of instant vanilla or instant chocolate pudding that has been mixed with 2 cups of cold milk and ⅓ cup of creamy peanut butter for the chocolate peanut butter pudding.

Jack Daniels Chocolate Ice Cream

When spirits are added to ice cream before freezing, the cold temperature subdues their strength just enough so that the flavor they impart is fine, subtle, and mellow.

YIELD: 6 servings

DIFFICULTY: ▬▬

PREPARATION TIME: 1 hour plus chilling and freezing times (allow at least 4 hours for the ice cream to freeze)

SPECIAL EQUIPMENT: ice cream maker

4 large egg yolks
⅔ cup granulated sugar
2 tablespoons nonalkalized cocoa powder
2 cups half-and-half
1 cup heavy (whipping) cream
6 ounces bittersweet chocolate, finely chopped
¼ cup Jack Daniels bourbon whiskey

1. In a medium bowl, whisk together the egg yolks, sugar, and cocoa until smooth. In a heavy, medium saucepan over medium-low heat, bring the half-and-half and heavy cream to a gentle boil. Remove the pan from the heat and gradually stir ½ cup of the hot half-and-half mixture into the egg yolk mixture until well blended. Gradually stir this mixture back into the saucepan. Continue cooking over medium-low heat, stirring constantly with a wooden spoon, until the custard is thick enough to coat the back of the spoon. Do not let the custard boil. Remove the pan from the heat and stir in the finely chopped chocolate until melted and smooth. Transfer the mixture to a large bowl. Put the bowl

over a larger bowl of ice water and stir the mixture occasionally for 15 to 20 minutes or until cold. Stir in the Jack Daniels.

2. Pour the mixture into the container of an ice cream maker and freeze according to the manufacturer's directions. Remove the container from the machine.

3. Scrape the ice cream into a medium bowl and smooth the top. Cover the bowl tightly with plastic wrap and aluminum foil. Freeze the ice cream for at least 4 hours or overnight, until firm.

4. Divide the ice cream among six chilled dessert bowls and serve.

～ Brownie Ice Cream Sandwiches ～

It is such a simple idea, you may be surprised you haven't thought of it before: an ice cream sandwich made with brownies rather than the soft chocolate wafer we usually see. The best thing about making your own ice cream sandwiches is that you can use any kind of ice cream you want. Be sure to let the ice cream soften, either in the refrigerator or in the microwave, so that it is easy to spread between the brownie halves. After they are assembled, the ice cream sandwiches should be left to firm up in the freezer for 8 hours or overnight.

YIELD: 16 brownie ice cream sandwiches

DIFFICULTY: ▬▬

PREPARATION TIME: 1 hour plus baking, cooling, and freezing times (allow the brownie ice cream sandwiches to freeze overnight)

Brownies:

¼ cup plus 2 tablespoons all-purpose flour
⅛ teaspoon baking soda
A large pinch of salt
5 ounces semisweet chocolate, finely chopped
5 tablespoons unsalted butter, cut into tablespoons
¼ cup granulated sugar
¼ cup packed light brown sugar
1 tablespoon light corn syrup
1 tablespoon water
½ teaspoon instant espresso coffee powder
1 large egg, at room temperature
1 teaspoon vanilla extract
¼ cup walnuts, finely chopped

To assemble:

3 pints coffee, vanilla, or chocolate chip ice cream (or your favorite flavor), softened (for instructions on softening ice cream, see page 21)

Make the brownies:

1. Position a rack in the center of the oven and preheat to 350°F. Line the bottom of a 10½-by-15½-by-1-inch jelly-roll pan with aluminum foil, leaving a 2-inch overhang on the short ends. Fold the overhang underneath the pan. Butter the aluminum foil and the sides of the pan.

2. In a small bowl, stir together the flour, baking soda, and salt. Put the chocolate in a medium bowl.

3. In a medium saucepan, combine the butter, sugars, corn syrup, water, and espresso powder. Cook over medium heat, stirring constantly with a wooden spoon, until the mixture comes to a boil. Remove the pan from the heat and pour the hot syrup over the chocolate. Let the mixture stand for 1 to 2 minutes to melt the chocolate, then whisk until smooth.

4. Whisk in the egg, blending until smooth. Stir in the vanilla and the flour mixture. Scrape the batter into the prepared pan and, using an offset metal spatula, spread in a thin, even layer. Sprinkle the walnuts over the top of the batter.

5. Bake the brownies for 10 to 12 minutes or until a cake tester or toothpick inserted into the center of the brownies comes out clean. Set the brownies in the pan on a wire rack to cool completely. Freeze the pan with the cooled brownies for 20 to 30 minutes or until firm.

Assemble the ice cream sandwiches:

6. Using the aluminum foil ends as handles, transfer the brownies to a flat baking sheet. Cover with a second baking sheet and invert the brownies. Carefully peel off the aluminum foil. Using a large sharp knife, cut the brownie rectangle in half crosswise so that you have two pieces that are almost square.

7. Line a 10½-by-15½-by-1-inch jelly-roll pan with plastic wrap. Put one of the brownie halves, walnut side down, into the lined jelly-roll pan. Using an offset metal cake spatula, spread the softened ice cream in an even layer over the brownie half. Put the second brownie, walnut side facing up, on top of the ice cream filling and press gently into place. Wrap the brownie ice cream sandwich in plastic and freeze overnight.

8. Remove the brownie ice cream sandwich from the freezer and unwrap. Using a large sharp knife, cut the brownie sandwich into 16 rectangles. Wrap the ice cream sandwiches individually in plastic and store in an airtight container in the freezer for up to 1 month.

∾ *Chocolate Mint Ice Cream Pie* ∾

This ice cream pie is a symphony of textures, beginning with the crispy, crunchy chocolate pie shell. The shell is topped with soft ice cream that encases a fudgy filling. Next, the pie is topped with light, airy cream and decorated with melt-in-the-mouth chocolate curls. Mint gently flavors the whole dessert, making it a refreshing and appealing proposition.

YIELD: 8 to 10 servings

DIFFICULTY: ▬▬

PREPARATION TIME: 1 hour plus cooling and freezing times (allow the pie to freeze for 8 hours)

SPECIAL EQUIPMENT: pastry bag fitted with a star tip (such as Ateco #5)

Chocolate mint fudge filling:

½ cup heavy (whipping) cream
3 tablespoons light corn syrup
5 ounces semisweet chocolate, finely chopped
1½ tablespoons crème de menthe
½ teaspoon vanilla extract

Chocolate pie shell:

8 ounces semisweet chocolate, coarsely chopped
4 tablespoons (½ stick) unsalted butter, cut into tablespoons
1½ tablespoons crème de menthe
1 teaspoon vanilla extract
1 cup crisped rice cereal

Mint ice cream filling:

2 pints vanilla ice cream, softened (for instructions on softening ice cream, see page 21)
3 tablespoons crème de menthe

Crème de menthe whipped cream:

½ cup heavy (whipping) cream
1½ teaspoons granulated sugar
2 teaspoons crème de menthe
½ teaspoon vanilla extract

Chocolate curls:

4 ounces semisweet chocolate curls (for instructions on making chocolate curls, see page 21)

Make the chocolate mint fudge filling:

1. In a medium saucepan over medium heat, bring the cream and corn syrup to a gentle boil. Remove the pan from the heat and add the chocolate. Let the mixture sit for 1 to 2 minutes to melt the chocolate, then whisk until smooth. Stir in the crème de menthe and vanilla. Cover the surface of the filling with plastic wrap and cool the filling to room temperature.

Make the chocolate pie shell:

2. Line a 10-inch pie plate with aluminum foil, leaving a 2-inch overhang around the entire edge of the pie plate. Fold the overhang underneath the pie plate.

3. In the top of a double boiler over hot, not simmering, water, melt the chocolate with the butter, stirring occasionally, until smooth. Remove the top part of the double boiler from the bottom and stir in the crème de menthe and vanilla. Stir in the cereal.

4. Scrape the chocolate mixture into the prepared pie plate. Using a small offset metal cake spatula, spread the chocolate mixture in a thin, even layer over the bottom and up the sides of the pie pan. Freeze the chocolate shell for 20 to 30 minutes or until firm.

5. Remove the firm pie shell from the freezer. Using the aluminum foil as handles, remove the chocolate shell from the pie plate. Invert the pie

shell and carefully peel off the aluminum foil. Put the chocolate pie shell back in the pie plate. Return the pie plate to the freezer.

Make the mint ice cream filling:

6. In a large bowl, stir together the softened ice cream and the crème de menthe. Remove the pie plate from the freezer and quickly spread half of the ice cream mixture into the chocolate pie shell. Pour the chocolate mint fudge filling over the layer of ice cream and spread evenly with a spatula. Spread the remaining ice cream over the chocolate filling. Cover the pie with plastic wrap and freeze for at least 8 hours or overnight.

Make the crème de menthe whipped cream:

7. In a chilled, large bowl, using a hand-held electric mixer set at medium speed, beat the cream and sugar until soft peaks start to form. Add the crème de menthe and vanilla and continue beating until stiff peaks start to form.

8. Fill a pastry bag fitted with a star tip (such as Ateco #5) with the crème de menthe whipped cream. Pipe a shell border around the edge of the pie. If desired, pipe a large rosette in the center of the pie.

9. Using a metal cake spatula or a large spoon, scoop up some of the chocolate curls and sprinkle them over the top of the ice cream pie, avoiding the areas with the piped whipped-cream decoration. Freeze the pie. Put the ice cream pie in the refrigerator for 30 minutes before serving.

∽ *Frozen Chocolate Mint Soufflé* ∼

Infused with the cool taste of mint, this high-standing frozen chocolate soufflé is garnished with jewel-like candied mint leaves and swirls of whipped cream. Both the soufflé and the mint leaves must be prepared well ahead of serving—the soufflé needs a night in the freezer to set and the leaves require a night or 8 hours to dry.

YIELD: 6 servings

DIFFICULTY: ▬▬

PREPARATION TIME: 30 minutes plus freezing time (allow at least 8 hours for the soufflé to freeze)

SPECIAL EQUIPMENT: pastry bag fitted with a large star tip (such as Ateco #5)

Chocolate mint soufflé:

8 ounces bittersweet chocolate, finely chopped
1 cup water
¼ cup granulated sugar
7 large egg yolks
¼ cup green crème de menthe
1½ cups heavy (whipping) cream

Candied mint leaves:

6 small sprigs of fresh mint
1 large egg white
½ cup granulated sugar

Decoration:

½ cup heavy (whipping) cream
1 tablespoon granulated sugar

Make the frozen soufflé:

1. Fold a 12-by-22-inch piece of heavy-duty aluminum foil four times lengthwise to form a 3-by-22-inch quadruple-thick piece of foil. Wrap and tape the foil tightly around the outside of a 1-quart soufflé dish, making sure that it extends at least 2 inches above the rim of the dish. Oil the inside of the foil collar lightly with flavorless vegetable oil.

2. In the top of a double boiler over hot, not simmering, water, melt the chocolate, stirring occasionally, until smooth. Remove the top part of the double boiler from the bottom and cool the chocolate for 5 to 10 minutes or until tepid.

3. In a heavy, small saucepan over medium-high heat, bring the water and sugar to a boil, stirring constantly, just until the sugar is dissolved. Boil the syrup, without stirring for 4 to 5 minutes or until a candy thermometer inserted into the syrup reads 220°F.

4. In a large bowl set in a larger bowl filled with ice water, using a hand-held electric mixer set at medium-high speed, beat the egg yolks for 30 to 50 seconds or until foamy. Still beating, slowly add the hot syrup in a slow stream. Continue beating for 2 to 3 minutes or until the mixture is cool and forms a thick ribbon when the beaters are lifted. Beat in the melted chocolate and the crème de menthe just until blended. The egg yolk mixture will deflate.

5. In a chilled, large bowl, using a hand-held electric mixer set at medium speed, beat the cream until soft peaks begin to form. Fold one fourth of the whipped cream into the chocolate mixture to lighten it. Gently fold in the remaining whipped cream.

6. Transfer the chocolate mixture to the prepared soufflé dish. Loosely cover the top of the dish with plastic wrap. Freeze the soufflé for at least 8 hours or overnight, until firm.

Make the candied mint sprigs:

7. Rinse the mint sprigs under cold running water and dry well with paper towels.

8. In a small bowl, using a wire whisk, lightly beat the egg white until frothy. Using a small artist's brush, paint the mint sprigs with the egg white. Place the sugar in a small bowl. Holding a mint sprig over the bowl, sprinkle the sprig with the sugar until the sprig is lightly coated. Place the mint on a sheet of waxed paper. Repeat the procedure with the remaining sprigs and sugar. Let the mint sprigs dry overnight.

Assemble the soufflé:

9. In a medium bowl, using a hand-held electric mixer set at medium speed, beat the cream with the sugar just until stiff peaks begin to form. Fit a pastry bag with a large star tip (such as Ateco #5) and fill with the whipped cream.

10. Carefully remove the foil collar from the frozen soufflé. Pipe large, swirled rosettes around the circumference of the frozen soufflé and garnish with the mint springs.

⌒ *Crème de Menthe Ice Cream* ⌒

YIELD: Approximately 2 quarts	
DIFFICULTY: ◼◼	
PREPARATION TIME: 20 minutes plus chilling and freezing times (allow at least 10 hours for the ice cream to freeze)	
SPECIAL EQUIPMENT: ice cream maker	

3 large eggs
⅓ cup granulated sugar
2 cups heavy (whipping) cream
1 cup half-and-half
¾ cup sweetened condensed milk
½ cup green crème de menthe
¼ cup light corn syrup
1 teaspoon vanilla extract
⅛ teaspoon salt
2 ounces semisweet chocolate, finely chopped

(continued)

1. In a large bowl, using a hand-held electric mixer set at high speed, beat the eggs for about 1 minute or until thickened and pale yellow. Beat in the sugar 1 tablespoon at a time. With a spoon, stir in the heavy cream, half-and-half, condensed milk, crème de menthe, corn syrup, vanilla, and salt until well combined. Cover and refrigerate for at least 4 hours or overnight, until well chilled.

2. Pour the mixture into the container of an ice cream maker and freeze according to the manufacturer's instructions. Add the chopped chocolate to the container and process briefly until evenly distributed in the ice cream.

3. Transfer the ice cream to a freezer container. Cover and freeze the ice cream overnight or for at least 6 hours before serving.

Vanilla Ice Cream with ～ Chocolate Chunks ～

Stir nice big chunks of bittersweet chocolate into rich custard-based vanilla ice cream for plenty of chocolate wallop with every smooth, creamy spoonful.

YIELD: Approximately 1½ quarts

DIFFICULTY: ▬▬

PREPARATION TIME: 45 minutes plus chilling and freezing times (allow at least 4 hours for the custard to chill and for the ice cream to freeze)

SPECIAL EQUIPMENT: ice cream maker

2 cups half-and-half
2 cups heavy (whipping) cream
1 cup granulated sugar, divided
1 vanilla bean, split in half lengthwise
4 large egg yolks
Pinch of salt
8 ounces bittersweet chocolate, cut into ¼-inch chunks

1. In a large, heavy saucepan, combine the half-and-half, heavy cream, and ½ cup of the sugar. Scrape the tiny black seeds from inside the vanilla bean into the cream mixture. Place the saucepan over medium-low heat and bring the mixture to a gentle simmer, stirring occasionally. Remove the pan from the heat.

2. Meanwhile, in a large bowl, using a hand-held electric mixer set at medium-high speed, beat the egg yolks with the remaining ½ cup of sugar and the salt for 2 to 3 minutes or until a thick ribbon forms when the beaters are lifted.

3. While beating the egg yolk mixture at low speed, slowly add half of the hot cream mixture, mixing until well blended. Pour this mixture back into the saucepan of cream. Continue cooking over medium-low heat, stirring constantly with a wooden spoon, for 2 to 4 minutes or until the custard is thick enough to coat the back of the spoon. Do not let the custard come to a boil. Immediately strain the custard into a bowl and set over a bowl of ice water. Stir the custard for 10 minutes or until cool. Remove the bowl from the ice water and cover the surface of the custard with plastic wrap. Refrigerate for 2 hours or until thoroughly chilled.

4. Pour the chilled custard into the container of an ice cream maker and freeze according to the manufacturer's instructions. Remove the paddle from the ice cream maker and stir the chocolate chunks into the ice cream. Transfer the ice cream to a freezer container. Cover and freeze for at least 2 hours or until firm.

Chocolate Ice Cream with White ⌒ *Chocolate Chunks* ⌒

Here is the reverse of the previous recipe . . . almost. But this time, because the chunks are made of white chocolate and the ice cream is flavored with dark chocolate, there is a double dose of chocolate. We suggest using this recipe *without* the chunks when you want "straight" chocolate ice cream, such as ice cream to make the Raspberry Chocolate Ice Cream Soda on page 340.

YIELD: Approximately 1½ quarts

DIFFICULTY: ▰▰

PREPARATION TIME: 30 minutes plus chilling and freezing times (allow at least 4 hours for the custard to chill and for the ice cream to freeze)

SPECIAL EQUIPMENT: ice cream maker

2 cups half-and-half
1½ cups heavy (whipping) cream
½ cup granulated sugar, divided
3 large egg yolks
Pinch of salt
8 ounces bittersweet chocolate, finely chopped
2 teaspoons vanilla extract
8 ounces white chocolate, cut into ¼-inch chunks

1. In a large, heavy saucepan, combine the half-and-half, heavy cream, and ¼ cup of the sugar. Put the saucepan over medium-low heat and bring the mixture to a gentle simmer, stirring occasionally. Remove the pan from the heat.

2. Meanwhile, in a large bowl, using a hand-held electric mixer set at medium-high speed, beat the egg yolks with the remaining ¼ cup of sugar and the salt for 2 to 3 minutes or until a thick ribbon forms when the beaters are lifted.

3. While beating the egg yolk mixture at low speed, slowly add half of the hot cream mixture, mixing until well blended. Pour this mixture back into the saucepan of cream. Continue cooking over medium-low heat, stirring constantly with a wooden spoon, for 2 to 3 minutes or until the custard is thick enough to coat the back of the spoon. Do not let the custard come to a boil. Immediately strain the custard into a bowl. Stir in the bittersweet chocolate and vanilla and blend until smooth. Set the custard over a bowl of ice water and stir for 10 minutes or until cool. Remove the bowl from the ice and cover the surface of the custard with plastic wrap. Refrigerate the custard for 2 hours or until thoroughly chilled.

4. Pour the chilled custard into the container of an ice cream maker and freeze according to the manufacturer's instructions. Remove the paddle from the ice cream maker and stir the white chocolate chunks into the ice cream. Transfer the ice cream to a freezer container. Cover and freeze the ice cream for at least 2 hours or until firm.

～ *Crispy Sugar Cones* ～

When you're in the mood for a cone with your ice cream, try these tasty spiraled twists of crispy sweetness. A scoop of any sort of ice cream tastes terrific in one of these cones, but we think chocolate tastes best—particularly if you decide to embellish the cones with melted chocolate, nuts, jimmies, and coconut.

YIELD: 8 cones
DIFFICULTY: ■■■
PREPARATION TIME: 45 minutes

2 large eggs, at room temperature
¾ cup sifted confectioners' sugar
½ teaspoon vanilla extract
⅛ teaspoon ground cinnamon (optional)
Pinch of salt
½ cup plus 2 tablespoons all-purpose flour
8 teaspoons finely chopped nuts, such as hazelnuts, pecans,
 peanuts, walnuts, or macadamia nuts (optional)
1 pound semisweet chocolate, melted (optional)
6 tablespoons finely chopped nuts or 6 tablespoons shredded
 sweetened coconut or 4 tablespoons jimmies or any combi-
 nation of these (optional)

1. Position two racks in the top two thirds of the oven and preheat to 425°F. Lightly butter and flour two baking sheets, tapping off any excess flour. Using a 6-inch pan lid, bowl, or plate and the tip of a sharp knife, trace two circles into the butter-flour coating on each sheet.

2. In a medium bowl, whisk together the eggs and sugar until smooth. Stir in the vanilla, cinnamon, salt, and flour to make a smooth batter.

3. Put 2 level tablespoons of the batter in the center of one of the circles. Using a small offset metal spatula or an artist's palette knife, spread the batter to completely coat one circle in an even layer. Repeat for the second circle on the same sheet. Sprinkle each circle with 1 teaspoon of nuts, if

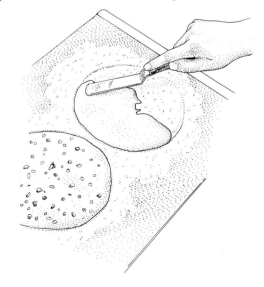

desired. Bake for 4 to 6 minutes or just until the circles are golden brown around the edges and beginning to change color in the center. If the circles are browning too quickly, reduce the oven temperature by 10° to 25°F. It is important to watch these cookies as they bake at such a high temperature—they should bake through but not become too dark.

4. Run a thin-bladed knife under one cookie. Working quickly, roll the cookie into a cone shape, rolling so that the side that was against the baking sheet is the outside of the cone for the plain cones. If you have sprinkled the cookie with chopped nuts, roll it so that the nut-coated side faces outward. Place the cone upright in a small glass to cool. Immediately shape the second one. If the cookies begin to cool, they cannot be rolled without breaking.

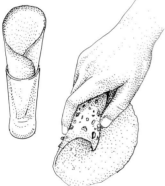

5. Using the remaining batter (and nuts, if desired), make the cones, 2 at a time, using a cool baking sheet each time.

6. When the cones are cool, coat the entire inside of each cone with chocolate. Or you can coat just the edges, if you prefer. Then the edges can be sprinkled with nuts, coconut, or jimmies. To coat the entire inside of the cones with chocolate, spoon about 1 tablespoon of the melted chocolate into each cone. Tilt the cone and, using an artist's palette knife or a pastry or paintbrush, spread the chocolate in a thin, even layer. Put the cone back in the glass upright. Repeat with the remaining cones. If just decorating the edges of the cones, place half of each quantity of the "sprinkling" ingredients in separate small shallow dishes (to avoid getting any chocolate in the ingredients).

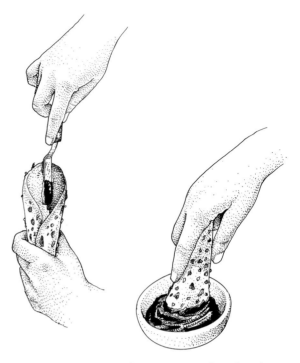

Dip the open end of a cone into the chocolate, tilting it around so that it forms a scant ½-inch band of chocolate around the edge of the cone. Let any excess run back into the pot of chocolate. Roll the edge of the chocolate-coated cone in the desired "sprinkling" ingredient and return the decorated cone to the glass to harden. Repeat with the remaining cones.

7. Fill the cones with ice cream and serve in tall, stemmed glasses or wrapped in waxed paper.

Charleston Cobblestone Ice
～ Cream ～

When you add raisins to this chunky ice cream, it takes a detour from extraordinarily good (but nevertheless familiar) rocky road to another street entirely. Developed by a reader from South Carolina, the ice cream is named in honor of that state's most graceful city.

YIELD: Approximately 1½ quarts

DIFFICULTY: ▬▬

PREPARATION TIME: 30 minutes plus chilling and freezing times (allow at least 10 hours for the ice cream to freeze)

SPECIAL EQUIPMENT: ice cream maker

1 cup half-and-half

1½ ounces unsweetened chocolate, finely chopped

1 cup heavy (whipping) cream

⅔ cup granulated sugar

6 large egg yolks

4 tablespoons (½ stick) unsalted butter, softened, cut into tablespoons

1 teaspoon vanilla extract

¾ cup lightly roasted unblanched almonds, coarsely chopped (for roasting instructions, see page 20)

3 ounces (about ¾ cup) dark raisins

¾ cup mini-marshmallows

5 ounces (about ¾ cup) semisweet miniature chocolate chips

1. In a small saucepan, combine the half-and-half and the unsweetened chocolate. Cook over very low heat, stirring often, until the chocolate is melted. Remove the pan from the heat.

2. In a medium saucepan, combine the heavy cream with ⅓ cup of the sugar. Over medium heat, cook until the mixture is very hot, but not boiling, stirring often. Reduce the heat to very low. In a medium bowl, with a hand-held electric mixer set at high speed, beat the egg yolks with the remaining ⅓ cup of sugar for about 1 minute or until thickened and pale yellow. Gradually stir about ½ cup of the cream mixture into the egg yolk mixture until it is well blended. Pour this mixture back into the pan of hot cream. Continue cooking over very low heat, stirring constantly with a wooden spoon,

until the mixture is thick enough to coat the back of the spoon. Remove the pan from the heat and stir in the butter and vanilla. Stir in the chocolate mixture until well combined. Cool the mixture to room temperature. Transfer to a medium bowl, cover, and refrigerate overnight or for at least 4 hours or until well chilled.

3. Pour the ice cream mixture into the container of an ice cream maker and freeze according to the manufacturer's instructions. Add the chopped almonds, raisins, marshmallows, and chocolate chips to the container and process briefly until evenly distributed in the ice cream.

4. Transfer the ice cream to a freezer container. Cover and freeze the ice cream for at least 6 hours or overnight before serving.

～○ *Milk Chocolate Ice Cream* ○～

From Lora Brody, author of *Growing Up on the Chocolate Diet,* comes a treat as rich and creamy as milk chocolate ice cream ought to be.

YIELD: 1¾ quarts
DIFFICULTY: ■
PREPARATION TIME: 20 minutes plus chilling and freezing time (allow at least 4 hours for the custard to chill and overnight for the ice cream to freeze)
SPECIAL EQUIPMENT: ice cream maker

4 cups heavy (whipping) cream
4 extra-large eggs
½ cup granulated sugar
2 teaspoons vanilla extract
12 ounces milk chocolate, chopped into ½-inch chunks

1. In a 2-quart saucepan over medium heat, bring the cream to a simmer.

2. In a large bowl, combine the eggs and sugar. Beat by hand or with an electric mixer for about 5 minutes or until a ribbon forms when the beaters are lifted. Slowly pour in the hot cream and beat for about 30 seconds. Return the mixture to the saucepan and add the vanilla. Cook over low heat, stirring constantly with a wooden spoon, for about 5 minutes or until the mixture is thick enough to coat the back of the spoon. Do not let the mixture boil.

3. Remove the pan from the heat. Add the chocolate chunks and stir until they melt completely.

4. Cool over a bowl of ice water. Refrigerate overnight or for at least 4 hours. When thoroughly chilled, pour the mixture into the container of an ice cream maker and freeze according to the manufacturer's instructions.

Bailey's Irish Cream Chocolate ∽ Chip Ice Cream ∽

You do not need an ice cream maker to whip up this smooth frozen dessert—all you need is a good home freezer and plenty of time. The dessert is enriched with a mixture of cream and egg yolks, a fair share of whipped cream, and softly beaten egg whites. When melted chocolate, still warm and liquid, is added to the chilled cream mixture, it separates into tiny chips. Bailey's Irish Cream flavors the ice cream, which is frozen in the freezer—no fuss, no bother.

YIELD: Approximately 2 quarts
DIFFICULTY: ▬
PREPARATION TIME: 30 minutes plus freezing time (allow at least 8 hours for the ice cream to freeze)
SPECIAL EQUIPMENT: ice cream maker

3 large eggs, separated
¾ cup granulated sugar
1 teaspoon vanilla extract
2½ cups heavy (whipping) cream, divided
¼ cup Bailey's Irish Cream
4 ounces semisweet chocolate, melted and kept warm

1. In a double boiler over simmering water, combine the egg yolks, sugar, vanilla, and ½ cup of the heavy cream. Whisk for 8 to 10 minutes or until the mixture is hot and the sugar has dissolved.

2. Fill a medium bowl halfway with ice and water and set it on a wet towel. Pour the hot egg yolk mixture into a smaller bowl and place the bowl in the ice bath. Spin the warm bowl and stir with a rubber spatula for about 10 minutes or until the yolk mixture becomes thick and very cold.

3. Stir in the Bailey's Irish Cream. Add the warm melted chocolate and, using a rubber spatula, quickly incorporate it into the yolk mixture (the chocolate will clump into small chips). Keep the mixture in the ice bath and set aside.

4. In a large bowl, using a hand-held electric mixer set at medium speed, whip the remaining 2 cups of cream until soft peaks form. Refrigerate.

5. In a large bowl, beat the egg whites until they form stiff peaks. Gently fold the whites into the refrigerated whipped cream.

6. Pour the chocolate mixture over the egg white mixture and carefully fold together.

7. Pour the mixture into a 2- to 3-quart aluminum bowl or rectangular glass dish and freeze for about 8 hours or until firm. Remove from the freezer 5 to 10 minutes before serving.

Peanut Butter Chocolate Chunk
⌒ *Ice Cream* ⌒

If you like peanut butter and chocolate together, try this ice cream. One of our readers came up with the idea of chopping up a few chocolate peanut butter cups and adding them to homemade peanut butter ice cream—and then for good measure she tossed in a handful of chopped chocolate. We like the way she thinks!

> YIELD: Approximately 1½ quarts
>
> DIFFICULTY: ▄▄
>
> PREPARATION TIME: 30 minutes plus chilling and freezing times (allow at least 10 hours for the ice cream to freeze)
>
> SPECIAL EQUIPMENT: ice cream maker

1½ cups heavy (whipping) cream
1½ cups half-and-half
½ cup plus 1 tablespoon granulated sugar
½ cup creamy peanut butter
2 1.6 ounce packages Reese's Peanut Butter Cups
2 ounces semisweet chocolate, finely chopped

1. In a large saucepan, combine the heavy cream, half-and-half, sugar, and peanut butter. Over medium heat, bring the mixture to a simmer, stirring often. Remove the pan from the heat and cool to room temperature.

2. Transfer the mixture to a medium bowl. Cover and refrigerate overnight or for at least 4 hours, until well chilled.

3. Pour the ice cream mixture into the container of an ice cream maker and freeze according to the manufacturer's instructions. Chop the 4 peanut butter cups into ½-inch chunks. Add the chunks and the chopped chocolate to the container and process briefly until evenly distributed in the ice cream.

4. Transfer the ice cream to a freezer container. Cover and freeze the ice cream overnight or for at least 6 hours before serving.

~ Chocolate Ginger Ice Cream ~

For a sophisticated ice cream to serve after the most elegant of dinners, try Barbara Kafka's recipe for a rich dessert gently flavored with ginger.

YIELD: Approximately 1 quart

DIFFICULTY: ◼

PREPARATION TIME: 30 minutes (allow 6 hours for the ice cream to chill and additional time for the ice cream to freeze)

SPECIAL EQUIPMENT: ice cream maker

---

2 cups heavy (whipping) cream

2 cups milk

¾ cup granulated sugar

6 quarter-size slices fresh ginger, peeled and lightly crushed
     with the side of a knife blade

4 large egg yolks

2 ounces semisweet chocolate, finely chopped

2 ounces unsweetened chocolate, finely chopped

1. In a heavy, medium saucepan, heat the heavy cream, milk, sugar, and ginger over medium heat, stirring occasionally with a wooden spoon to dissolve the sugar. Bring the cream mixture to a gentle boil. Remove the pan from the heat.

2. Put the egg yolks and chocolates in a large bowl. Slowly pour in the hot cream mixture, whisking constantly, until the chocolate has melted and the mixture is thoroughly blended.

3. Return the custard mixture to the saucepan. Stir over very low heat for about 4 minutes or until thick enough to coat the back of a spoon. Do not let the custard boil. Remove from the heat. Transfer the custard to a medium, nonaluminum metal bowl. Set the bowl of custard over a larger bowl, one-third full of ice water. Stir the custard frequently for 15 to 20 minutes or until chilled. Remove the bowl from the ice water. Cover the surface of the custard with plastic wrap and refrigerate for at least 4 hours or overnight.

4. Strain the chilled custard into the container of an ice cream maker and freeze according to the manufacturer's instructions. Chill for at least 6 hours or overnight.

∽ *Swiss Chocolate Cherries Jubilee* ∾

When it is warm, ganache—a combination of cream and chocolate—is liquid enough to pour or spoon, as does Rose Levy Beranbaum over vanilla ice cream in this recipe. Once the chocolate is in place, she instructs us to top the dessert with hot, sweet cherries jubilee. One taste and you will understand how the topping earned its exuberant name.

YIELD: 8 servings

DIFFICULTY: ◢

PREPARATION TIME: 30 minutes plus macerating time

Macerated cherries:

1 16-ounce can pitted Bing cherries in syrup
6 tablespoons kirsch or cognac

Ganache:

4 ounces bittersweet chocolate, chopped
¾ cup heavy (whipping) cream

To assemble:

¼ cup red currant jelly
¼ cup crème de cassis
1 quart vanilla ice cream

Macerate the cherries:

1. Drain the cherries, reserving 2 tablespoons of the syrup. Dry the cherries well on paper towels. Put the cherries in a small bowl and add the kirsch. Set aside to macerate for at least 1 hour.

Prepare the ganache:

2. In a food processor, process the chocolate until it forms very fine particles.

3. In a saucepan over medium heat, heat the cream just to the boiling point. With the motor running, pour the hot cream through the feed tube in a steady stream. Blend until smooth.

Assemble the dessert:

4. In a small saucepan, heat the currant jelly, crème de cassis, and the reserved 2 tablespoons of cherry syrup, stirring until the jelly is melted and the mixture is smooth. Set aside.

5. Drain the macerated cherries, reserving the kirsch. In a chafing dish or sauté pan, combine the cherries and 2 tablespoons of the reserved kirsch over medium heat. Cook for 1 minute and add the currant jelly mixture. Cook, stirring constantly, until the liquid bubbles, then reduce the heat to low.

6. In large ladle or small saucepan, warm the remaining reserved kirsch over low heat. Ignite the kirsch and pour it over the cherries, shaking the pan until the flames subside.

7. Divide the ice cream among eight stemmed glasses. Spoon 2 tablespoons of the warm ganache over the ice cream and top with the hot cherries.

Mocha Chocolate Chip Ice ～ Cream Sandwiches ～

Both the ice cream and the cookies are grand on their own. When matched in an ice cream sandwich they are spectacular.

YIELD: Approximately 1 dozen ice cream sandwiches

DIFFICULTY: ◼

PREPARATION TIME: 35 minutes plus baking and freezing times (allow at least 4 hours for the custard to chill and the ice cream to freeze)

SPECIAL EQUIPMENT: ice cream maker

Chocolate ice cream:

2 cups half-and-half
1½ cups heavy (whipping) cream
½ cup granulated sugar, divided
3 large egg yolks
Pinch of salt
8 ounces bittersweet chocolate, finely chopped
2 teaspoons vanilla extract

Mocha chocolate chip cookies:

8 tablespoons (1 stick) unsalted butter
4 ounces unsweetened chocolate, coarsely chopped
18 ounces (about 3 cups) semisweet chocolate chips
½ cup all-purpose flour
½ teaspoon double-acting baking powder
½ teaspoon salt
4 large eggs
1½ cups granulated sugar
1½ tablespoons instant coffee powder
2 teaspoons vanilla extract
2 cups chopped, roasted pecans (for roasting instructions, see page 20)

Make the ice cream:

1. In a large, heavy saucepan, combine the half-and-half, heavy cream, and ¼ cup of the sugar. Put the saucepan over medium-low heat and bring the mixture to a gentle simmer, stirring occasionally. Remove the pan from the heat.

2. Meanwhile, in a large bowl, using a hand-held electric mixer set at medium-high speed, beat the egg yolks with the remaining ¼ cup of sugar and

the salt for 2 to 3 minutes or until a thick ribbon forms when the beaters are lifted.

3. While beating the egg yolk mixture at low speed, slowly add half of the hot cream mixture, mixing until well blended. Pour the mixture back into the saucepan of cream. Continue cooking over medium-low heat, stirring constantly with a wooden spoon, for 2 to 3 minutes or until the custard is thick enough to coat the back of the spoon. Do not let the custard come to a boil. Immediately strain the custard into a bowl. Stir in the bittersweet chocolate and vanilla and blend until smooth. Set the custard over a bowl of ice and stir it for 10 minutes or until cool. Remove the bowl from the ice, and cover the surface of the custard with plastic wrap. Refrigerate the custard for 2 hours or until thoroughly chilled.

4. Pour the chilled custard into the container of an ice cream maker and freeze according to the manufacturer's instructions. Transfer the ice cream to a freezer container. Cover and freeze the ice cream for at least 2 hours, until firm.

Make the cookies:

5. Preheat the oven to 350°F. Line two baking sheets with baking parchment or waxed paper.

6. In a double boiler over hot, not simmering, water, melt the butter, unsweetened chocolate, and 1½ cups of the chocolate chips. Stir until smooth. Remove the top part of the double boiler from the bottom and cool the chocolate for 5 to 10 minutes or until tepid.

7. In a medium bowl, stir together the flour, baking powder, and salt.

8. In a large bowl, beat together the eggs, sugar, coffee powder, and vanilla. Blend in the chocolate mixture. Add the flour mixture, then stir in the nuts and the remaining chocolate chips.

9. Use 2 rounded tablespoons of dough for each cookie. Drop them 1 inch apart on the prepared baking sheets. Bake the cookies for 10 minutes or until they are cracked and shiny on the outside and soft inside. Cool completely on the baking sheets.

Assemble the ice cream sandwiches:

10. Remove the ice cream from the freezer 5 minutes before assembling the sandwiches.

11. Put about ½ cup of ice cream on the flat side of one cookie. Cover with another cookie and press the sandwich together gently. Serve immediately or store tightly covered in the freezer until ready to use.

∽ *Mile-High Ice Cream Pie* ∽

With three kinds of ice cream layered in a pie shell and a topping of billowing meringue, this pie comes by its name honestly. After the meringue is spread over the pie, the whole thing is put under a hot broiler for a few seconds so that the top of the meringue turns golden—similar to a Baked Alaska. The pie is then returned to the freezer until it is time to serve it with chocolate sauce. The longer it freezes, the easier it is to slice.

<table>
<tr><td>YIELD: 8 servings</td></tr>
<tr><td>DIFFICULTY: ▰▰</td></tr>
<tr><td>PREPARATION TIME: 30 to 35 minutes plus freezing time (allow at least 4 hours to freeze the pie)</td></tr>
</table>

Crust:

1½ cups sifted all-purpose flour
½ teaspoon salt
½ cup solid vegetable shortening, chilled
4 to 5 tablespoons ice water

Pie filling:

1 pint vanilla ice cream, softened (for instructions on softening
   ice cream, see page 21)
1 pint chocolate ice cream, softened
1 pint peppermint-stick ice cream, softened

Meringue:

8 egg whites, at room temperature
¼ teaspoon cream of tartar
½ cup granulated sugar
½ teaspoon vanilla extract

Chocolate sauce:

1½ cups half-and-half
1 cup granulated sugar
5 ounces unsweetened chocolate, coarsely chopped
5 ounces German sweet chocolate, coarsely chopped

Make the pie crust:

1. Position a rack in the center of the oven and preheat to 450°F.

2. In a large bowl, stir together the flour and salt. Sift the mixture. Using a pastry blender or two knives held scissor fashion, cut in the shortening until the mixture resembles small peas. Sprinkle 1 tablespoon of the ice water over the flour-shortening mixture and toss gently with a fork. Continue to add ice water a tablespoon at a time until the mixture is moistened and the dough forms a ball.

3. Put the dough on a lightly floured surface and roll it out until ⅛-inch thick. Fit it loosely into a 9-inch pie plate. Trim the uneven edges and prick the dough several times with a fork.

4. Bake the pie crust for 10 to 12 minutes or until it is golden. Remove the crust from the oven and let it cool completely.

Fill the pie:

5. Working quickly, spread the vanilla ice cream in an even layer in the bottom of the cooled pie shell, being careful not to break the crust. Spread the chocolate ice cream in a layer on the vanilla, then top with the peppermint-stick ice cream. Put the filled pie in the freezer until ready to bake.

Make the meringue:

6. Set the oven to broil. In a large bowl, using hand-held electric mixer set at medium speed, beat the egg whites until frothy. Beat in the cream of tartar and gradually add the sugar. Increase the speed to medium high and add the vanilla. Continue beating until stiff, shiny peaks form.

7. Remove the filled pie from the freezer and spread the meringue over the ice cream out to the edges of the pie crust, mounding the meringue into a dome shape. Broil the pie for 30 seconds to 1 minute or until the meringue is just browned.

8. Put the baked pie in the freezer for at least 4 hours or overnight.

Make the chocolate sauce:

9. In a heavy saucepan over low heat, combine the half-and-half, sugar, and chocolates. Stir until the chocolate is melted and the sauce is smooth and thick.

10. Serve each slice of frozen ice cream pie with a drizzle of the warm chocolate sauce.

⌒ Raspberry Sauce ⌒

Spoon this fresh-tasting sauce over ice cream or pound cake and use it to make the Raspberry-Chocolate Ice Cream Soda in chapter 11.

YIELD: 1 cup

DIFFICULTY: ◼

PREPARATION TIME: 15 minutes

2 10-ounce packages frozen red raspberries in light syrup, thawed
2 tablespoons granulated sugar
1 tablespoon cornstarch

1. In a food processor fitted with the metal chopping blade, process the raspberries and syrup for 5 to 10 seconds, until liquefied. Strain the raspberry puree through a fine sieve into a bowl.

2. Combine the sugar and cornstarch in a medium, noncorrosive saucepan. Whisk a small amount of the puree into the sugar-cornstarch mixture to make a paste. Stir in the remaining puree. Cook over medium heat, stirring constantly, for 3 to 4 minutes or until the sauce thickens slightly and comes to a rolling boil. Remove the pan from the heat and transfer the sauce to a noncorrosive bowl. Set the bowl over ice water and stir the sauce for 5 to 10 minutes or until chilled.

Chocolate Caramel-Praline Ice Cream Terrine with Warm ～ Caramel Sauce ～

Chocolate and caramel are a sweet pairing. The combination works very well in this pretty terrine of luscious chocolate ice cream enriched with bits of chopped praline—the sort of praline which is made with cream and pecans and is native to the South. When it is served, each slice of the terrine sits in a small pool of caramel sauce. The sauce, which can be made a day ahead of time and gently reheated in a double boiler, is good on plain ice cream, sundaes, or any time you are in the mood for a hot, buttery caramel sauce.

YIELD: 6 to 8 servings

DIFFICULTY: ■■■

PREPARATION TIME: 1 hour plus roasting (the nuts), cooling, and freezing times (allow at least 8 hours for freezing the terrine)

SPECIAL EQUIPMENT: 5-by-9-by-3-inch loaf pan; ice cream maker

Caramel praline:

1 cup granulated sugar
⅛ teaspoon fresh lemon juice
1 cup roasted pecan pieces (for roasting instructions, see page 20)
¼ cup heavy (whipping) cream

Ice cream terrine:

6 large egg yolks, at room temperature
½ cup granulated sugar
2½ cups milk
1 cup heavy (whipping) cream
6 ounces bittersweet chocolate, finely chopped
2 ounces unsweetened chocolate, finely chopped

Caramel sauce:

1 cup granulated sugar
⅛ teaspoon fresh lemon juice
¾ cup heavy (whipping) cream

To assemble:

White and dark chocolate curls, for garnish (optional; for instructions on making chocolate curls, see page 21)
Roasted pecan halves, for garnish (optional; for roasting instructions, see page 20)

Make the caramel praline:

1. Generously butter a baking sheet. In a heavy, small saucepan over medium-high heat, melt the sugar ¼ cup at a time, stirring constantly. Add the lemon juice and cook, stirring constantly, for about 1 minute or until the mixture is a light caramel color. Remove the pan from the heat and put it in a metal bowl of cold water briefly to stop it from cooking any longer. Stir in the pecan pieces and the cream. Pour the mixture onto the prepared baking sheet. Refrigerate for 1 hour or until the mixture is cold and brittle.

2. Break the praline into medium-sized pieces. In a food processor fitted with the metal chopping plade, process the praline pieces, pulsing 8 to 10 times, until the praline is coarsely chopped.

Make the ice cream terrine:

3. Line the bottom of a 5-by-9-by-3-inch loaf pan with baking parchment or waxed paper. In a medium bowl, whisk together the egg yolks and sugar. In a heavy, medium, nonaluminum sauce-pan, bring the milk and cream to a gentle boil over medium heat. Remove the pan from the heat and gradually stir ½ cup of the hot milk mixture into the egg yolk mixture until well blended. Gradually stir this mixture back into the saucepan. Continue cooking over medium-low heat, stirring constantly with a wooden spoon, for 2 minutes or until the custard is thick enough to coat the back of the spoon. Do not let the custard boil. Remove the pan from the heat, add the chopped chocolates, and stir until melted and smooth. Transfer the mixture to a large bowl. Put the bowl over a larger bowl of ice water and stir the custard occasionally for 15 to 20 minutes or until cold.

4. Pour the mixture into the container of an ice cream maker and freeze according to the manufac-turer's directions. Remove the container from the machine and stir in the praline pieces until well mixed. Pour the ice cream into the prepared loaf pan and smooth the top. Cover the pan tightly with plastic wrap and aluminum foil. Freeze the ice cream terrine overnight or for at least 8 hours.

Make the caramel sauce:

5. In a heavy, small saucepan, melt the sugar ¼ cup at a time, stirring constantly, over medium-high heat. Add the lemon juice and cook, stirring constantly, for about 1 minute or until the mixture is a light caramel color. Remove the pan from the heat and quickly and carefully stir in the cream. Keep the sauce warm in the top part of a double boiler over hot water.

Assemble the terrine:

6. Run a thin knife around the edges of the terrine to loosen it. Dip the pan, up to the rim, in a bowl of warm water for 5 seconds. Dry the outside of the pan and invert the loaf onto a chilled serving plate. Slice the loaf into servings with a thin sharp knife. Divide the caramel sauce between the dessert plates. Put a slice of the terrine on top of the sauce. Garnish with chocolate curls and pecan halves, if desired.

NOTE: The caramel sauce can be made up to 1 day ahead, covered, and refrigerated. Reheat in the top part of a double boiler over hot water.

Chocolate Sherbet with Pistachio
～ Sauce ～

This delicate dessert is an appealing contrast of textures and flavors. Small balls of icy chocolate sherbet are served with a smooth chilled sauce made by infusing a light custard with ground pistachios. The nuts lend their incredible buttery flavor to the sauce, which enhances the subtle flavor of the chocolate sherbet. Be sure you buy unsalted, shelled pistachios.

YIELD: 6 servings
DIFFICULTY: ■■
PREPARATION TIME: 1 hour plus chilling and freezing times (allow time for the sherbet to freeze overnight)
SPECIAL EQUIPMENT: ice cream maker

Chocolate sherbet:

6 ounces bittersweet chocolate, finely chopped
½ cup unsweetened alkalized cocoa powder
2 cups water
1 cup granulated sugar

Pistachio sauce:

1 cup unsalted, shelled pistachio nuts
3 cups boiling water
3 large egg yolks
⅓ cup granulated sugar
Few grains of salt
1¼ cups half-and-half

Make the sherbet:

1. In a medium bowl, combine the chocolate and cocoa. In a medium saucepan, combine the water and sugar. Cook over medium heat, stirring constantly, until the sugar dissolves. Bring the syrup to a simmer and remove the pan from the heat. Pour the hot syrup over the chocolate and cocoa. Whisk until smooth. Put the bowl over a larger bowl of ice water and stir the mixture occasionally for 20 minutes or until cold.

2. Pour the mixture into the container of an ice cream maker and freeze according to the manufacturer's instructions. Freeze the sherbet overnight.

Make the pistachio sauce:

3. Blanch the pistachios in the boiling water for 1 minute and drain. Wrap the pistachios in a clean dish towel. Pinch the nuts, one at a time, between two fingers to slip off their skins. Set the nuts aside in a bowl.

4. In a medium bowl, whisk together the egg yolks, sugar, and salt. In a heavy, medium, non-corrosive saucepan, bring the half-and-half to a gentle boil over medium heat. Remove the pan from the heat and gradually stir ½ cup of the hot half-and-half into the egg yolk mixture until well blended. Pour this mixture back into the saucepan. Continue cooking over medium-low heat, stirring constantly with a wooden spoon, for 2 minutes or until the custard is thick enough to coat the back of the spoon. Do not let the custard boil. Immediately pour the custard into a large measuring cup to stop the cooking process.

5. Put the pistachio nuts in a food processor fitted with the metal chopping blade. Process the

nuts for 10 seconds or until they are coarsely chopped. Remove 2 tablespoons of the nuts to use later as a garnish. Pour the hot custard through the feed tube with the motor running and blend for 45 seconds or until the mixture is creamy and the pistachios are finely ground. Using a fine-meshed sieve, strain the mixture into a bowl. Cover and refrigerate for 30 minutes or until cold.

Assemble the dessert:

6. Divide the chilled pistachio sauce among six serving bowls. Using two soup spoons, form the frozen chocolate sherbet into 18 small egg-shaped ovals. Put 3 in each bowl and sprinkle with the chopped pistachio nuts.

D and D (Dark and Delicious) 〜 Chocolate Sauce 〜

This is one of our favorite, low calorie chocolate sauces. We include it in this chapter because we know how very good it tastes liberally spooned over ice cream.

> YIELD: Approximately 1 cup
>
> DIFFICULTY: ▰
>
> PREPARATION TIME: 15 minutes plus cooling and chilling times

¾ cup granulated sugar
½ cup water
½ teaspoon fresh lemon juice
⅓ cup plus 1 tablespoon unsweetened nonalkalized cocoa
    powder, sifted
1 tablespoon unsalted butter
½ teaspoon vanilla extract

1. In a small saucepan, combine the sugar, water, and lemon juice. Cook over medium heat, stirring with a wooden spoon, until the sugar dissolves. Increase the heat to high and bring the syrup to a boil. Boil for 1 minute.

2. Remove the pan from the heat. Whisk in the cocoa powder and butter until blended and slightly thickened.

3. Cool the sauce to room temperature. Strain into a serving bowl and stir in the vanilla. Cover with plastic wrap and refrigerate until ready to serve. The sauce will keep for up to 2 weeks in the refrigerator.

9

Chocolate Candies

All-American Candy Bars
Magic Mocha Fudge
Maui Mounds
Peanut Butter Balls
Chunky Chocolate Fruit-and-Nut Squares
Milk Chocolate and Praline Truffles
Cabernet Truffles
Chocolate Walnut Fudge
    Rochers
Mocha Pralinés
Orange Pralinés
Fruit-and-Nut Medallions
Mocha Truffles
Gianduja Truffles
Grand Marnier Whipped-Cream
    Truffles
Raspberry Chambord Chocolate Balls
Chocolate Caramel Apples
Cashew Buttercrunch

ookies, cakes, and brownies are just fine, but there are times when only candy will do. Chocolate candies are the best. Sweet and dark, they melt on our tongues and linger in our mouths with a delicious warm creaminess that is part taste, part memory.

The popularity of chocolate candies is obvious to anyone who has perused the candy rack of a supermarket or newsstand. And while a store-bought chocolate bar is a good way to satisfy many a chocolate craving, it cannot compare with the taste of homemade chocolate candy. As lovely and tempting as a chocolate shop is, with pristine glass cases filled with trays of pretty truffles, the confections rarely hold a candle to the truffles you can make in your own kitchen with your favorite kind of chocolate and just a little practice.

In this chapter we explain how to make chocolate candies of nearly every description. Beginning with a chocolate bar similar to the ever-popular Snickers, we take you through candies such as fudge, buttercrunch, truffles, and French-style pralines. Some of the candies are simple to make—Maui Mounds and Peanut Butter Balls, for instance—while others require some skill at working with chocolate. Since many of the candies call for tempered chocolate, we urge you to read the section on tempering found on page 22 before you begin. Tempering is not difficult, but you must exercise care and steady surveillance to keep the chocolate in temper as you work.

～ *All-American Candy Bars* ～

Ever since Milton S. Hershey made the first 2 chocolate candy bars in 1894, Americans have had a nonstop love affair with them. Hershey's earliest creations were an almond bar and a milk chocolate bar, both sold almost exclusively to the baseball fans who gathered at ball parks on lazy summer afternoons. What may have started as a small idea, a sideline perhaps for Hershey, quickly blossomed into big business, and today we find candy bars in every supermarket, candy store, and newsstand in the country. Among the most popular is the Snickers bar made by the Mars Candy Company. Its delectable combination of chocolate, nougat, and peanut caramel has melted more than one sweets-loving heart. We developed our own version of a chocolate-covered nougat and peanut-caramel bar. You may enrobe it entirely with chocolate or decide to cover only the top and bottom of the bar with chocolate. Making candy bars at home takes time but is lots of fun. And we think it is pure pleasure to wrap the pretty bars in clear plastic or colorful foil and give them to friends. It is also pure pleasure to eat them.

YIELD: 36 candy bars

DIFFICULTY: ■■■

PREPARATION TIME: 4½ hours plus cooking, cooling, and setting times (allow 2 days to prepare the candy bars)

SPECIAL EQUIPMENT: heavy-duty stand-up electric mixer with wire whip and paddle attachments; candy thermometer; heating pad; 2 4-pronged professional dipping forks; cotton gloves, for handling coated bars

Peanut caramel:

2 cups heavy (whipping) cream
1½ cups light corn syrup
1½ cups sifted granulated sugar
½ cup packed light brown sugar
2 tablespoons unsalted butter, cut into ½-inch cubes
⅛ teaspoon salt
1 tablespoon vanilla extract
3½ cups salted roasted peanuts

Peanut butter nougat:

2 cups light corn syrup
2 cups sifted granulated sugar
1 cup packed light brown sugar
¾ cup water
2 large egg whites, at room temperature
Pinch of cream of tartar
2½ cups chunk-style peanut butter
¾ cup finely chopped salted, roasted peanuts
1 tablespoon vanilla extract

Coating:

3½ pounds milk or semisweet chocolate couverture, tempered,
*   or 1½ pounds if not coating the entire bar (for tempering*
*   instructions, see page 22)*

Make the peanut caramel:

1. Line the bottom and sides of a 10½-by-15½-inch jelly-roll pan with heavy-duty aluminum foil, leaving a 2-inch overhang on the short ends. Fold the overhang underneath the pan. Butter the bottom and sides of the foil-lined pan. Butter the bottom of the blade of an offset metal cake spatula.

2. Lightly butter the sides of a heavy 3½- or 4-quart saucepan. Add the cream, corn syrup, sugars, butter, and salt. Stirring constantly with a wooden spoon, cook the mixture over medium-low heat for 5 to 10 minutes or until the sugar is completely dissolved. Dip a clean pastry brush in water and wash down the sides of the pan to remove any sugar crystals. Raise the heat to medium and bring the mixture to a boil. Insert a candy thermometer into the mixture, but do not let it touch the bottom of the pan. (If using a thermometer mounted on a metal frame, the frame may touch the bottom of the pan.) Cook the caramel mixture, stirring constantly to prevent the caramel from scorching, for 30 to 40 minutes or until the thermometer registers 246°F (firm-ball stage). Remove the pan from the heat and stir in the vanilla and peanuts. Quickly pour the mixture into the prepared pan (do not scrape out the caramel that sticks to the bottom of the pan) and spread with the buttered offset spatula. Set the pan of caramel on a wire rack for 2 to 3 hours to cool completely.

Make the peanut butter nougat:

3. Butter the bottom of the blade of an offset metal cake spatula.

4. In a heavy 3½- or 4-quart saucepan, combine the corn syrup, sugars, and water. Stirring constantly with a wooden spoon, cook the mixture over

medium-low heat for 5 to 10 minutes or until the sugar crystals are dissolved. Dip a clean pastry brush in water and wash down the sides of the pan to remove any sugar crystals. Raise the heat to medium and bring the syrup to a boil. Insert a clean candy thermometer into the boiling syrup. (Sugar crystals from a used, unwashed candy thermometer contaminate the sugar syrup.) Cook the syrup without stirring for 18 to 22 minutes or until the thermometer registers 246°F (firm-ball stage). When the syrup reaches 242°F, start beating the egg whites (see instructions in the following step).

5. In a grease-free bowl of a heavy-duty stand-up electric mixer, using the wire whip attachment, beat the egg whites at low speed until frothy. Add the cream of tartar. Gradually increase the speed to medium high and continue beating the whites until stiff, shiny peaks form. By this point the sugar syrup should register 246°F on the candy thermometer. Remove the pan from the heat and transfer the hot syrup to a heat-resistant 1-quart measuring cup.

6. With the mixer set at low speed, gradually pour the hot syrup down the side of the bowl into the beaten egg whites. Continue beating for 3 to 5 minutes or until the mixture forms a thick, shiny ribbon. Remove the wire whip from the mixer and attach the paddle. At low speed, beat in the peanut butter, peanuts, and vanilla. Scrape down the sides of the bowl and mix just until blended. Quickly scrape the nougat over the cooled peanut caramel and spread with the buttered offset spatula in a smooth and even layer. If necessary, butter the spatula two to three more times during the spreading process to prevent the nougat from sticking. Cover the surface of the nougat with plastic wrap and refrigerate for 2 to 3 hours until the nougat is firm. Remove the peanut-caramel nougat from the refrigerator and leave at room temperature overnight.

Coat the peanut-caramel nougat:

7. Temper the chocolate (for tempering instructions, see page 22).

8. Remove the plastic wrap from the nougat. Invert the peanut-caramel nougat onto a large

cutting board. Peel the aluminum foil from the peanut-caramel layer. Invert the peanut-caramel nougat again so that the nougat side is facing upward. Using a large sharp knife, trim a ½-inch strip from each side of the candy rectangle so that it measures 9½ inches by 14½ inches. Cut it in half to form two 7¼-by-9½-inch rectangles.

9. Cover two 7¼-by-9½-inch cardboard rectangles with aluminum foil. Put one of the candy rectangles on one of the foil-covered bases so that the peanut-caramel layer is facing up.

10. Holding a metal cake spatula at a slight angle, spread about ¾ cup of the tempered chocolate in a thin, even layer over the top of the peanut-caramel layer. Still holding the spatula at a slight angle, scrape the excess chocolate back into the bowl. Refrigerate the rectangle for 1 to 2 minutes to set the chocolate. Invert the chocolate-covered rectangle onto the second foil-covered base. Spread about ¾ cup of the tempered chocolate over the nougat layer. Refrigerate for 1 to 2 minutes to set the chocolate. Coat the top and bottom of the second candy rectangle in the same manner.

11. Using a large sharp knife, trim ⅛ inch off the short sides of each chocolate-coated rectangle to remove the chocolate drips. Trim ¼ inch off the long sides of each rectangle so that they measure 7 inches by 9 inches.

12. Using a ruler and a small knife, mark the long edges of one of the rectangles into nine 1-inch segments. Using the marks as guides, score the surface of the chocolate into nine 1-inch-wide strips. Cut the rectangle along the score lines into 1-inch wide strips.

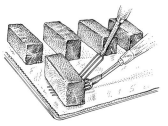

13. Working with three strips at a time, trim ⅛ inch off both short ends. Cut the three strips in half to make 6 candy bars. Trim the remaining six strips, three at a time, and cut into 12 bars. Mark, trim, and cut the remaining candy rectangle in the same manner.

remove any excess chocolate. Using a second fork, ease the coated bar onto the foil-lined baking sheet and carefully remove both forks. Decorate the top

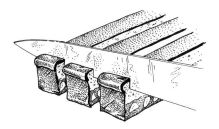

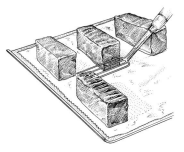

of the bar by gently touching the top with the prongs of the fork. Lift the fork with an upward

Dip the peanut caramel nougat candy bars:

14. Set the bowl of tempered chocolate over a smaller bowl that is two-thirds full of 86° to 91°F water. The bottom of the bowl containing the chocolate must touch the water to maintain the correct temperature. Put the simulated double boiler on a heating pad. To facilitate the coating process, tilt the larger bowl so the chocolate forms a pool that is almost level with the rim of the bowl.

15. Line two baking sheets with aluminum foil and set one of them next to the heating pad. With your fingers, put one of the candy bars on the surface of the tempered chocolate. Using a 4-pronged professional dipping fork, press down on the bar so that its sides are completely submerged in the chocolate. Using the fork, sweep some of the chocolate over the top of the bar to cover it. Lift the coated bar out of the chocolate and gently tap the fork several times on the side of the bowl to release any air bubbles in the chocolate. Remove the fork at a slight angle following the curve of the bowl to

motion and then pull toward you to create a fork pattern in the chocolate. Repeat two more times across the top of the candy bar. Dip and decorate the remaining bars in the same manner. Let the peanut-caramel-nougat candy bars set at room temperature for 1 hour or until they can be lifted from the aluminum foil without sticking and the tops and undersides of the bars are shiny.

16. Wrap the candy bars individually and store at room temperature in airtight containers for up to 2 weeks. The bars can also be frozen for up to 2 months. Thaw the frozen bars in the refrigerator overnight before bringing them to room temperature.

～◯ *Magic Mocha Fudge* ◠～

Thanks to the marshmallow cream, this recipe for creamy, smooth fudge is just about foolproof. The candy requires only a quick stint in the freezer to firm up, so that in a flash you have a sampling of an old-fashioned fudgy treat.

YIELD: 16 squares

DIFFICULTY: ◣

PREPARATION TIME: 30 minutes plus freezing time

SPECIAL EQUIPMENT: candy thermometer

---

12 ounces semisweet chocolate, finely chopped
1 cup marshmallow cream
½ cup coarsely chopped walnuts
2 teaspoons instant coffee powder
½ teaspoon vanilla extract
2 cups granulated sugar
¾ cup evaporated milk
4 tablespoons (½ stick) unsalted butter, cut into tablespoons
Dash of salt

1. Line a 9-inch square baking pan with aluminum foil so that the foil extends 2 inches beyond two opposite sides of the pan. Lightly butter the bottom and sides of the foil-lined pan. Put the pan directly on the floor of the freezer while preparing the fudge.

2. In a medium bowl, combine the chocolate, marshmallow creame, walnuts, coffee powder, and vanilla.

3. Lightly butter the sides of a heavy, noncorrosive 2-quart saucepan. Combine the sugar, evaporated milk, butter, and salt in the saucepan. Stirring constantly with a wooden spoon, cook the mixture over medium-low heat for 8 to 10 minutes or until the sugar is completely dissolved.

4. Increase the heat to medium and bring the syrup to a boil. Insert a candy thermometer, taking care that it does not touch the bottom of the pan. (If using a thermometer mounted on a metal frame, the frame may touch the bottom of the pan.) Cook the syrup without stirring for 5 to 7 minutes or until the candy thermometer registers 236°F (softball stage).

5. Pour the hot syrup over the chocolate-marshmallow mixture and let it stand for 2 minutes. Stir the mixture with a wooden spoon until the chocolate is melted and the mixture is smooth.

6. Scrape the fudge into the prepared pan. Using an offset metal spatula, smooth the top of the fudge. Cover the pan with plastic wrap and return to the freezer floor. Freeze the fudge for 30 to 40 minutes or until firm.

7. Using the two ends of the aluminum foil as handles, lift the fudge out of the pan. Invert the fudge onto a small cutting board and carefully peel off the foil. Invert again onto a smooth cutting surface. Using a large knife, score the fudge into 16 pieces. Cut the fudge, rinsing the knife with hot water and wiping dry between each cut. Store the fudge in an airtight container for up to 5 days.

Fudge Flavors

In most people's minds, fudge is linked with chocolate, and this is undoubtedly the most popular flavor for the candy. But fudge can also be flavored with vanilla, maple, or peanut but- ter. Thrifty cooks who hate to waste leftover food reportedly have concocted mashed potato fudge and a ground beef variety called Ranch Fudge.

⌒ *Maui Mounds* ⌒

Coconut, dried pineapple, and macadamia nuts combine with chocolate in one of the easiest candies we have ever made. Simply drop the mixture from a spoon onto baking sheets and freeze them for 20 to 25 minutes. Presto! Pop a few in your mouth and indulge in the rich flavors of the tropics.

YIELD: Approximately 24 candies
DIFFICULTY: ◼
PREPARATION TIME: 20 minutes plus chilling time

¾ cup sweetened condensed milk
8 ounces semisweet chocolate, finely chopped
½ cup sweetened flaked coconut
½ cup unsalted macadamia nuts
¼ cup dried pineapple, coarsely chopped
2 tablespoons coarsely chopped crystallized ginger

1. Line a baking sheet with aluminum foil.

2. In a medium, heavy-bottomed saucepan, bring the milk to a boil over medium-low heat. Add the chocolate to the hot milk and let stand for 2 to 3 minutes. Using a wooden spoon, stir the milk-chocolate mixture until the chocolate is melted and the mixture is smooth. Stir in the coconut, nuts, pineapple, and ginger.

3. Drop the mixture by heaping tablespoons onto the prepared baking sheet. Freeze the mounds, uncovered, for 20 to 25 minutes or until firm enough to lift from the foil. Store the Maui mounds in an airtight container and refrigerate for up to 1 week.

⌒ *Peanut Butter Balls* ⌒

These candies start with a smooth nut butter base and are then cloaked with chocolate—easy to make and so good to eat!

YIELD: Approximately 45 candies

DIFFICULTY: ◼

PREPARATION TIME: 50 minutes plus chilling time

SPECIAL EQUIPMENT: 3-pronged candy fork

9 ounces bittersweet chocolate, coarsely chopped
2 tablespoons solid vegetable shortening
1 cup plus 2 tablespoons (1 12-ounce jar) chunky peanut butter
5 tablespoons unsalted butter, softened
2 cups confectioners' sugar
1½ cups crispy rice cereal

1. In the top of a double boiler over hot, not simmering, water, melt the chocolate with the vegetable shortening, stirring until smooth. Remove the top part of the double boiler from the bottom. Transfer the chocolate mixture to a small glass or metal bowl and cool slightly while preparing the peanut butter balls.

2. In a medium bowl, cream together the peanut butter and butter with a wooden spoon. Gradually add the confectioners' sugar and mix until smooth. Stir in the cereal. (The cereal will break up.) Press a heaping tablespoon of the mixture together with your fingertips and then roll it between the palms of your hands to form a smooth ball. Repeat with the remaining mixture.

3. Line a baking sheet with aluminum foil and set it next to the bowl of chocolate. With one hand, tilt the bowl of chocolate so the chocolate forms a pool that is almost level with the rim of the bowl. With the other hand, put a peanut butter ball on the surface of the chocolate. Using a professional 3-pronged candy fork or a regular fork, press down on the peanut butter ball so that the sides are completely submerged in the chocolate. Turn the ball over. Lift the coated ball out of the chocolate mixture. Gently tap the fork on the side of the bowl and scrape it along the rim to remove any excess chocolate. Put the coated ball on the prepared baking sheet. Continue the process with the remaining balls and chocolate.

4. Freeze the balls on the baking sheet for 15 to 20 minutes or until the chocolate is set and the balls may be lifted easily from the aluminum foil. Store the peanut butter balls in an airtight container and refrigerate for up to 1 week.

Chunky Chocolate
⌒ *Fruit-and-Nut Squares* ⌒

Have you ever imagined creating your own chocolate candies, packed with precisely the amount and sort of nuts you want, the right ingredient for crunch, and your favorite dried fruit? In this recipe we offer lots of options. Once you have the combination customized to your liking, you can then select the sort of chocolate you want—dark, white, or milk. We explain how to make these dream candies using tempered couverture chocolate, which is important here, since it retains its gloss, firmness, and snap at room temperature. Be sure the nuts and fruit are dry and at room temperature when you fold them into the tempered chocolate. The squares will taste best if you let them age for 24 hours, so that the flavors of the ingredients have time to mingle with the chocolate.

YIELD: 16 squares (about 2½ pounds of candy)

DIFFICULTY: ▰▰▰

PREPARATION TIME: 1 hour plus chilling and setting times

1¼ pounds white, milk, or dark chocolate couverture
2½ cups nuts (walnuts, pecans, pistachios, or roasted almonds, cashews, brazil nuts, hazelnuts, macadamia nuts, or peanuts)
1 cup oven-roasted rice cereal, cookie crumbs, or toasted coconut
1½ cups raisins, currants, candied orange peel, or other coarsely chopped dried fruit

1. Temper the chocolate (for tempering instructions, see page 22.)

2. Line a 9-inch square baking pan with aluminum foil so that the foil extends 2 inches beyond two opposite sides of the pan.

3. In a large bowl, combine the nuts, cereal, cookie crumbs, or coconut, and the fruit. Using a clean, dry rubber spatula, fold in all but 3 tablespoons of the tempered chocolate until the nut-and-fruit mixture is completely coated. Quickly scrape the mixture into the prepared pan and spread evenly with the spatula. Dip a clean spatula into the remaining chocolate and drizzle it over the top of the candy. Refrigerate for 10 to 15 minutes or until the candy starts to set.

4. Remove the pan from the refrigerator. Using the two ends of the aluminum foil as handles, lift the candy out of the pan. Using a large, sharp knife, score the surface of the candy into 16 pieces. Let the candy set completely at room temperature for 1 hour. Cut the candy into 16 pieces. Store in an airtight container for up to 1 month.

Milk Chocolate and Praline
⟳ Truffles ⟲

If you like milk chocolate and hazelnuts together, you will love these truffles. The centers, which are quite easy to make, are rolled in the chopped praline and then refrigerated until you are ready to serve them. Packed in an airtight container, they will keep for a week. Or you may freeze them for as long as a month.

YIELD: Approximately 24 truffles	
DIFFICULTY: ▬▬	
PREPARATION TIME: 1 hour plus cooling and chilling times	

Hazelnut praline:

¾ cup granulated sugar

⅓ cup water

1 cup whole hazelnuts, roasted (for roasting instructions, see page 20)

Milk chocolate truffles:

½ cup heavy (whipping) cream

12 ounces Swiss milk chocolate, finely chopped

1 tablespoon unsalted butter, softened

2 teaspoons hazelnut liqueur, such as Frangelico (optional)

Make the hazelnut praline:

1. Lightly butter an 8-inch square on a baking sheet. In a small, heavy saucepan, combine the sugar and water. Cook over medium heat, stirring constantly, for 3 to 5 minutes or until the sugar dissolves. Increase the heat to high and bring the syrup to a boil. Cook without stirring for 4 to 8 minutes or until an amber-colored caramel forms. Immediately add the hazelnuts and stir to coat with the syrup. Quickly transfer the praline mixture to the prepared baking sheet and cool for 20 minutes or until hardened.

2. Break the hazelnut praline into pieces. Using a food processor fitted with the metal blade, pulse the praline pieces 15 to 20 times or until finely chopped. Measure ½ cup of the praline for the truffle filling. Reserve the remaining praline to coat the truffles.

Make the milk chocolate truffles:

3. In a small saucepan over low heat, bring the heavy cream just to a simmer. Remove the saucepan from the heat and add the chocolate, stirring until the chocolate is melted and smooth. Add the butter and hazelnut liqueur to the chocolate mixture and stir until the butter is melted. Stir in the ½ cup of hazelnut praline. Transfer the mixture to an 8-inch square baking pan. Cover the pan tightly with aluminum foil and freeze for about 1 hour or until the mixture is firm enough to roll.

4. Put the remaining hazelnut praline in a small bowl. Using a melon baller, scoop up about 1 tablespoon of the chilled chocolate mixture for each truffle. Roll the chocolate mixture between your palms to form round truffles. Roll the truffles in the praline, pressing the praline gently into the truffles. Transfer the truffles to an airtight container and refrigerate for at least 8 hours or overnight. Allow the truffles to stand at room temperature for 10 minutes before serving.

～◯ *Cabernet Truffles* ◯～

Cabernet Sauvignon gives these simple truffles a fruity character distinctly different from other liquor-flavored truffles.

YIELD: 30 truffles
DIFFICULTY: ▬
PREPARATION TIME: 30 minutes plus chilling time

¼ cup heavy (whipping) cream
8 ounces bittersweet chocolate, finely chopped
2 tablespoons dry, fruity red wine, such as Cabernet Sauvignon
4 tablespoons (½ stick) unsalted butter, softened
½ cup unsweetened alkalized cocoa powder

1. In a medium saucepan over medium-high heat, bring the cream to a simmer. Reduce the heat to low and cook the cream for 2 to 4 minutes or until it is reduced to 2 tablespoons.

2. In the top of a double boiler over hot, not simmering, water, melt the chocolate with the reduced cream and the wine, stirring frequently until smooth. Remove the top part of the double boiler from the bottom. Stir the butter into the chocolate mixture until smooth. Cover the surface of the truffle mixture with plastic wrap and refrigerate for 4 hours or until firm.

3. Put the cocoa in a small, shallow bowl. Using a melon baller or a teaspoon, scoop the truffle mixture and roll into irregularly shaped 1-inch balls. Roll each truffle in the cocoa to coat completely. The truffles may be stored in an airtight container in the refrigerator for up to 2 weeks.

～ *Chocolate Walnut Fudge* ～

Chocolate fudge has been a favorite American candy since the turn of the century. It is a simple, bold confection, intensely sweet and bursting with rich chocolate flavor. No one agrees on the origin of fudge. It may have been discovered by a Philadelphia candy maker who accidentally overcooked a batch of caramel; or, as another story goes, it was devised by college girls who cooked up concoctions of cream, sugar, and chocolate over the gaslights that hung from the ceilings of their dormitories. While its beginnings may have been accidental or crude, to make a stellar batch of fudge takes practice and patience. Many a novice has set out with high hopes of smooth, rich fudge only to be rewarded with a grainy, greasy mess. Follow our instructions, choosing the method that best suits you for cooling and creaming the fudge, and we promise you spectacular results. The fudge will be velvety, creamy, and wonderfully chocolaty—just as the old-fashioned confection should be.

YIELD: 16 pieces

DIFFICULTY: ▰▰

PREPARATION TIME: 20 minutes plus cooking, cooling, creaming, and setting times

---

SPECIAL EQUIPMENT: Candy thermometer; 8-inch square flan form (optional); 5- to 6-inch wide flexible "broad" metal knife (available at hardware stores), necessary for the jelly-roll pan or marble-slab cooling and creaming methods only

---

3 cups sifted granulated sugar
1¼ cups half-and-half
⅓ cup light corn syrup
Pinch of salt
7 ounces unsweetened chocolate, finely chopped
3 tablespoons unsalted butter, cut into ½-inch cubes
1½ teaspoons vanilla extract
2 cups walnut halves, coarsely broken

1. Put a 10-inch square piece of heavy-duty aluminum foil on a baking sheet. Butter an 8-inch square in the center of the foil. Lightly butter the insides of an 8-inch square flan form and set it on top of the buttered square. Alternatively, line an 8-inch square baking pan with foil so that the foil extends 2 inches beyond two opposite sides of the pan. Lightly butter the bottom and sides of the foil-lined pan.

2. Lightly butter the sides of a heavy, non corrosive 2-quart saucepan. Add the sugar, half-and-half, corn syrup, and salt. Stirring constantly with a wooden spoon, cook the mixture over medium-low heat for 5 to 10 minutes or until the sugar crystals are completely dissolved. Do not let the mixture boil. Remove the pan from the heat and, using a damp towel, wipe the sides above the liquid to remove any undissolved sugar crystals. Add the chocolate and stir until completely smooth.

3. Return the pan to the heat and insert a candy thermometer, taking care that it does not touch the bottom of the pan. (If using a thermometer with a metal frame, the frame may touch the bottom of the pan.) Bring the syrup to a gentle boil over medium-low heat. Cook the syrup without stirring for 1 hour to 1 hour and 20 minutes or until the

thermometer registers 234°F (soft-ball stage). If necessary, adjust the heat to low and use a Flame Tamer; the surface of the syrup must boil evenly and gently to avoid scorching the fudge. Carefully take the pan off the heat and remove the candy thermometer. Immediately wash the thermometer in hot water.

4. Refer to one of the following methods for cooling and creaming the fudge.

Pot Method

The pot method for cooling and creaming fudge is a common method often described in household cookbooks. It is more time-consuming than the other two methods described here and takes patience and a strong forearm. The advantage is that the cooling and creaming are done in the same pot the syrup was cooked in. Allow 50 to 70 minutes for the fudge to cool and 25 to 35 minutes to cream the fudge.

5. Set the pot containing the hot fudge on a cooling rack. Prop one side of the pot on a folded dish towel so that it is tilted. Replace the thermometer in the fudge. The tilted pot will ensure that the mercury bulb of the thermometer is adequately covered. Distribute the butter cubes evenly over the top of the hot fudge. Cool the fudge for 50 to 70 minutes or until the temperature registers 110°F on the candy thermometer and the bottom of the pot feels lukewarm to the touch. Do not disturb the fudge during the cooling process.

6. Using a wooden spoon, stir in the vanilla. Beat the fudge with the spoon for 25 to 35 minutes or until it starts to thicken and lose its shine. Stir in the walnuts. Scrape the fudge into the prepared pan and spread it evenly with a small metal spatula. Put the pan on a wire rack. Let the fudge set for 1 to 2 hours at room temperature until firm.

7. If using the square flan form, take a warm, sharp knife and run it around the edges of the fudge to loosen it. If using the baking pan, lift the fudge out of the pan, using the two ends of aluminum foil as handles. Invert the fudge onto a small cutting board and carefully peel off the foil. Invert again onto a smooth cutting surface. Using a large knife, score the fudge into 16 pieces. Cut the fudge, rinsing the knife with hot water and wiping dry between each cut.

Jelly-Roll Pan Method

The cooling procedure in the jelly-roll pan method is twice as fast as the pot method. The hot fudge mixture is poured out onto a dampened jelly-roll pan and cooled for 30 to 40 minutes. With this method, it is not possible to use the candy thermometer when cooling down the fudge syrup—you must rely on your sense of touch. The fudge is creamed with a broad, flexible knife directly in the jelly-roll pan. Creaming will take 15 to 25 minutes.

5. Run a heavy 11½-by-17½-inch jelly-roll pan under cold water. Invert the pan and shake off the excess moisture. Set the pan on top of a large wire rack.

6. Holding the saucepan containing the hot fudge close to the surface of the jelly-roll pan, slowly pour the fudge into the pan. Do not scrape out the fudge that clings to the bottom and sides of the pan. Evenly distribute the

butter cubes over the surface of the hot fudge. Cool the fudge for 30 to 40 minutes or until the bottom of the pan and the surface of the fudge feel lukewarm (110°F).

7. Sprinkle the vanilla over the surface of the fudge. Using a 5- or 6-inch-wide flexible "broad" metal knife (available at hardware stores), scrape the cooled fudge together and blend in the butter and vanilla by lifting and folding the fudge toward the center. When the butter and vanilla are completely incorporated, spread the fudge evenly across three fourths of the length of the jelly-roll pan. Scrape the fudge back together and lift and fold the edges toward the center. Continue this spreading, scraping, lifting, and folding process for 15 to 25 minutes or until the fudge thickens and starts to lose its shine. Blend in the walnuts. Quickly scrape the fudge into the prepared form or pan and spread it evenly with a small metal spatula. Put the pan on a wire rack. Let the fudge set for 1 to 2 hours at room temperature until firm. Unmold and cut the fudge as described in step 7 of the pot method.

Marble-Slab Method

The marble-slab method is a traditional method preferred by most professional fudge makers. The temperature of the marble will be a few degrees cooler than room temperature. It will absorb the heat from the hot fudge mixture quickly and evenly, resulting in a shorter cooling time than the two preceding methods. Allow 15 to 20 minutes for the fudge to cool and 10 to 20 minutes for creaming.

5. Lightly sprinkle a marble slab with water and spread the water with your hand so that a thin film of water covers the surface. Hold the saucepan of hot fudge close to the surface of the marble and slowly pour the fudge onto it. Do not scrape out the fudge clinging to the bottom and sides of the pan. Evenly distribute the butter cubes over the top of the hot fudge. Cool the fudge for 15 to 20 minutes or until the surface of the fudge feels lukewarm (110°F).

6. Sprinkle the vanilla over the surface of the fudge. Using a 5- or 6-inch-wide flexible metal "broad" knife, scrape the cooled fudge together and blend in the butter and vanilla by lifting and folding the fudge toward the center. When the butter and vanilla are completely incorporated, spread the fudge out into a 12-inch rectangle. Scrape the fudge back together and lift and fold the edges of the fudge back into the center. Continue working the fudge in this manner for 10 to 20 minutes or until the fudge thickens and starts to lose its shine. Blend in the walnuts. Quickly scrape the fudge into the prepared form or pan and spread it evenly with a small metal spatula. Put the pan on a wire rack. Let the fudge set for 1 to 2 hours at room temperature or until firm. Unmold and cut the fudge as described in step 7 of the pot method.

Fudge-Making Tips

Fudge is not the easiest of candies to make. To ensure success, we have compiled a list of tips—on techniques and equipment—as well as special instructions if you want to make fudge and live high in the mountains. Read these over and be sure to follow the recipe very carefully. If you do, you will surely be rewarded with creamy, rich fudge—just the way you like it!

Techniques

• Sift the sugar to cut down the time it takes it to dissolve. Be sure the sugar dissolves completely—you should not be able to feel any grittiness when you rub the sides of the pan with a wooden spoon.

• Butter the sides of the pan before cooking the syrup. This makes it easier to wipe sugar crystals from the sides before adding the chocolate and helps prevent crystals from forming during cooking.

• Be sure the chocolate is completely melted and blended into the hot syrup before bringing the mixture to a boil. Unmelted bits of chocolate can scorch and ruin the fudge.

• Fudge tastes even richer if you let it ripen in an airtight container for 1 or 2 days.

Equipment

• A straight-sided saucepan made of heavy-gauge noncorrosive metal (such as anodized aluminum or stainless steel) is the best choice for making fudge. Do not use a copper sugar pot—the chocolate will pick up an unpleasant aftertaste from the metal.

• Be sure the pan is of appropriate size. If it's too large, you will not be able to submerge the bulb of the candy thermometer sufficiently in the boiling fudge. If the pan is too small, you may have to cook the fudge mixture too long before it reaches the correct temperature and you also run the risk of messy, dangerous boil over.

Making Fudge at High Altitudes

• Liquid evaporates more quickly at high altitudes than it does at sea level, which means the cooking time will be shorter.

• If you follow sea-level instructions, the mixture will be too concentrated by the time the fudge reaches the given temperature. To adjust a fudge recipe for high-altitude cooking, deduct 2° from the required temperature for every thousand feet of altitude above sea level.

Rochers

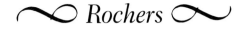

These little rock-shaped chocolates are surprisingly light and creamy. Made with whipped gianduja centers and coated with crisp shells of milk or semisweet chocolate, they finally are studded with roasted almond cookie crunch. Cocoa butter, which you will need for the recipe, is sold in some pharmacies and specialty food shops and is also available from mail order sources. The uncoated gianduja centers can be stored at room temperature for up to 48 hours in an airtight container. To keep finished rochers, freeze them or hold them at room temperature in an airtight container for up to 2 months.

YIELD: Approximately 3 dozen chocolates plus 1 pound of almond bark

DIFFICULTY: ■■■

PREPARATION TIME: 2 hours plus setting time

SPECIAL EQUIPMENT: pastry bag fitted with a large plain tip (such as Ateco #6)

Filling:

6 ounces gianduja, finely chopped (see page 18 for an explanation of gianduja)
2 ounces bittersweet chocolate, finely chopped
¾ cup heavy (whipping) cream
½ ounce cocoa butter, finely chopped
1½ teaspoons Italian nut liqueur, such as Capella or Frangelico
Confectioners' sugar

Coating:

1¼ cups roasted slivered almonds, (for roasting instructions, see page 20)
6 sugar cookies (such as Pepperidge Farm Bordeaux)
1½ pounds milk or semisweet chocolate couverture, tempered (for tempering instructions, see page 22)
1 cup roasted unblanched almonds (for roasting instructions, see page 20)

Make the filling:

1. In a medium metal bowl, combine the gianduja and chocolate.

2. In a small saucepan, combine the cream and cocoa butter. Over medium-low heat, slowly bring the mixture to a gentle boil. Pour the hot cream mixture over the gianduja and chocolate and whisk until smooth. Stir in the liqueur.

3. Fit a pastry bag with a large plain tip (such as Ateco #6). Line a baking sheet with aluminum foil.

4. Set the bowl containing the chocolate mixture over a bowl of ice water. Using a hand-held electric mixer set at medium speed, beat the filling for 1 to 2 minutes or until it is light in color and forms soft peaks when the beaters are lifted. Do not overbeat, or the filling will harden too quickly and have a

grainy texture. Remove the bowl from the ice water. Immediately spoon the whipped filling into the pastry bag.

5. Pipe ¾-inch mounds with pointed peaks onto the foil-lined baking sheet. Chill the centers for 10 to 15 minutes or until firm. (Do not overchill, or they will become too stiff to form the rounds.)

6. Sift a light dusting of confectioners' sugar over the chilled centers. With your fingertips, form each mound into a ¾-inch ball. Let the centers set, uncovered, at room temperature for at least 1 hour.

Prepare the coating:

7. Finely chop the roasted slivered almonds and put them in a small bowl. Using a rolling pin, crush the cookies into coarse crumbs. Combine the cookie crumbs with the almonds.

8. Temper the chocolate (for tempering instructions, see page 22). Stir the almond-cookie mixture into the tempered chocolate until evenly mixed.

9. Line a baking sheet with aluminum foil. Lift a rocher center with your forefinger and second finger and dip it into the tempered chocolate mixture. Toss the center between your fingers on the surface of the tempered chocolate to get an even coating. Lift up the center. Move your fingers in a scissorlike motion to release any drips, and scrape any excess chocolate from your fingers onto the edge of the bowl. Put the rocher on the foil-lined baking sheet, withdrawing your last finger with a twisting motion.

10. When all the rochers are coated, let them set at room temperature for 20 to 30 minutes or until they can be lifted from the aluminum foil without sticking and the tops and undersides of the chocolates are shiny. Store the rochers in an airtight container at room temperature for up to 1 week.

11. If desired, make almond bark with the leftover tempered chocolate. Line a baking sheet with aluminum foil. Using a small knife, trace a 9-inch square onto the foil. Stir the roasted unblanched almonds into the chocolate. Scrape the chocolate mixture into the center of the traced square. Using a metal cake spatula, quickly spread the chocolate mixture to fill the square. Refrigerate the bark for 8 to 10 minutes or until firm. Using a sharp knife, cut the bark into 36 1½-inch squares. Let the squares set at room temperature for 30 minutes before removing them from the foil. Store the bark in an airtight container at room temperature for up to 3 weeks.

◠ *Mocha Pralinés* ◠

Gianduja makes another appearance in these exquisite dipped candies, called pralinés (and pronounced "pra-leen-ay"), which in this case means chocolate candy, as it does in France. The centers are made from gianduja that has been mixed with espresso powder for subtle mocha flavor. If you prefer the flavor of orange to mocha or want to make two kinds of pralinés, we have a variation on the recipe in which the pralinés are perfumed with orange zest.

YIELD: 49 pralinés
DIFFICULTY: ▰▰▰
PREPARATION TIME: 2 hours plus overnight for the filling to set
SPECIAL EQUIPMENT: 3-pronged professional dipping fork; 7-inch square flan form; heating pad

Mocha-gianduja ganache:

9 ounces gianduja, finely chopped
4 ounces bittersweet chocolate, finely chopped
1 cup heavy (whipping) cream
1½ ounces cocoa butter, finely chopped
1½ teaspoons instant espresso coffee powder

Coating:

1½ pounds milk chocolate couverture, tempered (for tempering
instructions, see page 22)

Decoration:

Chocolate-covered coffee beans

Make the mocha-gianduja ganache:

1. In a medium bowl, combine the gianduja and bittersweet chocolate.

2. In a small saucepan, combine the cream and cocoa butter. Over medium-low heat, slowly bring the mixture to a gentle boil. Remove the pan from the heat and stir in the espresso powder. Pour the hot cream mixture over the gianduja and chocolate. Whisk until the mixture is smooth.

3. Put a 9-inch square of aluminum foil on a baking sheet. Set a 7-inch square flan form on top of the aluminum foil. Pour the ganache into the form and cover the surface with a piece of plastic wrap. Using a plastic scraper, smooth the surface of the ganache. Let the ganache set overnight at cool room temperature or refrigerate for 3 hours, until firm. (If refrigerated, let the ganache come to room temperature before coating.)

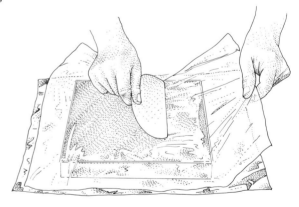

Prepare the coating:

4. Temper the milk chocolate (for tempering instructions, see page 22).

5. Remove the plastic wrap from the ganache. Using a small sharp knife, cut around the edges of the flan form to loosen the ganache. Remove the form.

6. Using a metal cake spatula, spread 3 table-spoons of the tempered chocolate in a thin, even layer over the top of the ganache. Let the chocolate set for 1 to 2 minutes or until firm. Invert the ganache square onto a work surface and carefully remove the aluminum foil. Spread 3 tablespoons of the tempered chocolate over the surface of the ganache. Let the chocolate set for 1 to 2 minutes or until firm.

7. Using a ruler and a small knife, mark all four edges of the ganache square into 7 1-inch segments. Using the marks as guides, score the surface of the chocolate into 49 1-inch squares. Dip the blade of a large, sharp knife in hot water and wipe it dry. Cut the ganache along the score lines into squares. Dip the knife in hot water and dry it after each cut.

8. Line a baking sheet with aluminum foil and set it next to the heating pad on which you have put the tempered chocolate (see tempering instructions, page 22). With your fingers, put one of the ganache centers on the surface of the pool of tempered chocolate. Using a 3-pronged professional dipping fork, press down on the ganache center so that the sides are completely submerged in the chocolate, and turn the center over. Lift the coated center out of the chocolate and gently tap the fork on the side of the bowl. Remove the fork at a slight

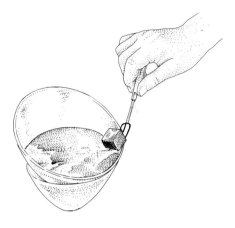

angle following the curve of the bowl to release any excess chocolate. Put the coated center on the foil-lined baking sheet and carefully remove the dipping fork. Dip a second ganache center into the chocolate and set it on the baking sheet. Decorate the top of the first mocha praliné by gently touching it with the prongs of the fork. Lift the fork with an upward motion and slightly forward to create the fork pattern in the chocolate. Top with a chocolate bean. Dip a third ganache center in the chocolate and set it on the baking sheet. Decorate the second mocha praliné with the fork and top with a chocolate coffee bean. Continue to alternate the dipping and decorating process until all the mocha pralinés have been coated. Let them set at room temperature for 20 to 30 minutes or until they can be lifted from the aluminum foil without sticking and the tops and undersides of the pralinés are shiny.

9. Line a second baking sheet with aluminum foil. Pour the leftover tempered chocolate onto the foil and spread evenly. Refrigerate for 10 minutes or until firm. Let the chocolate stand at room temperature for 30 minutes. Break the chocolate into small pieces and store to use again baking or candy making.

10. Store the mocha pralinés in an airtight container at room temperature for up to 1 week or freeze them for up to 2 months.

∽ *Orange Pralinés* ∽

Follow the ingredient list for Mocha Pralinés (see page 300), making these substitutions:

Orange-gianduja ganache:

Substitute 3 ¾-by-2-inch strips orange zest for the instant espresso coffee powder

Coating:

Substitute 1½ pounds semisweet chocolate couverture for the milk chocolate couverture

Make the orange-gianduja ganache:

1. In a medium bowl, combine the gianduja and bittersweet chocolate.

2. In a small saucepan, combine the heavy cream, cocoa butter, and orange zest. Over medium-low heat, slowly bring the cream mixture to a gentle boil. Remove the pan from the heat and let the mixture steep for 15 minutes. Return the pan to the heat and bring the mixture to a second boil. Remove the pan from the heat and discard the orange zest. Pour the hot cream mixture over the gianduja and chocolate. Whisk until the mixture is smooth. Proceed as in step 3 of the recipe for Mocha Pralinés.

Prepare the coating:

3. Proceed as in steps 4 through 10 of the recipe for Mocha Praliné. Decorate the tops of the orange pralinés with the fork pattern only.

∽ *Fruit-and-Nut Medallions* ∽

We developed these waferlike candies as an exercise for working with milk chocolate couverture. Attractively decorated with dried fruit and nuts, the medallions quickly became one of our favorites—shiny, smooth candies that keep very well and make wonderful gifts.

YIELD: 2 dozen chocolates
DIFFICULTY: ▰▰
PREPARATION TIME: 1 hour plus cooling time
SPECIAL EQUIPMENT: 24 1⅛-by-2¾ (3-ounce) muffin cups

24 whole blanched almonds
1¼ pounds milk chocolate couverture, tempered (for tempering instructions, see page 22)
48 dark raisins
6 large dried apricots, cut into quarters
24 pecan halves

1. Position a rack in the center of the oven and preheat to 350°F. Put the almonds in a single layer on a baking sheet and bake for 8 to 10 minutes, shaking the sheet a couple of times, until the nuts are barely golden. Transfer the nuts to another baking sheet to stop the cooking process and cool completely.

2. Wipe the inside bottoms and sides of 24 2¾-by-1⅛-inch (3-ounce) muffin cups with a lint-free cloth.

3. Spoon 2 teaspoons of the tempered chocolate into 6 of the muffin cups and spread the chocolate evenly to make a thin layer. Working quickly before the chocolate sets, gently press the fruits and nuts into each of the chocolate rounds, making an attractive design. Refrigerate the muffin tin for 10 to 12 minutes or until the chocolate rounds set and start to contract from the edges of the cups.

4. Gently tap the muffin tin over a cloth-covered work surface to release the chocolates. If the chocolates do not release with a gentle tap, return the tin to the refrigerator for a few more minutes. The chocolates must be completely set before they will unmold.

5. Continue making and unmolding the medallions in the same manner. Store the chocolates in an airtight container at room temperature for up to 3 weeks.

⌒ *Mocha Truffles* ⌒

These simple uncoated truffles—made with chocolate chips and rolled in cocoa—are a breeze to make, since you use the microwave to melt the chocolate and heat the liqueur.

YIELD: 3½ dozen truffles
DIFFICULTY: ◣
PREPARATION TIME: 30 minutes plus chilling time

12 ounces (about 2 cups) semisweet chocolate chips
½ cup coffee liqueur, such as Kahlua or Tía Maria
4 large egg yolks, at room temperature
½ cup unsweetened alkalized cocoa powder

1. Put the chocolate chips in a microwave-safe 1-quart glass measuring cup. Heat in the microwave oven on medium (50 percent) power for 3 to 5 minutes or until the chocolate turns shiny. Remove the container from the microwave and stir the chocolate until it is completely melted.

2. In a 2-cup glass measuring cup, heat the coffee liqueur in the microwave oven on high (100 percent) power for 1 to 2 minutes or until it comes to a simmer. Remove the container from the microwave.

3. In a large bowl, using a hand-held electric mixer set at medium-high speed, beat the egg yolks for 2 minutes or until the mixture forms a thick yellow ribbon when the beaters are lifted. Continue to beat the yolks while very slowly adding the hot liqueur. Beat in the melted chocolate at low speed and continue mixing for 30 seconds, until the mixture is smooth. Cover the surface of the truffle mixture with plastic wrap and refrigerate for 1½ hours or until firm.

4. Put the cocoa in a shallow bowl. Using a melon baller or a teaspoon, scoop the truffle mixture and roll it into irregularly shaped 1-inch balls. Roll each truffle in the cocoa. Store the truffles in an airtight container in the refrigerator for up to 2 weeks.

～ *Gianduja Truffles* ～

These are classic truffles, made as you might find them in fashionable candy shops in Europe. Their centers are made from gianduja, and the milk chocolate exteriors are coated with cocoa.

> YIELD: Approximately 4 dozen truffles
>
> DIFFICULTY: ▰▰▰
>
> PREPARATION TIME: 2 hours plus setting time
>
> SPECIAL EQUIPMENT: pastry bag fitted with a large plain tip (such as Ateco #6); heating pad

Filling:

9 ounces gianduja, finely chopped
3 ounces bittersweet chocolate, finely chopped
1 cup heavy (whipping) cream
1 ounce cocoa butter, finely chopped
1 tablespoon Italian nut liqueur, such as Capella or Frangelico
Confectioners' sugar

Coating:

1½ pounds milk chocolate couverture, tempered (for tempering instructions, see page 22)
4 cups unsweetened alkalized cocoa powder

Make the filling:

1. In a medium metal bowl, combine the gianduja and chocolate.

2. In a small saucepan, combine the cream and cocoa butter. Over medium-low heat, slowly bring the mixture to a gentle boil. Pour the hot cream mixture over the gianduja and chocolate. Whisk until the mixture is smooth. Stir in the liqueur.

3. Fit a pastry bag with a large plain tip (such as Ateco #6). Line a baking sheet with aluminum foil.

4. Set the bowl containing the chocolate mixture over a bowl of ice water. Using a hand-held electric mixer set at medium speed, beat the filling for 2 or 3 minutes or until it is lighter in color and forms soft peaks when the beaters are lifted. Do not overbeat, or the filling will harden too quickly and the texture of the truffles will be grainy. Remove the bowl from the bowl of ice water. Immediately spoon the whipped filling into the pastry bag.

5. Pipe 1-inch mounds with pointed peaks onto the foil-lined baking sheet. Chill the centers for 10 to 15 minutes or until firm. Do not overchill, or they will become too stiff to form into rounds.

6. Sift a light dusting of confectioners' sugar over the chilled centers. With your fingertips, form each center into an irregularly shaped ball. Let the centers set, uncovered, at room temperature for at least 1 hour (see Note).

Prepare the coating:

7. Temper the milk chocolate (for tempering instructions, see page 22).

8. Put the cocoa in a 9-by-13-inch baking pan.

Make troughs 9-inches long by 1 inch wide in the cocoa.

9. Lift a truffle center with your forefinger and second finger. Toss the center between your fingers on the surface of the chocolate to get an even coating. Lift up the center. Move your fingers in a scissorlike motion to release any drips, and scrape any excess chocolate from your fingers onto the edge of the bowl. Put the truffle in a cocoa trough, withdrawing your last finger with a twisting motion. Cover the truffle with cocoa. Continue dipping the remaining truffles in the chocolate and putting them in the cocoa troughs. Let the truffles sit in the cocoa for 5 to 20 minutes or until the chocolate sets.

10. Line a baking sheet with aluminum foil. Pour the leftover tempered chocolate onto the foil and spread evenly. Refrigerate the chocolate for 10 minutes or until firm. Let the chocolate stand at room temperature for 30 minutes. Break the chocolate into small pieces and store to use again in baking or candy making.

11. Remove the truffles from the cocoa and put in an airtight container at room temperature for up to 1 week.

NOTE: The uncoated centers may be stored in an airtight container and kept at room temperature for up to 48 hours before coating. Finished truffles can be frozen in an airtight container for up to 2 months.

Grand Marnier Whipped-Cream Truffles

To form these deliciously creamy truffles, simply pipe the chocolate mixture into foil cups, finishing each one with a jaunty peaked mound.

YIELD: 24 truffles

DIFFICULTY: ◼

PREPARATION TIME: 30 minutes plus chilling time

SPECIAL EQUIPMENT: 24 1½-inch-diameter foil candy cups; 12-inch pastry bag without a tip

Confectioners' sugar, for dusting the cups
12 ounces bittersweet chocolate, coarsely chopped
1 cup heavy (whipping) cream
2 tablespoons orange liqueur, such as Grand Marnier

1. Set the foil cups on a baking sheet. Using a fine sieve or sifter, sift a heavy layer of confectioners' sugar into the cups.

2. In the top of a double boiler over hot, not simmering, water, melt the chocolate, stirring frequently until smooth. Remove the top part of the

double boiler from the bottom and set aside to cool for 5 to 10 minutes or until the chocolate is tepid.

3. In a large bowl, beat the cream until it begins to form soft peaks. Beat in the orange liqueur and the melted chocolate all at once, just until mixed.

(continued)

4. Working quickly, since the mixture hardens rapidly, spoon the mixture into the tipless pastry bag and pipe it into the foil cups in peaked mounds. Sift a light layer of confectioners' sugar onto each, if desired.

5. Refrigerate the truffles for at least 1 hour before serving. The truffles may be covered and refrigerated for up to 5 days.

Raspberry Chambord Chocolate ⟳ Balls ⟲

Once you have purchased the chocolate truffle shells, these candies are not difficult to make. As devised by Rose Levy Beranbaum, each one is filled with a single fresh raspberry awash in Chambord liqueur. Truffle shells, which are used to form the balls, are available through mail order and some candy supply houses. They are made from milk, semisweet, or white chocolate and generally are packaged in four-tray cases with more than 200 balls in a case. They keep well, and if you want, you can mix the varieties of chocolate in a case when you order. When making the balls, it is a good idea to keep the plastic trays to support the balls as you fill them.

> YIELD: 48 chocolates
>
> DIFFICULTY: ◼◼◼
>
> PREPARATION TIME: 2 hours plus chilling time
>
> SPECIAL EQUIPMENT: milk chocolate truffle shells; heating pad

48 fresh raspberries (see Ingredient Note)
48 large-opening milk chocolate truffle shells
1 cup Chambord
⅛ cup melted cocoa butter, for sealing (optional)
1¼ pounds milk chocolate couverture, tempered, for coating
  (for tempering instructions, see page 22)

INGREDIENT NOTE: You may substitute frozen raspberries by defrosting and draining them well before using, but the texture is best with fresh raspberries.

1. Cut the raspberries in half and put 2 halves in each chocolate shell. Carefully fill each one almost to the top with Chambord.

Seal the chocolate balls:

2. If you are using cocoa butter, put the butter in the top part of a double boiler over hot, not simmering, water. Keep it warm and fluid. Using a paper cone with a tiny opening cut in the point, drop a small amount (about ¼ teaspoon) of the melted cocoa butter into each shell. Chill for 10 minutes. The cocoa butter will rise to the top and harden, forming a perfect seal. Alternatively, seal the openings with tempered chocolate. First, cut small squares of waxed paper and using the tip of a spoon, drop a small pool of tempered chocolate onto each waxed paper square. Invert the square over the opening of the ball. Chill for 10 minutes or until set. Peel off the waxed paper and trim away the excess chocolate.

Coat the balls:

3.   Temper the chocolate (for tempering instructions, see page 22).

4.   Line a baking sheet with aluminum foil. Check that the sealed balls are completely dry before coating. Remove about 1½ tablespoons of the tempered chocolate and put it in the palm of one hand.

5.   Pick up a chocolate ball and press it on top of the tempered chocolate in the palm of your hand. Gently roll the ball between both palms until it is evenly coated with a thin layer of chocolate. Using your fingers, put the coated ball on the foil-lined baking sheet, withdrawing your fingers with a twisting motion.

6.   Dab the palm of one hand with more chocolate and continue coating the remaining balls. After coating 12 balls, remove the chocolate from your hands to ensure that hot hands will not overheat the tempered chocolate and cause the coating to streak as it sets.

7.   When all the balls are coated, refrigerate them for 10 minutes to set the chocolate. Store the chocolate balls in an airtight container and keep them in a cool, dark, dry place. The chocolates can be stored for up to 3 months before the liqueur starts to evaporate.

～ *Chocolate Caramel Apples* ～

Remember the caramel-covered apples that were so popular at carnivals and autumn festivals before the days of fast-food vendors? We have re-created them here but with an inspired addition: a coating of bittersweet chocolate. Bite through the smooth chocolate exterior to the chewy caramel below and then into the crisp juicy apple beneath it all. This is no ordinary caramel apple—it is something truly special.

YIELD: 10 to 12 apples

DIFFICULTY: ▄▄

PREPARATION TIME: 1 hour plus cooking and setting times

SPECIAL EQUIPMENT: wooden sticks; candy thermometer

10 to 12 medium apples, washed and dried
Vegetable oil
2¼ cups heavy (whipping) cream
1½ cups light corn syrup
1 cup superfine sugar
½ cup packed dark brown sugar
3 tablespoons unsalted butter, cut into tablespoons
⅛ teaspoon salt
2 teaspoons vanilla extract
3 ounces bittersweet chocolate, coarsely chopped
Finely chopped walnuts (optional)

1. Insert a wooden stick into the stem end of each apple. Oil a baking sheet.

2. In a large, heavy saucepan, combine the cream, corn syrup, sugars, butter, and salt. Cook over medium-low heat, stirring constantly with a wooden spoon, for about 4 minutes or until the sugars dissolve. Raise the heat to medium and bring the mixture to a boil. Insert a candy thermometer into the caramel mixture, being careful that it does not touch the bottom of the pan. (If you are using a thermometer with a metal base, it may touch the bottom of the pan.) Continue to cook the mixture, stirring frequently, for 25 to 30 minutes or until the thermometer registers 240°F (soft-ball stage). Immediately transfer the hot caramel to a small saucepan to stop the cooking process. Cool the caramel to 220°F. Stir in the vanilla.

3. Using the wooden sticks as handles, dip each apple into the hot caramel, turning until coated. Scrape the excess caramel from the bottom of the apple onto the edge of the pot. Put the apple on the prepared baking sheet. If the caramel becomes too thick, heat it gently until it reaches the correct consistency. Let the apples sit for 10 minutes or until the caramel hardens.

4. In the top of a double boiler over hot, not simmering, water, melt the chocolate, stirring frequently, until smooth. Remove the top part of the double boiler from the bottom. Dip the top one third to one half of each apple in the chocolate. Dip the chocolate-coated apples in the walnuts, if desired. Set aside to cool.

⌒ *Cashew Buttercrunch* ⌒

This candy, developed by Cathy Ziolkowski of West Chester, Ohio, blends the warm smoothness of milk chocolate with the full flavor of cashews, and was a first-place winner in one of our recipe contests. It takes only one taste of a bite-sized morsel to understand why we awarded a blue ribbon to this recipe.

YIELD: 81 pieces	
DIFFICULTY: ▬▬	
PREPARATION TIME: 50 minutes plus chilling time	

8 tablespoons (1 stick) unsalted butter
1 cup granulated sugar
2 tablespoons water
1 tablespoon light corn syrup
2½ cups unsalted cashews, finely chopped
12 ounces milk chocolate, coarsely chopped

1. Line a 9-inch square baking pan with aluminum foil so that the foil extends 1 inch beyond two opposite ends of the pan. Lightly butter the bottom and sides of the foil-lined pan.

2. In a heavy, medium saucepan, combine the butter, granulated sugar, water, and corn syrup. Cook over medium-high heat, stirring constantly, until the mixture comes to a boil.

3. Attach a candy thermometer to the pan so that it does not touch the bottom. (if you are using a candy thermometer that has a metal base, it may touch the bottom of the pan.) Continue to cook the mixture over medium-high heat, stirring constantly, for about 15 minutes or until the thermometer registers 300°F.

4. Remove the pan from the heat and quickly stir in 1 cup of the cashews. Spread the mixture into the prepared pan.

5. Cool the mixture in the pan on a wire rack for about 5 minutes. With a buttered metal spatula, score the buttercrunch into 1-inch pieces. So that the pieces will break apart easily, continue to score along the same lines until the buttercrunch is cool and you have reached the bottom of the pan. Using the two ends of the foil as handles, lift the buttercrunch out of the pan and invert it onto a wire rack. Peel off the foil and break the pieces apart.

6. In a heatproof metal bowl over a pan of hot, not simmering, water, melt the chocolate, stirring frequently until smooth. Remove the bowl from the pan of hot water, and set it over a pan of warm water so that the water touches the bottom of the bowl. Tilt the bowl on the edge of the pan to create a deep pool of chocolate for dipping. Put the remaining 1½ cups of cashews in a shallow bowl.

7. Using a fork, dip each buttercrunch piece into the melted chocolate, turning it so that it is fully coated. Lift the coated piece out of the chocolate and scrape off the excess chocolate from the fork onto the edge of the bowl. Roll the buttercrunch in the chopped nuts, turning it to coat completely. Put the candy on a wire rack set over a baking sheet and refrigerate for about 30 minutes or until the chocolate is set. Store the buttercrunch in an airtight container in a cool place.

10

Chocolate in a Hurry

Chocolate Mint Wafers
Chocolate Champagne Zabaglione
Fruit-and-Chocolate Club Sandwiches
Chocolate Chip Pie
Mississippi Mud
Ice Cream Sundae Cake
Meringue Kisses
Brownie Cookies
Chocolate-Flecked Peanut Butter Cookies
Chocolate Fondue with Fresh Fruit
Dark Chocolate Madeleines
Mexican Chocolate Soufflé
Black and White Chunk Cookies
Maria's Mocha Chip Cookies
Extra-Special Chocolate Chunk Cookies
Chocolate Walnut Sundae
Hazelnut and Chocolate Chunk Cookies

hances are you're never in too much of a hurry for chocolate, but for those times when you do not have the energy or hours to bake a deep, dense cake or make a satiny mousse, there is no reason to content yourself with a handful of chocolate chips grabbed on the run. There are plenty of tasty quick treats, easy to make and definitely easy to eat.

In this chapter we have collected some of our favorite quick recipes. Many have appeared in the magazine in the section called "Short & Sweet"; others have been in the section featuring recipes developed around a mix. The rest have been gleaned from a variety of articles with three things in mind: they are fast, they are easy, and they taste *very* good.

～ *Chocolate Mint Wafers* ～

Wafers are thin crisp cakes, crackers, or, in this case, cookies with good chocolate flavor and a hint of mint.

> YIELD: Approximately 2 dozen wafers
>
> DIFFICULTY: ▄
>
> PREPARATION TIME: 15 minutes plus baking and cooling times

2 ounces semisweet chocolate, coarsely chopped
8 tablespoons (1 stick) unsalted butter, softened
½ cup granulated sugar
Pinch of salt
1 large egg white
2 teaspoons vanilla extract
½ teaspoon mint extract
¾ cup all-purpose flour

1. Position two racks in the top two thirds of the oven and preheat to 350°F. Lightly butter two baking sheets. In the top of a double boiler over hot, not simmering, water, melt the chocolate, stirring frequently until smooth. Remove the top part of the double boiler from the bottom and let the chocolate cool for 5 to 10 minutes or until tepid.

2. In a food processor fitted with the metal chopping blade, combine the butter, sugar, and salt, and process for 5 seconds or just until combined. Scrape down the sides of the bowl. Add the egg white and the vanilla and mint extracts, and process for about 5 seconds or until smooth. Scrape

down the sides of the bowl, add the melted chocolate and flour, and blend for about 5 seconds or until even in color.

3. Using 1 level tablespoon of dough for each wafer, drop the wafers onto the prepared sheets, leaving 3 inches between each wafer. Bake for 12 to 14 minutes or until the wafers are just beginning to crisp around the edges. The wafers will be soft in the center and will firm up as they cool. Remove the baking sheets to wire racks and cool the wafers on the sheets for 1 minute. Using a spatula, transfer the wafers to paper towels and cool completely. Repeat with the remaining dough.

Chocolate Champagne
～ *Zabaglione* ～

The chocolate and champagne transform a classic velvety egg-based pudding into something completely different.

YIELD: 4 servings

DIFFICULTY: ▰

PREPARATION TIME: 20 minutes

1 tablespoon heavy (whipping) cream
3 tablespoons granulated sugar, divided
1 ounce bittersweet chocolate, finely chopped
2 tablespoons unsalted butter, softened
1 teaspoon vanilla extract
3 large egg yolks
Pinch of salt
½ cup extra-dry champagne

1. In a small, heavy saucepan over medium heat, combine the heavy cream and 1 tablespoon of the sugar. Stir until the mixture is hot and the sugar is dissolved. Remove the pan from the heat. Stir in the chocolate until melted. Add the butter and vanilla and stir until smooth.

2. In the top of a double boiler over simmering water, combine the egg yolks, salt, and the remaining 2 tablespoons of sugar. With a hand-held electric mixer set at high speed, beat the mixture for 2 to 3 minutes or until it is very light in color. Gradually beat in the champagne. With the mixture still over simmering water, continue beating for 3 to 5 minutes or until soft mounds form. Do not overcook, or the mixture may curdle and the volume will decrease. Reserve ½ cup of the zabaglione for a garnish.

3. Stir a large spoonful of the zabaglione into the chocolate mixture to lighten it, then fold in the remaining zabaglione until the color is almost even but a few streaks remain. Quickly spoon the chocolate-champagne zabaglione into four 6-ounce stemmed glasses. Garnish each serving with a dollop of the reserved plain zabaglione. Serve immediately.

Fruit-and-Chocolate
～ *Sandwiches* ～

Exotic tropical fruits such as kiwifruit and papaya are commonly found in supermarkets and specialty stores around the country. Here, we pair them with bright-red strawberries, pound cake, and chocolate sauce to make a colorful, pretty, and easy-to-assemble dessert.

YIELD: 4 servings

DIFFICULTY: ▰

PREPARATION TIME: 20 minutes

(continued)

Passionate chocolate sauce:

⅓ cup plus 1 tablespoon heavy (whipping) cream
1 tablespoon unsalted butter
1 tablespoon granulated sugar
3 ounces bittersweet chocolate, finely chopped
1 tablespoon passion fruit liqueur, such as La Grande Passion

Club sandwiches:

2 kiwifruit, peeled
¼ papaya, peeled and seeded
8 strawberries
1 9-by-5-inch loaf pound cake, preferably homemade
4 teaspoons passion fruit liqueur, such as La Grande Passion

Make the passionate chocolate sauce:

1. In a small, heavy saucepan, combine the cream, butter, and sugar. Set the pan over medium heat and bring the mixture to a gentle boil. Remove the pan from the heat and add the chocolate, stirring until smooth. Blend in the liqueur. Keep the sauce warm while preparing the club sandwiches.

Make the club sandwiches:

2. With a sharp thin-bladed knife, cut the kiwifruit crosswise into ⅛-inch thick slices. Cut the slices in half crosswise. Cut the papaya lengthwise into ⅛-inch thick wedges. Cut the wedges in half crosswise. Hull 4 of the strawberries and cut them lengthwise into ⅛-inch thick slices.

3. Preheat the broiler. Position a broiler rack about 4 inches from the heat.

4. Cut the pound cake into twelve ⅜-inch slices. Arrange the slices on a baking sheet and toast them under the broiler for 30 to 60 seconds or until lightly browned. Turn the slices over and toast the other side. Be careful not to let the slices burn.

Assemble the club sandwiches:

5. Divide the chocolate sauce among four dessert plates. Put one slice of cake on the sauce. Arrange four slices of kiwifruit on one half of the slice; arrange four strawberry slices on the other half. Top the fruit with a second slice of cake and sprinkle the slice with 1 teaspoon of liqueur. Arrange four slices of papaya on half of the second slice; arrange four slices of kiwifruit on the other half. Top the fruit with a third slice of cake. Repeat the process to assemble the other 3 club sandwiches.

6. With a small sharp knife, leaving the stems attached, slice each of the 4 remaining strawberries about three quarters of the way through. Spread the slices slightly to form a fan shape. Top each club sandwich with a strawberry fan and serve immediately.

⌒ *Chocolate Chip Pie* ⌒

This pie without a crust is more like one giant and wonderful chocolate chip cookie, cut into wedges and served with chocolate sauce and ice cream.

YIELD: 8 servings

DIFFICULTY: ◣

PREPARATION TIME: 30 minutes plus baking time

Pie:

2 cups all-purpose flour
1¼ teaspoons double-acting baking powder
½ teaspoon salt
1½ cups packed light brown sugar
7 tablespoons unsalted butter, melted, divided
2 large eggs, at room temperature, lightly beaten
1 teaspoon vanilla extract
4 ounces (about ⅔ cup) semisweet chocolate chips
¾ cup walnuts, coarsely chopped

Hot fudge sauce:

⅓ cup water
1 tablespoon unsalted butter
2 ounces unsweetened chocolate, coarsely chopped
1 cup granulated sugar
2 tablespoons light corn syrup
A few grains of salt
1 teaspoon vanilla extract

2 pints vanilla ice cream

Make the pie:

1. Position a rack in the center of the oven and preheat to 350°F. Lightly butter a 10-inch pie plate.

2. In a large bowl, stir together the flour, baking powder, and salt. Blend in the brown sugar. Stir in 6 tablespoons of the melted butter, the eggs, and vanilla. Add the chocolate chips and walnuts and work into a stiff batter. Transfer the batter to the prepared pie plate and spread evenly.

3. Bake for about 30 minutes or until a cake tester or toothpick inserted into the center comes out clean. Brush the top with the remaining 1 tablespoon of melted butter and let the pie cool for a few minutes while making the fudge sauce.

Make the hot fudge sauce:

4. In a heavy 1-quart saucepan over medium-high heat, bring the water and butter to a simmer and heat until the butter is melted. Remove the pan from the heat and stir in the chocolate. Stir until smooth. Add the sugar, corn syrup, and salt, and mix well. Return the pan to the heat and bring the mixture to a boil without stirring. Cover and cook for 3 minutes. Uncover and simmer for 2 minutes longer. Remove the pan from the heat, cool for 5 minutes, and stir in the vanilla.

5. Cut the pie into 8 slices. Serve each slice with a large scoop of ice cream and top with hot fudge sauce.

～◯ *Mississippi Mud* ◯～

Almost anyone who has eaten in a school cafeteria has memories of a thick chocolate concoction affectionately (or derisively) called Mississippi Mud. Leave any preconceived notions with the rest of your school-day memories and try this very dense, very moist, and very chocolaty cake. It is made from a mix and is as easy to put together as paddling downstream.

> YIELD: 8 to 10 servings
>
> DIFFICULTY: ▰
>
> PREPARATION TIME: 15 minutes plus baking time

1 21.5-ounce box fudge brownie mix
8 tablespoons (1 stick) unsalted butter, melted
2 cups water
2 teaspoons vanilla extract
2 large egg whites, at room temperature
9 ounces (about 1½ cups) semisweet chocolate chips
1 cup walnuts, coarsely chopped

1. Position in a rack in the center of the oven and preheat to 350°F. Butter the bottom and sides of a 9-by-13-inch baking pan.

2. In a large bowl, stir together the brownie mix, melted butter, water, and vanilla until blended.

3. In a grease-free bowl, using a hand-held electric mixer set at high speed, beat the egg whites until they form soft, shiny peaks. Fold them into the brownie mixture. Pour the batter into the prepared pan and spread evenly. Sprinkle the chocolate chips and walnuts over the top. Bake for about 25 minutes or until the surface of the cake is puffed and slightly firm. A cake tester or toothpick inserted into the center of the cake will come out wet. Do not overbake. Serve warm.

～◯ *Ice Cream Sundae Cake* ◯～

Few desserts are faster to put together and better satisfy an after-dinner craving for something sweet than slices of pound cake topped with ice cream. We have taken the idea a couple of steps further by adding fresh fruit and a quick and creamy fudge sauce. If you have homemade pound cake on hand, use it, but if not, many store-bought brands are very good, too.

> YIELD: 8 servings
>
> DIFFICULTY: ▰
>
> PREPARATION TIME: 15 minutes plus cooling and assembly times

Hot fudge sauce:

2 ounces unsweetened chocolate, coarsely chopped
1 cup granulated sugar
6 ounces evaporated milk

½ teaspoon vanilla extract

To assemble:

1 9-by-5-inch loaf pound cake, preferably homemade
1 quart ice cream
Fresh fruit, for garnish (optional)

Make the hot fudge sauce:

1. In the top of a double boiler over hot, not simmering, water, melt the chocolate. Stir frequently until smooth. Remove the top part of the double boiler from the bottom and cool the chocolate for 10 to 12 minutes or until tepid.

2. In a heavy, medium saucepan over low heat, combine the sugar and evaporated milk. Using a wooden spoon, stir for 2 to 3 minutes or until the sugar has dissolved. Bring the mixture to a boil and cook for 8 to 10 minutes or until it is thick enough to coat the back of the spoon.

3. Remove the mixture from the heat and whisk in the melted chocolate. Continue stirring until the sauce is smooth. Cool the sauce slightly and stir in the vanilla. Transfer the sauce to a pitcher or serving bowl.

Assemble the dessert:

4. Slice the pound cake and divide it among individual serving plates. Top with scoops of ice cream and warm fudge sauce. Garnish with fresh fruit, if desired, and serve immediately.

━━ *Meringue Kisses* ━━

A kiss (when it refers to a meringue, anyhow) is a swirl of sweetened egg white with a peaked tip. These bite-sized morsels, full of chocolate chips, make a chewy snack or an elegant accompaniment to after-dinner coffee. They are easy to form with a plain pastry bag—you do not even need a tip for the bag.

> YIELD: Approximately 45 kisses
>
> DIFFICULTY: ◤
>
> PREPARATION TIME: 10 minutes plus baking time
>
> SPECIAL EQUIPMENT: pastry bag with a 1-inch opening (a metal tip is not necessary)

3 large egg whites, at room temperature
⅛ teaspoon cream of tartar
⅛ teaspoon salt
¾ cup granulated sugar
1 teaspoon vanilla extract
12 ounces (about 2 cups) semisweet chocolate chips

1. Position one rack in the top third and another rack in the bottom third of the oven and preheat to 300°F. Line two baking sheets with baking parchment.

2. In a large, grease-free bowl, using a hand-held electric mixer set at high speed, beat the egg whites, cream of tartar, and salt until the whites begin to form soft peaks. Add the sugar slowly, a tablespoon at a time. Continue beating for 2 minutes or until the egg white mixture forms stiff, shiny peaks.

3. Using a large rubber spatula, gently fold the vanilla and the chocolate chips into the meringue.

(continued)

4. Spoon half the mixture into a pastry bag with a 1-inch opening. It is not necessary to use a metal tip. Secure the parchment to the baking sheets by piping dabs of meringue beneath the paper in the four corners of each sheet. Finally, pipe 1-inch round kisses on the sheets, 22 to 23 per sheet.

5. Bake the kisses for about 25 minutes or until their tips are just beginning to brown. They should feel firm if gently touched and should be easy to remove from the parchment. Remove the kisses and cool on wire racks. Serve when they are completely cool or store them in airtight containers.

⬿ *Brownie Cookies* ⬿

These chewy, chocolaty cookies are similar to brownies in texture and taste. But instead of cutting a panful of brownies into squares, you form them into cookies before they are baked. The result? Mouthfuls of intense chocolate flavor.

YIELD: 3 dozen cookies

DIFFICULTY: ◼

PREPARATION TIME: 15 minutes plus baking time

12 ounces (about 2 cups) semisweet chocolate chips
1 ounce unsweetened chocolate, finely chopped
2 tablespoons unsalted butter
1 teaspoon instant coffee powder
3 large eggs, at room temperature
1 cup plus 2 tablespoons granulated sugar
1 teaspoon vanilla extract
½ cup plus 2 tablespoons unbleached all-purpose flour
½ teaspoon double-acting baking powder

1. Position one rack in the top and the other in the bottom third of the oven and preheat to 350°F.

2. In the top of a double boiler over hot, not simmering, water, melt the chocolates and the butter, stirring frequently until smooth. Add the coffee powder and stir well. Remove the top part of the double boiler from the bottom and cool the mixture to room temperature.

3. In a large bowl, using a hand-held electric mixer set at medium speed, beat the eggs until foamy. Add the sugar 2 tablespoons at a time while continuing to beat for about 2 minutes or until the mixture is light and fluffy. Add the vanilla and the cooled chocolate mixture. Mix well.

4. Sift the flour and baking powder into the egg-chocolate mixture and mix well.

5. Drop the dough in rounded teaspoons onto two ungreased baking sheets, leaving 2 inches between cookies. Bake for 8 to 10 minutes or until the cookies are just set. Halfway through baking, switch the positions of the baking sheets so that the cookies brown evenly. Do not overbake. Remove them from the oven and cool for 5 minutes. Using a spatula, transfer the cookies to a wire rack and cool completely.

Chocolate-Flecked Peanut Butter
⌒ *Cookies* ⌒

Grated chocolate speckles the cookie dough, forming little flecks of good chocolate flavor.

YIELD: About 2½ dozen 3-inch cookies

DIFFICULTY: ◣

PREPARATION TIME: 20 minutes plus baking and cooling times

1½ cups all-purpose flour
2 tablespoons cornstarch
1 teaspoon baking soda
¼ teaspoon salt
8 tablespoons (1 stick) unsalted butter, softened
½ cup granulated sugar
½ cup packed light brown sugar
1 large egg, at room temperature
1½ teaspoons vanilla extract
¾ cup creamy peanut butter
4 ounces semisweet chocolate, coarsely grated
Granulated sugar, for dipping the fork

1. Position the racks in the top two thirds of the oven and preheat to 350°F. In a medium bowl, stir together the flour, cornstarch, baking soda, and salt.

2. In a large bowl, using a hand-held electric mixer set at medium-high speed, cream the butter for about 1 minute or until creamy. While beating, gradually add the granulated sugar and then the brown sugar until blended. Beat in the egg and vanilla and continue beating the mixture for 2 to 3 minutes or until it is thick and light colored. Beat in the peanut butter. Using a wooden spoon, stir in the dry ingredients just until smooth. Stir in the grated chocolate.

3. Put the granulated sugar (about 2 to 3 tablespoons) in a small, shallow dish. Using 1½ tablespoons of dough for each cookie, roll the dough between the palms of your hands into 1¼-inch balls. Put the balls on an ungreased baking sheet, leaving 2½ to 3 inches between the cookies. Dip the tines of a fork into the sugar and press the fork into the top of each cookie. Dip the fork back into the sugar and, in the opposite direction, press the tines into the top of each cookie to make a crisscross pattern. The cookies will be about 2 inches in diameter. Repeat for all the cookies. Bake the cookies for about 12 minutes or until they are light golden around the edges. Using a spatula, transfer the cookies to paper towels for 2 to 3 minutes and then to a wire rack to cool completely.

Chocolate Fondue with Fresh ～ Fruit ～

We suggest serving this deep, rich fondue with bright, pretty fruits such as kiwifruit, starfruit, papaya, and strawberries, since tropical fruits are increasingly easy to find in markets everywhere (even exotic starfruit, which is shaped like a star and is reddish brown on the outside and dark yellow inside) and strawberries are available most of the year. If you prefer, dip squares of pound cake into the fondue or different fruits—sliced bananas, apple wedges, orange sections, or sliced pears, for example.

YIELD: 6 servings

DIFFICULTY: ▬

PREPARATION TIME: 15 minutes

½ cup half-and-half
4 ounces bittersweet chocolate, finely chopped
1 ounce milk chocolate, finely chopped
¼ teaspoon vanilla extract
2 starfruit, cut into 12 slices
12 strawberries
2 kiwifruit, pared and cut into 12 slices
½ papaya, peeled, seeded, and cut into 12 slices

1. In a small saucepan, bring the half-and-half to a gentle boil. Remove the pan from the heat. Stir in the chocolates until melted. Stir in the vanilla until smooth.

2. Pour the chocolate fondue into four small cups. Put the cups in the center of four plates and arrange the prepared fruit around each cup of fondue. Serve the fondue warm or at room temperature.

⌢ *Dark Chocolate Madeleines* ⌢

Madeleines are small shell-shaped cakes baked in specially formed molds. They have been made in France for years, but traditionally are not flavored with chocolate. We took matters into our own hands and developed an easy recipe for chocolate madeleines. Try them with a cup of tea or as an accompaniment to fresh berries and fruit.

YIELD: 12 madeleines

DIFFICULTY: ▬

PREPARATION TIME: 30 minutes plus baking and cooling times

SPECIAL EQUIPMENT: 1 madeleine mold, with each shell measuring 3 inches by 2 inches

3 ounces bittersweet chocolate, coarsely chopped
⅓ cup sifted all-purpose flour
½ teaspoon double-acting baking powder
Pinch of salt
5 tablespoons unsalted butter, softened
¼ cup superfine sugar
1 large egg, at room temperature, separated
1 tablespoon milk, at room temperature
2 teaspoons vanilla extract

1. Position a rack in the center of the oven and preheat to 375°F. Generously butter the twelve indentations of the madeleine mold pan. Dust the indentations with flour and tap out the excess.

2. In the top of a double boiler over hot, not simmering, water, melt the chocolate, stirring frequently until smooth. Remove the top part of the double boiler and let the chocolate cool for 5 to 10 minutes or until tepid.

3. In a small bowl, stir together the flour, baking powder, and salt.

4. In a medium bowl, using a hand-held electric mixer set at medium-high speed, beat the butter with the sugar for 30 to 60 seconds or until creamy. Add the egg yolk and continue mixing for 20 to 30 seconds or until light. Beat in the melted chocolate. Reduce the speed to low and mix in the milk and vanilla. Add the flour mixture and mix just until smooth.

5. In a medium bowl, using a hand-held electric mixer set at low speed, beat the egg white until frothy. Gradually increase the speed to medium high and continue beating the egg white until stiff, shiny peaks form when the beaters are lifted. Fold the egg white into the chocolate mixture until evenly mixed.

6. Divide the batter among the buttered molds. Smooth the batter so that it is level with the top of each mold. Bake the madeleines for 12 to 15 minutes or until they spring back when gently pressed with a finger. Do not overbake, or the madeleines will lose their moist, almost fudgy texture. Cool them in the pan on a wire rack for 10 minutes. Release the madeleines by inverting the pan on a work surface and gently tapping the bottom. Serve them warm or cool them completely and store in an airtight container.

～ *Mexican Chocolate Soufflé* ～

The cinnamon and the strong coffee give this soufflé its distinctive flavor, making it reminiscent of a light airy dessert from down Mexico way.

> YIELD: 6 servings
>
> DIFFICULTY: ◼
>
> PREPARATION TIME: 20 minutes plus baking time

Soufflé:

2 tablespoons unsalted butter
2 tablespoons cornstarch
½ cup milk, at room temperature
4 ounces (about ⅔ cup) semisweet chocolate chips
3 large egg yolks plus 6 large egg whites, at room temperature
1 tablespoon strong brewed coffee
¾ teaspoon ground cinnamon
Pinch of salt
⅓ cup granulated sugar
Confectioners' sugar, for dusting (optional)

Ice cream sauce:

1 pint vanilla ice cream
3 tablespoons coffee liqueur

Make the soufflé:

1. Position a rack in the lower third of the oven and preheat to 350°F. Generously butter a 1½-quart soufflé dish. Fold a 24½-by-8-inch piece of aluminum foil in half. Butter one side of the foil strip and wrap it around the soufflé dish with the buttered side facing inward, to create a 2-inch collar above the upper edge of the dish. Secure the collar with paper clips.

2. In a heavy, medium saucepan set over medium-low heat, melt the butter. Whisk in the cornstarch and continue cooking for 1 to 2 minutes or until the mixture is well blended and comes to a boil, forming small bubbles. Whisk in the milk. Continue to stir for 1 to 2 minutes or until the mixture starts to thicken. Remove the pan from the heat. Stir in the chocolate chips until melted.

Whisk in the egg yolks, coffee, and cinnamon until smooth. Transfer the mixture to a large bowl.

3. In a large, grease-free bowl, using a hand-held electric mixer set at low speed, beat the egg whites until frothy. Add the salt and gradually increase the speed to medium high. Continue beating the whites until soft peaks begin to form. Beat in the sugar 1 tablespoon at a time. Continue beating the whites until they form stiff, shiny peaks.

4. Fold one fourth of the egg whites into the chocolate mixture to lighten. Fold in the remaining whites. Gently scrape the batter into the prepared soufflé dish. Put the dish on a baking sheet and bake for 30 to 35 minutes or until a cake tester or toothpick comes out clean when inserted into the outer edge of the soufflé, and moist when inserted into the center of the soufflé. While the soufflé is baking, make the ice cream sauce.

Make the ice cream sauce and serve the soufflé:

5. Let the ice cream soften at room temperature for 15 minutes. Scrape it into a medium bowl and stir in the coffee liqueur until blended.

6. When the soufflé is done, dust it with confectioners' sugar, if desired, and serve immediately. Transfer the sauce to a sauce bowl and serve with the soufflé.

⌒ *Black and White Chunk Cookies* ⌒

The dough for these simple cookies is chock-full of chocolate chunks—white and bittersweet—and plenty of pecans.

YIELD: Approximately 2½ dozen cookies
DIFFICULTY: ◼
PREPARATION TIME: 25 minutes plus baking and cooling times

1 cup all-purpose flour
⅓ cup unsweetened nonalkalized cocoa powder
½ teaspoon baking soda
¼ teaspoon salt
8 tablespoons (1 stick) unsalted butter, softened
½ cup granulated sugar
½ cup packed light brown sugar
1 large egg, at room temperature
1 teaspoon vanilla extract
6 ounces semisweet chocolate, cut into ¼-inch chunks
5 ounces white chocolate, cut into ¼-inch chunks
⅓ cup pecans, coarsely chopped

1. Position a rack in the center of the oven and preheat to 325°F. Line two baking sheets with baking parchment or aluminum foil.

2. In a small bowl, stir together and then sift the flour, cocoa, baking soda, and salt.

3. In a large bowl, using a hand-held electric mixer set at low speed, beat the butter for 30 to 45 seconds or until creamy. Gradually add the sugars and beat at medium speed for 1 to 2 minutes or until light and fluffy. Beat in the egg and vanilla.

Using a wooden spoon, stir in the flour mixture. Add the semisweet and white chocolate chunks and the pecans, and stir until well combined.

4. Drop the dough a tablespoon at a time onto the baking sheets, leaving about 1 inch between cookies. Bake for 10 to 15 minutes or until the cookies are puffed and lightly browned around the edges. Cool the cookies on the baking sheets for 3 to 5 minutes, then transfer them to wire racks to cool completely.

⟶ *Maria's Mocha Chip Cookies* ⟳

Here is another chunky cookie that uses two kinds of chocolate—bittersweet and milk chocolate—as well as nuts for super flavor and lots of texture.

> YIELD: Approximately 5 dozen cookies
>
> DIFFICULTY: ◼
>
> PREPARATION TIME: 30 minutes plus baking and cooling times

2½ cups all-purpose flour
1 teaspoon baking soda
½ teaspoon salt
¼ cup chocolate liqueur
1 tablespoon instant coffee powder
1 cup (2 sticks) unsalted butter, softened
¾ cup granulated sugar
¾ cup packed light brown sugar
2 large eggs, at room temperature
1½ cups walnuts, coarsely chopped
6 ounces (about 1 cup) semisweet chocolate chips
6 ounces (about 1 cup) milk chocolate chips

1. Position a rack in the center of the oven and preheat to 375°F. Line two baking sheets with baking parchment or aluminum foil.

2. In a medium bowl, stir together the flour, baking soda, and salt. Sift the mixture.

3. In a small bowl, combine the chocolate liqueur and coffee powder. Stir until the powder is dissolved.

4. In a large bowl, using a hand-held electric mixer set at low speed, beat the butter for 30 to 45 seconds or until creamy. Gradually add the sugars and beat at medium speed for 1 to 2 minutes or until light. Beat in the eggs and the liqueur-coffee mixture. Using a wooden spoon, stir in the flour mixture. Add the walnuts and the chocolate chips and stir until well combined.

5. Using about 2 tablespoons of dough for each cookie, drop the dough onto the baking sheets, leaving about 2 inches between the cookies. Bake for 10 to 12 minutes or until the cookies are lightly browned around the edges. Cool the cookies on the baking sheets for 3 to 5 minutes, then transfer them to wire racks to cool completely.

Extra-Special Chocolate Chunk ⌒⌒ *Cookies* ⌒⌒

Buttery macadamia nuts and pecans blend with white chocolate chunks in these big, rich cookies. For uniformly sized cookies, we suggest packing the dough into a quarter-cup measure, but you may choose to drop the cookies onto the baking sheets free-form and shape them with your fingers or two spoons.

YIELD: Approximately 2 dozen cookies

DIFFICULTY: ◣

PREPARATION TIME: 30 minutes plus baking and cooling times

---

2 cups all-purpose flour
1 teaspoon baking soda
½ teaspoon salt
12 tablespoons (1½ sticks) unsalted butter, softened
1 cup packed light brown sugar
¾ cup granulated sugar
2 large eggs, at room temperature
1 teaspoon vanilla extract
12 ounces white chocolate, cut into ¼-inch chunks
1 cup macadamia nuts, coarsely chopped
½ cup pecans, coarsely chopped

1. Position a rack in the center of the oven and preheat to 300°F. Line two baking sheets with baking parchment or aluminum foil.

2. In a medium bowl, stir together the flour, baking soda, and salt. Sift the mixture.

3. In a large bowl, using a hand-held electric mixer set at low speed, beat the butter for 30 to 45 seconds or until creamy. Gradually add the sugars and beat at medium speed for 1 to 2 minutes or until light and fluffy. Add the eggs one at a time, beating well after each addition, then add the vanilla. Using a wooden spoon, stir in the flour mixture. Add the white chocolate chunks, macadamia nuts, and pecans, and stir until well combined.

4. Form the cookies by packing the dough into a ¼-cup measuring cup so it is even with the edge of the cup. Drop the formed dough onto the baking sheets, leaving about 3 inches between cookies. Flatten the dough slightly with the palm of your hand. Bake the cookies for 20 to 25 minutes or until lightly browned around the edges but still slightly soft in the center. Cool the cookies on the baking sheets for 3 to 5 minutes. Transfer the cookies to wire racks to cool completely.

⌒ *Chocolate Walnut Sundae* ⌒

Since both the sauce and the brittle can be prepared ahead of time (the brittle up to a week ahead), we thought they could be paired together and given as a gift to a sundae-loving friend. All he or she would need is the ice cream and the cherry. The sauce should be stored in an airtight container in the refrigerator and can be reheated in the microwave on high (100 percent) power for 1½ minutes. Stir it well. The brittle should be kept in an airtight container at room temperature. Both are made in the microwave.

YIELD: 4 to 6 servings
DIFFICULTY: ◼
PREPARATION TIME: 20 minutes plus cooling time

Chocolate sauce:

9 ounces semisweet chocolate, coarsely chopped
½ cup half-and-half
2 to 3 tablespoons strong freshly brewed coffee (optional)

Walnut brittle:

1 cup granulated sugar
½ cup light corn syrup
½ teaspoon baking soda
1 cup walnuts, coarsely chopped

To assemble:

1 pint vanilla ice cream, or flavor of your choice
Whipped cream (optional)

Make the chocolate sauce:

1. Put the chopped chocolate and half-and-half in a microwave-safe 2-cup glass bowl. Microwave on high (100 percent) power for 1 minute. Stir until smooth. Stir in the coffee, if desired.

Make the walnut brittle:

2. Generously butter an 8-inch square in the center of a baking sheet. In a microwave-safe 2-quart bowl, stir together the sugar and corn syrup. Microwave on high (100 percent) power for 1½ to 2 minutes or until the sugar boils. Stir well. Microwave, uncovered, on high (100 percent) power for 5 to 6 minutes longer or until a candy thermometer registers between 290° and 300°F (hard-crack stage). If the syrup is not hot enough, return it to the microwave and cook on high (100 percent) power for 20 to 30 seconds longer. Do not overcook.

3. Stir in the baking soda. The syrup will foam. Add the walnuts. Spread the mixture out on the prepared baking sheet and let it cool until it lifts off the sheet in one firm piece. Break the brittle up into small pieces or chop it coarsely in a food processor or blender.

Assemble the sundae:

4. Divide the ice cream among four ice cream dishes. Spoon the sauce over each, and top with broken or ground brittle. Spoon a dollop of whipped cream on each sundae, if desired.

Variations for the chocolate sauce:
Substitute one of the following for the brewed coffee: ½ teaspoon almond extract; 1 teaspoon vanilla extract; or 2 to 3 tablespoons coffee liqueur, orange liqueur, or cognac.

Hazelnut and Chocolate Chunk
〜 *Cookies* 〜

Fewer cookies are easier or quicker to make. You start with a mix, add only a few ingredients, including some chopped chocolate and roasted nuts to make them extra good, and mix the cookie dough with a few strokes of a wooden spoon. You don't even have to butter the baking sheet—just line it with foil.

YIELD: Approximately 3 dozen cookies
DIFFICULTY: ◣
PREPARATION TIME: 15 minutes plus roasting, baking, and cooling times

1 21.5-ounce box fudge brownie mix
½ cup water
⅓ cup vegetable oil
1 large egg, at room temperature
3 tablespoons all-purpose flour
9 ounces bittersweet chocolate, coarsely chopped, divided
1½ cups roasted hazelnuts, coarsely chopped, divided (for roasting instructions, see page 20)

1. Position a rack in the center of the oven and preheat to 350°F. Line a baking sheet with aluminum foil.

2. In a medium bowl, using a wooden spoon, stir together the brownie mix, water, oil, egg, and flour just until combined. Fold in all but ¼ cup of the chocolate and ¼ cup of the hazelnuts. Drop the cookie dough a rounded tablespoon at a time onto the prepared baking sheet, leaving at least 1 inch between cookies. Gently press several pieces of both the reserved chocolate and the reserved hazelnuts into the top of each cookie.

3. Bake the cookies for 13 to 15 minutes or until your fingertip leaves a slight indentation on the center of a cookie. Transfer the cookies to a wire rack and cool completely. (The cookies may stick slightly to the aluminum foil, but they will loosen when gently nudged with a spatula.)

11

Michael Harris

Chocolate
Drinks

Mocha Shake
Orange Mocha Velvet
Rich, Rich Chocolate Malt
Spiced Chocolate Coffee
Minted Hot Cocoa
Chocolate Egg Cream
Frappé au Chocolat
Mock Mexican Hot Chocolate
Nun's Habit
Café Olé
Monastery Madness
The Beverly Hills Hotel Milkshake
Domaine Chandon's Raspberry Milkshakes
Debbie's Mocha Delight
Drostaretto
Raspberry Chocolate Ice Cream Soda
Café Mocha
Chocolate Eggnog

*W*hether your preference is hot chocolate, a chocolate milkshake, or a bubbly chocolate soda, beverages made with chocolate are among the best around. Here you will find a number of hot and cold coffee-based drinks, as well as variations on creamy cocoa, everybody's favorite comfort libation. We have chocolate milkshakes of every description and, for urban dwellers, have included a recipe for egg cream, which will satisfy the most fervent fan of that candy store tradition. We also have our own version of eggnog, guaranteed, we think, to make your holidays especially jolly.

Chocolate drinks are pure pleasure. You can make them one at a time to quell a craving instantly or make them in batches. Hot drinks warm us right down to our toes and are the perfect friend when we're tucked into our favorite easy chair with a good novel. Cold chocolate drinks are festive enough to serve at a party where the guests range from nine to ninety and the order of the hour is for something delicious, slightly indulgent, and definitely chocolaty.

~ Mocha Shake ~

If you're in the mood for something creamy, rich, cold, and delicious—but low in calories—try this shake. It's barely 150 calories a serving!

YIELD: 1 serving	
DIFFICULTY: ◼	
PREPARATION TIME: 5 minutes	

½ cup chocolate ice milk
½ cup cold skim milk
⅛ teaspoon instant coffee powder

Process all ingredients in a blender for 10 to 15 seconds or until mixed. Serve immediately in a chilled glass.

~ Orange Mocha Velvet ~

This recipe was developed for a magazine story about warming up after a day on the slopes. The orange- and cinnamon-scented coffee would taste good anytime you needed a quick warm-up.

YIELD: 8 servings	
DIFFICULTY: ◼	
PREPARATION TIME: 10 minutes	

½ cup heavy (whipping cream), for garnish
½ cup ground French roast coffee beans
2 teaspoons grated orange zest

1 cinnamon stick, broken

3 tablespoons granulated sugar

2 tablespoons unsweetened alkalized cocoa powder

5 cups water, boiled and cooled for 1 minute

8 cinnamon sticks or ground cinnamon, for garnish

1. In a chilled bowl, using a hand-held electric mixer set at medium-high speed, beat the cream for 2 to 3 minutes or until soft peaks just begin to form.

2. In a filter-lined brew basket of a manual drip coffee maker, combine the ground coffee, orange zest, and cinnamon stick. In the carafe of the coffee maker, combined the sugar and cocoa. Pour the hot water through the brew basket in two additions. Remove the basket and stir the coffee until the sugar is completely dissolved.

3. Divide the hot coffee mixture among eight small coffee cups. Garnish each cup with a dollop of whipped cream and a cinnamon stick, or dust the top of the whipped cream with ground cinnamon. Serve immediately.

⌐⌐ *Rich, Rich Chocolate Malt* ⌐⌐

Malted milk powder is available at most supermarkets. This malted will bring back memories (real or imagined) of stopping by the malt shop with your Saturday night date.

YIELD: 2 servings
DIFFICULTY: ◼
PREPARATION TIME: 15 minutes

Chocolate syrup:

1½ ounces bittersweet chocolate, finely chopped

¼ cup plus 2 tablespoons skim milk, divided

Malted milk:

¾ cup skim milk

2 cups vanilla ice cream, divided

¼ cup malted milk powder

Whipped cream, for garnish (optional)

Make the chocolate syrup:

1. Put the chocolate in a small bowl. In a small saucepan over medium heat, bring ¼ cup of the milk to a boil. Remove the pan from the heat and pour the hot milk over the chocolate. Let the mixture stand for 1 to 2 minutes and then whisk until smooth. Stir in the remaining 2 tablespoons of milk.

Make the malted milk:

2. In a blender, combine the milk, 1 cup of the ice cream, the malted milk powder, and the chocolate syrup. Blend at high speed for 20 to 30 seconds or until smooth. With the motor running, gradually add the remaining 1 cup of ice cream. Blend until smooth. Pour into two chilled glasses and top with whipped cream, if desired. Serve immediately.

⟿ *Spiced Chocolate Coffee* ⟿

We have discovered that there are lots of ways to make hot coffee-based drinks. This one, with a hint of cinnamon and nutmeg, is one of our favorites.

YIELD: 1 serving
DIFFICULTY: ▰
PREPARATION TIME: 10 minutes

⅛ teaspoon ground cinnamon
Pinch of ground nutmeg
8 ounces hot freshly brewed coffee
2 tablespoons cacao liqueur
¼ cup whipped heavy cream
3 chocolate-covered coffee beans, for garnish (optional)

In a large mug, combine the cinnamon and nutmeg. Stir in the coffee and liqueur. Top with the whipped cream, and garnish with chocolate-covered coffee beans, if desired.

⟿ *Minted Hot Cocoa* ⟿

A trace of mint in hot chocolate only makes this soothing drink better than ever.

YIELD: 1 serving
DIFFICULTY: ▰
PREPARATION TIME: 10 minutes

1¼ teaspoons unsweetened nonalkalized cocoa powder
2½ teaspoons granulated sugar
Pinch of salt
1 cup plus 2 teaspoons milk, divided
1 tablespoon plus 1 teaspoon cacao liqueur
1 teaspoon crème de menthe
¼ cup whipped heavy cream
Mint leaves, for garnish (optional)

1. In a large mug, stir together the cocoa, sugar, salt, and 2 teaspoons of the milk until smooth.

2. In a small, heavy saucepan over medium heat, heat the remaining cup of milk until small bubbles start to form around the sides of the pan. Add the hot milk to the cocoa mixture and stir until well combined. Stir in the liqueurs. Top with the whipped cream and garnish with mint leaves, if desired.

⌒ *Chocolate Egg Cream* ⌒

Egg creams have neither eggs nor cream, but they do have a lot of history. They are unique to New York, found most frequently in the boroughs of New York City, where they were served up in candy stores from the Bronx to Brooklyn. Marian J. Betancourt, who provided us with this authentic re-creation of a real egg cream, describes their flavor as being "refreshing and thirst-quenching but not heavy and sweet. The taste of chocolate will be in the neighborhood, not knocking on your front door." Alas, egg creams, like the corner candy store, are a thing of the past in most of New York City, but with a little practice you can concoct the drink at home. Set the glass in the sink so you can perform with style without making a mess.

YIELD: 1 serving
DIFFICULTY: ◼
PREPARATION TIME: 1 minute

1 cup cold milk
7 ounces cold seltzer
3 tablespoons chocolate syrup

1. Put a 16-ounce round-topped glass (such as a Coca-Cola glass) in the sink. Pour the milk into the glass.

2. Holding a bottle of seltzer a foot or two above the glass, pour the seltzer into the glass until it is full and has a foamy head. Add the syrup all at once. Using a long-handled spoon, stir the egg cream quickly, being careful to preserve the head. Serve immediately.

⌒ *Frappé au Chocolat* ⌒

Most of us think of a frappé as being a thick milkshake. This one has no milk, but it sure is thick.

YIELD: 1 serving
DIFFICULTY: ◼
PREPARATION TIME: 5 minutes

1¼ cups vanilla or chocolate ice cream
⅓ cup chocolate liqueur

In a food processor or blender, process the ice cream and chocolate liqueur for 30 to 60 seconds or until very smooth. Serve immediately.

～◯ *Mock Mexican Hot Chocolate* ◯～

Long ago, the Spanish missionaries and nuns who settled in Mexico added sugar and cinnamon and other spices to the native chocolate, which otherwise was extremely bitter. Mexican chocolate—chocolate that has been processed and flavored similarly to the old way—tastes quite different from European and American chocolate. Many people prefer it. Here, we have simulated its flavor in a recipe for frothy hot chocolate. This basic recipe is embellished upon in the following three recipes.

YIELD: 5 cups

DIFFICULTY: ◼

PREPARATION TIME: 10 minutes plus cooking time

4 cups milk
½ cup packed dark brown sugar
2 ounces unsweetened chocolate, coarsely chopped
2 large egg whites
¾ teaspoon ground cinnamon
¾ teaspoon vanilla extract
¾ teaspoon almond extract

1. In a large, heavy saucepan over medium heat, cook the milk, brown sugar, and chocolate until smooth, stirring frequently.

2. Increase the heat and bring the mixture to a gentle boil. Remove the pan from the heat.

3. In a small bowl, beat the egg whites for 30 seconds or until frothy. Using a hand-held electric mixer, gradually beat the whites into the chocolate mixture. It will be frothy. Stir in the cinnamon, vanilla, and almond extract and return the pan to the heat for 1 minute.

4. Pour the hot chocolate into a heatproof pottery pitcher and serve.

∽ *Nun's Habit* ∽

YIELD: 1 serving
DIFFICULTY: ◼
PREPARATION TIME: 10 minutes

1 cup hot Mock Mexican Hot Chocolate (see recipe, page 334)
4 tablespoons orange liqueur, such as Grand Marnier
¼ cup whipped cream
Pinch of ground cloves
Bittersweet chocolate shavings, for garnish (optional)
Strip of orange zest, for garnish (optional)

In a warmed, heatproof mug or glass, mix together the hot chocolate and Grand Marnier. Top the drink with the whipped cream and sprinkle with the cloves. Garnish with the chocolate shavings and the strip of orange zest, if desired.

∽ *Café Olé* ∽

YIELD: 1 serving
DIFFICULTY: ◼
PREPARATION TIME: 10 minutes

½ cup hot coffee
½ cup hot Mock Mexican Hot Chocolate (see recipe, page 334)
2 tablespoons crème de cacao
1 tablespoon dark rum
1 tablespoon brandy
¼ cup whipped cream
6 chocolate-covered coffee beans, for garnish (optional)
Cinnamon stick, for garnish (optional)

In a warm, heatproof mug or glass, mix together the coffee, hot chocolate, crème de cacao, rum, and brandy. Top the drink with the whipped cream. Garnish with the chocolate-covered coffee beans and a cinnamon stick, if desired.

～ *Monastery Madness* ～

YIELD: 1 serving

DIFFICULTY: ▬

PREPARATION TIME: 10 minutes

1 cup hot Mock Mexican Hot Chocolate (see recipe, page 334)
2 tablespoons hazelnut liqueur, such as Frangelico
3 tablespoons brandy
¼ cup whipped cream
6 roasted hazelnuts, for garnish (optional) (for roasting instructions, see page 20)
Cinnamon stick, for garnish (optional)

In a warm, heatproof mug or glass, mix together the hot chocolate, hazelnut liqueur, and brandy. Top the drink with the whipped cream. Sprinkle with the hazelnuts and garnish with a cinnamon stick, if desired.

The Beverly Hills Hotel ～ *Milkshake* ～

This milkshake is served at the famous California hotel. We can only imagine the bevy of beauties it has tempted. And we confess . . . we've succumbed to this rich, smooth milkshake on more than one occasion.

YIELD: 2 servings

DIFFICULTY: ▬

PREPARATION TIME: less than 5 minutes

Chocolate curls:

4 ounces semisweet chocolate

Milkshake:

1¼ cups vanilla ice cream
½ cup cold milk
⅓ cup chocolate syrup

Make the chocolate curls:

1. In the top of a double boiler over hot, not simmering, water, melt the chocolate.

2. On an ungreased baking sheet, spread a ¹⁄₁₆-inch-thick layer of chocolate into a 6-inch square. Refrigerate the baking sheet for 2 to 4 minutes or until the chocolate just starts to set.

3. Remove the baking sheet from the refrigerator. Using a ruler and a sharp knife, cut the chocolate into ¼-by-6-inch strips. Holding a thin baker's scraper or metal spatula at a 45° angle, push upward and against the chocolate strips so that each one forms a curl. Store extra curls in an airtight container in the refrigerator until ready to use.

Make the milkshake:

4. In the container of a food processor or blender, process the ice cream, milk, and chocolate syrup for about 1 minute or until very smooth. Pour the milkshake into chilled glasses. Add two straws to each glass and encircle each straw with a chocolate curl, if desired.

Domaine Chandon's Raspberry 〜 *Milkshakes* 〜

These raspberry milkshakes are actually served inside edible chocolate bags. It is a bit tricky to make bags, but with enough tempered chocolate and patience (and the right sort of paper bag for the mold), you will be able to make the whimsical containers in your kitchen. Be sure your refrigerator has enough room in it for the bags (you do not want to have to wedge them in between the milk cartons) and give yourself plenty of time. After you have mastered making the bags, you may want to fill them with candies, ice cream, or fresh berries as well as the milkshake described here.

YIELD: 4 servings

DIFFICULTY: ▰▰▰

PREPARATION TIME: 40 minutes; allow 1 hour for tempering the chocolate

SPECIAL EQUIPMENT: 4 small paper bags, 3 inches tall with 4-by-2-inch bases, lined with a coated surface (bags used for freshly ground coffee work well), each bag trimmed with pinking shears to a 3-inch height (if using unlined bags, line them with waxed paper)

Chocolate bags:

2¼ pounds semisweet chocolate couverture, tempered (for tempering instructions, see page 22)

Raspberry milkshake:

1 pint fresh raspberries or 2 10-ounce packages frozen raspberries in light syrup, thawed and drained
2½ cups vanilla ice cream
⅓ cup cold milk
¼ cup raspberry liqueur, such as Chambord or Framboise
2 to 4 tablespoons superfine sugar
Fresh raspberries, for garnish (optional)

Make the chocolate bags:

1. Temper the chocolate.

2. Open the paper bags and stand them upright

on a baking sheet. Pour about ¼ cup of the tempered chocolate into each bag. With a small pastry brush and using long, swift strokes, brush the chocolate up from the bottom of the bags until the inside of each one is evenly coated. Apply a little extra chocolate in each corner. Refrigerate the bags for 10 minutes or until the chocolate is set. Keep the remaining chocolate at the correct temperature for tempered chocolate, as explained on page 22.

3. Pour about 3 tablespoons of the tempered chocolate into each bag and brush a second coat on the inside of the bags. Brush extra chocolate on the base of the bags. Reserve the leftover tempered chocolate. Refrigerate the bags for 15 minutes or until the chocolate is set.

4. One at a time, remove the bags from the refrigerator. Turn each one upside down and, starting at the bottom, very carefully peel away the paper bag from the chocolate. If necessary, make any minor repairs with a small pastry brush and the

reserved tempered chocolate. Refrigerate the chocolate bags for 10 minutes or until the chocolate is completely set. Store the tempered chocolate bags at room temperature.

Make the raspberry milkshake:

5. In a food processor or blender, process the raspberries for 30 seconds or until pureed. Strain the berries through a fine sieve into a medium bowl. Return the raspberry puree to the processor or blender and add the ice cream, milk, and raspberry liqueur, and process for 1 minute or until very smooth. Add sugar to taste and process for 15 seconds longer. Evenly divide the milkshake among the chocolate bags. Top each serving with fresh raspberries, if desired. Serve immediately with straws.

⬿ Debbie's Mocha Delight ⬾

Liqueur-spiked ice cream balls make these milk-shakes extra delicious. These are for the adults in the crowd.

> YIELD: 4 servings
>
> DIFFICULTY: ■■
>
> PREPARATION TIME: 15 minutes

3 cups coffee ice cream, divided
8 teaspoons chocolate liqueur
½ cup heavy (whipping) cream
1 teaspoon granulated sugar
½ teaspoon unsweetened nonalkalized cocoa powder
2 cups strong brewed coffee, chilled
1 cup cold milk
¼ cup chocolate syrup
Ground cinnamon, for garnish

1. Using an ice cream scoop, make 4 ice cream balls, each one with about ½ cup of ice cream. Put the balls on a baking sheet covered with plastic wrap and freeze for about 1 hour or until very solid.

Using a chopstick, make a hole about 1 inch deep and ½ inch wide in each ball. Pour 2 teaspoons of chocolate liqueur into each hole. Return the balls to the freezer.

2. In a chilled small bowl, using a hand-held electric mixer set at medium-high speed, whip the cream with the sugar and cocoa powder until stiff peaks form.

3. In a blender, mix the coffee, milk, chocolate syrup, and the 1 cup of remaining ice cream until smooth.

4. Divide the coffee mixture among four chilled glasses. Perch an ice cream ball on the edge of each glass. Garnish with the cocoa whipped cream and sprinkle with cinnamon. Serve immediately.

Drostaretto

Here's another chilled coffee-based drink for the over-twenty-one set.

YIELD: 4 servings

DIFFICULTY: ◼

PREPARATION TIME: 10 minutes plus chilling time

1½ cups hot strong freshly brewed coffee
2 tablespoons unsweetened alkalized cocoa powder
2 tablespoons packed light brown sugar
¾ cup heavy (whipping) cream
½ cup milk
½ cup almond-flavored liqueur, such as amaretto
¾ cup vanilla ice cream
4 teaspoons chocolate syrup or 2 ounces milk chocolate, grated,
  for garnish

1. In a medium bowl, combine the coffee, cocoa, and brown sugar. Whisk until the ingredients are well combined and the brown sugar is dissolved. Cover and refrigerate for 2 hours or until very cold.

2. Stir the coffee mixture to recombine the ingredients. In a blender or food processor, process the chilled coffee mixture, heavy cream, milk, and almond-flavored liqueur for 5 seconds. Add the ice cream and process for 10 seconds or until very smooth.

3. Pour immediately into chilled glasses. Drizzle the chocolate syrup across the top of each serving or sprinkle with the grated milk chocolate. Serve immediately.

Raspberry Chocolate Ice Cream ～ Soda ～

Raspberries and chocolate are a divine combination and never more heavenly than in this spectacular ice cream soda put together by Barbara Kafka. It is best made with homemade ice cream, but your favorite store-bought will do just fine, too.

YIELD: 1 soda

DIFFICULTY: ◼

PREPARATION TIME: less than 5 minutes

½ cup Raspberry Sauce (see recipe, page 277)
½ cup whipped cream, divided
2 scoops (⅔ cup) Milk Chocolate Ice Cream (see recipe, page 269) or store bought
Soda water or seltzer water from a siphon
Fresh raspberries, for garnish (optional)

1. Pour the raspberry sauce into a tall ice cream soda glass. Add ¼ cup of the whipped cream.

2. Put 1 scoop of the chocolate ice cream on top of the whipped cream. Fill the glass with soda water.

3. Top with the remaining scoop of chocolate ice cream, the remaining ¼ cup of whipped cream, and fresh raspberries, if desired.

4. Serve the soda with a long-handled spoon and a straw.

～ Café Mocha ～

Deceptively creamy and quick to make (use the microwave), this hot coffee is made with skim milk that has been heated and then put in a blender to make it foamy. Since the recipe was developed in our test kitchens as an idea for a midnight libation, we made it with decaffeinated coffee—but substitute the real thing if you are so inclined.

YIELD: 1 serving

DIFFICULTY: ◼

PREPARATION TIME: 5 minutes

2 teaspoons unsweetened nonalkalized cocoa powder
1 to 2 teaspoons granulated sugar
1½ teaspoons instant decaffeinated coffee powder
Pinch of ground cinnamon
¾ cup water
2 tablespoons coffee or chocolate liqueur (or a combination of both)
½ teaspoon vanilla extract
½ cup skim milk
½ teaspoon grated semisweet chocolate (optional)

1. In a microwave-safe 10-ounce mug, combine the cocoa, sugar, coffee, and cinnamon. Gradually stir in the water until the mixture is smooth. Stir in the liqueur and vanilla. Microwave for 2 to 3 minutes at high (100 percent) power, until the mocha mixture is very hot but not boiling. Remove the mug from the microwave.

2. Put the milk in a microwave-safe 2-cup measuring cup. Microwave for 1 to 2 minutes on high (100 percent) power, until the milk comes to a boil. Immediately pour the hot milk into a blender and process at high speed for 30 to 40 seconds or until foamy. Top the hot mocha mixture with the foamed milk. Sprinkle with grated chocolate and serve immediately.

⌒ *Chocolate Eggnog* ⌒

Don't let the holidays go by without trying our customized version of eggnog. It is as rich and creamy as the more traditional brew, but we have added an ingredient we're sure you will agree makes it a lot better. What else but chocolate?

YIELD: 10 cups
DIFFICULTY: ■
PREPARATION TIME: 10 minutes plus chilling time

6 large eggs
¼ cup granulated sugar
Pinch of salt
1½ cups chocolate syrup
2 tablespoons vanilla extract
2 cups heavy (whipping) cream, chilled
½ cup cognac
¾ cup amaretto
Grated chocolate, for garnish (optional)

1. In a very large bowl, using a hand-held electric mixer set at medium-high speed, beat the eggs with the sugar and salt for 5 to 7 minutes or until a thick yellow ribbon forms when the beaters are lifted.

2. Slowly beat in the chocolate syrup and vanilla. In a chilled, large bowl, using a hand-held electric mixer set at medium speed, beat the cream for 1 to 2 minutes or just until soft peaks form.

3. Using a rubber spatula, fold the whipped cream into the chocolate mixture. Stir in the cognac and amaretto. Chill, stir, and serve the eggnog in a chilled punch bowl or chilled punch glasses. Top each serving with grated chocolate, if desired.

Mail Order Sources

Albert Uster Imports, Inc.
9211 Gaither Road
Gaithersburg, MD 20877
(301) 258-7350

* Carma chocolate couverture
and gianduja, chocolate molds,
chocolate-dipping forks, marzipan roses, disposable pastry bags

Assouline and Ting, Inc.
926 Allegheny Avenue
Philadelphia, PA 19133
(800) 521-4491

* Cocoa Barry gianduja and
chocolate couverture

Bridge Kitchenware Corporation
214 East 52nd Street
New York, NY 10022
(212) 688-4220

* Chocolate-dipping forks, charlotte molds, square flan forms,
chocolate molds

Maid of Scandinavia
3244 Raleigh Avenue
Minneapolis, MN 55416
(800) 328-6722

* Cocoa butter, chocolate-dipping forks, paste food color, gum
paste cutters, silver dragées,
disposable pastry bags, meringue powder, rose nails, decorating tips, Plexiglas separator
tiers; Callebaut, Lindt, and
Nestlé chocolate couvertures;
chocolate molds

Hauser Chocolatier
18 Taylor Avenue
Bethel, CT 06801
(203) 794-1861

* Lindt chocolate couverture

Tomric Plastics, Inc.
136 Broadway
Buffalo, NY 14203
(716) 854-6050

* Chocolate molds

Creative Foodcrafts
P.O. Box 44
Stoneham, MA 02180
(800) 343-5815

* Chocolate molds

International Pastry Arts
Center
526 Executive Boulevard
Elmsford, NY 10523
(914) 347-3737

* Chocolate molds

Paradigm Chocolate Company
5775 S.W. Jean Road, #106A
Lake Oswego, OR 97035
(503) 636-4880

* Guittard and Lindt chocolate
couvertures

Williams-Sonoma Mail Order
Department
P.O. Box 7456
San Francisco, CA 94120-7456
(415) 421-4242

* Callebaut chocolate couverture

A Cook's Wares
3270 37th Street
Beaver Falls, PA 15010
(412) 846-9490

* Callebaut and Lindt chocolate
couvertures

Recipe Credits

Chocolatier *wishes to thank the following people, restaurants, and hotels for the truly outstanding recipes included in this book.*

Adrienne's Tea Garden, Victoria British Columbia: *Belgian Mousse Parfaits*
Barbara Albright: *Fudgy Food-Processor Brownies; Two-Tone Cutout Cookies; Chocolate Chip Banana Muffins; Chocolate Muffins with White Chocolate Chunks; Chocolate Peanut Butter Pudding Pops; Mocha Shake; Brownies in the Round*
Barbara Albright and Adrienne Welch: *Chocolate Eggnog*
Melanie Barnard and Brooke Dojny: *Chocolate Linzer Bars; Peanut Butter Chocolate Chip Bars; Orange Mocha Velvet*
Alan Barone: *Chocolate Custard with Raspberries*
Hotel Bel Air, Los Angeles, CA: *Chocolate Orange Truffle Cake*
Cile Bellefleur-Burbidge: *Cile's Daisy Chocolate Wedding Cake*
Rose Levy Beranbaum: *White Chocolate Nostalgia Cake; Swiss Chocolate Cherries Jubilee; Raspberry Chambord Chocolate Balls*
Adriane Berman: *Cashew-Praline Blondies*
Marian J. Betancourt: *Chocolate Egg Cream*
Beverly Hills Hotel, Los Angeles, CA: *The Beverly Hills Hotel Milkshake*
Rachel Binah: *Chocolate Almond Shortbread*
Karl Bissinger: *Grand Marnier Whipped-Cream Truffles*
Flo Braker: *California Linzertorte*
Lora Brody: *Milk Chocolate Ice Cream*
Sidney Burstein: *Hollywood Hills*
Hans Bussinger: *Chocolate Valentine Box*
Beryl Byrd: *Bailey's Irish Cream Chocolate Chip Ice Cream*
Ann Byrn: *Chocolate Chess Pie; Double Fudge Pie; Chocolate Bourbon Pecan Pie with Bourbon Butter Crust; Chocolate Banana Cream Pie*
Jayne Church: *The Most Chocolate Chip Cookies*
City Restaurant, Los Angeles, CA: *City Chocolate with Espresso Crème Anglaise*
Donna Covrett: *Chocolate Chunk Sour Cream Coffee Cake*
Susan Crowther and Norma Saunders: *Mocha Chocolate Chip Ice Cream Sandwiches*
Delores Custer and Mariann Sauvion: *Chocolate Tulips with Raspberry Bavarian Cream; Chocolate Cream Puffs with Capuccino Cream; D and D (Dark and Delicious) Chocolate Sauce*
Marcel Desaulniers: *Chocolate Cashew Dacquoise; Chocolate Caramel-Praline Ice Cream Terrine with Warm Caramel Sauce*
Jim Dodge: *White Chocolate and Coconut Pie*
Restaurant Domaine Chandon, Los Angeles, CA: *Domaine Chandon's Raspberry Milkshakes*
Janet Dresden, Incredible Edibles, Stamford, CT: *Incredible Chocolate Cake*
Major Margo Duckett: *Drostaretto*
Maurice Dufour: *Florentine Chocolate Cake*
Maria Elena Eichwald: *Maria's Mocha Chip Cookies*
Essex House, New York, NY: *Frozen Chocolate Mint Soufflé*
Melanie Falick: *Scones with Chocolate and Ginger; Hazelnut and Chocolate Chunk Cookies*
Barbara Feldman: *San Francisco Fudge Foggies®*
Gail Feyer: *White Chocolate Lemon Cheesecake*
Kathy Fleegler: *Kathy Fleegler's Chocolate Strawberry Patch*
Helen Fletcher: *Charlotte Royale*
Jim Fobel: *Chunky Peanut Butter Chocolate Chunk Cookies; Mocha Macadamia Nut Chocolate Chunk Cookies; Oatmeal Bittersweet Chocolate Chunk Cookies: Chocolate-Dipped Chocolate Chunk Cookies; Chocolate Orange Marble Cake; Chocolate Butter; Chocolate Ice Cream with White Chocolate Chunks; Vanilla Ice Cream with Chocolate Chunks; Crispy Sugar Cones; Chocolate Mint Wafers; Chocolate Champagne Zabaglione; Chocolate-Flecked Peanut Butter Cookies*
Margaret Fox,' Cafe Beaujolais, Mendocino, CA: *Chocolate Coffee Cake*
Ray Freese: *Aloha Peanut Pie; Baked Chocolate Mousse with Rum Sauce*
Cathy Garvey: *Peanut Butter Cupcakes; Chocolate-Speckled Banana Loaves; Spiced Chocolate Coffee; Minted Hot Cocoa*
Bruce Gleeman: *Chocolate Lovers' Wedding Cake*
Bert Greene: *Chocolate Angel Pie*
Graves Mountain Lodge, Syria, VA: *Ice Cream Sundae Cake*
Karl Beckley, Green Lake Grill, Seattle, WA: *Chocolate Indulgence*
Mary Goodbody: *Chocolate Walnut Sundae*
Groths Vineyards and Winery, Oakville, CA: *Cabernet Truffles*
Lynn Hagee: *Choclava*
Thomas Harte: *Mexican Chocolate Soufflé*
Janice Wald Henderson: *White Chocolate Pound Cake*
Amy Hodgett: *Extra Special Chocolate Chunk Cookies*
Lucinda Hutson: *Mock Mexican Hot Chocolate; Nun's Habit; Café Olé; Monastery Madness*

Adrienne Islin: *Triple Chocolate Espresso Cake*
Deborah Ingrassia: *Deborah's Chocolate Brunch Cake*
John Isom: *White Chocolate Almond Ice Cream*
Martin Johner: *Cocoa Blackout Cake*
Betsy Jordan: *Chocolate Cheesecake Triangles; Betsy's Best Wishes Cake; Boston Cream Pie; All-American Dixie Devil's Food Cake; Chocolate Cream Pie*
Barbara Kafka: *Chocolate Ginger Ice Cream; Raspberry Chocolate Ice Cream Soda*
Jean Kaynes: *Meringue Kisses*
Mary Ann King: *Crème de Menthe Ice Cream*
Abigail Kirsch Culinary Productions: *Chocolate Timbales with Warm Cherry Compote*
Daniel Kucharski: *Chocolate Fondue with Fresh Fruit*
Patisserie Lanciani, New York, NY: *Gâteau Charlene Blanche*
Andria Leduc: *Black and White Chunk Cookies*
Marion L. McCathron: *Ever-So-Delicious Brownies*
Bernadette McKelvey: *Crème de Menthe Brownies*
Michael McLaughlin: *Classic Chocolat Mousse; Dark Chocolate Raspberry Mousse; Orange White Chocolate Mousse with Fresh Strawberry Sauce*
Nicholas Malgieri: *Chocolate Almond Wedding Cake*
Amelia P. Morehead: *Brownie Cookies*
Norma Mullin: *Rich, Rich Chocolate Malt*
Linda d'Orlando: *Peanut Butter Chocolate Chunk Ice Cream*
Jean Louis Palladin: *Chocolate Sherbet with Pistachio Sauce*
Constance Parriott, Belltown Cafe, Seattle, WA: *Andrea's Fudge Cake*
Patsy Pearson: *Milk Chocolate and Praline Truffles*
Margaret P. Perrone: *Chocolate Chubbies*
Karen Peterson: *Reverse Chocolate Hazelnut Cookies*
Ponchartrain Hotel, New Orleans, LA: *Mile High Ice Cream Pie*
Thelma Pressman: *Mocha Truffles*
Randall Price: *Chocolate Walnut-Praline Cake*
Red Lion Inn, Stockbridge, MA: *Chocolate Chip Pie*
Janet Riches: *Walnut Brownies*
Lois Ringelheim: *Chocolate Toffee Torte*
Ritz Cafe, New York, NY: *Jack Daniels Chocolate Ice Cream*
Michael Roberts: *Trump's Mini-Cupcakes*
Rick Rodgers: *Magic Mocha Fudge; Maui Mounds; Peanut Butter Balls; Fruit-and-Chocolate Club Sandwich; Frappé au Chocolat*

Andy Rolleri: *Chocolate Hazelnut Terrine*
Debbie Russell: *Debbie's Mocha Delight*
Salisbury House, Los Angeles, CA: *Macadamia Chocolate Chip Streusel Coffee Cake*
Richard Sax: *The World's Best Rugelach; Chunky Chocolate Coconut Bars; Chocolate-Dipped Peanut Brittle Fingers*
Eileen Schofield: *Chocolate Orange Marble Cake*
Phillip Stephen Schulz: *Cherry Bread Pudding with Chocolate Sauce*
Bev and John Shaffer: *Double Chocolate Raspberry Tart*
Stanley Shear: *Chocolate Coffee Twist*
Stephen Shern: *Chocolate Marble Cheesecake*
Sinclair's American Grill, Hilton Hotel, Jupiter Beach, FL: *Chocolate Fig Cake with Gianduja Glaze*
Spa at Palm-Aire, Pompano Beach, FL: *Chocolate Chip Banana Bran Muffins*
Susan Spedalle: *Chilled Peanut Butter Brownies*
Karen Stolz Spence: *Karen's Chocolate Sin-amon Bundt Cake*
Mark Spiegel: *Cupid's Delight Wedding Cake*
Steamboat Inn, Idleyld Park, OR: *Chocolate Mousse Tart*
Thirtyone Northwest, Portland, OR: *Oregon Hazelnut Pavé*
Marcia Tonison: *White Chocolate Cocomacs*
Brian Vaughan: *Buffalo Chip Cookies*
Leslie Weiner: *Mocha Mousse Pie*
Adrienne Welch: *Cocoa Layer Cake; Rigo Jancsi; Chocolate Walnut Torte; White Chocolate Strawberry Obsttorte; Microwave Walnut Brownie Cake; Microwave Walnut Brownie Cake à la Mode; Microwave Walnut Brownie Cake with Whipped-Cream Frosting; White Chocolate Sour Cream Cheesecake; Triple Chocolate Sour Cream Cake; Mocha Pudding; Chocolate Alpine Cake; White Chocolate Citrus Roulande; Chocolate Kugelhupf; Chocolate Doughnuts; Chocolate Stollen; Whole Wheat Tea Scones; Chocolate Mint Ice Cream Pie; Brownie Ice Cream Sandwiches; Fruit-and-Nut Medallions; Gianduja Truffles; Rochers; Mocha Pralinés with an Orange Pralinés Variation; Chocolate Walnut Fudge; All-American Candy Bars; Chunky Chocolate Nut-and-Fruit Squares; Chocolate Caramel Apples; Dark Chocolate Madeleines; Hazelnut-Praline Ganache Cake; Mohr Im Hemd; Raspberry Sauce; Mississippi Mud; Café Mocha; Chocolate Raspberry-Ganache Cake*
Leslie Wiener: *Chocolate Chip Granola; Banana Chocolate Chip Pancakes; Coconut Chocolate Streusel Coffee Cake*
Elaine Witt: *Charleston Cobblestone Ice Cream*
Cathy Ziolowski: *Cashew Buttercrunch*

INDEX